Louisiana
Retirement
and
Estate Planning
6th Edition

John E. Sirois,
JD, MBA, CFP®, CIMA, CIMC
Estate and Elder Law Attorney
CERTIFIED FINANCIAL PLANNER™
Certified Investment Management Analyst
Certified Investment Management Consultant

John E. Sirois, A Professional Law Corporation
1356 B West Tunnel Boulevard
Houma, Louisiana 70360
985-580-2520
john@jsiroislaw.com
www.LouisianaEstatePlanner.com
www.HoumaEstatePlanningAttorney.com

Securities offered through
Raymond James Financial Services, Inc.
Member FINRA/SIPC
Investment Advisory Services offered through
Raymond James Financial Services Advisors, Inc.
One Galleria Boulevard, Suite 735
Metairie, Louisiana 70001
504-837-1733
john.sirois@raymondjames.com

In Baton Rouge and other areas call:
1-888-JSIROIS (574-7647)

1356 B. West Tunnel Boulevard
Houma, Louisiana 70360
985-580-3322
john.sirois@raymondjames.com
www.raymondjames.com/johnsirois

Louisiana
Retirement

and

Estate Planning

6th Edition

The essential financial planning
book for retirees, pre-retirees and seniors

John E. Sirois, JD, MBA, CFP®, CIMA, CIMC
Estate and Elder Law Attorney
CERTIFIED FINANCIAL PLANNER™
Certified Investment Management Analyst
Certified Investment Management Consultant

Published by
John E. Sirois
1356 B West Tunnel Boulevard
Houma, Louisiana 70360
1-888-574-7647

Printed in the United States of America

ISBN 978-0-578-54331-6

For my lovely wife, Katherine, for her love, support and limitless patience without which this book would not have been possible; my daughter, Sophia, and step-daughter, Lauren, for their patience and understanding during the many hours that went into this book.

Table of Contents

xi

List of Tables

Preface

Many Louisiana residents are confused or outright misinformed when it comes to the laws, rules, regulations, and planning strategies that affect their retirement and estate planning endeavors. When approaching retirement and throughout the retirement years, Louisiana residents are faced with numerous complex planning issues. Many of these issues are unique to Louisiana and our Civil Code from which much of our law is derived. In addition, the tax code has more than its share of traps for the unwary. The laws governing estate taxation, retirement distributions, income taxation and long-term care planning are complex and frequently change. To make matters worse these laws were not designed to work harmoniously. Transitioning into retirement involves some of the largest if not the largest financial transaction you will encounter in your lifetime. Even small mistakes can be very costly; therefore, you must get it right the first time.

As you are probably aware, there are few financial planning resources that are specific to Louisiana residents. This book will hopefully help to fill that void. This book is an attempt to shed some light on the common issues facing Louisiana residents when planning for retirement and for their estate. The concepts and strategies presented in this book come from some of my experiences helping retirees and pre-retirees as an attorney and CERTIFIED FINANCIAL PLANNER™ Professional.

Although there are many basic resources available online or in print, most merely scratch the surface of retirement and estate planning. This book provides both basic information and a more detailed analysis of the planning issues facing retirees and pre-retirees. Therefore, some of the topic areas covered in this book are rather complex. To make it easier to find the information you are seeking, each chapter may be read as a stand-alone module. Hopefully this book will provide an awareness of the complex nature of the planning issues you will face throughout your retirement years.

This book is by no means a do-it-yourself manual to retirement, estate and eldercare planning. You should leave that to the experts. However, I hope this book will empower you with enough information to know which questions to ask and to identify and avoid the numerous pitfalls you will encounter as a retiree and pre-retiree. I also hope this book will serve as your roadmap to help you navigate your retirement years. If you have any retirement, investment or estate planning questions or if I can be of assistance to you, call or E-mail.

Successful planning,

John Sirois

1

Retirement and Estate Planning

RETIREMENT PLANNING AND ESTATE PLANNING are more about people than they are about investments and legal documents. Sure, retirement planning and estate planning involve money, taxes, investments, wills, trusts, IRAs, insurance, and many other areas of financial planning, but planning is really about you and your family. Of course you plan for retirement to provide income after your paycheck stops. But you also plan to provide you and your family with security and peace of mind. Peace of mind knowing that you will have a lifetime of adequate retirement income, and family harmony is maintained after your death.

Retirement planning and estate planning are intertwined and should not be viewed independently of each other. For example, retirement assets with beneficiary designations must be coordinated with your estate plan as they are not controlled by your will. If done properly, planning your retirement and your estate can help foster worry-free golden years. If planning is done haphazardly or not at all, you may run out of money, pay unnecessary taxes, or leave your children fighting over their inheritance. Neglecting to plan will likely create a financial and legal mess that your spouse or your children will have to clean up.

The biggest threat to your retirement and to your estate comes from within…procrastination. Both retirement planning and estate planning are easy to put on the back burner—in particular estate planning. After all, who wants to think about their own death? It is common for people to admit they have procrastinated when it comes to planning their estate. When people talk about procrastinating, I often jokingly tell them to come see me a month before they meet their demise, and we will get all of their affairs in order. Of course no one knows when they will die. Due to the uncertainties of life, do not procrastinate when it comes to your retirement plan or your estate plan!

Retirement! ... Now What?

Retirement! You've pursued this goal your entire working life. Whether you intend to adopt a hobby, play golf, go fishing, plant a garden, volunteer in your community, travel the U.S. or the world or simply relax, you need a reliable income plan. Your work paycheck will end and must be replaced with a retirement "paycheck" from retirement assets. Producing a lifetime retirement "paycheck" requires planning before and throughout retirement. Even though retirement means different things to each person, all successful retirements require a plan—a well thought out plan.

Some retirees work part time, not only to make use of their acquired knowledge and skills but also to earn additional income. Others are adamant about never working again. Whatever your ideal retirement looks like, it should be about spending your remaining years doing the things you've always wanted to do but never had the time. It should be about enjoying life!

Your most important retirement goal should be enjoying your remaining years free from financial stress and worry, not maximizing the return on investments or minimizing taxes. To enjoy retirement and achieve your retirement dreams, you need an adequate monthly income that continues throughout your lifetime, taking into consideration rising costs due to inflation. Ensuring this income requires proper planning during your working years and proper implementation afterward. Both planning periods include a series of objectives: maintaining consistent investing and savings, maximizing investment return within your risk tolerance, protecting your portfolio from healthcare and long-term care expenses, minimizing taxes and protecting your loved ones through estate planning. Achieving these objectives is necessary because you will not enjoy retirement if you lose sleep over your dwindling portfolio, the vacillating stock market or whether your money will last through your and your spouse's lifetime.

The best years of your life should be relatively trouble free if you give your finances appropriate attention before and during your retirement. Without proper planning, however, your retirement years can be difficult, frustrating and downright frightening. You must navigate complex tax laws, minimize risk to your portfolio during volatile markets and ensure adequate income for rising medical costs and other living expenses. Although no one has a crystal ball that shows where to invest or whether inflation will dramatically increase in the future, a thorough plan will allow you to weather the many unknowns ahead of you. Your transition into retirement is not an event; rather, it is a journey that sometimes requires you to make adjustments to your course. For example, the proper adjustments to your portfolio allocation can enhance performance, and adjustments in spending, if necessary, can help ensure that your portfolio lasts.

Are you prepared for your retirement journey? Are you on track with your retirement savings? Do you know how to make your portfolio last? Do you know how to protect your family when you are no longer with them? Do you know what steps to take now to ensure a smooth transition into retirement? Have you protected your assets from potential long-term care expenses? Do you know without a doubt that you will have enough to live comfortably throughout retirement? Do you have an up-to-date estate plan? If you answered "no" to one or more of these questions, you are not adequately prepared for retirement. You should take steps to turn any "no" answers into "yes" answers to help ensure a enjoyable, worry-free retirement.

Not Your Parents' Retirement

Your retirement years will not be wholly comparable to your parents'. Prior generations relied primarily on Social Security and pension income. As a result, producing an adequate retirement income was not their responsibility. We have experienced and will continue to experience dramatic shifts in the sources of retirement income. Employers continue to eliminate or reduce pension benefits, thereby shifting the retirement savings burden to employees. Your 401(k) account (or other defined contribution plan) and private savings will play a more important role. Unlike most previous generations' retirees, you will be primarily responsible for producing a "paycheck" for the remainder of your life.

As a retiree, you will want the financial freedom to travel or to pursue a favorite extra-curricular activity. Today's retirees live more active lifestyles, which generally require more income than might be anticipated. To keep up with your lifestyle, your income requirements will demand a solid investment strategy that manages portfolio risk and ensures sufficient growth.

Reaching the Summit: Transitioning into Retirement

Your transition into retirement is an increasingly complex journey with many pitfalls along the way. Imagine you are a mountain climber standing at the foot of Mount Everest. What is your goal? To reach the peak, right? Well, reaching the peak should be half of the answer. The whole answer is to reach the peak and return safely. Most of the accidents on Mount Everest occur after the summit is reached and the journey down the mountain has begun.

Your retirement is similar. The day you retire is like reaching the summit. The easier part of retirement planning—the accumulation phase—ends the day you retire. The more difficult part of retirement planning—the distribution phase—begins the day you retire. The accumulation phase is easier because you are still working and contributing to your retirement accounts. The distribution phase is more difficult because your retirement portfolios must grow to hedge inflation risk, provide an income stream and avoid severe market losses. During the distribution phase, you cannot replace large losses to your retirement account through salary deferrals or other contributions because you are no longer receiving a paycheck. The retirement portfolio must provide the paycheck. Attempting to grow your portfolio, withdraw an income stream and protect it from market volatility is not an easy task. This is why retirement's distribution phase is the journey's more difficult part.

Start Planning Early

Ensuring adequate income for your lifetime and your spouse's lifetime doesn't just happen. You must set the wheels in motion for a comfortable and enjoyable retirement long before reaching retirement age. Without goals and a plan to reach your goals, your retirement success will be left to chance. You probably would not embark on a vacation with no idea of which road to take to reach your destination. You should likewise not embark on your retirement journey without a plan to reach your destination—a comfortable retirement.

It is never too early to start planning for retirement or planning your estate. If you are within five years of retirement, it is extremely important that you get your financial "closet" in order. This means consolidating accounts scattered among different financial institutions and developing a plan for retirement. Your plan should include steps to ensure your portfolio will grow to at least the minimum amount to provide income for your lifetime. To achieve your goal, additional saving or cutbacks in spending before and during retirement may be required.

The main planning issues facing retirees include retirement income planning, healthcare cost planning, long-term care planning and estate planning. Rapidly increasing life expectancies may require that your retirement portfolio provide inflation-adjusted income for 30 to 40 years or more. Therefore, retirement is a long-term planning process that merely begins another phase at the start of retirement.

This book is a guide to successfully transitioning into and completing the second part of the retirement planning journey—the retirement years. It is designed to provide you and other Louisiana residents with the information needed to make informed decisions when entering retirement and navigating through retirement. It is also designed to help you plan your estate. Above all, it is designed to make you aware of the numerous planning issues—traps for the unwary—that you will encounter.

Your Retirement Paycheck

Your retirement "paycheck" must provide sufficient income to maintain your desired standard of living for your life and your spouse's life. You have spent considerable time and energy accumulating retirement assets during your working years. However, you probably put little thought and planning into preserving and distributing your retirement assets in a manner that will provide the highest probability of producing lifetime income. As you approach retirement, you must answer two questions: Do I have sufficient assets to support my desired standard of retirement living? How will I produce sufficient income to support my desired standard of living?

Defining your standard of living during retirement requires developing ideas of your ideal retirement. You likely have big plans in store for your golden years. Your plans may include extensive traveling, purchasing a second home, or pursuing your favorite hobbies. All of these activities require additional income. Ideally you develop an impression of your desired retirement lifestyle many years prior to retirement and plan for and accumulate sufficient assets to support your retirement dreams. Although baby boomers anticipate a very active retirement, one survey found that 50 percent expected their retirement income needs to be 70 percent or less of their pre-retirement income. However, nearly 62 percent of current retirees spend 70 percent or more of their pre-retirement income.[1] This is an example of why you should use caution when relying on rule-of-thumb estimates. Your retirement is unique to you; therefore, you need a plan that fits your needs and retirement goals. A retirement cash flow analysis can help determine a suitable withdrawal rate and required rate of return to avoid running out of money.

Managing Risk to Your Nest Egg

Your investment management plan is another critical area of retirement planning. Unfortunately, most individuals take a haphazard approach to investment management by not having a strategy to manage risk to their retirement assets. Not planning can lead to purchasing the day's "hot" investment or experiencing large losses. In addition, haphazard planning may lead to accounts scattered across many brokerage firms with no consolidated game plan to manage all the assets. If this describes your investment situation, the first step to managing risk is to consolidate your accounts and define a strategy to manage your retirement assets.

Your retirement portfolio must grow in value and produce income, but it must also be protected against significant losses. If your nest egg dwindles significantly due to market losses, you may never recover, especially when withdrawals are taken from your portfolio. Large losses to your retirement portfolio may cause you to run out of money or to experience a reduced standard of living. Either will result in stress and worry and may mean an unenjoyable retirement. Unfortunately, this is exactly what happened to many people who retired from the late 1990's through 2008 and who did not have a plan to manage risk to their portfolios. Many portfolios were reduced by a third to a half or more after the technology bubble burst in 2000 and during the great recession from 2007-2009 following the real estate bubble. This is not the way to begin retirement.

Managing risk should not begin during your retirement years. If you have not yet retired, a plan to manage risk to your 401(k), 403(b),

457, IRAs or other taxable or tax-deferred plans is paramount. Managing risk is a recurring thread in Chapter 3 of this book.

Healthcare Costs

Rising healthcare costs is another threat to retirement security. As of 2019, there is still much uncertainty about the future landscape of the healthcare system after the enactment of The Patient Protection and Affordable Care Act (Obamacare). Although insurability due to pre-existing conditions is no longer an issue, estimating the future out of pocket cost of retiree healthcare is a formidable task. Much of the uncertainty has risen from the frequent changes to the implementation and enforcement of the law. Hopefully we soon will have more clarity about the future of healthcare.

A recent study found that a couple age 65, retiring in 2018, needs approximately $399,000 to have a 90 percent chance of covering health insurance premiums and out-of-pocket health expenses.[2] The study assumed both spouses had drug expenses at the 90th percentile throughout retirement. These estimates are based on Medicare beneficiaries. Another study found that a 65 year old couple retiring in 2019 will need approximately $285,000 for medical costs during retirement.[3] Neither of these studies included long-term care expenses in their calculations. Similar to the rising costs of company-sponsored pension plans, the rising costs of healthcare will cause employees and retirees to carry more of the financial burden. Some estimates suggest that by 2031 employers will be paying less than 10 percent of retirees' healthcare costs. Rising healthcare costs present additional planning challenges for early retirees who may have to pay out-of-pocket for health care insurance before they become eligible for Medicare. You should plan for healthcare costs to consume a greater proportion of your retirement income when determining your income needs. This may avoid unpleasant surprises from healthcare costs in later years. What is your health insurance game plan prior to Medicare eligibility?

Long-Term Care Expenses

An extended long-term care need can wipe out retirement funds, leaving your spouse with insufficient means to maintain his or her standard of living. Increasing life expectancies raise the odds that you or your spouse will need long-term care; therefore, consider the effects an extended long-term care need will have on your retirement funds.

Regular health insurance and Medicare generally do not pay for long-term care services. As a result, without proper planning, you pay out-of-pocket and are at risk of depleting, because of an extended long-term care stay, all or a significant portion of your retirement assets. Due to this danger, planning for long-term care expenses is a key component of retirement planning.

What Happens After I Die?

Who will inherit your estate? Will my estate go through a lengthy and expensive succession? How will you provide for your surviving spouse without interference from the children? Will my spouse be able to sell the family home and other assets without permission from the children? Should you use trusts to protect assets left to your children or grandchildren? Are there special issues regarding children from a previous marriage? Do any children or grandchildren have special needs? These are common estate planning issues that, if not already addressed, should be considered when planning for retirement.

Top Retirement and Estate Planning Mistakes

Retirement planning and estate planning require some of the most important decisions you will make during your lifetime. In addition, the transactions associated with your retirement will likely involve the largest transactions of your lifetime. Mistakes can be devastating and can drastically affect your standard of living during retirement as well as the legacy you intend to leave your children and grandchildren. It is highly recommended that you seek competent advice when transitioning into retirement, as well as throughout retirement, to help prevent the following mistakes.

Failing to Prepare a Comprehensive Plan

Retirement planning, estate planning, long-term care planning, and investment planning cannot be dealt with in isolation because they are intertwined with one another. You may already seek advice from an investment broker, a financial planner, an insurance agent, an attorney and/or a CPA. Although it is often necessary to seek advice from different professionals, you should have a comprehensive plan to coordinate the different areas of planning. In addition, you should have a CERTIFIED FINANCIAL PLANNER^{TM} coordinate the efforts of your team of professional advisors. Without a comprehensive plan, recommendations from different professionals may cause you to drift aimlessly or change directions too frequently, resulting in no plan at all. A comprehensive retirement, estate and investment plan can prevent this outcome and bring the other professionals "together" as your planning team.

Failing to Prepare a Retirement Cash Flow Analysis

A retirement cash flow analysis will help determine your proper portfolio withdrawal rate. It will also help determine the required rate of return on your investments. The analysis considers portfolio values, pension payments, Social Security benefits, duration of retirement, living expenses, inflation and income tax rate. The cash flow analysis may reveal that you should wait a year or more to retire or that you must reduce your expected standard of living to avoid running out of money during retirement. Ideally, a retirement cash flow analysis should be performed far ahead of your projected retirement date. The information provided by the analysis may show that an increase in your saving rate is necessary to retire with sufficient assets by your selected retirement date. Without a cash flow analysis, you will have no idea whether you have sufficient resources to retire or whether you may run out of money. It can also help prevent "getting behind the eight ball" by withdrawing too much during early retirement years. Because of these benefits, a retirement cash flow analysis is a critical step for every retiree and pre-retiree.

Failing to Protect Your Retirement Nest Egg from Market Risk

Managing market risk is one of the most important and most difficult aspects of retirement planning. Failure to manage retirement portfolio investment risk may cause you to have a reduced standard of living during retirement or cause you to run out of money. Although either outcome is unacceptable, the vast majority of retirees and pre-retirees and their advisors do not have a solid strategy to manage risk. Unfortunately, managing risk is not as simple as buy-and-hold asset allocation. Ask anyone who used a standard buy-and-hold asset allocation strategy during the 2000-2002 or 2007-2009 market meltdowns. The market environment is constantly changing, so your investment strategy must adapt to these changes. Avoid being lulled into a false sense of security by using asset allocation programs or target retirement portfolios. Professional assistance to help you manage investment risk is highly recommended. It is important that you select a competent advisor with a solid plan to manage risk, rather than a salesperson concerned only with making the sale.

Failing to Prepare a Will or a Revocable Trust

One of the worst estate planning mistakes is dying without a will or a revocable trust. If you die without a will or a revocable trust, your estate goes through an intestate succession. In this case, the State of Louisiana has a will for you; however, the intestacy laws may not distribute your estate as you may have intended. If you die without a will or a revocable trust, you lose all control over the distribution of your assets, and your loved ones may have to pay estate taxes that could have been avoided.

Failing to Update Your Will or Revocable Trust

After your will or revocable trust has been drafted, it should not be filed away and forgotten. As a rule of thumb, your will or revocable trust should be reviewed and, if necessary, updated every five years. Of course, changes in Louisiana law, federal and state tax laws, size and composition of your estate, personal and family situations and financial situations require an immediate review of your existing will or trust. A will that was properly drafted in your state of residence will be valid in other states. However, if you change residence to another state, your will or trust should be reviewed, and it may be advisable to execute a new will or trust in accordance with the state laws of your new residence.

Failing to Name Primary and Contingent Beneficiaries

Perhaps the most important election you can make is the designation of primary and contingent beneficiaries for your life insurance policies, IRAs, employer retirement plans and annuities. If you do not designate appropriate beneficiaries for your retirement plan, your beneficiaries may lose the benefit of distributions over their life expectancy. As a result, your retirement assets will be distributed and subjected to taxation very rapidly. Thus, the primary benefit, the extended tax-deferred growth, offered by these tax-advantaged vehicles may be lost.

Failing to Place Certain Assets in Trust

If minor children, grandchildren or others with special needs require assistance with the management of inherited assets, you should place these assets in trust for their benefit. You should place inherited assets which are large in value in trust regardless of your heirs' ages if the heirs lack maturity and/or experience to prudently manage a large sum of money.

Failing to Prevent Unsuccessful Retirement Rollovers and Transfers

When you roll over your employer plan, properly completing the paperwork is a must. The same holds true for IRA transfers. An error in the paperwork may result in a full taxable distribution and a 10 percent early withdrawal penalty.

Failing to Avoid Probate

You may wish to design your estate plan to avoid the cost and delay of probate. Revocable (or irrevocable) trusts, beneficiary designated accounts, and payable on death designations for bank accounts transfer your assets to your loved ones without the need for probate. Avoiding probate can also help keep your private matters and financial information private. If you own real estate in another state, you should consider using a revocable trust to avoid ancillary probate.

Failing to Explore Your Options with Employer Stock

If you have a significant amount of employer stock, it may be advantageous to elect net unrealized appreciation treatment for all or a portion of it. Mistakes may cause unwanted tax consequences, so competent advice is a must.

Failing to Follow the Rules for Premature IRA Distributions

If you are taking IRA withdrawals pursuant to an exception to the 10 percent premature distribution penalty, you must adhere strictly to the rules. Failure to properly calculate or withdraw the correct distribution amount will cause unwanted taxes and penalties. The rules are rather technical, so consult a competent advisor.

Failing to Select the Right Pension Option

Pensions provide a variety of payment options which are usually irrevocable. Prior to selecting a pension option, have a retirement cash flow analysis prepared to help identify your best option.

Failing to Protect Assets from Creditors

You should protect your assets to hinder a creditor's attempt to seize your assets due to a personal injury, malpractice, or other liability. Adequate liability insurance, limited liability companies, family limited partnerships, trusts, life insurance and annuities can help reduce your liability exposure and frustrate a creditor's attempt to seize your assets.

Failing to Prepare for Long-Term Care Expenses

The dangers of expenses associated with long-term care are often not addressed or fully appreciated by retirees. Without proper planning, long-term care expenses can devastate your retirement plan. Most retirees should insure against this risk just as homeowners insure against the risk of fire. The strict asset and income limitations of the Medicaid laws require planning well ahead of a long-term care need for optimal results. With advance planning, all of your assets can be protected from long-term care expenses.

Failing to Prepare for Incapacity

You should have general powers of attorney and powers of attorney for healthcare drafted to enable someone to manage your affairs in the event you are incapacitated. Revocable trusts also provide for the management of your affairs if you become incapacitated.

Failing to Fully Enjoy Your Retirement

Proper planning prior to and during retirement will increase your odds of enjoying a fulfilling and worry-free retirement. Proper planning can alleviate stress and worry by having a plan to manage market risk, thereby giving you peace of mind that your retirement portfolio will last and that your loved ones will be taken care of.

The chapters in this book will address all of these issues as well as other topics critical to your retirement and estate planning endeavors.

---

1 Many Americans' Retirement Hopes are Filled with Holes, EBRI, 2006 Retirement Confidence Survey, April 4, 2006.
2 EBRI Issue Brief, Savings Medicare Beneficiaries Need for Health Expenses: Couples Could Need as Much as $400,000, up From $370,000 in 2017, October 8, 2018.
3 Fidelity Investments, 2019.

2

Optimal Retirement Withdrawal Rates

Chapter Highlights

❖ The correct portfolio withdrawal rate is one of the most important retirement decisions.

❖ Caution should be used when relying on average rates of return and average historical inflation rates to calculate portfolio withdrawal rates.

❖ A retirement cash flow analysis is needed to determine <u>your</u> correct portfolio withdrawal rate.

❖ Retirees may experience retirements exceeding 40 years in length.

❖ Academic studies have shown that the maximum safe initial withdrawal rate ranges from under 3 percent to 6 percent. A 4 percent inflation-adjusted withdrawal rate is a standard rule of thumb for many retirees.

❖ Severe market losses and abnormally high inflation are the primary culprits of running out of money. Inflation cannot be controlled. However, risk can be reduced and inflation hedged through proper portfolio management.

❖ Avoiding severe market losses, especially near the beginning of retirement, is vital to long-term portfolio survival. Unfortunate retirees who experience severe market losses near the onset of retirement often have to either reduce their portfolio withdrawal rate or risk running out of money.

❖ Annuitizing a portion of the portfolio may increase portfolio survivability.

WHEN YOU RETIRE, your money must last to provide lifetime income—a task that is easier said than done. The primary obstacles to sustaining lifetime income are inflation, poor or negative investment returns, a lengthy retirement, the increasing costs of healthcare and long-term care and poor decision making. Due to poor planning and inadequate advice, retirees are prone to making many mistakes when taking retirement distributions. For example, many retirees make the mistake of withdrawing too much from their portfolios in the early years of retirement. In addition, many retirees fail to protect their portfolios from significant market losses, such as during the market slides from 2000 through 2002 and the Great Recession of 2007-2009. Another common mistake is assuming an investment return that is overly optimistic due to the memory bias of the 1980's and 1990's bull market. Any one of these errors may put your retirement dreams in jeopardy. To make matters worse, some retirees are likely, without competent advice and adequate planning, to commit multiple distribution planning errors. The end result is usually a reduction in standard of living, running out of money or both.

Despite the widespread publicity of the difficult decisions facing retirees, many are unprepared for the challenges of developing and maintaining a successful retirement distribution plan. One study found that many pre-retirees were gravely uninformed and unprepared to successfully shift from the accumulation phase to the distribution phase of retirement planning.[1] The study found that

- Approximately 73 percent of pre-retirees are confident that they will retire as planned, but only 43 percent actually retired when they expected.

- More than half of pre-retirees believed that retirement will involve a reduction in living expenses, but 77 percent reported that their expenses increased during retirement.

- Even among people that worked with a financial expert, only 50 percent had a written retirement plan.

Is your situation similar to the findings of this study?

How Long Must My Retirement Portfolio Last?

Obviously, you cannot know how long you will live; therefore, you must look to life expectancy trends to determine how long retirement is likely to last. Underestimating the length of your retirement may cause your retirement portfolio to be exhausted prematurely. It is far better to overestimate the length of retirement; unfortunately, many retirees underestimate. In 2017, the average life expectancy in the United States was 78.6 years. Male average life expectancy was 76.1 years, while female average life expectancy was 81.1 years. Keep in mind that these are average life expectancies. You have a 50 percent chance of living beyond the average life expectancy. The following statistics provide some insight on current life expectancies:[2]

- Once age 65 is reached, a man has a 37 percent chance of living to age 85 and a 17 percent chance of living to age 90.

- Once a woman reaches age 65, she has a 28 percent chance of living to age 90 and a 10 percent chance of living to age 95.

- For married couples, once age 65 is reached, there is a 65 percent chance of one spouse living to age 85 and a 10 percent chance of one spouse living to age 95.

The Bottom Line

Earlier retirements and increasing life expectancies will equal longer retirements for many individuals. Many workers retire in their mid to late fifties or early sixties rather than age 65. The continued rapid increase in life expectancy and earlier retirement has a clear impact: Many retirees will experience 40 or more years of retirement. If you are one of these fortunate retirees, your retirement portfolio must last longer and provide more retirement income. A longer retirement also means that erosion of purchasing power from inflation will have a more severe impact than shorter retirement periods. As a result, making portfolios last through retirement will be more difficult than for prior generations of retirees.

Balancing Current Income Needs and the Effects of Inflation

Your top investment objective is likely receiving reliable income from your retirement nest egg for the remainder of your lifetime. As a result, you may be tempted to invest heavily in bonds to produce income. Keep in mind that "income" from retirement portfolios may consist of capital appreciation, interest and/or dividends. Yes, you need "income" from your portfolio, but the "income" does not have to come from bond income or stock dividends. As discussed in this chapter, a large portion of your "income" should consist of portfolio growth from investing in stocks, depending on your length of retirement, portfolio size and risk tolerance. The growth potential of stocks should help protect your purchasing power many years into retirement.

Potential Pitfalls of Investing too Conservatively

Many retirees (and many financial advisors) believe the beginning of retirement means moving out of stocks and into fixed-income investments.[a] If your retirement will be short (less than 20 years) an over-weighted allocation to fixed income may be a viable option. However, today's retirees are retiring sooner and living longer, which requires retirement portfolios to last 30 to 40 years or longer. Although the traditional view is that capital appreciation (growth) is not as important during retirement as current income, studies suggest that capital appreciation (through stock investing) during retirement is critical to portfolio survival for most individuals with extended retirements.

The Inflation Factor

Although inflation from January 1, 1926 through 2018 averaged 2.9 percent[3], inflation can trend much higher for extended periods. For example, from 1970 through 2006, inflation averaged 4.67 percent. Inflation was generally below average (2.4 percent) from 1993 through 2012, but it averaged 7.4 percent in the 1970s and 5.1 percent in the 1980's.[4] Admittedly, estimating future inflation trends is difficult, but

---

[a] Fixed income investments generally refer to bonds, bond mutual funds, certificates of deposit, and fixed annuities.

do not underestimate the effect of inflation on future expenses. Consider a hypothetical example of a retiree experiencing a 3 percent rate of inflation. A retiree requiring $40,000 annually from their retirement portfolio at the onset of retirement will need over $97,000 annually in year 30. Remember to use caution when using the long-term average of 3 percent when estimating long-term income needs. Inflation can and has deviated from this average for long periods—the 1950's, 1970's and 1980's experienced an average inflation rate of over 5 percent. If you retire during a period of above average inflation, the long-term average inflation rate of 3.0 percent will underestimate the inflation rate for your retirement. Your future living costs will be underestimated, and you may run out of money during retirement.

Consider the Real Return

Many investors believe that risk management is simply investing in CDs[b] or bonds[c] because there is no risk to principal with these investments. Unfortunately, an allocation entirely of fixed-income securities will erode purchasing power in future years. The real return[d] is the best measurement of investment return. The real return of fixed-income investments after taxes and inflation is generally very low and often negative. For example, Ibbotson data[e] revealed that the average return of intermediate government bonds from 1926 through 2018, was 5.5 percent. After adjusting for inflation the return for the same period

---

[b] CDs are insured by the FDIC and offer a fixed rate of return, whereas the return and principal value of investment securities fluctuate with changes in market conditions.
[c] Bonds are subject to credit and interest rate risk. Timely payments of interest and principal payments are based on the financial condition of the issuer. Yield and market value will fluctuate with changes in market conditions.
[d] The return after taxes and inflation.
[e] Ibottson Associates is a leading authority on asset allocation with expertise in capital market expectations and portfolio implementation. Ibottson Associates publishes historical capital market data.

was 2.5 percent. <u>Large company stocks represented by the S&P 500[f] experienced a return of 10.0 percent from 1926 through 2018. After inflation, the return was 6.9 percent.</u>[g] The bottom line is that fixed-income investments such as bonds and CDs do not provide an adequate hedge against the eroding effects of inflation. One option to consider, depending on your situation, is to hedge against inflation by investing in stocks, real estate, commodities and other investments that provide capital appreciation potential. Regardless of which asset classes are used in your portfolio, risk management is of paramount importance.

So How Much Should I Invest in Stocks?

An analysis of historical market returns[h] shows that holding too few stocks will shorten your portfolio's minimum life in most cases.[5] Therefore, depending on your situation, it may be detrimental to hold less than 50 percent stocks. Unless your retirement will be short (less than 20 years) or your withdrawal requirements are less than 3 percent, the higher return potential of stocks will be essential to help maximize portfolio survivability. Of course, increasing your portfolio allocation to stocks may cause you to assume more risk. One study suggested that portfolio mixes ranging from 50 percent stocks and 50 percent bonds to 75 percent stocks and 25 percent bonds were an optimal mix for many portfolios. As usual, many exceptions to these guidelines exist. For example, higher withdrawal rates generally require greater percentages of stocks and market conditions may dictate a different asset mix.[6]

Retirees must be concerned with the effects of inflation over a long retirement. Unfortunately, heavily investing in bonds, CDs or fixed annuities may not provide adequate real returns. Retirees must rethink traditional methods of investing for retirement and avoid haphazardly overweighting bonds in their portfolios. In addition, retirees must invest to support sufficient withdrawals and to provide adequate

---

[f] The S&P 500 is an unmanaged index of 500 widely held stocks that is generally considered representative of the U.S. stock market. Keep in mind that individuals cannot invest directly in any index, and index performance does not include transaction costs or other fees, which will affect actual investment performance. Individual investor's results will vary.

[g] Past performance is not indicative of future results.

[h] Past performance is not indicative of future results.

Diversification and asset allocation do not ensure a profit or protect against a loss.

portfolio growth to hedge against inflation. Capital appreciation (growth) can also help ensure the portfolio will not be prematurely exhausted and help increase the odds that some assets are left to transfer to children and grandchildren.

How Much Can I Withdraw?

One of the most significant and often debated numbers in retirement planning is the appropriate withdrawal rate of retirement assets. You must determine your "personal withdrawal rate"—the maximum amount you can withdraw from your portfolio without running out of money during your lifetime. Your personal withdrawal rate will also determine the minimum portfolio size required to support your desired level of income during retirement. For this reason, your personal withdrawal rate is important to know while accumulating retirement assets. If you know how much income you will need during retirement, your personal withdrawal rate can be used to determine the required size of your retirement portfolio.

Determining your personal withdrawal rate is one of the most critical decisions you will face as a retiree because a withdrawal rate that is too high may prematurely exhaust your portfolio. On the other hand, a withdrawal rate that is too low may result in a reduced standard of living during retirement. When calculating portfolio survivability, you should assume a target rate of investment return and the required withdrawals to maintain your standard of living. Your personal withdrawal rate, whether based on a percentage or dollar amount, should be adjusted annually for inflation.

Your personal withdrawal rate will help determine how your portfolio must be invested during retirement to support your income needs without prematurely exhausting your portfolio. Obviously higher withdrawal rates require higher investment returns and/or larger portfolios. Pre- and post-retirement planning is critical to help ensure sufficient lifetime income. You need a well thought out retirement plan and the discipline to follow it. For example, many retirees increased their withdrawal rate during the 1995-1999 time frame because they assumed the bull market would continue. A disciplined and well-informed retiree would have accumulated these extraordinary returns in the portfolio to help cushion periods of poor returns such as the below average market returns from 2000-2008. In such a situation,

competent professional advice can make the difference between
running out of money and having a nest egg that lasts through
retirement.

Withdrawal rate decisions along with investment decisions are
where you are most likely to run into trouble. A retirement cash flow
analysis is a tool that financial planners use to determine your personal
withdrawal rate on an inflation-adjusted basis. Many variables come
into play when determining your optimal personal withdrawal rate,
such as portfolio size, projected and actual investment returns,
inflation, taxes, standard of living, Social Security payments, pension
payments and life expectancy. Due to the complexity and importance
of withdrawal rate decisions, a professionally prepared retirement cash
flow analysis is highly recommended.

Will You Be Lucky?

A major wildcard in determining your personal withdrawal rate is
luck. Specifically, does luck place the beginning of your retirement at
or near the start of a secular bull market? In other words, is your
retirement starting at a time of historically low or historically high
stock and/or bond values? If luck is in your favor and you retire near
the start of a secular bull market (historically low values), your
portfolio should last longer and/or your personal withdrawal rate
should increase. However, if you are unlucky and retire near the start
of a secular bear market (historically high values), your portfolio will
not last as long and withdrawal rates should be more conservative.
Unfortunately, no one is able to predict when bull and bear markets
will begin or end. Only hindsight can tell us that. To mitigate the
negative effect of the risk to retiring at the start of a period of poor
returns, consider adjusting the withdrawal percentage as market returns
suggest, adjusting the portfolio allocation to reduce exposure to
negative market returns, and/or beginning with a more conservative
approach to initial portfolio withdrawals.[7]

Academic Research of Withdrawal Rates

Numerous academic studies attempt to identify the optimal
portfolio withdrawal rate during retirement. A quick overview of some
of the research may help set proper expectations regarding portfolio
withdrawal rates under different market conditions using various asset

mixes. As a rule of thumb, a 4 percent inflation-adjusted withdrawal rate is a good starting point for a 30 year retirement.[i,8,9,10] Of course, the results of these studies may not reflect your own situation. Keep in mind that these studies, although insightful, are academic; therefore, they should not be used as a cookie cutter approach to determining your personal withdrawal rate. The withdrawal rate studies examined in this chapter were based on assumptions that may not apply to your retirement. These studies may be used as a starting point to determine your personal withdrawal rate rather than as a turn-key solution to your retirement withdrawal plan. Because your personal situation and retirement income needs are unique, your personal withdrawal rate must be tailored to meet your goals. In addition, the optimal mix of your portfolio will depend on your personal investment suitability.

One study was based on actual historical returns from a portfolio consisting of 50 percent common stocks and 50 percent intermediate U. S. Treasury notes. It provides insight on sustainable withdrawal rates and the impact of severe portfolio losses near the onset of retirement. The study found that an initial inflation adjusted withdrawal rate of 4 percent resulted in the portfolio lasting at least 35 years regardless of the year retirement began, going back to 1926. Caution should be used with a 50 percent common stock and 50 bond portfolio if initial withdrawal rates exceed 4 percent.[11]

The same study found that retirees who began retirement at anytime from 1964 through 1969 with a 50 percent stock and 50 percent Intermediate U.S. Treasury bond portfolio and who withdrew 5 percent per year[j] ran out of money in approximately 20 years—an unacceptable outcome. The severe market slide of 1973 and 1974 combined with high inflation were the primary reasons for the shorter portfolio life.

If retirement is to last 30 years, a 6 percent inflation-adjusted withdrawal rate causes the retiree to run out of money over 60 percent of the time based on the study's assumptions. The study indicated that increasing the stock weighting to 75 percent improved the portfolio survivability for initial withdrawal rates of 4 and 5 percent.[12,13]

---

[i] The studies assumed a 30 year retirement and a portfolio allocation of at least 50 percent to stocks.
[j] Adjusted for inflation

Another observation is that your maximum personal withdrawal rate will decline with longer retirements. Successful personal withdrawal rates range from under 3 percent to 5.5 percent, depending on retiree age, asset valuations, and portfolio growth rate. In addition, portfolios with lower withdrawal rates, especially in the early years of retirement, are better able to weather difficult market periods. During the 1980's and 1990's bull market, larger withdrawal rates were supported while retirees experienced above average portfolio growth. Unfortunately, bull markets do not last forever, and retirees will experience both bull and bear markets. A 4 percent (or lower) initial withdrawal rate will increase the odds of portfolio survivability during difficult market periods.[14]

Another study using all of the major asset classes (large and small cap, growth and value, international, real estate, fixed income and cash) suggested that retirement portfolios of at least 65 percent stocks were able to support an initial inflation adjusted withdrawal rate between 5.2 percent and 5.6 percent for 40 years with a 99 percent degree of certainty. If a slightly lower degree of certainty is acceptable, an initial inflation adjusted withdrawal rate between 5.7 percent and 6.2 percent was sustainable for 40 years with a 95 percent degree of certainty. An additional observation was that initial safe withdrawal rates were lower for portfolios allocated to 50 percent stocks than for portfolios allocated with 65 percent or 80 percent stocks. This study reinforces the need to allocate a sufficient portion of your portfolio to stocks to help sustain a prolonged retirement.

A later study compared the effect of different allocations of stocks[k], bonds[l] and cash[m] on portfolio longevity using Monte Carlo simulation[15]. Monte Carlo simulation is a random sampling of historical market returns taken 5,000 to 10,000 times to simulate the probability of random market returns. The study concluded that based

---

[k] Represented by the S&P 500
[l] Represented by intermediate government bonds
[m] Represented by 30-day T-Bills

on a 4.5 percent inflation adjusted withdrawal rate and a 30-year retirement period, a conservative portfolio[n] failed to survive a 30-year retirement period 67 percent of the time. This means that if you retire with a $500,000 portfolio, invest it conservatively and withdraw $22,500 per year for 30 years, you would run out of money two-thirds of the time. You probably agree that a 2 out of 3 chance of running out of money during retirement is unacceptable. An aggressive portfolio[o] survived the 4.5 percent distribution rate for 30 years 91.6 percent of the time. These odds are much more acceptable. In addition, the aggressive portfolio survived a 40-year retirement period with a 4.5 percent distribution rate 85 percent of the time.[16]

Therefore, portfolios more heavily weighted to stocks are more likely to survive longer retirement periods with withdrawal rates of 4.5 percent or more. Keep in mind that a portfolio withdrawal rate that is too aggressive may cause you to invest too aggressively (and possibly assume too much risk), run out of money, or both.[17]

For shorter retirement periods, a 4.5 percent withdrawal rate from conservative portfolios had better chances of survival and more consistency than more aggressive portfolios. The probability of failure for conservative portfolios increases dramatically for retirement periods in excess of 20 years. Therefore, if your retirement is not likely to last longer than 20 years, a more conservative portfolio (more bonds and less stocks) may provide adequate longevity with less volatility than a more aggressive portfolio. On the other hand, if your retirement is likely to last longer than 20 years, a more aggressive portfolio (more stocks and less bonds) may provide better portfolio survivability.[18]

If you require withdrawal rates greater than 6 percent, you dramatically increase the odds of running out of money. Using Monte Carlo simulation, the chance of failure rate can be calculated for a given withdrawal rate and rate of investment return. For example, you may require a 6 percent initial withdrawal rate, and based on your investment assumptions, Monte Carlo simulation may reveal that a 30 percent chance of running out of money during a 30-year retirement exists. Some retirees accept these odds considering their need for a higher withdrawal rate. If investment performance exceeds the projected returns, you may not run out of money. On the other hand, if

---

[n] 20 percent stocks, 50 percent bonds and 30 percent cash (30-day T-Bills)
[o] 85 percent stocks and 15 percent bonds

investment performance lags, you may run out of money well short of 30 years. You have the option of reducing the withdrawal rate during retirement if the investment returns are not sufficient.

The 2007-2009 financial crisis and ensuing low bond yields have sparked additional analysis of safe portfolio withdrawal rates. For example, in January 2013, intermediate-term bond real interest rates were about 4 percent less than the historical average used in prior withdrawal simulations. When using January 2013 bond rates, failure rates for retirement account withdrawals jumped to over 50 percent. With no real bond yield, retirees faced a one in three chance of running out of money after 30 years with a 50 percent stock portfolio.[19] This study serves as another lesson about the dangers of relying on historical data for future estimates of asset risk and return. The study also questioned the safety of the 4 percent withdrawal rule when bond yields are historically low. One way to deal with this problem is by adjusting the withdrawal rate over time when market conditions are poor.[20] Another caveat concerning the 4 percent rule of thumb is its increased failure rate when equity price-earnings ratios are high and dividend[p] yields are low. A 2011 study found that in projecting long-term sustainability, a 4 percent withdrawal rate cannot be considered safe when the cyclically adjusted price-earnings ratio has experienced historical highs and dividend yield has experienced historical lows. Therefore, use caution with the 4 percent rule when markets are expensive. Alternatives to common stocks and assets that are not historically expensive can be added to the portfolio when common stocks are richly priced. The bottom line is do not blindly follow the 4 percent withdrawal rule![21]

Your suitable withdrawal rate will depend on the size of your portfolio, investment return, inflation, required income and desired degree of certainty that you will not run out of money. A higher degree of certainty requires a lower withdrawal rate, all else being equal. If you are willing to accept a certain percentage of failure (i.e. running out of money), a higher withdrawal rate may be used. A higher initial withdrawal rate may also be used if you are willing to reduce the withdrawal rate in the future if investment returns are not sufficient. Although these retirement withdrawal studies provide some guidance, every retiree's situation is unique and requires a custom cash flow

---

[p] Dividends are not guaranteed and will fluctuate.

analysis. Regardless of your initial withdrawal rate, unusually low returns and abnormally high inflation for prolonged periods are the usual culprits of running out of money during retirement. If you are faced with this devastating duo, you may have to reduce withdrawals to avoid running out of money.[22]

Beware of Averages

Averages can often be misleading; therefore, always look to the underlying numbers used to determine the average. For example, a city might have an average annual temperature of 65 degrees, which sounds like a very comfortable climate. However, if half of the year the temperature is 30 degrees and the other half of the year the temperature is 100 degrees, the climate no longer seems comfortable. The average temperature, however, is 65 degrees. To avoid making invalid assumptions which lead to poor decision making, you must look beyond the average to the underlying numbers.

Frequently, the financial press and investment sales people will state that the stock market's long-term average is, for example, between 10 percent and 12 percent. That sounds pretty good; however, we must drill deeper. Whether you begin retirement near the start of a bear market or a bull market has a huge influence on investment strategy. To illustrate the impact of the sequence of returns on investment strategy and the danger of relying on the average return, consider the following example.

A 62-year-old retiring in 1983 with a $2 million retirement portfolio requires $150,000 of pre-tax income per year, adjusted annually for inflation. If the portfolio were allocated to the S&P 500[q] for a 20-year retirement period ending in 2002, the average annual return would have been 12.71 percent. A total of $4.2 million would have been distributed, and the retiree would have had an ending portfolio balance of $8.6 million. That is a very good result by any standard. However, if we reverse the order of returns and begin with the losses first (the returns from 2000-2002), the return was the same, 12.71 percent, but the total distributions were $2.5 million and the portfolio was exhausted in 14 years![23] In the second scenario, the portfolio never recovers from the poor market returns during the early

---

[q] The S&P 500 is an unmanaged index of the 500 largest domestic companies by market capitalization. Individuals cannot invest directly in any index.

years of retirement. This example also emphasizes the danger of relying on the average return, and the disastrous result of experiencing large market losses near the start of retirement.

Do not assume that the long-term average will apply to your retirement years. Inflation, like investment returns, changes with economic forces. Although the average long-term inflation rate is 2.9 percent, the average inflation rate from 1973 to 2004 was 4.7 percent. If you retired in the mid 1970's and used the average long-term inflation rate, you would have severely underestimated the inflation rate, which is the danger of using long-term assumptions for a specific retirement period. Beware of averages!

Consistency of Returns

The consistency of returns is also critical to your portfolio survivability. If we expand on the most recent example but split the portfolio between the S&P 500 and bonds, the rate of return is slightly lower at 12.29 percent (compared to 12.71 percent without bonds), but the standard deviation drops from 16.91 to 11.57 (a lower number means less variability and more consistent returns). Adding bonds to the portfolio results in much more level annual returns and provides total distributions of $4.2 million instead of $2.5 million. The portfolio also lasts 20 years, ending with a balance of $902,142 rather than running out of money after 14 years.[24] The bonds helped to dampen the stock market decline's effects. Keep in mind that portfolio survivability during retirement requires return consistency and the ability to avoid large losses.

Should a Portion of my Portfolio be Annuitized?

Another consideration is using an immediate fixed annuity for a portion of your retirement portfolio to extend portfolio longevity. An immediate fixed annuity can provide a guaranteed income stream for the life of you and your spouse. In most cases, for example, the annuity should pay out for life and period certain of 20 years. Because the annuity payments are for life, neither you nor your spouse can outlive the income stream. If, however, you and your spouse die 5 years after the annuity payments begin, your beneficiaries will receive payments for the remaining 15 years of the 20-year period. If a period-certain annuity is not used, payments will cease upon the last spouse's death, even if the payments began a short time prior to death. Careful analysis of the benefits of annuitizing a portion of your portfolio is needed as the decision to annuitize is irrevocable.

Studies using Monte Carlo simulation returns have shown that portfolios using a 4.5 percent withdrawal rate last longer and have a higher probability of survival by adding an immediate annuity to the allocation to hedge against longevity risk.[25] Longevity risk is the risk that you or your spouse will run out of money. In the following study, stocks were represented by the S&P 500; bonds were represented by intermediate government bonds; and cash was represented by 30-day T-bills[26]. Without an immediate fixed annuity, a conservative portfolio[r] using a 4.5 percent withdrawal rate fails 67.4 percent of the time using a 30-year retirement period. If 25 percent of the retirement portfolio is annuitized, the failure rate drops to 46.7 percent for the 30-year retirement period. If 50 percent of the portfolio is annuitized, the failure rate drops to 18.7 percent for a 30-year period.[27]

Similar results occur for balanced portfolios,[s] growth portfolios,[t] and aggressive portfolios.[u] Without the immediate fixed annuity, the balanced portfolio fails 23.7 percent of the time for 30-year retirement periods. With 25 percent annuitization, the failure rate drops to 14.9 percent, and for 50 percent annuitization, the failure rate drops to 5.5 percent. The growth portfolio fails 12.9 percent of the time for a 30-year retirement period. If 25 percent of the portfolio is annuitized, the failure rate drops to 7.8 percent. With 50 percent annuitization, the failure rate fell to 3.3 percent.[28] The aggressive portfolio fails a 30-year withdrawal period 8.4 percent of the time without annuitizing part of the portfolio. If 25 percent of the aggressive portfolio is annuitized, the failure rate drops to 5.4 percent for a 30-year withdrawal period. With 50 percent annuitization, the failure rate drops to 2.5 percent.

A downside to using an immediate fixed annuity is that there is less opportunity for your portfolio to appreciate in value as with unannuitized portfolios. By annuitizing a portion of the portfolio, you are trading some growth potential for a guaranteed lifetime income stream and a reduction in the portfolio failure rate. With the aggressive

---

[r] 20 percent stocks, 50 percent bonds and 30 percent cash Diversification and asset allocation do not ensure a profit or protect against a loss.
[s] 40 percent stocks, 40 percent bonds and 10 percent cash
[t] 60 percent stocks, 30 percent bonds and 10 percent cash
[u] 85 percent stocks and 15 percent bonds

portfolio allocation, the decrease in portfolio growth potential is not as pronounced as with the conservative, balanced or growth portfolios.[29]

The size of your portfolio, the investment return, the estimated length of retirement, and the withdrawal rate will influence whether you should annuitize a portion of your portfolio. In summary, the study revealed that annuitizing a portion of the portfolio reduces the failure rate for retirement periods longer than 25 years.

Will Spending Decrease in Later Years?

Another consideration is that spending habits change over the course of retirement. Retirees through their mid 70's are generally very active and are likely to have more discretionary spending. Retirees from their mid 70's to their mid 80's typically become less active and expenses usually tend to decline as discretionary spending diminishes. Retirees from their mid 80's and beyond are usually more passive and have few discretionary expenditures. Using this line of thought, retiree expenses may actually tend to decrease (disregarding inflation) as retirees age. One study estimated that at age 75 spending is approximately 20 percent less than initial spending levels at age 65.[30] For example, travel and vehicle purchases are scalable and can be expected to decline during later retirement years.[31] Keep in mind that health and long-term care expenses unfortunately may offset any reduction in active, discretionary spending.

The U.S. Bureau of Labor's Consumer Expenditure Survey also shows decreasing expenditures with increasing age. The 2012 survey revealed a 17 percent reduction in the average annual expenditures between the 55- to 64-year-old age group and the 65- to 74-year-old age group. In addition, there was a 27 percent reduction in spending between the 65- to 74-year-old age group and the over-age-75 group. The only category of expenses that did not decrease was healthcare. Use caution with these statistics as future inflation trends and investment returns are unknown. When calculating retirement withdrawals, the more conservative route is to assume living expenses will continue to increase. Furthermore, long-term care costs were not included in the survey.[32]

Unfortunately, no black box answer to your correct retirement withdrawal rate exists. The correct answer will only be found through proper planning and thorough analysis of your unique situation;

therefore, a retirement cash flow analysis is critical when determining your portfolio withdrawal rate. Due to the many unknowns and variables involved, professional help is recommended. Once you determine your optimal portfolio withdrawal rate, investment returns and/or spending habits may cause you to adjust the withdrawal rate. The rate of retirement portfolio withdrawals must be monitored on an ongoing basis. As such, retirement truly is a process rather than an event.

---

[1] http://www.comparelongtermcare.org/genworth-study-finds-lack-of-awareness-about-cost-of-retirement, November 8, 2013.

2 Centers for Disease Control and Preventiion, National Center for Health Statistics.

[3] Ibbotson Stocks, Bonds, Bills and Inflation 1926-2015.

[4] U.S. Department of Labor, Bureau of Labor Statistics, 2007.

[5] William Bengen, Conserving Client Portfolios During Retirement, Part III, Journal of Financial Planning, December 1997.

[6] William Bengen, Determining Withdrawal Rates Using Historical Data, Journal of Financial Planning October 1994.

[7] Larry R. Frank, CFP, and David M. Blanchett, CFP, CLU, AIFA, QPA, CFA, The Dynamic Implications of Sequence Risk on a Distribution Portfolio, Journal of Financial Planning, June 2010.

[8] William Bengen, Determining Withdrawal Rates Using Historical Data, Journal of Financial Planning, October 1994.

[9] Phillip L. Cooley, Carl M. Hubbard, and Daniel T. Walz, Retirement Savings: Choosing a Withdrawal Rate That is Sustainable, American Association of Individual Investors Journal, February 1998.

[10] David M. Zolt, CFP, EA, ASA, MAAA, Retirement Planning by Targeting Safe Withdrawal Rates, Journal of Financial Planning, October 2014.

[11] William Bengen, Determining Withdrawal Rates Using Historical Data, Journal of Financial Planning October 1994.

[12] William Bengen, Baking a Withdrawal Plan "Layer Cake" for Your Retirement Clients, Journal of Financial Planning, August 2006.

[13] William Bengen, Conserving Client Portfolios During Retirement, FPA Press 2006.

[14] William P. Bengen, Asset Allocation for a Lifetime Journal of Financial Planning, August 1996.

[15] Monte Carlo simulations are used to show how variations in rates of return each year can affect your results. A Monte Carlo simulation calculates the results of your Plan by running it many times, each time using a different sequence of returns. Some sequences of returns will give you better results, and some will give you worse results. These multiple trials provide a range of possible results, some successful (you would have met all your goals) and some unsuccessful (you would not have met all your goals). The percentage of trials that were successful is the probability that your Plan, with all its underlying assumptions, could be successful. The Results Using Monte Carlo Simulations indicate the likelihood that an event may occur as well as the likelihood that it may not occur. In analyzing this information, please note that the analysis does not take into account actual market conditions, which may severely affect the outcome of your goals over the long-term.

[16] John Ameriks, Ph.D., Robert Veres and Mark J. Wasrshowsky Ph.D., Making Retirement Last a Lifetime, Journal of Financial Planning, December 2001.

[17] Id.

[18] Id.

[19] Michael Finke, Ph.D. CFP; Wade D. Pfau, Ph.D., CFA; and David M. Blanchett, CFP, CFA, The 4 Percent Rule is Not Safe in a Low-Yield World, Journal of Financial Planning, January 2013.

[20] Jonathan T. Guyton, Decision Rules and Portfolio Management for Retirees: Is the "Safe" Initial Withdrawal Rate Too Safe?, Journal of Financial Planning, 2004.

[21] Wade D. Pfau, Ph.D., Can We Predict the Sustainable Withdrawal Rate for New Retirees?, Journal of Financial Planning, August 2011.

[22] Jonathan T. Guyton, Decision Rules and Maximum Initial Withdrawal Rates, Journal of Financial Planning, March 2006.

[23] John Nersesian, Hatching a Nest Egg, www.Financial-Planning.com, 2006.

[24] Id.

[25] See Ameriks note 1.

[26] Intermediate Government bonds, 30-day T-bills and S&P 500 return data are from Ibbotson Associates.Inclusion of these indexes is for illustrative purposes only. Keep in mind that individuals cannot invest directly in any index, and index performance does not include transaction costs or other fees, which will affect actual investment performance. Individual investor's results will vary. Past performance does not guarantee future results.

[27] See Ameriks note 1.

[28] Id.

[29] Id.

[30] Tacchino and Saltzman, Do Accumulation Models Overstate What's Needed to Retire? Journal of Financial Planning 1999.

[31] Michael Finke, Ph.D. CFP; Wade D. Pfau, Ph.D., CFA; and Duncan Williams, CFP, Spending Flexibility and Safe Withdrawal Rates, Journal of Financial Planning, March, 2012.

[32] Ty Bernicke, Reality Retirement Plannning: A New Paradigm for an old Science, Journal of Financial Planning, June 2005.

Wade D. Pfau, Ph.D., CFA, Capital Market Expectations, Asset Allocation, and Safe Withdrawal Rates, Journal of Financial Planning, January, 2012.

3

Retirement Investments

Chapter Highlights

❖ Investing for retirement distributions requires a different strategy than investing for retirement accumulation.

❖ Risk management is vital to the success of any investor; however, during retirement, risk management is more important than ever because you do not have the luxury of waiting for the market to bail you out of investing mistakes.

❖ One of your most difficult challenges during retirement is controlling your emotions when making investment decisions.

❖ Your risk tolerance is closely related to your required return, and you must have a clear understanding of the amount of risk you are willing to assume while attempting to achieve your required rate of return.

❖ An investment policy statement serves as a road map that will define your current situation, short- and long-term goals, investment time horizon, risk tolerance, required returns and asset allocation parameters.

❖ Asset allocation involves diversification and potentially maximizing returns for your risk tolerance. The benefits of diversification through asset allocation are indisputable but will not guarantee a gain or protect against a loss.

❖ Strategic asset allocation invests in a constant mix portfolio regardless of changes in economic conditions. Your risk tolerance and required return determine your suitable investment allocation.

❖ Tactical asset allocation uses a portfolio based on your risk tolerance and required return; however, the portfolio mix is not static. Changes are made to your portfolio to reflect changes in economic conditions, returns, correlations between asset classes and standard deviation (risk).

❖ Tactical asset allocation may provide a better opportunity than strategic asset allocation to help achieve your desired return in range-bound or bear-trending markets. Tactical asset allocation provides flexibility to adjust the portfolio in light of changing market conditions. A tactical approach may also result in a portfolio that is more aggressive and more volatile than one using strategic asset allocation.

❖ Passive portfolio management (indexing) does not attempt to add value by providing returns in excess of a benchmark index (e.g. S&P 500) or by reducing risk.

❖ Active portfolio management attempts to achieve a return that is in excess of a benchmark index or to achieve a similar return with less risk than the benchmark index.

❖ Relative strength allows you to make tactical decisions regarding which market areas should be over-weighted and which areas should be under-weighted or avoided altogether.

❖ Standard Deviation is a measure of total variability of returns from the average return. It is a measure of risk and provides a range of possible future returns in relation to the average return.

❖ Beta measures volatility (risk) relative to the market. For example, an investment with a beta of 1.0 has the same volatility as the market, and an investment with a beta of 1.2 is 20 percent more volatile than the market.

❖ The Sharpe, Treynor and Sortino ratios measure risk-adjusted return.

❖ If you are paying portfolio managers for active management, you want to find highly skilled portfolio managers. Alpha provides a measure of manager skill as it compares the actual return with the return that you should have earned for the level of risk you undertook. Higher alphas indicate the manager is producing a higher return than anticipated from the level of investment risk assumed.

ONE OF THE MOST DAUNTING TASKS you will face as a retiree is investing your retirement portfolio to provide a lifetime of income. You must make many decisions such as how to protect your portfolio from market risk, how to use asset allocation, when to make portfolio changes and how to select the best investments for your retirement. Unfortunately, investing to produce retirement income is more challenging than investing to accumulate your retirement portfolio. The rules and objectives change when you transition from the accumulation phase (your working years) to the distribution phase (retirement). During retirement, risk management is more important than ever because you do not have the luxury of waiting for the market to bail you out of investing mistakes. In addition, you probably will not earn sufficient income to rebuild your portfolio if you experience large losses. The inability to recuperate from significant losses may cause you to run out of money early, to experience a drastically reduced standard of living, or to suffer both. Warren Buffet's rules to investing provide some wisdom: 1. Don't lose money. And 2. Don't forget rule number one.

An additional challenge is the need to grow your portfolio to hedge against inflation while withdrawing income from the portfolio. Unfortunately, investing for income and investing for portfolio growth are conflicting objectives requiring different investment strategies. You must obtain a balance between these two objectives within your risk tolerance.

Do not be lulled into a false sense of security by assuming that retirement investing is a simple task to be addressed once at the onset of retirement. The financial planning industry has created many risk profile questionnaires that will suggest one of several asset allocation pie chart portfolios based on your risk profile score. Typically, the suggested portfolio is to be held long-term and changed only when your risk profile changes. Although determining your risk profile is an important step when designing your portfolio, investing during retirement is more complex than the cookie cutter approach used by most investors and brokers alike.

Unfortunately, many financial advisor representatives do no more than determine the retiree's risk score and plug the retiree into a set-it-and-forget-it pie chart asset allocation. To the detriment of retirees, this approach fails to adequately address how risk is to be managed. Remember, avoiding large losses to your retirement portfolio is paramount when investing during retirement. The reason much of the advice is cookie-cutter asset allocation is that usually the person recommending buy-and-hold strategic asset allocation is a salesperson rather than a true investment professional. You must be able to distinguish the professional investment advisor representative from the salesperson. There can be a big difference between the two. An initial sign of a salesperson is a lack of a strategy to help manage risk to your retirement nest egg.

The most common method of managing risk is to adjust the percentage of bonds in the portfolio. But what if bonds perform poorly due to an adverse interest rate environment or other economic factors? Or what if allocating too much to bonds causes the portfolio return to drop too low or rising interest rates cause bond values to drop? True risk management involves more than adding bonds to your portfolio. Investment management is both an art and a science, and for many investors, it is not as simple as a buy-and-hold asset allocation. Investing is a complex process, and the underlying factors affecting investment decisions are constantly changing. For these reasons, a strategic buy-and-hold asset allocation portfolio may not be an adequate strategy to manage risk during retirement, especially during bear or sideways-trending markets.

This chapter does not cover all aspects of investing. Rather, it points out major investment mistakes and misconceptions. This chapter also describes tools and strategies that may be used to increase the odds of investing success. Hopefully, it will enlighten you to the importance of going beyond sole reliance on long-term historical returns to create a buy and hold portfolio and will encourage you to take the steps necessary to protect your portfolio—steps that most investors and advisors never take.

A Few Common Mistakes to Avoid

The most difficult challenge facing retirees is controlling the emotional aspect of investing. But you must control your emotions, or your emotions will control you. All investors suffer from investment mistakes due to our psychological "wiring." In other words, we are pre-programmed to make many common investment mistakes, but knowing about them may help you avoid them. For example, fear and greed are two of the most powerful human emotions, and they run rampant in the investment world. The 2007-2009 market decline is a prime example of fear controlling investment decisions. When the market drops, many investors fear that the market will continue to drop. If this fear is not controlled, it can cause an investor to abandon a sound investment strategy. Greed, on the other hand, often causes investors to abandon their risk management plan when the market rises to extended levels. The "irrational exuberance of the late 1990s is a good example of investors throwing caution to the wind. Human nature or not, emotions and investing do not mix and, if not controlled, create a disastrous combination. Awareness of the problems that emotions and flawed logic may cause when making investment decisions is a step toward controlling those emotions as an investor.

Riding the Emotional Rollercoaster

Unfortunately, the failure to keep emotions in check often leads to poor investment decisions. The market and the various market sectors constantly experience up and down trends. Price fluctuation is a normal part of the stock and bond markets. If you invest in the stock market, you must accept some degree of risk and fluctuation even if your portfolio is very conservative. There are no free lunches in the investment world. If your portfolio allocation is suitable for your risk tolerance, problems generally do not arise from the portfolio or the market but from how you react to rising and falling markets.

When faced with a difficult market, irrational decision making causes many investors to veer from their game plan. Historically, any given market index typically has a negative return once every three or four years. Although market pullbacks and corrections are normal, emotions may cause investors to fear that the market will continue to fall. The further the market falls, the greater the influence of emotions on investor decision making. The typical "falling market" emotions in sequential order are anxiety, denial, fear, panic, capitulation, despondency, desperation and depression. Like clockwork, many investors who attempt to buy and hold will sell when the pain from losses is overwhelming (selling low). This usually occurs anywhere from the panic stage to the depression stage. Selling most likely occurs near the end of a market correction when the market is washed-out and about to start rebounding. The end result is that many investors sell at or near the market cycle's bottom.

When a market selloff ends and the market begins to go up, investors feel the following "rising market" emotions in sequential order: hope, relief, optimism, excitement, thrill and euphoria. By the time thrill and euphoria set in, the market has usually had a nice run; the media is reporting that the economy is great; and many people feel the market will continue to rise. At this stage, many investors feel comfortable investing. Like clockwork, not long after they get back into the market (and are buying at higher prices), the market starts to go down again. After a good run, the market is usually due to pullback; it is a normal market process. When the market begins to go down, "falling market" emotions come into play again, and the cycle is repeated.

After experiencing this buy high, sell low cycle a few times, an investor may be left bewildered, not knowing what to do. Following a few bad investment experiences, investors may feel like a deer in headlights and do nothing to manage risk to their portfolio, or they may get completely out of the market. For example, during severe corrections like 1973-1974, 2000-2002 and 2007-2009, many growth-oriented investors got out of the market completely and turned to bonds, CDs and money market investments. Unfortunately after 2008, historically low interest rates have provided little return to investors in many fixed income investments. To make matters worse many investors failed to have a strategy to reinvest in stocks when the market outlook improved. Such action is a sign of irrational, emotion-driven behavior. It is also a result of not having a strategy to manage risk.

Investing too Conservatively

Investing too conservatively out of fear of market volatility is another emotional mistake. Investors who do not have a plan to manage risk typically make this mistake. One way many investors deal with market volatility is to avoid it by investing too heavily in CDs, fixed annuities or bonds. This is a classic example of the fear of loss overriding rational decision making. Investing too heavily in bonds and other fixed-income investments (e.g. CDs) may calm the fears of a nervous investor but will not provide a hedge against inflation for later years.

To get an idea of inflation's effects, you need only know that $1 will be worth $.41 in 30 years, assuming a 3 percent inflation rate. Put another way, a $1 million portfolio 30 years into the future is worth

$410,000 after adjusting for a 3 percent inflation rate. This means that, over 30 years, purchasing power can be cut in half. Although we typically do not notice inflation's effects as they are occurring, consider that many people paid more for the car they drive today than they paid for their first home. That is inflation's effect over time. In the end, without a sound strategy to manage risk, you are likely to invest too heavily in bonds and CDs in an attempt to protect your portfolio from market risk during volatile markets. Do not be drawn into a false sense of security by overweighting bonds or CDs. Although the risk of losing money is real, especially in volatile markets, inflation risk should not be underestimated, for it is a very serious threat to retirement security.

Following the Herd

The herd mentality is another common, emotion-driven investor mistake. The herd mentality occurs when investors gravitate to what the majority of other investors are doing. For example, when the market has experienced a good run to the upside, investors who are on the sidelines want a part of the action. As investors continue to bid stocks higher, more investors continue to jump into the market for fear of missing out on the gains. The market continues to be driven up by investors joining the herd and entering the market. A problem arises, however, for investors who arrive late to the party. When market prices reach extreme levels, investors begin to sell to lock in their profits. Once the selling begins, prices begin to drop. The herd mentality begins to work in the opposite direction as more investors begin to sell. The selling accelerates as prices continue to drop and as fear and panic set in. As more investors join the selling herd, prices often reach oversold levels. If you followed the herd into the market and bought high, you are likely to follow the herd out of the market and sell low. The herd mentality has a huge effect when the market is at extreme levels, near market tops and market bottoms. Investors without a risk management strategy who follow the market's every move are particularly prone to the herd mentality.

Lacking Patience

Successful investing requires patience to allow the investment strategy to work. Many investors trade too frequently due to a lack of patience and discipline. However, patience is difficult without a sound strategy for investment decision making; therefore, a sound strategy is a must. Many investors make decisions based on market "noise" by placing too much emphasis on every market up tick and down tick. Although we live in an instant gratification society, exercising patience when investing is a must so long as investment decisions are based on a sound strategy. Daily and weekly trends change frequently and are very difficult to forecast with any degree of confidence. In essence, the short-term market trend is random, but the intermediate and longer-term trends last months to years. For this reason, intermediate and long-term trends are much more important and may be used to guide investment decisions. Unfortunately, most individual investors focus on the short-term. This behavior renders many investors unable to see "the forest for the trees."

Having Memory Biases

Another common investor mistake is recency bias which causes investors to place more emphasis on recent investment experiences than on more distant experiences. Recency bias may cause an investor to extrapolate recent experiences into faulty long-term forecasts. For example, it causes investors to become unreasonably optimistic in rising markets and unreasonably pessimistic in falling markets.

Ignoring Mistakes

Many investors also have difficulty admitting to a wrong decision. Regret aversion may cause this difficulty. Regret aversion is problematic because it may cause an investor to hold on to a losing investment in an attempt to "get back to even." Or, regret aversion may prevent an investor from getting back into the market after a correction or pullback when prices are low. It is a fact of life that some investment decisions will be wrong. Too many unknowns exist about the future to always make the right investment call. The key is to recognize a wrong decision and correct it before too much damage occurs to your portfolio. It is okay to make a wrong investment decision, but it is not okay to stay wrong. The ability to admit a mistake and correct it is essential for investment success.

Using Mental Accounting

If your portfolio is truly diversified, some investments will go up while others are going down (or at least not all will be moving up or down at the same rate). Due to the effect of negatively correlated assets discussed further herein, a properly diversified portfolio will hold investments that typically do not move in the same direction at the same time. Mental accounting will cause an investor to look at the investments individually, rather than as a combined portfolio. Invariably, the investments experiencing losses or which are lagging in the short-term when the overall market it going up are deemed not worthy of investing. These same investments are usually the ones that will begin to go up when the overall market is going down. This is a result of negative or nonperfect correlation. Although a diversified portfolio cannot guarantee a profit or protect against a loss, a diversified portfolio potentially reduces the impact of market downtrends through negative or nonperfect correlation. To stay on track, avoid mental accounting and look at your portfolio as a whole.

Individual Investors' Track Records

If you need additional proof that investment decisions are often driven by emotion rather than logic, consider these findings. Studies have shown that investors (and many advisors) continue to do a poor job of investment management. For example, the 20-year average annual return ending in 2017 for equity investors was 5.29 percent. During that same time frame, the S&P 500 had an average annual return of 7.20 percent, and inflation averaged 2.15 percent.[1] The average equity investor return was dramatically lower than the S&P 500 due to the following types of irrational decision making: buying high and selling low, chasing returns, following the herd, mental accounting, a lack of risk management and not employing a sound strategy when making investment decisions.

Even bond investors performed poorly. The average fixed-income investor's return for the 20-year period ending in 2017 was 0.44 percent. During the same period, long-term government bonds returned an average of 4.60 percent. The take-away from the study is that underlying stock and bond portfolios performed much better than the average investor whose decisions about when to buy and sell investments were poor.[2]

As mentioned earlier, we are hard-wired to react to the market in an irrational, emotion-driven fashion. This is why it is critical to remove emotions from the investment decision making process. The best way to remove emotions is to have a plan for navigating the capital markets and for managing risk.

Designing Your Portfolio

Designing a portfolio and implementing an investment strategy is an ongoing process, not a one-time event. The first step to designing your portfolio is to determine your required rate of return. The required rate of return is the return you must receive (or anticipate receiving) for assuming the investment risk of a particular portfolio. Your required rate of return may be stated as a flat percentage or range such as 6 percent to 8 percent. In the alternative, your required rate of return may be stated as a certain percentage over the rate of inflation such as 4 percent over the Consumer Price Index[a] (CPI). A retirement cash flow analysis is needed to determine your required portfolio return and the amount of risk you must assume as determined by your retirement goals.

Risk Tolerance

Your risk tolerance is closely related to your required return, and you must have a clear understanding of the amount of risk you are willing to assume while attempting to achieve your target return rate. Your risk tolerance and investment experiences are unique and vary widely from other individuals'. Remember not to invest too conservatively, which may not provide an adequate hedge against inflation, or too aggressively, which may increase your chance of losses. You must have a balance that helps protect against both of these risks. Determining your risk tolerance is an important step because it will help to determine your appropriate investment strategy and mix of asset classes. It will also help to determine the appropriate investment vehicles.

Many investors desire a high rate of return but are unwilling to accept the price volatility (risk) associated with that level of return. Investors seeking higher returns must accept a higher degree of price volatility. However, the risk of more aggressive portfolios can and should be managed. For example, an aggressive investor would have

[a] The Consumer Price Index is a measure of inflation and is compiled by the US Bureau of Labor Studies.

had a large allocation to technology stocks in the late 1990s. The same aggressive investor should have managed the risk to his or her portfolio by not riding these stocks down from 2000 through 2002. Although you may be a long-term investor, you should still manage risk rather than merely "hang in there for the long haul."

Time Horizon

Your appropriate time horizon, like risk tolerance, will vary from other investors' time horizons. Because time horizon and risk tolerance are closely related, all else being equal, a shorter time horizon typically suggests a lower risk tolerance, and a longer time horizon typically suggests a higher risk tolerance. Your time horizon can be expressed as when retirement distributions must begin as well as how long distributions must last. If distributions are to begin sooner rather than later, your time horizon is usually shorter, and your risk tolerance generally should be lower. Like risk tolerance, your time horizon is a primary factor in determining the mix of stocks and bonds in your portfolio and in establishing the weights between the asset classes. Risk tolerance and time horizon also help determine the types of managers, and the amount of risk the managers assume, that will be used in your portfolio.

Some investors segregate their retirement portfolios into different pools or portions, each with a different time horizon. For example, income for the next three years would be taken from the short-term pool, which is usually invested in money market accounts, CDs and/or short-term bonds. The next pool is earmarked for intermediate-term use (e.g. four to eight years) and is usually invested more aggressively than the short-term pool. The final pool of money is for long-term use and is invested more aggressively than the intermediate-term pool. Assets from the longer term pools are used to replenish the shorter term pools as these assets are spent on retirement expenses. Many variations on this concept exist; however, all are designed to encourage more aggressive investments in the long-term pool to hedge against inflation, while protecting the short-term pool from risk of loss. Because the long-term pool is not used for immediate income needs, the retiree is less likely to draw down or sell these assets when the market is down.

The first two steps to developing your investment strategy— determining your risk tolerance and determining your time horizon—

are often overlooked. Investors often skip these steps and go straight into selecting their investments. Do not make this common mistake. Put adequate thought into defining your risk tolerance and time horizon to design a portfolio within your comfort range.

Asset Classes

A fundamental investment issue is how much to invest in the various asset classes. Asset classes include stocks, bonds, cash, real estate, and commodity related investments. Your time horizon, risk tolerance and income needs are among the primary drivers determining the asset classes to consider for your portfolio. Investors with shorter time horizons and lower risk tolerances may choose to reduce or eliminate exposure to more risky asset classes and sub-classes. Commodity and real estate investments are considered riskier asset classes. Riskier asset sub-classes include, but are not limited to, emerging markets, international stocks and bonds[b], small and medium sized companies, and high-yield (junk) bonds[c]. Investors with longer time horizons and higher risk tolerances should consider increasing exposure to riskier asset classes and sub-classes in their investment mix. If the risks are correctly managed, emerging market, international and commodity related investments, small company stock[d] and real estate may enhance the portfolio's risk-to-return attributes. The "sleep factor" must also be considered. More aggressive investments may cause too much stress and worry, resulting in the inability to stick to the game plan. Investments that cause you to lose sleep may be too aggressive for your risk tolerance.

---

[b] There are special risks involved with global investing related to market and currency fluctuations, economic and political instability, and different financial accounting standards.

[c] High-yield bonds are not suitable for all investors. The risk of default may increase due to changes in the issuer's credit quality. Price changes may occur due to changes in interest rates and the liquidity of the bond. When appropriate these bonds should only comprise a modest portion of a portfolio.

[d] Investing in small company stocks generally involves greater risks, and therefore, may not be appropriate for every investor.

The Investment Policy Statement (IPS)

An investment policy statement (IPS) establishes the framework for managing your portfolio. It also provides a sound, well thought out process for making investment decisions. The IPS serves as a road map that will define your current situation, short- and long-term goals, investment time horizon, risk tolerance and asset allocation guidelines.

Benefits of an IPS

An IPS provides a set of policies and procedures that can help you "stay the course" with investment decisions in difficult markets. It serves as a reminder of why a particular investment strategy was implemented and of the risk/reward tradeoffs. As a result, an IPS may help you subdue emotions to prevent irrational decision making. For example, a conservative investor may be enticed by a rising market to invest more aggressively and beyond the limits stated in his or her IPS. If this occurs, the IPS should be amended to reflect an increase in risk tolerance. In most cases, the investor will realize that he or she does not want to invest more aggressively and will stick to the original IPS game plan. In addition, an IPS may prevent second guessing of investment decisions in difficult markets. It also provides procedures and benchmarks to monitor portfolio investment performance and individual investment managers.

Elements of an IPS

IPS elements include but are not limited to

- Investment goals for appreciation, yield and capital preservation
- A target rate of return
- Restrictions on allowable investments (Are below investment grade bonds allowed, and if so are there limitations to amounts? Will limitations be placed on the use of indexing or active management of portfolios? Will restrictions be placed on investments in foreign jurisdictions?)
- The allowing or disallowing of short selling or option strategies
- Minimum and maximum limits to allocate to asset classes
- Criteria for hiring and firing investment managers

- Evaluation procedures for investment managers, including appropriate benchmarks to measure quarterly, annual, three-year, five-year and ten-year returns

- Guidelines for portfolio rebalancing (Will rebalancing occur monthly, quarterly, or annually? In the alternative, will the portfolio be rebalanced when asset classes are beyond percentage limitations set by the IPS? This is typically used for strategic asset allocation portfolios.)

Asset Allocation and Modern Portfolio Theory

Many investors use some form of asset allocation when making investment portfolio decisions. Asset allocation is primarily concerned with using diversification to help reduce risk and assist in maximizing returns for your risk tolerance. Asset allocation and Modern Portfolio Theory (MPT) define the level of risk you are willing to assume while attempting to achieve a given rate of return. Your portfolio is then designed to best reflect this optimal risk/return relationship[3]. This is sometimes referred to as investing on the efficient frontier.

The benefits of diversification through asset allocation are undisputable. Nobel Laureate Harry Markowitz proposed that investors should focus on the risk/reward relationship of an entire portfolio rather than each investment individually. His ground-breaking work detailed the mathematics of why diversification works. Although diversification does not ensure a profit or guarantee against losses, it helps to reduce volatility. Reducing volatility means reducing risk and can help you achieve your investment goals. Thus, diversification can help improve the risk-adjusted returns and is designed reduce the risk of "putting all of your eggs in one basket." The debate arises with how to implement asset allocation. Later, this chapter will cover the two primary types of asset allocation: strategic asset allocation and tactical asset allocation.

Modern Portfolio Theory emphasizes the importance of diversification when investing. Through diversification, a portfolio can be created that is typically less risky than the individual investments due to security prices that do not move in the same direction at the same time. This means they are not perfectly correlated. The correlations between asset classes enable diversification to help reduce risk. Correlation may range from -1 (perfect negative correlation) to +1 (perfect positive correlation). Negatively correlated security prices generally move in opposite directions; however, to achieve diversification, prices need not have a perfect negative correlation. Portfolio volatility (risk) can be reduced by adding securities with a correlation of less than 1.0 (e.g. 0.4). An example of low correlation is that when stocks go down in value, bonds often go up in value. Assets with a low correlation help to eliminate some volatility and provide diversification in various market conditions. Furthermore, due to a low correlation between assets, a diversified portfolio is often less risky than the least risky asset in the portfolio[e]. For example, a portfolio composed of 60 percent bonds and 40 percent stocks is less risky[f] than a portfolio of 100 percent bonds, even though the portfolio contains 40 percent stocks.

Strategic vs. Tactical Asset Allocation

Although asset allocation is in widespread use, there is much disagreement over how it is best implemented. Part of the confusion arises from the various definitions of asset allocation. Asset allocation can be defined as determining the mix of stocks and bonds in a portfolio. It can also be defined as the entire process of determining the mix of stocks to bonds, selecting investments to construct the portfolio and rebalancing the investments when needed. Regardless of how you define and implement asset allocation, you should generally use some form of asset allocation due to the advantages of diversification. The asset allocation debate circles around the two primary types of asset allocation: strategic asset allocation and tactical asset allocation.

Strategic asset allocation uses a constant mix portfolio that is not changed with changes in economic conditions. The portfolio establishes long-term target allocations to stocks, bonds and cash based on the investor's risk tolerance and historical long-term returns, correlations and standard deviations of all of the asset classes. Unlike a tactical asset allocation portfolio, the portfolio's allocation does not change unless the investor's risk tolerance changes. Typically, the portfolio is rebalanced several times a year to realign the portfolio with the original suggested long-term target asset allocation.

---

[e] Risk meaning volatility as measured by standard deviation.
[f] Risk meaning volatility as measured by standard deviation.

Tactical asset allocation creates a portfolio based on the investor's risk tolerance; however, the portfolio mix does not remain constant. Changes are made to the portfolio to reflect changes in economic conditions, valuations, price trends, returns, correlations and standard deviation. For example, if a certain asset class is overpriced (e.g. large-cap growth in 1999 or real estate in 2006), this asset class may be underweighted until it is no longer overpriced. Underpriced asset classes or asset classes that are poised to appreciate in value may be overweighted. Tactical asset allocation seeks to determine the market areas or sectors that are most likely to outperform over the intermediate and long-term. These areas are overweighted while the market areas likely to underperform are underweighted.

Strategic Asset Allocation

Most investors use strategic asset allocation as it is easy to implement and maintain. Because no decisions need to be made regarding current economic conditions, intermediate or long-term trends, or changes in various asset classes' future return prospects, once the allocation is established, very little needs to be done other than to rebalance the portfolio. A fixed buy-and-hold strategic asset allocation portfolio attempts to provide a target rate of return with a portfolio that is held through all market conditions. The investing public accepted this strategy as the markets generally rose during the 1980's and 1990's secular bull market. Stocks experienced unprecedented gains, and portfolios generally rose with the stock market. Any drop in the market provided opportunities to add money while stock prices were lower (i.e. buy on pullbacks). Unfortunately, bull markets do not last forever.

Strategic asset allocation (i.e. buy and hold investing) has been used by most investment advisors for decades and is based on Modern Portfolio Theory. The foundation for Modern Portfolio Theory was laid in 1952 with work by Harry Markowitz.[4] Markowitz's work explained how combining risky assets in a diversified portfolio can reduce risk. Later, William Sharpe developed the Capital Asset Pricing Model which conveys that the expected return for a portfolio is determined by its overall exposure to risk.[5] Sharpe's work explained that investing in riskier assets should reward the investor with higher returns. In 1986, Brinson, Hood and Beebower (BHB) published a study of the asset allocation of 91 large pension funds from 1974 to 1983.[6] Their study is widely cited for its findings that 93.6% of the variation in investment returns is explained by the asset allocation policy.[7] The BHB study was also used for building the case for setting a strategic asset allocation and avoiding changes to the portfolio unless the investor's risk tolerance changes. Proponents of strategic asset allocation have and continue to rely on the belief that because 93.6% of the return is determined by the asset allocation, attempts to change the asset mix in light of economic, political, investment trend or business cycle changes are futile.

Armed with the works of Markowitz, Sharpe and BHB, the investment industry embraced and promoted strategic asset allocation for its ease of implementation and its "set it and forget it" approach, and the "pie chart" was born. Since the BHB study, strategic asset allocation buy and hold has spread across the investment world. It does not take much thought to determine your risk tolerance and a strategic asset allocation portfolio to match. Then the investor should periodically rebalance the portfolio and hold it for the long-term. There are numerous shortcomings and misrepresentations when applying strategic asset allocation which will be discussed in the next section.

Myths and Misconceptions of Strategic Asset Allocation

In the real world of investing there are numerous problems with the application of Modern Portfolio Theory and strategic asset allocation to your portfolio as it misrepresents the importance of asset allocation policy in determining portfolio performance and the likelihood of attaining your investment goals. The investment industry has provided investors with a false sense of security by taking certain interpretive liberties with the findings of Markowitz, Sharpe and BHB.[8]

Over the past two to three decades half-truths and investment myths have permeated the investing world. To the detriment of investors, these myths have become so commonplace that most investors have accepted them and believe them to be true.

The Pie Chart Myth

You are probably familiar with a pie chart allocation that divides the portfolio between various asset classes as determined by a risk profile questionnaire. For the investor using strategic asset allocation, conventional wisdom says that the most important factor to investment success is the mix of stocks, bonds and cash (i.e. the asset allocation). It is common in today's financial literature and among investors and professionals alike to rely on the assumption that 93.6 percent of portfolio returns are explained by the asset allocation. Put another way, the investor's allocation to stocks, bonds and cash will determine 93.6 percent of the return. This line of reasoning is based on the BHB study that the investor's allocation to stocks, bonds and cash will determine 93.6 percent of the portfolio's return. The investment industry has used the BHB study to suggest that tactical changes to the portfolio such as raising cash when market risk is high or changing the asset mix does not contribute to return and should be avoided.[9]

In examining the BHB study, we find that the asset allocation policy of the 91 pension funds examined explained an average of 93.6 percent of the <u>total variation in quarterly returns</u>. There is a huge difference between 93.6 percent of the total variation in quarterly returns and 93.6 percent of the return. Actual returns and quarterly variation of returns are two different things. Making the leap to suggest that this study shows that 93.6 percent of the return is determined by the asset allocation is flawed. Wall Street and many advisors have relied on the BHB study to suggest that successful investing is simply a matter of completing a risk profile questionnaire and dividing the assets among the various asset classes. The assumption is that once the risk profile determines the correct strategic asset allocation pie chart, 93.6 percent of the return will be explained. The remaining 6.4 percent is market timing and security selection and is ignored. Do not be lulled into a false sense of security by thinking a strategic pie chart allocation will be successful through all market conditions.

Investors should use caution when applying the BHB study findings, which were based on pension portfolios, to their retirement portfolios. Pensions invest differently from the way a retiree should invest. Institutional portfolios include pensions, foundations, endowments, large trusts and portfolios of $10 million to $100 billion or more. Institutional portfolios have a time horizon that is much longer than a retiree's time horizon. Often they have a perpetual existence. Their size and extended (or perpetual) time horizon are two of the reasons that institutional portfolios have the ability to better withstand extended market downturns and ride out long bear market trends. In addition, pension and other institutional portfolios frequently receive additional assets. For these reasons, a strategic asset allocation buy-and-hold strategy is often an institutional portfolio's optimal strategy.

As an individual investor, you do not have the luxury of riding out a 10- to 15-year flat market such as the 1966 to 1982 period discussed further herein. A more recent example is the S&P 500's average annual return of -0.95% from 2000 to 2009. In most cases, such a dismal investment experience would cause you to run out of money in a relatively short amount of time. In addition, unlike large pension funds, typically no additional funds are normally added to your portfolio once retirement begins.

The Historical Data Problem with Strategic Asset Allocation

Developing a strategic asset allocation requires assumptions to be made regarding future returns, correlations and standard deviations. To determine the optimal portfolio, strategic asset allocation relies on historical data as the input data for the various asset classes' expected future returns, correlations and standard deviations. Common sense tells us that these variables for each investment class change over time, and the historical average may not be reflective of the current environment.[10] What is the impact on the portfolio if the historical intermediate term corporate bond return is 5.5 percent, but the current rate of return is 2 percent? In addition, there is no way to accurately predict these changes many years into the future. If you cannot accurately predict the long-term returns, correlations and standard deviations of the various asset classes, the future performance of a strategic asset allocation portfolio is unknown. If the future returns, standard deviations and correlations are different from the assumption used to create the asset allocation model, the results forecasted by the asset allocation model will also be different. Failing to change the portfolio in light of changes in economic cycles may lead to disappointing results. If you have not had success with forecasting long-term future events relating to the economy and the stock market, don't feel bad. Economists also have great difficulty projecting long-term forecasts. Predicting the future is impossible. Basing investment decisions on intermediate and long-term trends is more reliable than trying to predict the return of the S&P 500 twenty years in the future or assuming the returns of the next twenty years will resemble the past twenty years.

If we examine historical returns, we find that they are not a reliable predictor of future returns. For example, let's assume you retired in 2000 and are designing a portfolio for retirement. Let's also assume that you are a buy-and-hold strategic asset allocation investor, which means that your portfolio mix will not change unless your risk tolerance changes. If you assumed that large-cap growth stocks would have continued to perform as in the 1980s (+17.55% annually) and the 1990s (+18.21% annually) or even tracked their long-term average of 9.8% from 1926 through 2009 your market assumptions would have been off...way off from 2000 through 2009. The S&P 500 was virtually flat during that time frame. Unfortunately, during 2000-2009 large capitalization stocks returned far less than their historical average. In fact, the average return for large capitalization stocks during this period was -0.95%![g] Typical of strategic asset allocation, a significant portion of the portfolio is allocated to large-cap growth stocks and large-cap value stocks. Small cap stocks and emerging market stocks typically compose 10-15 percent of a strategic asset allocation. By locking into this strategic buy-and-hold asset allocation portfolio based on historical returns, the portfolio would have over-weighted one of the worst performing asset classes (large-cap stocks) and underweighted two of the best performing asset classes. Small capitalization stocks returned 5.8% annually during the 2000-2009 period. Emerging market stocks returned 10.2% annually during the same period.[h] Strategic asset allocation requires that you hold on to underperforming asset classes. Some investors are better served by underweighting or eliminating underperforming asset classes until these asset classes show signs of improvement. Retirees who invested heavily in large-cap stocks from 2000 through 2009 were in for a rough ride as these assets drastically underperformed other market segments.

Is Diversification Enough to Protect Against Market Declines?

Strategic Asset Allocation is based on the premise that diversification is the optimal way to manage risk. By diversifying among different assets, as one asset goes down, another is likely going up, so they offset each other. By diversifying portfolios, investors

---

[g] As measured by the S&P 500.
[h] As measured by the MSCI Emerging Market Index.

believe the risk is being "managed". Is diversification enough, however?

The degree to which diversification works is dependent upon correlation. Correlations range between -1.0 (negative correlation meaning prices move in opposite directions); 0.0 (no relationship between price movement); to +1.0 (perfect correlation meaning prices move in tandem together). When analyzing correlations of asset prices, as correlations move above 0.5, the benefits of diversification are reduced. Correlations above .80 represent a very high degree of correlated price movement, and thus, a low amount of correlation. The correlation between asset classes changes over time and often increases during falling markets. When correlations increase, diversification is less effective.[11] A classic example was 2008 when domestic stocks, international stocks, real estate, commodities and even most bonds all moved down together.

The problems with changes in correlations are not isolated to events like the market crash in 2008. Correlations between asset classes change daily and often change dramatically over time. Strategic asset allocation models assume a future fixed correlation between asset classes. If the assumed correlations vary from the actual correlations, the portfolio will not deliver the risk/return that was intended. Strategic asset allocation models rely on historic asset correlations and returns to determine the optimal investment mix. Correlations, like returns, are not constant and it is impossible to predict future correlations. Correlations among asset classes are unstable which complicate asset allocation decisions.[12] For example, the correlation of international stocks to the S&P 500 was 0.48 from 1970 to 1997, but from 1998 to 2002 it was 0.83. As a result, international stocks and the S&P 500 were much more likely to move together from 1998 to 2002 which drastically increased portfolio volatility. A rise in correlation results in a reduction in the benefits of diversification causing an unintended increase in risk to your portfolio. Therefore, diversification may not be enough to adequately manage investment risk.

Two More Faulty Assumptions

If the historical data problem were not enough, there are additional assumptions that must hold up for your strategic asset allocation model to work in the real world of investing. We will review two to the most blatantly incorrect assumptions about investing on which strategic asset allocation is based.

The first assumption is: All investors are rational decision makers. We know from behavioral finance that investors behave irrationally when making investment decisions. One example is the desire to buy more stocks when prices are high and fewer when prices are low. Additional examples of irrational decision making were explored in the section *A Few Common Mistakes to Avoid* in this chapter.

A second assumption is: The markets are efficient which means all information about a stock or bond is already factored into its price. The capital markets are efficient, but not perfectly efficient. Warren Buffet once stated, "I'd be a bum on the street with a tin cup if markets were efficient." Buffet built his fortune buying stocks overlooked by a majority of his peers.[13] In fact, there would be no insider trading if all information were already factored into the price.

Strategic Asset Allocation and Bear Markets

Strategic asset allocation may not provide the desired returns during extended bear markets. The "lost decade" beginning after 2000 where equity returns, correlations and volatility deviated from their long-term averages is not an isolated phenomenon. Since 1900 there have been four secular bear markets each with unique return, correlation and volatility characteristics.[14] Consider a longer-term analysis of large-cap blue chip stocks represented by the Dow Jones Industrial Average (DJIA).[i] Large-cap blue chip stocks are generally considered safer than other stock classes and comprise the vast majority of the equity investment portion for strategic asset allocation portfolios. The average annual DJIA return from November 1982 through August 2000 was 13.95 percent.[15] This time period included the greatest bull market in U.S. history. Because most large-cap stocks (as well as stocks in general) went up significantly during this time period, a strategic asset allocation buy-and-hold strategy was a viable plan for many investors. Unfortunately, just as trees do not grow to the sky, the market does not always go up.

What if the market remains in a bearish or sideways trending market for an extended period (a secular bear market)? Secular bear markets have occurred several times this past century. For example, if

---

[i] The DJIA is a diversified group of 30 blue chip stocks in the United States.

we consider the DJIA's return from February 1966 through October 1982, the average annual return was 0.05 percent. The cumulative return during that 18-year secular bear market was 1.62 percent.[16] This is a shocking fact for most investors because conventional wisdom is that the market generally goes up. During this time frame, the market was bearish more often than bullish. A buy-and-hold strategic asset allocation strategy in that type of market was not as viable a strategy as during the 1980's and 1990's secular bull market. Remember the vast majority of the equity portion of strategic asset allocation portfolios is invested in large-cap stocks which comprise the DJIA.

Imagine retiring in 1966: inflation was high; income taxes were higher than today's taxes; and for the first 18 years of your retirement, blue chip stocks as measured by the DJIA index returned an average of 0.05 percent per year.[17] If you are a long-term buy-and-hold strategic asset allocation investor and the majority of your portfolio is in large-cap stocks, obviously, it would not take long to exhaust your retirement portfolio. What if your retirement begins at or near the start of a secular bear market similar to 1966? Will your strategy adjust to navigate adverse market conditions?

Tactical Asset Allocation

The alternative to strategic asset allocation is tactical asset allocation. Tactical asset allocation may better serve some investors especially in difficult markets. A tactical approach considers market trends and cycles, investor behavior and the valuation of asset classes to make investment decisions. A tactical approach recognizes that the market and the economy are constantly changing, and therefore, changes are made to the portfolio allocation to take advantage of opportunities ushered in by market or economic changes and to protect the portfolio. Tactical decisions should only be made according to a disciplined strategy, not by shooting from the hip. One way of implementing a more tactical approach is through the use of forward-looking market assumptions to make portfolio adjustments in light of changing market conditions. Another way is to use intermediate- and long-term relative strength to guide portfolio adjustments to exploit intermediate- and long-term market trends. The stock market is constantly shifting, and the most promising areas in which to invest today may not be the best market areas to invest in six months or a year from now. This is why a tactical approach to asset allocation helps to navigate difficult markets. Your portfolio should continue to be diversified; however, the optimal investment choices change over time as do the proportions between investment choices.

For example, although secular bear markets are difficult times for the market as a whole, strategies such as sector rotation and managing risk can help you navigate that type of market. Sector rotation involves investing in the strongest market areas and avoiding the weaker areas. When various market areas (small cap, large cap, value, growth, international, bonds, etc.) rotate in and out of favor, the portfolio can be changed to overweight the favored areas. As the market changes, adjustments are made to take advantage of these changes and to protect the portfolio. This is a tactical asset allocation approach. Some investors prefer to take a more tactical approach to investing, especially during difficult markets.

The take away of this section is that a more tactical approach rather than a strategic asset allocation buy-and-hold approach may provide a better opportunity to achieve the desired return in range-bound or bear-trending markets. Tactical asset allocation is not market timing; rather, it is involves making portfolio changes when the market conditions change. The market is random in the short term (days to weeks) which is why market timing is not a viable strategy. However, the market is cyclical in the intermediate term (months) and trending in the long term (years). Tactical asset allocation attempts to exploit intermediate-term cycles and long-term trends.

Tactical asset allocation is not without its challenges. Foremost is the ability to correctly overweight the areas of the market that are likely to outperform and correctly underweight the areas of the market that are likely to underperform. Improper implementation of tactical asset allocation may lead to market timing and could end up doing more harm than good. A disciplined approach utilizing tools such as relative strength is vital to implementing tactical asset allocation. Professional guidance is highly recommended when using tactical asset allocation.

Forward-Looking Market Assumptions

It is common knowledge that price to earnings (P/E) ratios expand and contract, correlations between asset classes change, and economic conditions constantly evolve around the business cycle. Some asset allocation models deal with the problems associated with relying on historical returns by making adjustments to intermediate-term market assumptions. These are sometimes called forward-looking market assumptions. Forward-looking market assumptions make adjustments to the factors affecting the market and returns of various asset classes. Forward-looking market assumptions attempt to mitigate the problems associated with the long-term market assumptions of traditional strategic asset allocation.

Many asset allocation programs use purely historical data. Using historical data assumes the future will resemble the past. Over the very long term, returns usually revert to the average. However, for periods of time, sometimes exceeding 18 years, market sectors can provide flat or negative returns. This is typical of a long-term bear market trend. Would you like to buy and hold those underperforming asset classes for the long haul?   In addition, returns and correlations in short and intermediate periods are often dramatically different than their long-term averages. As an investor, the intermediate term is more important than a 75 year long-term average.

The market five to seven years ago looked dramatically different than it does today, and it will likely look very different five to seven years in the future. Forward-looking market assumptions typically result in portfolios that are more "in tune" with current and near future market conditions. Because the market is constantly changing, prior periods' market data should not be a driving factor when developing an allocation for the future. Rule-of-thumb assumptions and purely historical data may not accurately reflect economic conditions over the next three to five years. Unfortunately, many investors rely solely on very long-term (75 years or more) historical data to develop their portfolios. Not surprisingly, they are disappointed if their assumptions do not match current market conditions.

Forward-looking assumptions recognize that the past is not necessarily a reliable guide to the future. For example, forward-looking capital market assumptions would have made an adjustment to the future returns of large-cap stocks due to the late 1990's market bubble. Purely historical data would not include this type of adjustment and would likely result in using an over-inflated rate of return for large-cap growth stocks during the years immediately following the market bubble. Purely historical returns tend to skew the asset allocation in the direction of whichever asset class has been recently performing the best. This trend-chasing effect of strategic asset allocation is a major source of risk and poor performance in many investment portfolios.

Foundations, endowments, pensions and other very large institutional portfolios have long realized the flaws of relying solely on historical data and have utilized forward-looking market assumptions for years. The more sophisticated forward-looking assumptions used by the largest institutions are now available to individual investors.

Institutional research firms create forward-looking capital market assumptions by examining the fundamental economic variables that influence risk and return in the capital markets and by estimating the impact of those variables on future returns. Forward-looking capital market assumptions also use historical returns, possible economic scenarios, long-term market equilibrium results and market correlations.

For example, the returns for domestic large-cap stocks are composed of four factors: (1) the income return (dividend yield plus share repurchase); (2) real earnings growth; (3) inflation; and (4) P/E expansion or contraction. If the price to earnings ratio (P/E ratio) is expanding, the prices of stocks go up without a proportional increase in earnings. This is due to investor demand driving stock prices higher. If the P/E ratio contracts, stock prices drop without a proportional drop in earnings. The phenomenon of P/E expansion and contraction played a significant role in the 1990's market bubble and its subsequent decline. After 1999, significant P/E expansion or contraction was not anticipated; therefore, returns were expected to be more consistent with economic fundamentals. This means that increases or decreases in stock prices are more closely tied to increases or decreases in earnings. Forward-looking market assumptions would have made an adjustment to the asset allocation model to reflect the lack of P/E expansion or contraction for the foreseeable future.

Using Relative Strength to Make Tactical Allocation Decisions

Asset classes move into and out of favor for significant periods of time. For example, domestic stocks may outperform international stocks or small company stocks may outperform large company stocks. The ability to identify these intermediate to long-term trends can be exploited to improve returns and reduce risk. Relative strength allows you to make tactical decisions regarding the market areas that should be overweighted and the areas that should be underweighted or avoided altogether. Relative strength analysis enables the comparison of two investments, indexes or portfolio managers (e.g. large-cap stocks vs. small cap stocks) to determine which has a positive relative strength. The investment, index or portfolio manager with a positive relative strength will outperform the investment, index or portfolio manager with which it was compared.

An old saying on Wall Street is, "The trend is your friend." Relative strength is a great tool to identify intermediate- and long-term trends. Relative strength does not guarantee a positive return but can help to identify the strongest areas in which to invest. Relative strength is also helpful because it indicates when major changes in market leadership occur. When a major change in market leadership occurs, the portfolio should typically be adjusted to reflect these changes.

Relative strength analysis is an intermediate- to long-term tool which identifies trends typically lasting from two to seven years. It allows intelligent decisions to be made regarding where to allocate investment capital by investing in favorable sectors and avoiding unfavorable sectors. It also provides a plan of action for when to change the allocation. When an investment's relative strength turns negative, the portfolio is reallocated to market areas demonstrating a positive relative strength. If the stock market is falling and too few areas of the market are exhibiting favorable relative strength, cash or bonds likely will have a positive relative strength versus stocks and may be overweighted until conditions improve for stocks. This is a form of tactical asset allocation.

Manager Returns are Related to the Asset Class

Many investors commit the error of mistaking a good money manager for that manager's primary asset class being in favor. Most of the success or lack thereof of portfolio managers has to do with whether the asset class in which they invest is in favor or out of favor (i.e. generally rising or generally falling). The large-cap growth managers and technology managers were some of the best performers during the latter half of the 1990's. From 2000 through 2005, these same managers were among the poorest performers. The reason is not that these managers suddenly turned into horrible stock pickers. Rather, large-cap growth and technology stocks were among the worst performing market areas from 2000 through 2005. In contrast, from 1995 through 1999, large-cap growth and technology were among the best performing market areas. The bottom line is that the majority of a portfolio manager's return is a result of how well or how poorly the portfolio manager's market area is performing. Again, relative strength can help determine which asset classes are in favor over the intermediate to long term.

Relative strength may also be used to determine which managers outperform their benchmark index. Managers with a positive relative strength versus their benchmark index will continue to outperform their benchmark index until their relative strength turns negative. In addition, relative strength may be used to compare two managers within the same asset class or the same style. All else being equal, the manager with the better relative strength should generally be selected. For example, two small-cap value managers with great track records may be compared using relative strength. The manager with the positive relative strength should continue to outperform the other until the relative strength turns negative.

What Does All of This Mean?

Regardless of which investment strategy you use, you should remain diversified to help reduce risk. During difficult markets, some investors will be better served by using a tactical asset allocation strategy rather than a strategic asset allocation strategy. If using tactical asset allocation, investors should not haphazardly make buy-and-sell decisions as this would be just as dangerous as shooting from the hip. Instead, investors must have a game plan to determine when tactical adjustments to the portfolio should be made. A game plan should include tactical asset allocation guided by forward-looking market assumptions and relative strength analysis. These tools can help determine which market areas to overweight and which to avoid. Above all, the allocation should remain flexible enough to change with changing market conditions.

Measuring Performance and Risk

Numerous statistical tools are available to measure and evaluate return, risk and manager performance. Sole reliance on historical returns is often a recipe for failure because it often causes investors to chase returns. To avoid chasing a manager with a "hot hand," a number of criteria should be evaluated. In addition, when comparing managers, it is critical to use techniques that provide an apples-to-apples comparison.

Average vs. Geometric Returns

Volatility and deviation from the average return have a significant impact on returns. An understanding of the difference between average returns and geometric returns is vital. Higher volatility reduces geometric returns relative to the average return. For example, an investor invests $1000, and the portfolio is down 50 percent the first year and up 50 percent the second year. The average return is 0 percent, but the portfolio value at the end of year two is only $750 for an annualized geometric return of -13.4 percent. Geometric return measures compounded returns and provides a better measure of portfolio performance over time because it factors in the effects of losses.

Average returns should be used with caution because they may not provide a clear interpretation of actual returns. Consider this analogy: Boudreaux wants to cross Bayou Self, but he is unsure of its depth. He knows Thibodaux is familiar with Bayou Self, so he asks Thibodaux about the water's depth. Thibodaux tells him the water's depth averages four feet. Boudreaux assumes he can easily wade through the chest deep bayou but soon finds himself underwater. Although the average depth is four feet, the bayou is one foot deep along the banks and seven feet in the middle. Thus, the average depth is four feet. Average returns can similarly mislead.

Measuring and Controlling Risk

Because portfolio construction and investing rely heavily on defining and quantifying risk, it is important to have a basic understanding of risk as it relates to portfolio construction and investment selection. Risk means different things to different investors. Most investors define risk as risk of loss of principal, and for retirees a loss of principal is one of the most important risks to minimize. Unfortunately, retirees are faced with many other types of risk: purchasing power (inflation) risk, interest rate risk, volatility risk and the risk of running out of money.

The uncertainty that the realized return (the actual return on investment) is not usually guaranteed to equal the expected return received on the investment is also risk. For example, if you expect the future returns of an investment to average 8 percent, to the extent that actual returns may average 6 percent is risk. If the actual returns are 8 percent, there is no risk because the actual returns equaled the expected returns. The several types of risk can be broken down into two categories: diversifiable risks and nondiversifiable risks. The combination of these two types of risk is the total risk.

Diversifiable (unsystematic) risks are company, industry and/or region specific. These types of risks can be diversified away through proper portfolio construction and can be reduced or potentially eliminated by not "putting all of your eggs in one basket."

Nondiversifiable (systematic) risks are risks that cannot be diversified away, such as changes in interest rates, changes in exchange rates, general fluctuations in security prices due to market cycles and/or the economy and the effects of inflation. No amount of diversification can eliminate systematic risk.

Measuring Risk: Standard Deviation

Standard deviation is a common tool for measuring risk. It measures how much the actual returns differ from the average. Risk is generally measured as volatility or the variability of return. The standard deviation is the measurement used to determine the variability of returns. A higher standard deviation is a result of a higher degree of variability from the average return. A lower standard deviation means the actual returns are expected to be closer to the average return. Investments with a higher standard deviation are considered riskier because the returns deviate more from their average. The standard deviation of an individual security or a portfolio of securities may also be calculated.

For the statistically inclined, this example may help. Assuming that returns are normally distributed, 68 percent of returns will fall within one standard deviation; 95 percent of returns will fall within two standard deviations; and 99.75 percent of returns will fall within three standard deviations. If the standard deviation of an investment is 15 percent and its average return is 8 percent, 68 percent of the time the returns will be between -7 percent and +23 percent (8 percent and plus or minus 15 percent), and 95 percent of the time returns will be between

-22 percent and +38 percent (8 percent and plus or minus two times 15 percent).

Do not assume that a low standard deviation always means low risk. A portfolio with a lower standard deviation means the returns exhibit less variation from the average return and is generally considered less risky than a portfolio with a higher standard deviation. If the portfolio's return is -5 percent for eight years, the standard deviation will be zero because the return was the same each year. The portfolio was risky, however, because the investor lost 5 percent each year. Similarly, if an investment has very high positive returns in most years, but from time to time has very low negative return years, the standard deviation may be high, but many investors would not consider this a risky investment because it usually provides a high positive return with few low negative return years.

Measuring Risk: Beta

Another way of measuring risk is to consider volatility as measured by a portfolio's beta. Variability and volatility are not the same. Variability is the degree of deviation of returns from the average return. Volatility is the degree of deviation compared to a benchmark index (e.g. S&P 500). The volatility of returns compared to the market or the benchmark index is the beta coefficient (beta). A beta of one is a result of the portfolio's return moving lockstep with its benchmark index. A beta of 1.5 is the result of the portfolio moving 50 percent more than the market on the upside and the downside. If the beta is .5 the portfolio is moving half as much on the upside and downside. In addition, beta is a measure of systematic risk that cannot be diversified away. Generally, it is better to have a lower beta.

Active or Passive Management

When designing an investment strategy, in addition to selecting either strategic or tactical asset allocation, a decision must be made as to whether to use a passive indexing approach or an active management approach. An example of passive indexing is an investment that replicates the S&P 500. Passive indexing does not attempt to add return through buying and selling stocks or bonds in the portfolio. Rather, the portfolio remains fixed to match the index. Passive index investing has the primary advantage of being less expensive than active management. It is also generally more tax-efficient than active management. Tax efficiency is irrelevant for tax-deferred accounts because all gains are taxed as ordinary income when distributed.

Active management seeks to outperform a benchmark index by taking advantage of changes in market trends and economic conditions through superior stock and bond selection and the timing of buy-and-sell decisions. Active management may also seek to reduce risk while providing a similar return to its benchmark index. Most active managers underperform their benchmark index, so it is vital to identify managers that consistently outperform their benchmark index. It is difficult to beat the benchmark market index; however, some managers consistently outperform their benchmark index. For those who can identify active managers capable of consistently beating their benchmark index (i.e. beat the market), significant performance over the benchmark indexes may be achieved.

The additional cost of active management must be weighed against the potential additional performance over the index. If a portfolio manager does not consistently beat its benchmark index, the investor is paying for underperformance. However, if an active manager has beat the benchmark index consistently after factoring in management fees, the active manager is worth the additional fee. Another benefit of active management is that managers may provide returns comparable to their benchmark index but with a lower amount of risk. It is critical to use a process to identify managers who beat their index and/or reduce risk consistently. A process is needed to avoid "shooting from the hip" when selecting active managers.

Selecting Portfolio Managers

When selecting portfolio managers, an investor should employ a process to screen potential investments for inclusion in a portfolio allocation. To eliminate emotion when selecting portfolio managers, the process relies heavily on statistical analysis. Hopefully, an overview of the tools used to screen investments for inclusion in a portfolio will give you an understanding of the factors to consider and the questions to ask. Although the following is an attempt to explain in simple terms the screening process, it is still fairly technical.

You must first determine your appropriate asset allocation mix of stocks, bonds and cash. An investment risk profiler can help determine your appropriate risk tolerance by considering your required return, expectations of future returns of asset classes and time horizon. For example, a typical portfolio might consist of 45 percent domestic stock, 25 percent foreign stock, 25 percent bonds and 5 percent cash. Passive investors may stop there and allocate the portfolio among passive indexes as per their chosen asset allocation. For active investors, the analysis has just begun. Active investors must now select portfolio managers for each asset class. Active portfolio management is more expensive than passive portfolio management; therefore, it should add value. Investors should seek managers who can add return in excess of the index (e.g. S&P 500) and/or reduce risk compared to the index.

The selection of active managers should be driven by the value they add through their buy-and-sell decisions, isolated from the effects of the up and down movement of the market. The active manager should generate sufficient additional value when compared to passive indexing to compensate the investor for the incremental risk and additional costs of active management.

A robust process is needed to identify managers who consistently generate returns which exceed their benchmark indexes. The first step is to determine the appropriate benchmark index for comparison to the manager. Much of the analysis which follows relies on selecting the correct index for comparison to the portfolio manager.[j] For example, when analyzing a mid-cap value portfolio, it is best to compare it to a mid-cap value index (e.g. the S&P Midcap 400/Citigroup Value Index), rather than the S&P 500 (a large-cap blend index)[k18] to allow an apples-to-apples comparison. If the index and the portfolio are not a good fit, the additional risk and return measurements discussed herein will be meaningless. To ensure that the appropriate benchmark index is used, compare the manager's performance with the benchmark. Correlation squared (R^2) is used to determine whether the correct index is used to compare with the portfolio manager.

---

[j] The "correct" index or the closest fit index is referred to as the benchmark index.

[k] The S&P MidCap 400 provides investors with a benchmark for mid-sized companies. A market-capitalization-weighted index developed by Standard and Poor's consisting of those stocks within the S&P 500 Index that exhibit strong value characteristics. Citigroup Value Index uses a numerical ranking system based on four value factors and three growth factors to determine the constituents and their weightings.

Correlation squared is the proportion of the total variation in the manager's performance that is explained by variation in the benchmark index's performance. A high R^2 indicates that a manager's return is closely correlated to the benchmark, and it reflects the percentage of a manager's movements that can be explained by movements in the benchmark index. An R^2 of greater than .65 indicates that comparing the manager to the index benchmark is an apples-to-apples comparison. An R^2 of less than .65 indicates the benchmark index is not a good fit, and another benchmark index should be chosen for comparison. Statistical calculations on which appropriate benchmarks are based (e.g. alpha, beta and the information ratio) will have less credibility as R^2 drops below .65. The lower the R^2, the less relevant the beta is to the manager's performance. A high R^2 (high correlation) is, therefore, critical when evaluating beta.

Sources of Returns in Excess of the Index

Excess returns are an actively managed portfolio's returns that are in excess of its benchmark index's returns. Remember, if you are paying for active management, you want returns that are greater than the benchmark index or lower risk for the same return. The best managers provide returns in excess of their benchmark index with lower risk. Returns in excess of the benchmark index can be generated in two ways.

The first way to generate excess returns is to assume greater risk than the benchmark index. The beta is one way to measure the amount of risk relative to the benchmark index. Beta measures portfolio volatility or sensitivity relative to the portfolio's benchmark index or the overall market. Beta is calculated by comparing the manager's excess return over Treasury bills to the benchmark index's excess return over Treasury bills. The beta of the benchmark index is always 1.00.

Higher beta portfolios are more volatile, returning more than the benchmark index in up markets and declining more than the benchmark index in down markets. Lower beta portfolios move less than their benchmark index in both directions. Unfortunately, beta is a sword that cuts both ways. Therefore, the potential success of generating excess returns through beta depends on the market's direction. A beta of 1.50 shows that an investment is expected to perform 50 percent better than the benchmark index in up markets and 50 percent worse than the benchmark index in down markets. A beta of .90 shows that an investment is expected to perform 10 percent worse than the benchmark index in up markets and 10 percent better than the benchmark index in down markets. Keep in mind that a low beta reveals only that the manager's market-relevant risk is low. Total risk, as measured by the standard deviation, may still be very high.

Beta can be helpful when selecting an investment suitable for a particular level of risk. An investment with a low beta (less than 1) is generally less volatile than the market and may be better suited for more conservative investors. Unfortunately, lower volatility generally coincides with lower returns, and conservative investors should be willing to accept lower returns for less risk. On the other hand, investments with a beta of greater than one may be better suited for more aggressive investors. A beta of greater than one typically indicates that the investment is expected to provide returns greater than the overall market. However, higher amounts of risk must be assumed for these higher anticipated returns.

The Sharpe Ratio

The Sharpe ratio measures the risk-adjusted performance as it measures the manager's return efficiency per unit of risk. The Sharpe Ratio uses standard deviation as a measure of risk. When comparing investments, both the return and the amount of risk borne to achieve the return are important. The Sharpe Ratio can help determine whether returns are a result of good investment decisions or a result of assuming more risk. Generally, the higher the Sharpe ratio the better the portfolio performance considering the portfolio's degree of risk. When comparing Sharpe ratios, higher scores are more desirable than lower scores, all else being equal.

The Treynor Ratio

The Treynor Ratio is also a measure of risk-adjusted performance that uses beta as the measure of risk. The Treynor Ratio is similar to the Sharpe Ratio, and investors should seek investments with a higher, rather than a lower, Treynor Ratio.

Capture Ratios

There are two types of capture ratios: upside capture ratio and downside capture ratio. A portfolio manager that has an upside capture ratio of 1.20 means the portfolio performance has beat the market by 20 percent in rising markets. A portfolio manager has a downside capture ratio of .80 means the portfolio performance has fallen 20 percent less than the market in falling markets. Ideally, seek managers that have an upside ratio of greater than one and a downside ratio of less than one.

Alpha: A Measure of Investor Skill

Another way to generate excess returns is through superior stock and sector selection. The value a manager adds through superior buy-and-sell decisions can be measured by alpha. After adjusting the excess return for the beta or the market portion of the return, the remaining excess return can be attributed to the manager's buy-and-sell decisions. If you are paying a portfolio manager for active management, you want to find the most skilled portfolio managers available. Alpha provides a measure of manager skill and is a measure of the beta-adjusted excess return.

In addition, alpha is a measure of risk-adjusted return. It is a measure of the difference between the manager's actual performance and the performance anticipated in light of the manager's risk posture and the market's behavior. A positive alpha indicates that the manager is adding value through their buy-and-sell decisions. Higher alphas are desirable over lower alphas, and a negative alpha indicates the manager is doing more harm than good with their buy-and-sell decisions.

What is the importance of alpha? Alpha is independent of market direction, and it can help protect portfolios from market declines. Managers who consistently generate positive alpha should be able to outperform their benchmark index in all market environments. A positive alpha means the portfolio should go up more than the index in rising markets and fall less than the index in falling markets. Managers that are able to generate positive alpha have been successful with their buy-and-sell decisions and the trade timing, and they have produced a rate of return that is more than commensurate with the manager's risk posture.

Active Risk and Tracking Error

Just as <u>total return</u> can be broken down into beta (return from the market) and alpha (return generated by the portfolio manager's skill), <u>total risk</u> can be divided into market risk and active risk introduced by the manager. High beta managers typically bring high levels of market risk, resulting in a standard deviation greater than the benchmark. Active risk excludes market risk and is the measurement of risk introduced by the portfolio manager. Active risk is the extra volatility (risk) introduced by portfolio managers in pursuit of excess returns over the benchmark index. To beat their benchmark index, portfolio managers must do something different than the benchmark index. These differences introduce deviations from the benchmark index, which is the active risk. The annualized standard deviation of active risk is the tracking error. Put another way, tracking error is the standard deviation of the difference in returns between a portfolio and its benchmark index.[19]

The Information Ratio

The information ratio is a standardized measure of return per unit of risk. This measurement helps to determine the degree to which the portfolio manager's stock and sector selection and trade timing are paying off. The information ratio measures the manager's alpha versus the volatility of the manager's alpha. A higher information ratio is a result of consistently delivering alpha. The most desirable portfolio managers have a high alpha and low levels of active risk. Managers providing high levels of alpha with lower levels of active risk result in high information ratios. Because the information ratio is a standardized measure, it allows direct comparison of managers with different alpha and active risk characteristics. The information ratio is the best measure of manager skill that is isolated from fluctuations in the market. When selecting a portfolio manager, a high information ratio provides the best return for a given level of risk. As a result, a higher information ratio is better than a lower information ratio. <u>Managers with a high information ratio tend to track their benchmark and produce adequate excess return to justify the expense of active management (and deviation from the benchmark).</u>

Managers in higher-return asset classes (e.g. small cap, emerging market, and international stocks) are expected to add more alpha than lower return asset classes (e.g. bonds and large cap stocks). Riskier portfolios will contain a higher percentage of higher-return asset classes; therefore, the benefits of using active management increase as investors move into riskier portfolios. In addition, active management may provide more benefits for the portfolio's small cap and international portions. Therefore, if you wish to use passive indexing for a portion of the portfolio, the portfolio's large-cap stock and bond portions would typically be passively indexed. You may consider using active portfolio managers for the small cap and international portions. These are usually the riskier asset classes, and skilled investment managers can potentially add more value here than in the portfolio's large-cap or fixed-income portion.

Conclusion

This chapter has emphasized the importance of implementing a sound investment strategy. Remember that the market is constantly changing. Therefore, you must have a strategy to guide your investment decisions through both up and down markets. Above all, you should manage the risk to your portfolio. Finally, I hope you will focus on some of the important investment selection tools outlined herein to avoid making the mistake of relying solely on historical returns as past performance may not be indicative of future results.[1]

---

[1] The performance data quoted represents past performance. Past performance does not guarantee future results. Investment return and principal value of an investment will fluctuate so that an investor's shares, when redeemed, may be worth more or less than their original cost. Current performance may be lower or higher than the performance data quoted. The investment return and principal value of an investment security will fluctuate with market conditions so that when redeemed the value of the investment may be worth more or less than the original cost.

Opinions expressed are those of John Sirois and not necessarily those of RJFS or Raymond James. All opinions are as of this date and are subject to change without notice.

[1] Source Dalbar "Quantative Analysis of Investor Behavior" 2018.

[2] Source Dalbar "Quantative Analysis of Investor Behavior" 2018.

[3] Keep in mind that individuals cannot invest directly in any index, and index performance does not include transaction costs or other fees, which will affect actual investment performance.

[4] Harry Markowitz. "Portfolio Selection", Journal of Finance, March, 1952.

[5] William F. Sharpe. "Capital Asset Prices: A Theory of Market Equilibrium Under Conditions of Risk", *Journal of Finance,* September, 1964.

[6] Brinson, Gary, Randolph Hood and Gilbert Beebower. Determinants of Portfolio Performance", *Financial Analysts Journal*, July-August 1986, pp. 39-44.

[7] William W. Jahnke. "The Asset Allocation Hoax." *Journal of Financial Planning*, February, 1997, pp. 109-113.

[8] Id.

[9] Id.

[10] Michael E. Kitces, CFP, CLU, ChFC, RHU, REBC, The Rise of Tactical Asset Allocation, Journal of Financial Planning, June, 2012.

[11] William J. Coaker II. "The Volatility of Correlation, Important Implications for the Asset Allocation Decision", *Journal of Financial Planning*, February, 2006.

[12] Id.

[13] "The Value of Active Management", Capital Guardian, *Viewpoints*, April, 2011.

[14] "Solow, Kenneth R., and Michael E. Kitces. "Understanding Secular Bear Markets: Concerns and Strategies", *Journal of Financial Planning*, March 2006.

[15] Source: Rydex Investments "The 100 Year Dow Jones Chart".

[16] Source: Rydex Investments "The 100 Year Dow Jones Chart".

[17] Source: Rydex Investments "The 100 Year Dow Jones Chart".

[18] The S&P MidCap 400 provides investors with a benchmark for mid-sized companies. A market-capitalization-weighted index developed

by Standard and Poor's consisting of those stocks within the S&P 500 Index that exhibit strong value characteristics. Citigroup Value Index uses a numerical ranking system based on four value factors and three growth factors to determine the constituents and their weightings. Indexes are unmanaged and individuals cannot invest directly in any index

[19] Source: Raymond James Consulting Services, "An Innovative Approach to Building Investment Portfolios" 2006.

4

Individual Retirement Accounts

Chapter Highlights

❖ An IRA is a tax-deferred retirement account controlled by the owner.

❖ The IRA owner has a wide choice of investment options including mutual funds, stocks, bonds, certificates of deposit, options, exchange traded funds and real estate.

❖ The IRA owner may name one or more primary and contingent beneficiaries and may change beneficiaries at any time.

❖ Louisiana law protects IRAs from creditors, and Federal law protects IRAs from bankruptcy.

❖ Contributions to IRAs must be made by April 15 of the year following the contribution year; however, contributions are not mandatory.

❖ Contributions may not be made once age 70½ is attained.

❖ Deductible IRA contributions are limited by income thresholds for participants of qualified plans. Anyone may make a nondeductible contribution up to the lesser of the IRA contribution limit or the amount of his or her compensation for the year.

❖ Contributions made after age 70½ or in excess of the contribution limit are excess contributions. Excess contributions are subject to a 6 percent excise tax until corrected.

❖ To encourage IRA owners to use their IRA as a retirement account, distributions prior to age 59½ are subject to a 10 percent premature-distribution penalty unless an exception applies.

❖ Distributions from IRAs must begin by April 1 of the year following the owner's turning 70½ years of age.

❖ Distributions in excess of cost basis are taxed as ordinary income regardless of the holding period.

❖ An IRA rollover is the receipt of IRA assets and subsequent re-contribution to an IRA. Rollovers must be completed within 60 days to avoid taxation on the withdrawn assets.

❖ Only one IRA rollover per taxpayer is allowed in a 12-month period.

❖ An IRA transfer is a direct conveyance of IRA assets from one IRA to another. IRA transfers are not subject to the 60-day rule, and more than one transfer may occur within 12 months.

❖ An inherited IRA is an IRA received by a beneficiary from a deceased IRA owner. An inherited IRA must remain in the deceased IRA owner's name and cannot be rolled or converted into an IRA in the beneficiary's name.

❖ An inherited IRA may be moved only by direct custodian-to-custodian transfer.

❖ A special rule allows a surviving spouse to rollover a deceased IRA owner's IRA into his or her own IRA. In this case, the IRA need not remain in the deceased IRA owner's name.

❖ Prohibited transactions and self-dealing may cause an IRA to lose its tax-deferred status, resulting in immediate income taxation of the IRA assets.

INDIVIDUAL RETIREMENT ACCOUNTS ARE the most widely used private retirement accounts; however, very few people understand exactly what an Individual Retirement Account (IRA) is and what an IRA can and cannot do. This chapter will provide an explanation of IRAs, the types of IRAs, contribution limits, investment options, rollovers, transfers and prohibited transactions.

The Basics

An IRA is a type of tax-deferred retirement savings account controlled by the account owner. An IRA is not an investment but a type of account that may hold different types of investments (e.g. mutual funds stocks, bonds, exchange traded funds (ETFs), CDs, options, real estate, etc.). Features of IRAs over other types of retirement accounts such as 401(k) and 403(b) accounts are the almost unlimited investment options, the ease of transferring accounts and the beneficiary planning flexibility.

IRAs were created in 1974 to allow individuals to make contributions to a tax-deferred account for distribution during their retirement years. These are traditional IRAs. Today, many types of IRAs exist, such as Roth IRAs, SIMPLE IRAs, SEP IRAs, Education IRAs, Individual Retirement Annuities and Spousal IRAs. Unless otherwise noted, "IRA" refers to a traditional IRA.

The IRA participant is the account owner, and the assets in an IRA are fully vested at all times.[1] In contrast, ownership of assets in a 401(k) account is normally restricted by a vesting schedule. If employment terminates prior to the employee becoming fully vested in the 401(k) account, the employee forfeits the unvested portion of the account balance. An IRA cannot include vesting provisions because the absence of vesting provisions is a requirement of all IRAs.

Each IRA may have only one owner. Therefore, an IRA cannot be established as a joint IRA between two or more people. Annual contributions to IRAs are not mandatory, and any amount may be contributed as long as it does not exceed the maximum allowable annual contribution. You may own as many IRAs as you wish; however, you may not contribute more than the annual maximum allowable amount between all IRAs. In addition, an IRA is portable, which means you may freely transfer your IRA to another custodian.

IRAs also require an IRA governing document that defines the IRA owner's rights and obligations.[2] The governing document is sometimes called an IRA adoption agreement. This agreement defines the obligations of the custodian or trustee in custody of the IRA assets. For example, the adoption agreement determines whether the beneficiaries' distributions will be per capita (by heads) or per stirpes (by roots). It will also determine whether a trust may be named beneficiary and what happens if no beneficiary is named. You should read and understand the terms of your IRA adoption agreement because they will control most aspects of your IRA.

The most common IRA type is an individual retirement custodial account or a custodial IRA. If you have an IRA at a brokerage firm, it is most likely a custodial IRA. The brokerage firm or other institution acts as the IRA custodian. Some IRAs are established with a trustee rather than a custodian; however, in the context of IRAs, there is little distinction between the two. Lastly, an IRA may be established as an Individual Retirement Annuity issued by an insurance company.

All IRAs carry an "IRA maintenance fee," unless it is waived by the custodian or trustee. The custodian for accounts that are larger in value may waive the annual maintenance fee. The IRA maintenance fees are typically $30 to $40, which helps to offset the additional reporting and record keeping associated with IRAs.

Beneficiaries

An IRA owner is allowed to name one or more beneficiaries. As with any beneficiary designated asset, an IRA avoids probate and is not controlled by the will if there is a valid beneficiary designation. Typically, the owner's spouse is named the primary beneficiary, and the children are named the contingent (secondary) beneficiaries. The contingent beneficiaries take the primary beneficiary's place if the primary beneficiary is dead at the IRA owner's death. It is always a good idea to name contingent beneficiaries in the event that the IRA owner and the primary beneficiary die in a common accident. It also prevents the IRA from not having a designated beneficiary if the primary beneficiary dies and the IRA owner dies prior to naming a new primary beneficiary.

In the event that no designated beneficiary is named, the IRA owner's estate becomes the default beneficiary. If the estate is the beneficiary, the IRA owner's will or the intestacy laws typically determine who will receive the IRA assets. The IRA adoption agreement may prevent the beneficiary designation from defaulting to the estate if no beneficiary is named. For example, the IRA adoption agreement may provide that the IRA owner's surviving spouse or their descendants will receive the IRA if no beneficiary is named.

For IRA distribution and tax purposes, it is undesirable for the estate to be the IRA beneficiary. If the IRA owner does not have a designated beneficiary and dies <u>prior</u> to the required beginning date (April 1 after reaching age 70½), the entire IRA must be distributed by December 31 of the calendar year containing the fifth anniversary of the IRA owner's death (the five-year rule).[3] This means that if the IRA owner dies prior to beginning required minimum distributions from the IRA, the entire IRA must be distributed within five years after the IRA owner dies. Annual distributions are not required; however, the entire account must be distributed by December 31 of the year that contains the fifth anniversary of the owner's death.[4] If the IRA owner does not have a designated beneficiary and dies <u>after</u> the required beginning date, the five-year rule does not apply. The IRA must be distributed at least as fast as based on the deceased IRA owner's life expectancy.[5] However, if the IRA has a designated beneficiary, the beneficiary may take distributions based on his or her life expectancy rather than the deceased owner's life expectancy.[6] For younger beneficiaries, this outcome provides for smaller required distributions and much more tax-deferral. See Chapter 7 for more information regarding IRA required minimum distributions.

Creditor Protection

In Louisiana, IRAs are protected from seizure by creditors.[7] Protection from seizure by creditors applies to traditional IRAs, Roth IRAs, SIMPLE IRAs, SEP IRAs and any other pension or tax-deferred arrangement (such as 401(k), 403(b), 457 or other employer plan). Contributions to IRAs or other tax-deferred plans are exempt if made at least one year prior to filing for bankruptcy or one year from the date writs of seizure are filed against the tax-deferred account.

The 2005 Bankruptcy Act exempts IRAs from the bankruptcy estate up to an inflation-adjusted cap. As of April 1, 2016 the cap is $1,283,035. SEP IRAs and SIMPLE IRAs are not subject to the cap. In addition, assets in a traditional IRA that were rolled over from an employer plan (e.g. 401(k) or a 403(b)) are also not subject to the cap. Inherited IRA's, however, are not protected under Federal bankruptcy law. Regardless, Louisiana law provides tax-deferred accounts with unlimited protection from seizure.[8] See Chapter 25 on asset protection for more information.

Contributions to IRAs

IRA contributions must be made in cash.[9] Although noncash contributions will not disqualify the IRA for tax purposes, they are treated as excess contributions. The IRA contribution deadline is the income-tax-return deadline for the year.[10] For example, a 2019 contribution may be made anytime during 2019 or by April 15, 2020. If you obtain a tax-filing extension, you do <u>not</u> have additional time to make an IRA contribution. In addition, if you make a prior-year contribution before the tax-filing deadline, the contribution should clearly be identified as a prior year's contribution. You may claim a deduction for an IRA contribution even if the contribution has not yet been made.[11] Therefore, you may file your taxes in March and claim a deduction for the prior year's IRA contribution even if you have not yet made the IRA contribution. You have until April 15 to make the IRA contribution for the prior year.

In the year you reach age 70½, no additional IRA contributions may be made.[12] Contributions made after age 70½ are excess contributions. This age limitation does not apply to rollover contributions,[13] which are assets transferred from a 401(k), 403(b), 457, pension rollout to an IRA or transfer from one IRA to another.

In addition, contribution amounts are limited by compensation for the year.[14] Compensation includes salaries, wages, net earnings of a sole proprietor, partnership income of an active partner, professional fees and taxable alimony or separate maintenance payments.[15] However, rental income, pensions, interest income and dividend income are not considered compensation. If you do not have compensation for the year, you cannot make an IRA contribution. There is an exception to this rule called a spousal IRA.

If one spouse has little or no compensation, a spouse who has compensation can make a contribution to a spousal IRA for the spouse who has no compensation.[16] Only the spouse with the higher amount of compensation is allowed to make a spousal contribution.[17] For example, a spouse with $2000 of compensation cannot make a spousal IRA contribution for the spouse who has compensation of $40,000. In addition, the spouses must file taxes as married filing jointly and be married at the end of the year. Finally, a spousal contribution may be made if the contributing spouse is over age 70½ as long as the receiving spouse is under 70½.

You may make contributions to any number of IRAs; however, aggregate contributions to all IRAs cannot exceed the lesser of the IRA contribution limit or your compensation. If you make a maximum contribution to a traditional IRA, no Roth IRA contribution is allowed for that year. If you make a partial contribution to a traditional IRA, the maximum allowable Roth IRA contribution is equal to the difference between the annual IRA contribution limit and the amount of the traditional IRA contribution. For example, Thibodaux, age 40, makes a $2,500 traditional IRA contribution in 2019. He may also make a $3,500 Roth IRA contribution in 2019, as long as he has at least $6,000 of compensation in 2019.

The contribution limits are adjusted for inflation in $500 increments. (See Table 1.)

Table 1 - Total IRA Contribution Limits

Year	Maximum Contribution	Catch-Up Provision**	Total Contribution With Catch-Up
2019*	$6,000	$1,000	$7,000

* Contribution limits are adjusted for inflation in $500 increments.
** If age 50 or over at the end of the year.

Deductible IRA Contributions

Contributions to an IRA may be deductible depending on your level of income and on whether you participate in an employer plan. If neither you nor your spouse participates in an employer plan, the entire IRA contribution is deductible. If the IRA owner participates in an employer plan, the deductibility thresholds vary. (See Table 2.)

Table 2 - 2019 IRA Deduction Thresholds*

Filing Status	Limited Deduction if MAGI is Between	No Deduction if MAGI is Over
Single	$64,000-$74,000	$74,000
Joint**	$103,000-$123,000	$123,000
Married Filing Separately	$0-$10,000	$10,000

These thresholds are be indexed for inflation in $1,000 increments. Married Filing Separate limits are not adjusted for inflation.
**If you are not covered by an employer plan, but your spouse is, your deduction is phased out if your MAGI is between $193,000 and $203,000. No deduction is allowed if MAGI exceeds $203,000.

If your modified adjusted gross income[a] (MAGI) is less than the income threshold, a full deduction is allowed. If your MAGI falls between the income threshold and the phase out limit, you qualify for a partial deduction. Of course, if your MAGI exceeds the phase out limit, no deduction is allowed. You may still make an IRA contribution; however, the contribution is nondeductible.

---

[a] Modified adjusted gross income is adjusted gross income with the following items added back: IRA deductions, exclusions for foreign earned income, deductions for foreign housing, exclusions for Series EE bond, exclusions for employer-provided adoption assistance and deductions for student loan interest.

If the IRA owner's spouse is an active participant in an employer retirement plan but the IRA owner is not, the deduction phase out range is $193,000 to $203,000 of MAGI (2019). For individuals married filing separately, the deduction phase-out is $10,000 of MAGI if the IRA owner's spouse is a participant in an employer retirement plan. Employer retirement plans include 401(k), 403(b), profit sharing, pension, stock bonus, money purchase, Keogh, SEP and SIMPLE plans. You are generally considered covered by a defined contribution plan (profit sharing, stock bonus, money purchase plan, etc.) if money is contributed or allocated to your account. You are generally considered covered by a defined benefit pension plan if you are eligible to participate in the plan. Furthermore, you may be considered an active participant in the employer plan if you fit the definition of an active participant in the plan document even if contributions have not been made to your account.

When you make nondeductible IRA contributions, IRS Form 8606 must be filed with your federal income tax return. If you fail to file Form 8606, the nondeductible IRA contribution will be treated as a deductible contribution. Failing to file Form 8606 will result in paying taxes on portions of the IRA distribution that should have been a tax-free return of basis.

Certain IRA participants are allowed an income tax credit for contributions to traditional IRAs or Roth IRAs. The maximum annual contribution eligible for the credit is $2,000, and the maximum credit is $1,000 per taxpayer. The amount of credit available, if any, depends on the taxpayer's MAGI. (See Table 3)

Table 3 - Income Tax Credit Based on MAGI (2019)

Joint Filers MAGI	Head of Household Filers MAGI	Single Filers MAGI	Credit Rate	Maximum Credit
$0-$38,500	$0-$28,875	$0-$19,250	50%	$1,000
$38,501-$41,500	$28,876-$31,125	$19,251-$20,750	20%	$400
$41,501-$64,000	$31,126-$48,000	$20,751-$32,000	10%	$200
Over $64,000	Over $48,000	Over $32,000	0%	$0

Excess Contributions

If IRA contributions exceed the applicable annual thresholds, the contribution is considered an "excess contribution." Contributions after age 70½ and failed IRA rollovers are also considered excess contributions. In addition, an excess contribution may occur by rolling over a required minimum distribution.

Excess contributions that are not corrected are subject to a 6 percent excise tax per year. Fortunately, an excess contribution may be corrected if withdrawn prior to the IRA owner's income tax deadline (including extensions). Any earnings associated with the excess contribution must also be withdrawn. Furthermore, if the owner is under 59½, the 10 percent premature-distribution penalty will apply to the earnings.[18]

If an excess contribution and its associated earnings are not removed by the tax filing deadline, the excess contribution may be treated as an additional contribution for later years. For example, if Boudreaux, age 40, contributes $7,000 to his IRA in 2019, he has made an excess contribution of $1,000. If he withdraws the $1,000 excess contribution and any associated earnings prior to his tax filing deadline, he has corrected the excess contribution. If, however, he does not withdraw the excess contribution and does not make a 2020 contribution, the $1,000 excess contribution will be treated as a 2020 contribution. If Boudreaux makes a maximum IRA contribution in 2020, the $1,000 excess contribution will remain an excess contribution subject to the 6 percent excise tax. On the other hand, if Boudreaux makes a 2020 IRA contribution of at least $1,000 less than the maximum for that year, the $1,000 excess contribution will be treated as a 2020 contribution, and the 6 percent excise tax will no longer apply.

Distributions from IRAs

To encourage IRA owners to use their IRAs as retirement accounts, distributions prior to age 59½ are subject to a 10 percent premature-distribution penalty, unless an exception applies. The 10 percent penalty only applies to the distribution's taxable amount. For example, if Marie (age 45) withdraws $3,000 from her IRA of which $2,000 is taxable, the 10 percent penalty will be $200 ($2000 taxable portion x 10 percent). Many exceptions to the 10 percent premature-distribution penalty exist. See Chapter 6 for more details on exceptions to this penalty.

Taxation of IRA Distributions

IRA distributions are treated as ordinary income even if the assets are held longer than one year.[19] In contrast to assets which are not in a tax-deferred account, long-term capital gain rates may apply if assets are held longer than one year. Most IRAs consist of all deductible contributions, so 100 percent of every distribution is taxable. If nondeductible contributions have been made, a portion of each distribution will be treated as a return of basis and is not taxed. To compute the portion of an IRA distribution that is a non-taxable return of basis, add together all of the distributions for the year from all IRAs. Next, add together all of the nondeductible contributions made to all IRAs owned. The distribution's non-taxable portion is the portion of the year's distribution that has the same ratio to the total amount of the year's taxable distribution as the amount of the nondeductible contributions held in all IRAs bear to the total balance of all IRAs. The balances and amounts are as of the end of the calendar year.[20] For example, Thibodaux has made $10,000 of deductible contributions and $20,000 of nondeductible contributions to his IRA. The year-end value of his IRA is $50,000. If he withdraws $4,000 in a single year, $2,518.52 is taxable and $1,481.48 is non-taxable ([$20,000 \ ($50,000+$4,000)] x $4,000). Thibodaux's total nondeductible contributions now total $18,518.52 ($20,000 - $1,481.48).

Keep in mind that, when determining the IRA balance at the end of the year, any outstanding rollover amounts must be added to this total. An outstanding rollover balance is an IRA distribution made within 60 days of the end of the calendar year which is not rolled over into an IRA by the end of the year and is rolled into an IRA prior to the end of the 60-day window but in the following calendar year. For example, Boudreaux withdraws $20,000 from his IRA on December 15, 2018, and does not rollover this amount into an IRA by the end of the year. He does, however, complete the rollover on January 28, 2019, which is within the 60-day rollover time limit. Although the $20,000 withdrawal was not included in his IRA as of December 31, 2018, it is included in the year-end balance so long as the rollover is completed within 60 days.

Unfortunately, distributions from an IRA cannot be designated as taken solely from the nondeductible portion. An IRA owner may not attempt to distribute only the non-taxable portions, even if an IRA contains amounts characterized as nondeductible. Furthermore, an IRA owner may not attempt to rollover to another IRA only the deductible portion of an IRA. Amounts attributable to both deductible and nondeductible portions must be rolled over.[21]

Losses on IRA Investments

Because IRAs are tax-deferred accounts, losses on IRA investments are generally not tax deductible. However, losses on IRAs are deductible if all IRAs owned by the individual are fully distributed and there is a net loss on the combined amounts of all IRAs.[22] For example, assume Boudreaux contributed $3,000 to IRA X and the current value is $2,500. If he distributes the entire IRA, he can recognize a loss of $500 which can be deducted as a miscellaneous itemized deduction subject to the 2 percent AGI floor. However, assume Boudreaux also had IRA Y to which he contributed $6,000, and its current value is $8,000. Because he has two IRAs, he must aggregate both for the computation of gains and losses. Considering IRA X and IRA Y, Boudreaux has a net gain of $1,500. Thus, there is no tax loss available. Even if Boudreaux did not have a gain in IRA Y, which would have resulted in an aggregate loss of $500 from IRA X, it would not be in Boudreaux's best interest to liquidate both IRAs for the purpose of claiming a $500 loss. The benefits of tax-deferral on these accounts would be lost if the assets were distributed.

If you have both traditional IRAs and Roth IRAs, the loss rule applies separately to each type of IRA. Therefore, to claim a loss on a traditional IRA, only traditional IRAs need be distributed.

Rollovers and Transfers

When changing IRA custodians or when taking an IRA distribution with the intent to roll it back into an IRA within 60 days, you must understand the distinction between rollovers and transfers.[b] A <u>rollover</u> is a receipt of assets from an IRA or retirement plan and subsequent contribution of these assets to the same or a different IRA or retirement

---

[b] You should compare your current and prospective account's features, including fees and charges, before making a transfer decision. Distributions that are not properly rolled over to another retirement plan or account may be subject to withholding, income taxes, and if made prior to age 59 1/2, may be subject to a 10% penalty tax.

plan. Rollovers may be of any amount, and the amounts contributed to an IRA as a rollover are nondeductible.[23]

IRA owners should beware of a trap for rollovers occurring in the first distribution year. Required minimum distributions must begin by April 1 after the IRA owner's 70½ birthday. However, the first distribution year is the year the IRA owner turns 70½. Assume Boudreaux turns 70½ in 2019. His first required minimum distribution must be taken by April 1, 2020. Any withdrawals from the IRA in 2019 will first be considered a required minimum distribution and cannot be transferred or rolled over. Withdrawals that are rolled over will be considered excess contributions until the required minimum distribution is satisfied.[24]

You are not required to rollover the entire IRA into the same IRA; thus, a portion of an IRA may be rolled over to another IRA. In addition, amounts received as a rollover must be contributed to an IRA or other retirement plan within 60 days of receiving the distributed assets.[25] If the rollover amount is not contributed to an IRA within the 60-day time limit, a taxable distribution occurs. Furthermore, if you are under 59½, the 10 percent premature-distribution penalty will apply. Unlike a 401(k) and other employer plans, the mandatory 20 percent withholding does not apply to IRA rollovers.

The IRS has discretion to waive the 60-day rollover time limit where failure to waive the time limit would be against equity or good conscience. Events that are out of the IRA owner's control, including casualties or disasters, may provide grounds to waive the 60-day requirement. The IRS will consider the relevant facts and circumstances including errors by financial institutions, postal errors and the inability to complete the rollover due to death, disability, incarceration or hospitalization. On the other hand, the IRS is not very lenient in circumstances where the IRA owner withdrew funds as a personal loan with the intent to re-contribute the funds within the 60-day window but exceeded the 60-day time limit. For example, the IRS refused to approve a waiver of the 60-day time limit where the IRA owner withdrew funds to pay off large debts due to medical bills and home repairs in order to avoid bankruptcy. The IRA owner planned to re-contribute the funds within 60 days by using proceeds from a timber sale. Unfortunately, bad weather delayed the timber sale until after the 60-day time limit. The IRS determined that these circumstances were not the type that justified a waiver, and the withdrawal was treated as a taxable distribution.[26]

You are allowed one <u>rollover</u> during the 12-month period ending on the distribution day. The 12-month period begins when the IRA distribution is received, not on the date the distribution is rolled over into an IRA. The IRS has previously maintained the position that the 12-month restriction applies to each IRA independently. Therefore, an IRA owner with three IRAs may complete a rollover for each IRA within a 12-month period. <u>However, a 2014 Tax Court ruling held that the one rollover per year rule applies to all of a person's IRAs.</u>[27] If rollovers are taken from two different IRAs within a 12-month period, the one rollover per 12-month period is violated. Of course, two rollovers from the same IRA may not be taken within a 12-month period. If IRA funds are moved by way of direct custodian-to-custodian <u>transfer</u>, the 12-month restriction does not apply.[28]

A <u>transfer</u> is a direct custodian-to-custodian conveyance of assets. The IRA owner does not receive any portion of the assets that would require contribution to the same or another IRA. Transfers are generally preferable to rollovers as <u>the 12-month limitation and the 60-day rollover period do not apply to transfers.</u> As a result, transfers are less likely to result in a mistake that causes adverse tax consequences.[29] To avoid the 12-month limitation and 60-day rollover period, use a transfer instead of a rollover to move funds from one IRA to another.

The owner of multiple IRAs may transfer assets between each IRA freely without limitation. A single IRA may be split into multiple IRAs, and multiple IRAs may be consolidated into one or more IRAs. Some restrictions apply, however, with transfers involving SIMPLE IRAs. Traditional IRAs and SEP IRAs cannot be transferred or rolled into a SIMPLE IRA. After two years have elapsed since the original SIMPLE IRA contribution, a SIMPLE IRA may be rolled into a traditional IRA or SEP IRA.

Required minimum distributions may not be transferred or rolled into another IRA.[30] If a required minimum distribution is rolled over into another IRA, it is considered an excess contribution.

Transfers and Rollovers from 401(k) Plans to IRAs

Many 401(k) and other employer-plan participants elect to rollover or transfer their account balances to an IRA when they retire. Rolling an employer-plan balance into an IRA is typically the best choice for the vast majority of retirees, and it has many advantages. Chapter 8 discusses the pros and cons of 401(k) rollovers. For distributions on or after January 1, 2002, after-tax 401(k) contributions may also be rolled into an IRA. Participants in 403(b), 457 and other employer plans may also elect to rollover their accounts to an IRA. Lastly, lump sum pension payments may be rolled into an IRA, which provides more control over these assets.

Options with Inherited IRAs

An inherited IRA is an IRA received by a beneficiary from a deceased IRA owner. When an IRA owner dies, the beneficiaries receive the IRA as an inherited IRA. An inherited IRA must remain in the deceased IRA owner's name and cannot be rolled or converted into an IRA in the beneficiary's name.[31] For example, Marie (who is not Pierre's spouse) is the beneficiary of Pierre's IRA. When Pierre dies, the IRA should be titled "IRA in the name of Pierre Thibodaux, deceased, FBO (for the benefit of) Marie Thibodaux." If there is more than one beneficiary, each beneficiary may transfer his or her IRA portion to another IRA custodian; however, the IRA must remain in the deceased IRA owner's name. If a non-spouse beneficiary attempts to re-title the IRA into his or her name, the IRA will be fully distributed with taxes due on the entire amount.

An inherited IRA may be moved only by direct custodian-to-custodian transfer. In addition, the transfer should be completed by December 31 of the year after the IRA owner dies to take advantage of the Separate Account Rule. If the Separate Account Rule does not apply, required minimum distributions for all beneficiaries will be based on the oldest beneficiary's age. Unlike an IRA owner, the beneficiary may not take receipt of the IRA assets and rollover the assets to an IRA within 60 days. If the beneficiary attempts a rollover (as opposed to a custodian-to-custodian transfer), a full taxable distribution of the IRA occurs. In short, a financial disaster ensues.

If the surviving spouse is the beneficiary, a special rule allows a surviving spouse to rollover a deceased IRA owner's IRA into his or her own IRA. In this case, the IRA need not remain in the deceased IRA owner's name. The spouse may rollover the IRA into his or her own IRA as the IRA owner. See Chapter 7 for additional information regarding spousal rollovers.

Prohibited Transactions

Prohibited transactions should be avoided due to the effects of the IRA being disqualified as an IRA. If an IRA is disqualified, the IRA asset value on the first day of the taxable year in which the prohibited transaction occurred is treated as being distributed on that first day.[32] For example, Boudreaux has an IRA with a January 1 value of $300,000. He commits a prohibited transaction by borrowing $5,000 from his IRA on October 1. Boudreaux's entire IRA ceases to be an IRA, and he has constructive receipt of the entire IRA as of January 1. Therefore, the entire IRA is deemed distributed to him as of January 1. The entire IRA is taxable to Boudreaux, and if he is under age 59½, the 10 percent penalty will apply. Prohibited transactions include[33]

- Investing in collectables (e.g. art, antiques, rugs, gemstones). Although certain gold or silver coins held by the custodian are allowed if the custodial document permits;

- Purchasing life, health or accident insurance;

- Borrowing from the IRA;

- Pledging IRA assets as collateral. (A pledge of a portion of the IRA as collateral causes constructive receipt of the amount pledged, rather than constructive receipt of the entire IRA. The constructive receipt occurs on the date the collateral is pledged, rather than on the first day of the taxable year.)

Due to the severe consequences of a prohibited transaction, IRA owners should steer clear of any activity that may be considered a prohibited transaction.

Self-Dealing

Certain transactions between the IRA owner and "disqualified persons" are considered self-dealing and may cause an IRA to no longer be classified as an IRA. Disqualified persons include the IRA owner, the IRA beneficiaries and the IRA custodian or trustee. Prohibited transactions include but are not limited to[34]

- Lending money or extending credit between the IRA and a disqualified person;

- Furnishing goods, services or facilities between an IRA and a disqualified person;

- Selling, exchanging or leasing of property between the IRA and a disqualified person;

- Purchasing property for personal use with IRA funds. The money should first be withdrawn from the IRA.

If the IRA owner or the IRA beneficiaries receive some type of benefit from a transaction with the IRA, self-dealing is probably involved. Self-dealing occurs even if all transactions are at arm's length and the IRA ends up with the better deal.

An IRA may invest in real estate or a closely held business; however, the self-dealing rules may come into play. The rules can be rather complex and running afoul of the rules may cause the IRA to lose its tax-deferred status. For this reason, use non-IRA assets to purchase real estate or closely held business interests whenever possible.

---

[1] IRC § 408(a)(4); § 408 (b)(4).
[2] IRC § 408(a); Regs. § 1.408(2)(b).
[3] IRC §401(a)(9)(B)(ii); Reg. § 1.401(a)(9)-3, A-4, A-2.
[4] Reg. § 1.401(a)(9)-3, §54.4974-2, A-3(c).

[5] Reg. § 1.401(a)(9)-5, A-5(a)(2).
[6] Reg. § 1.401(a)(9)-5, A-5(a)(1).
[7] La. R.S. §13:3881.
[8] Id.
[9] IRC § 219(e)(1).
[10] IRC § 219(f)(3).
[11] Rev. Rul. 84-18, 1984-1 C.B. 88.
[12] IRC § 219 (d)(1); Prop. Regs. § 1.219(a)-2(b)(2).
[13] Regs § 1.408-8, Q&A A-3.
[14] IRC § 219(b)(1).
[15] Prop. Regs. § 1.219(a)-1(b)(3).
[16] IRC § 219(c)(1).
[17] IRC §219(c)(2).
[18] IRC §§ 408(d)(4); 4973(b).
[19] IRC § 408(d)(1).
[20] IRC §§ 408(d)(2)(B), (C)
[21] Notice 87-16, Q&A D-3, D-4.
[22] IRS Pub. 590.
[23] IRC § 219(d)(2).
[24] Reg. § 1.401(c)-2, A-7(a).
[25] IRC § 402(c)(3)(A).
[26] PLR 200433022.
[27] Alvan L. Bobrow, et ux. V. Commissioner, TC Memo 2014-21, January 28, 2014.
[28] IRC § 408(d)(3)(B).
[29] Rev. Rul. 78-406.
[30] IRC §§ 402(c)(4)(B), 408(d)(3)(E).
[31] IRC §§ 402(c)(9); 408(d)(3)(C.
[32] IRC § 408(e)(2)(B).
[33] IRS Pub. 590; § IRC 4975.
[34] IRC § 4975.

5

Roth IRAs

Chapter Highlights

- ❖ A Roth IRA is a tax-deferred retirement account controlled by the owner.

- ❖ Roth IRAs have the same creditor protection features, investment flexibility, and beneficiary options as traditional IRAs.

- ❖ Unlike traditional IRAs, qualified Roth IRA distributions are tax-free.

- ❖ As Roth contributions may be made at any age, contributions may be made after the owner attains 70½ years of age.

- ❖ Roth IRA contributions may not be made if the owner's income is above certain thresholds.

- ❖ Contributions to Roth IRAs are not tax deductible.

- ❖ Unlike traditional IRAs, Roth IRA owners are not subject to required minimum distributions. Thus, the account may continue to accumulate until the owner's death.

- ❖ Roth IRA beneficiaries are subject to tax-free required minimum distributions after the owner's death.

- ❖ If a beneficiary does not withdraw the required tax-free distribution, a 50 percent excise tax will be imposed on the amount that should have been withdrawn.

- ❖ A traditional IRA may be converted to a Roth IRA; however, income taxes must be paid on the conversion amount.

ROTH IRAS are a type of IRA that provides unique planning opportunities to eligible participants. Like traditional IRAs, Roth IRAs are designed to encourage retirement saving. However, unlike traditional IRAs, Roth IRA qualified distributions are tax free, and the

Roth IRA owner is never obligated to take required minimum distributions.[1] Individuals who are unable to make a deductible traditional IRA contribution should consider making a Roth IRA contribution, rather than a nondeductible traditional IRA contribution. All Roth IRA contributions are nondeductible, but all future growth of the Roth IRA is free from taxes to both the owner and the beneficiaries.

A Roth IRA may be created by making annual contributions. In addition, a Roth IRA may be created by converting a traditional IRA into a Roth IRA. Like traditional IRAs, Roth IRAs are a special type of account, not an investment. Rather, the account is used to purchase investments chosen by the Roth IRA owner who has complete flexibility to direct the investment mix and management of Roth IRA assets.

Roth IRA Contribution Limits and Eligibility

Similar to traditional IRAs, Roth IRAs are subject to maximum annual contribution amounts. In contrast to traditional IRAs, contributions may be made after April 1 following the owner reaching 70½ years of age.[2] A significant feature of Roth IRAs is that there are no age limitations on Roth IRA contributions or conversions.[3]

A Roth IRA contribution of $6,000[a] ($7,000 if over age 50) may be made by persons who are married and file jointly with a modified adjusted gross income (MAGI) that does not exceed $203,000. The $6,000 limit is phased-out for couples with MAGI between $193,000 and $203,000, and no contributions may be made if the couple's MAGI exceeds $203,000.[4] Because of the contribution limit, individuals with higher income levels will not be able to make a Roth IRA contribution. In contrast, individuals of any income level may make a nondeductible contribution to a traditional IRA.

For single individuals, a $6,000 ($7,000 if over age 50) contribution may be made if MAGI does not exceed $122,000.[b] The contribution limit is phased-out for individuals with MAGI between $122,000 and $137,000. If MAGI exceeds $137,000, no contribution may be made.[5] Individuals who are married filing single are not allowed to make a full Roth IRA contribution and may not make any contributions if MAGI exceeds $10,000.

---

[a] For 2019
[b] For 2019

For contribution eligibility for Roth IRAs, include required minimum distributions and income from Roth conversions in MAGI.[6] To determine MAGI for Roth IRAs, certain adjustments to adjusted gross income must be made.[7] These adjustments differ slightly from the adjustments made to determine MAGI for traditional IRA deductions. (See Table 4 and Table 5 below.)

Table 4 - Roth IRA Contribution Limits

Year	Maximum Contribution	Catch-Up Provision**	Total Contribution With Catch-Up
2019*	$6,000	$1,000	$7,000

* Contribution limits are adjusted for inflation in $500 increments.
** If age 50 or over at the end of the year.

Table 5 - 2019 Roth IRA Contribution Phase-Out Limits

Married Filing Jointly*	$193,000-$203,000
Single or Head of Household*	$122,000-$137,000
Married Filing Separately	$0-$10,000

*Indexed for inflation

Like traditional IRAs, even if all other criteria are met, the Roth IRA owner must have earned income of at least the contribution amount.[8] Spousal Roth IRA contributions are allowed. For example, if one spouse has earned income of at least $12,000 through 2019 ($14,000 through 2019 if age 50) and the couple files a joint return, both spouses can contribute $6,000 ($7,000 if age 50), even if one spouse has no earned income for the year.[9]

Total contributions to all IRAs cannot exceed the maximum annual allowable amount.[10] If an individual has made a maximum contribution to a traditional IRA, no Roth IRA contribution is allowed. If a partial contribution is made to a traditional IRA, the maximum allowable Roth IRA contribution is equal to the difference between the annual IRA contribution limit and the traditional IRA partial contribution amount.

Roth IRA Conversions

An eligible traditional IRA owner may elect to convert all or part of a traditional IRA to a Roth IRA as a qualified rollover contribution. Beginning in 2010, the $100,000 MAGI threshold was eliminated, allowing anyone to convert a traditional IRA to a Roth IRA.[11]

Roth IRA conversions may be made by rollover, by direct custodian-to-custodian transfer or by transferring a traditional IRA to a Roth IRA with the same custodian. A SEP IRA or a SIMPLE IRA may be converted to a Roth IRA; however, two years must elapse from the inception of the SIMPLE IRA.[12] An inherited IRA may not be converted to a Roth IRA.[13]

When converting a traditional IRA to a Roth IRA, income taxes must be paid on the converted amount.[14] An eligible IRA owner may elect to convert an entire IRA in one year or elect a partial conversion. Partial conversions may be spread over a number of years which may reduce the income tax burden. If electing a partial conversion of an IRA with deductible and nondeductible contributions, the conversion amount cannot be treated solely as coming from the nondeductible contributions to avoid taxes on the conversion. When converting (or withdrawing from) an IRA, the amount converted is deemed to consist of a pro-rata portion of taxable and nontaxable dollars. All IRAs (including SIMPLE and SEP IRAs) are aggregated to determine the pro-rata taxable amount of a distribution from any IRA. One option is to rollover the taxable portion of the IRA to a 401(k) or other qualified plan. By leaving only the nontaxable portion in the IRA, the IRA may be converted to a Roth IRA without paying taxes.

The Pension Protection Act of 2006 allows an employer plan participant to directly rollover employer plan funds to a Roth IRA. The benefit of a direct rollover is that the pro-rata rule for rollovers does not apply. Thus, by converting only the after-tax money in an employer plan to a Roth IRA by way of a rollover, the conversion is tax free.[15]

Factors to Consider When Converting to a Roth IRA

The decision to convert to a Roth IRA involves many factors, some of which are unknown. The decision should not be taken lightly because the wrong decision may put the IRA owner in a worse position after the conversion. The decision to convert a traditional IRA to a Roth IRA should be made after receiving competent professional advice. Questions to ask and factors to consider include

- Will taxes due upon conversion be paid with IRA proceeds or from non-IRA sources? It is typically advantageous to pay the taxes with non-IRA sources, as more is left in the IRA to grow tax deferred or tax free.

- Is the IRA owner's tax bracket likely to be the same or lower in future years? If the tax bracket will be higher when distributions are taken in later years, converting to a Roth IRA when in a lower tax bracket may be advantageous. If the tax bracket will be lower when distributions are taken in future years, converting when tax bracket is higher may cause more taxes to be paid than if there were no conversion.

- When will the owner require distributions from a converted Roth IRA? It is more advantageous to convert if distributions from a converted Roth IRA are needed later rather than sooner. Ideally, distributions from the Roth IRA will never be needed, and the Roth IRA is left to the beneficiaries who receive tax-free distributions over their life expectancy.

- What portion of the IRA, if any, consists of after-tax contributions? Upon conversion to a Roth IRA, after-tax contributions are not subject to taxes.

- If the estate is subject to estate taxes, paying income taxes on the conversion removes those dollars from the taxable estate.

- If the IRA owner is receiving Social Security benefits, the additional income realized in the year of the Roth conversion may cause otherwise un-taxable Social Security benefits to be taxable.

Roth IRA Distributions

Another significant feature of Roth IRAs is that qualified distributions are 100 percent free from federal income taxation.[16] Qualified distributions meet the following criteria:

- The distribution must be made after the owner is age 59½;

- or has become disabled;

- or has died; AND

- the distribution must occur after the end of the five-year holding period beginning with the first taxable year for which the first Roth IRA contribution had been made or for which a Roth IRA conversion had occurred, whichever is sooner (the five-year rule).

For example, if a Roth IRA contribution is made on March 1, 2019, for the 2018 tax year, the five-year rule is satisfied if the first Roth IRA distribution occurs after December 31, 2022.

For the purposes of the five-year rule, all Roth IRAs are aggregated (regular contributions and conversions).[17] Each Roth IRA owner has only one five-year holding period for taxation of <u>contributions</u>. However, there may be multiple five-year holding periods to determine the taxation of Roth IRA <u>conversions</u>.

<u>Nonqualified distributions</u> are subject to ordering rules that allow distributions to come first from contributions, rather than earnings.[18] Roth IRA <u>nonqualified distributions</u> are in the following order:

1. Regular contributions (not Roth conversions) are withdrawn.

2. Roth IRA conversion contributions are withdrawn on a first-in, first-out basis. Converted amounts that represent deductible contributions are distributed prior to nondeductible contributions.

3. Earnings are withdrawn.

If a withdrawal is a nonqualified distribution, the withdrawal's earnings portion is subject to taxes and the 10 percent premature-distribution penalty if under age 59½.[19] Prior to withdrawing earnings, all <u>contributions</u> made to the Roth IRA are distributed as a tax-free return of basis.[20] The 10 percent premature-distribution penalty does not apply to the tax-free return of basis portion of <u>contributions</u>.

A special rule applies to distributions from a Roth IRA that was converted from a traditional IRA. If the Roth IRA owner is under age 59½, a nonqualified withdrawal made within five years of the conversion may be subject to the 10 percent premature-distribution penalty, to the extent the distribution consists of converted funds that were taxed at the time of the conversion. For the purposes of this special rule, a new five-year holding period applies each time there is a conversion of traditional IRA funds to a Roth IRA. The special five-year holding period begins on January 1 of the year of the applicable conversion.[21]

For example, Boudreaux converts $25,000 from his traditional IRA to a Roth IRA in 2019. This is Boudreaux's first Roth IRA. He pays income taxes on the $25,000 conversion in 2019. In 2023, at age 57,

Boudreaux's Roth IRA is worth $30,000, and he withdraws $5,000. Because the five-year holding requirement from the date the Roth IRA was opened has not been met, the $5,000 withdrawal is not a qualified distribution. The 10 percent premature-distribution penalty will apply to the entire $5,000 withdrawal. This outcome is designed to prevent traditional IRA owners from circumventing the premature-distribution penalty by converting to a Roth IRA and then taking tax-free and penalty-free, pre-59½ distributions of the converted funds.

For example, Thibodaux opens a Roth IRA in 2015 with a $2,000 contribution and makes no additional contributions. In 2019 Thibodaux converts a $75,000 traditional IRA to a Roth IRA. In 2020, when Thibodaux is 62, he withdraws $10,000 from his Roth IRA. No taxes are due on the distribution because five years have elapsed since his first Roth IRA was opened and he is over age 59½. Although the withdrawal was within five years of the <u>conversion</u> from the traditional IRA, no penalty applies because he is over 59½.

Because Roth IRA contributions are made on an after-tax basis and distributions are taken first from contributions, all contributions to a Roth IRA may be withdrawn, even if the withdrawals are not qualified distributions. Because Roth IRA contributions are made on an after-tax basis, only the earnings are taxable for <u>nonqualified</u> distributions.

Roth IRA Required Minimum Distributions

While the Roth IRA owner is alive, required minimum distributions do not apply.[22] The Roth IRA owner is never required to take distributions from the Roth IRA, regardless of his or her age. Once the Roth IRA owner dies, the beneficiary must begin required minimum distributions[23] over the beneficiary's then remaining nonrecalculating single life expectancy. Distributions must begin by December 31 of the year following the Roth IRA owner's death. If distributions do not begin by this date, the five-year rule will apply and the entire Roth IRA must be distributed by the end of the fifth year beginning the year after the Roth IRA owner dies. The post death required minimum distributions for Roth IRAs are calculated the same as for traditional IRAs using the Single Life Table. After the beneficiary's death, distributions continue to be made based on the now deceased beneficiary's remaining life expectancy.

The five-year holding period will continue to apply to Roth IRA beneficiaries after the owner's death. Once the five-year holding period has been satisfied, all distributions to Roth IRA beneficiaries are free from income tax. If the five-year holding period has not elapsed and a Roth IRA beneficiary takes distributions from the Roth IRA, distributions are tax-free so long as distributions do not exceed the Roth IRA owner's original basis. If earnings are distributed prior to the five-year period elapsing, income taxes will be paid on the distributed earnings as income in respect of a decedent (IRD). Once the five-year holding period has been satisfied, all future distributions (including earnings) from the Roth IRA are free from taxation.

If the Roth IRA does not have a designated beneficiary, the inherited Roth IRA will be distributed under the five-year rule. If the surviving spouse is the sole beneficiary, the surviving spouse may roll the account into his or her own Roth IRA. If the spousal rollover is elected, the required-minimum-distributions rule and the pre-59½ premature-distribution penalty are applied to the surviving spouse as owner rather than as beneficiary. By electing a spousal rollover for an inherited Roth IRA, the spouse may choose not to take distributions. The surviving spouse is treated as the owner and is not subject to lifetime required minimum distributions. Once the surviving spouse dies, the Roth IRA beneficiary must begin distributions by December 31 of the year following the spouse's death.

Like traditional IRAs, an inherited Roth IRA remains in the deceased Roth IRA owner's name and may not be combined with other inherited Roth IRA accounts in other deceased owners' names. Inherited Roth IRAs in the same deceased owner's name may be combined.

Recharacterizations of Roth IRA Conversions and Contributions

If the participant wishes to undo a Roth IRA conversion or contribution, the assets may be recharacterized to a traditional IRA if the recharacterization is completed by the participant's income tax filing due date (plus extensions) for the year of the Roth IRA conversion or contribution.[24] A recharacterization may be desirable if an ineligible Roth IRA contribution was made. For example, the Roth

IRA owner had an income level that prevented a Roth IRA contribution.

A conversion or contribution to a Roth IRA followed by a recharacterization back to a traditional IRA can only be elected once per calendar year. Once recharacterized, the assets cannot be recontributed or reconverted back to a Roth IRA until the later of the beginning of the calendar year following the calendar year in which the conversion or contribution took place or the date that is 30 days after the date on which the Roth IRA had been recharacterized as a traditional IRA.[25]

Planning Ideas with Roth IRAs

Individuals who are not eligible to make a deductible, traditional IRA contribution should consider making a Roth IRA contribution if they are eligible.

If an individual has reason to believe he or she may be in a higher tax bracket when distributions from a traditional IRA will be taken, converting the traditional IRA to a Roth IRA now may be beneficial.

If the traditional IRA will not be needed for retirement income, converting to a Roth IRA eliminates RMDs and allows for tax-free distributions on the account, including all future growth. By paying income taxes on the conversion, the gross estate is reduced by the amount of income taxes paid. In addition, income taxes and calculations for Income in Respect of a Decedent (IRD) are eliminated for the Roth IRA beneficiaries. The taxes on conversion are paid by the Roth IRA owner. A child or grandchild beneficiary will receive tax-free growth on the Roth IRA, and all distributions are tax-free. No other planning vehicle can provide these benefits.

If an individual has a tax loss for the year, he or she should consider converting all or part of a traditional IRA to a Roth IRA. An amount equal to the tax loss may be converted, and no taxes will be due on the conversion.

---

[1] Unless certain criteria are met, Roth IRA owners must be 59½ or older and have held the IRA for five years before tax-free withdrawals are permitted. Additionally, each converted amount may be subject to its own five-year holding period. Converting a traditional IRA into a Roth IRA has tax implications. Investors should consult a tax advisor before deciding to do a conversion.

[2] IRC § 408A(c)(4).

[3] IRC § 408A(c)(4).

[4] IRC §408A(c)(3)(A) and (C).

[5] IRC § 408A(c)(3)(A) and (C).

[6] IRC § 408A(c)(3); Treas. Reg. § 1.408A-3, Q & A 5.

[7] To determine MAGI for Roth IRAs add the following items to AGI: Income from Roth IRA conversions; Tradition IRA deduction; student loan interest deduction; Income from U.S. savings bonds used to pay higher education expenses; Foreign earned income exclusion; Foreign housing exclusion; Employer reimbursed adoption expenses; and Deduction for qualified tuition and related expenses.

[8] IRC § 219(b)(1)(B).

[9] IRC § 219(C)(1).

[10] IRC § 408A(c)(2).

[11] The Tax Increase Prevention and Reconciliation Act (TIPRA).

[12] Reg. § 1.401A-4, A-4(b).

[13] IRC § 408(d)(3)(C).

[14] IRC § 408(A)(d)(3)(A)-(C).

[15] IRS Notice 2014-54.

[16] IRC §408(A)(d)(1).

[17] IRC §1.408A-6 (Q and A 9).

[18] IRC §408A(d)(4)(B).

[19] Reg. § 1.408A-6, A-5.

[20] IRC § 408A(d)(4)(B); Reg. 1.408A-6, A-9.

[21] Reg. 1.408A-6, A-5(b); IRC § 408A(d)(3)(F).

[22] IRC § 408(c)(5).

[23] Reg. § 1.408A-6, A-14(b).

[24] IRC §1.408A-5 (Q and A1)); IRC §1.408A-5(Q and A6(b).

[25] IRC §1.408A-5 (Q and A9)(a)(1).

6

Pre-59½, Penalty-Free Distributions

Chapter Highlights

❖ IRA participants are subject to a 10 percent penalty if distributions are taken from an IRA or employer plan prior to age 59½.

❖ Participants under age 59½ may avoid the premature-distribution penalty by qualifying for an exception.

❖ A series of substantially equal periodic payments under Section 72(t) of the Internal Revenue Code allows participants to take early penalty-free distributions prior to age 59½ if no other exception applies.

❖ A beneficiary is not subject to the premature-distribution penalty if the IRA owner dies.

❖ Exceptions exist for disability, qualified first-time home purchases, qualified educational expenses and medical expenses.

❖ Participants of 401(k) and 403(b) plans may take penalty-free distributions from their plan if they separate from service after attaining age 55.

❖ Certain federal, state and local public safely officials including firefighters, police officers, boarder protection officers, air traffic controllers and emergency medical personnel may take penalty-free distributions from government defined benefit and defined contribution plans upon separation from service after age 50 rather than age 55.

ACCOUNT OWNERS WISHING TO take distributions from their IRA prior to age 59½ will be subject to a 10 percent premature-distribution-penalty tax, unless an exception applies. This 10 percent early distribution penalty is applied to the distribution's taxable portion, and it is in addition to the ordinary income taxes due on the distribution. One of these exceptions to the premature-distribution penalty is a series of substantially equal periodic payments (SEPP) also known as 72(t) distributions.[1] Other exceptions are death, disability, first-time home purchases and medical expenses in certain situations.

Substantially Equal Payments Under 72(t)

Several requirements must be met to claim the substantially equal payments exception. Due to the complexity of this area of tax code, it is highly recommended that you seek expert advice prior to establishing a SEPP plan. You may be exposed to unnecessary taxes and interest penalties if you do not follow the 72(t) rules. Distributions under a SEPP plan are calculated using one of three IRS approved methods:[2] Annuity Method, Amortization Method or RMD Method.

The annuity and amortization methods are used more often because they produce larger distribution amounts for a given IRA value. IRA owners should seek to create the largest distributions possible from the smallest amount of IRA assets. The amortization and annuity methods have a fixed annual distribution amount. It is calculated once—at the beginning of the payment stream—and the annual distribution amount may not be modified. This is what distinguishes the amortization and annuity methods from the RMD method. The fixed annual distribution amount is easily matched to income needs. In addition, the amortization and annuity methods, due to their fixed distribution amount, may exhaust the IRA if the IRA asset value drops significantly.

Contrarily, the RMD method is typically not prone to this problem because the annual distribution is recalculated annually. The RMD method will result in a different amount each year depending on the increase or decrease in account value and the IRA owner's age. If the account has experienced a significant decline because of poor investment performance, the annual distribution amount will be automatically adjusted downward. This flexibility ensures that distributions continue at a rate the IRA asset value can sustain.

Calculating SEPP Distributions

Revenue Ruling 2002-62 provides the rules governing SEPP distributions. The amount that can be withdrawn each year is calculated by using one of three methods: annuity, amortization or RMD Method.

The variables included in the annuity and amortization calculations are the IRA owner's age, the IRA account value and a "reasonable" interest rate. A reasonable interest rate is any interest rate that is not more than 120 percent of the federal mid-term rate[a]. A lower rate may be used; however, it will result in lower annual distributions.

Because the amortization and annuity methods assume some account value growth due to the interest rate, larger distributions result. The RMD method uses the account balance (valued annually) and the IRA owner's life expectancy based on his or her age. The account balance is divided by the life expectancy factor to determine the annual required distribution. The following year the IRA owner's new age and new account value are used to determine his or her life expectancy to calculate that year's distribution. Each method will allow a different amount to be withdrawn from an IRA, and most individuals simply choose the method allowing for the distribution amount closest to their cash flow requirements. The amortization method always produces the largest distribution. A financial advisor with the use of software can perform these calculations for you. (See Table 6 on the next page.)

The recalculation or hybrid method appears to be another alternative allowed by the IRS.[3] The recalculation method allows the IRA owner to begin SEPP distributions using the amortization method to maximize annual withdrawals. The distribution amount is then recalculated each year based on the account value, the IRA owner's age and the applicable interest rate the following year. The recalculation method will enable larger distributions than the RMD method but will prevent the possibility of exhausting the IRA if the IRA value drops due to poor investment performance or due to withdrawals. If the account value goes up, a larger distribution will result for the year. If the account value goes down, a smaller distribution will result. The recalculation method must be selected in advance. (See Table 6) To use the recalculation method, you should

1. Select the amortization method

2. Determine a valuation date

---

[a] The mid-term rate is determined in accordance with §1274(d) for either of the two months immediately preceding the month in which the distribution begins.

3. Select an interest rate not exceeding 120 percent of the Federal Mid Term Rate for either of the two months preceding the distribution.

4. Reset the account value, account owner's age and interest rate on the same date each year.

Table 6 - Estimates of SEPP Distributions

IRA Balance	Calculation Methods		
	Annuity Method	Amortization Method	RMD Method
$100,000	$4,604	$4,626	$3,378
$200,000	$9,209	$9,253	$6,757
$400,000	$18,417	$18,506	$13,514

Calculations assume a 55-year-old IRA owner, single life table, and an interest rate of 2.19 percent.

Selection of Life-Expectancy Table

When calculating SEPP distributions, any of the three life-expectancy tables may be used.

The single-life table will create the largest payment from the smallest account balance. This is the same table IRA beneficiaries use to calculate RMDs from inherited IRAs. The single-life table will optimize the payments from any given account, so it is the most frequently used table and typically should be used by IRA owners.

The Uniform-Lifetime Table may also be used. This is the same table used to calculate RMDs for IRA owners.

The Joint-Life Table is the third option. This is the same table that may be used by IRA owners to take RMDs by the IRA owner if his or her spouse beneficiary is more than 10 years younger. For SEPP purposes, the Joint-Life Table may be used even if the beneficiary is not the IRA owner's spouse. Unlike lifetime RMDs where the sole beneficiary must be the IRA owner's spouse to use the Joint-Life Table, Revenue Ruling 2002-62 only requires that there be a named beneficiary to use the Joint-Life Table. If there is more than one beneficiary, use the oldest beneficiary's age when consulting the Joint-Life Table. If there is no named beneficiary, the Joint-Life Table may not be used.

Frequency of Payments

Distributions under the SEPP exception must be made "not less frequently than annually."[4] Although the tax code does specifically address monthly or quarterly payments, several private letter rulings acknowledged monthly payments.[5] It is generally accepted that payments may be made annually, quarterly or monthly. It is also generally accepted that payments may be changed from monthly to quarterly to annually and back so long as the annual distribution amount does not change. However, until the IRS provides guidance on this issue, it is best to play it safe by not altering the payment frequency.

The amortization method and annuity method enable the calculation of precise monthly, quarterly or annual payments. If payments begin in mid-year rather than on January 1, monthly or quarterly payments should be taken for the remainder of the year during the first year. For example, if payments are to begin on July 1, six monthly payments would be made the first year, twelve payments the second through fourth year, and six monthly payments in the fifth year (assuming only five years of payments were required).

The RMD method is an annual calculation, so taking less than the full year's distribution if payments began in mid-year would probably violate the 72(t) rules.

Duration of Payments

Once distributions have begun from the IRA under the SEPP exception, the payments generally must continue at least annually, unmodified, for the longer of five years or until the IRA owner reaches age 59½. In other words, if a 50-year-old IRA owner begins SEPP distributions under 72(t), distributions must continue until the individual attains age 59½ before the distribution amount may be modified or discontinued. On the other hand, if a 58-year-old IRA owner begins SEPP distributions under 72(t), distributions must continue for a minimum of five years before the distribution amount can be modified or discontinued.

Modification of Payments

It is important to note that if the payment amount is modified before the later of five years or attainment of age 59½, a 10 percent penalty, plus interest, will be applied retroactively to all current and previous distributions intended to qualify under the SEPP exception. Any retroactive penalties and interest are reported on the tax return of the year of the modification to the payments. Prior returns are not amended.

If you are taking SEPP distributions under the amortization or annuity methods, you have one chance to modify the payments by electing a one-time switch to the RMD method under Rev. Rul. 2002-62. Switching to the RMD method can help you avoid depleting the IRA under the amortization or annuity methods if, for example, the account value drops dramatically.

For example, if the IRA owner, began SEPP distributions based on the amortization method, a $500,000 IRA might have resulted in a required distribution of $23,132 per year. If the IRA account value dropped to $250,000 due to a market downturn, a $23,132 annual distribution from the IRA would cause disproportionately large distributions compare to the IRA's value. By switching to the RMD method, the annual distribution might be reduced to $8,961 for a 57 year old. To further reduce distributions under the RMD method, the joint life expectancy of the IRA owner and the owner's spouse may be used. The RMD method will also require a smaller distribution the following year if the IRA value drops.

Caution should be used because the RMD calculation will produce a much lower annual payment. In some cases it may be too low and will not provide sufficient income. Prior to making the election to switch to the RMD method, make sure there are sufficient resources to last until SEPP distributions terminate. This may mean that a few additional payments under the existing calculation may have to be taken and kept in reserve prior to switching to the RMD method.

Revenue Ruling 2002-62 also provided that IRAs that run out of money while taking SEPP distributions will not be subject to the 10 percent penalty.

A 2009 Tax Court decision held that an IRA distribution for higher education expenses did not result in a modification of the SEPP payment schedule. The court reasoned that the distribution for higher education expenses fell under another exception for the 10 percent premature distribution penalty.[6]

If the IRA owner dies or becomes disabled, distributions under SEPP from the IRA may be discontinued or modified.

Other Considerations

If you establish a SEPP plan, your IRA custodian will issue a 1099-R with box 7 coded with two, one or seven. If box 7 is coded with a two (early distribution with an applicable exception) you do not need to file anything else with the IRS. If box 7 is coded with a one (early distribution, no known exception) or a seven (normal distribution), you will need to file IRS form 5329 to obtain the SEPP exception.

IRA owners of any age may use the SEPP distribution option regardless of employment status. Distributions under SEPP may be made from a 401(k) but only after separation from service. Keep in mind that employees separating from service after age 55 may take penalty-free distributions from their 401(k) without using the SEPP exception.

If your IRA creates SEPP distributions that are too large, consider splitting the IRA into two. One IRA is funded with the amount of assets required to produce the desired amount of SEPP payments under the IRA owner's selected calculation method. The other IRA continues to grow tax deferred. If additional income is needed at a later time, split off another IRA and begin SEPP distributions from that IRA. IRAs are not aggregated to calculate SEPP distributions.

No contributions or rollovers may be added to the IRA once SEPP distributions begin. In addition, no amount may be transferred to another IRA. Any transaction causing a change in account value (such as additions or other withdrawals) will be considered a modification and will trigger the 10 percent penalty.

Several PLRs issued prior to Rev. Rul. 2002-62 allowed cost of living increases if they were included from the inception of the 72(t) payments. It appears that Rev. Rul. 2002-62 requires the same payments each year; therefore, cost of living increases are probably not allowed. Further guidance from the Service may clarify this issue.

Other Exceptions to the 10 percent Penalty

Use SEPP if no other pre-59½, penalty-free distribution exception applies. Some exceptions include death, disability, certain higher education expenses and qualified, first-time home purchases. IRAs and employer plans allow penalty-free, pre-59½ distributions as follows:

- In the event of the participant's death, the beneficiary may take penalty-free distributions from the deceased participant's IRA or employer plan.[7] This exception applies even if both the deceased participant and the beneficiary are under age 59½. If a surviving spouse beneficiary rolls the IRA or qualified plan into his or her own IRA, this exception to the premature-distribution penalty is no longer available. A spousal rollover converts the IRA or qualified plan of the deceased participant into the surviving spouse's IRA.

- If an IRA or employer-plan participant is disabled, the premature-distribution penalty does not apply.[8] Disabled is defined as "unable to participate in any substantial gainful activity by reason of any medically determinable physical or mental impairment which can be expected to result in death or to be of long-continued and indefinite duration."[9]

- For IRAs only, the premature-distribution penalty does not apply to qualified, first-time home buyers up to a $10,000 lifetime limit. The limit is for the participant, not the home purchaser. The distribution may be used to pay for qualified acquisition costs for the first home of the participant or the participant's spouse, child, grandchild, parent or grandparent. The distribution must be used to pay for qualified acquisition costs within 120 days of the distribution.[10]

- The premature-distribution penalty does not apply to medical expenses in excess of 10 percent of adjusted gross income for distributions taken during the taxable year the medical expenses were incurred.[11] Although the deductions need not be itemized as required by IRC §213, this exception applies only to medical expenses that would be deductible if itemized.

- For IRAs only, an unemployed IRA owner may take penalty-free distributions to pay for health insurance. The IRA owner must have separated from employment and have received unemployment compensation for 12 consecutive weeks. In addition, the distribution must occur during the year the unemployment compensation is received or the following year. Finally, the distribution must occur while the IRA owner is unemployed or within 60 days after employment resumes. This exception applies to medical insurance and long-term care insurance premium payments.[12]

- For IRAs only, distributions for qualified higher education expenses incurred by the IRA owner in the distribution year are also not subject to the premature-distribution penalty. Qualified higher education expenses for the IRA owner and his or her spouse, children and grandchildren qualify. The exception applies to tuition, books, fees, supplies and equipment required for virtually all accredited public, nonprofit and proprietary post-secondary institutions. Room and board also qualify if the student is enrolled at least half-time.[13]

- For qualified plan and 403(b) participants who separate from service after age 55, the premature-distribution penalty does not apply.[14] The order of events is important. The participant must turn age 55 first and then separate from service. Internal Revenue Service Publication 575 states separation from service after January 1 of the year the participant attains age 55; however, §72(t) uses the participant's actual birthday. To be on the safe side, wait until age 55 before relying on this exception.

- Government 457(b) plans are not subject to the 10% early withdrawal penalty. However, assets rolled from a governmental 457(b) plan to an IRA, 401(k) or other tax deferred plan or to a governmental 457 plan from an IRA, 401(k) or other tax deferred plan are subject to the 10% early withdrawal penalty.

- Certain federal, state and local public safely officials including firefighters, police officers, boarder protection officers, air traffic controllers and emergency medical personnel may take penalty-free distributions from government defined benefit and defined contribution plans upon separation from service after age 50 rather than age 55. Any distribution that qualifies for the public safety worker exception will not be considered a modification for 72(t) purposes. The exception does not apply to IRAs.[15]

[1] IRC § 72(t)(2)(A)(iv).
[2] Rev. Rul. 2002-62.
[3] PLRs 200432021, 200432032 and 200432024.
[4] Rev. Rul. 2002-62.
[5] PLRs 8919072, 9050030, 200105066.
[6] Benz v. Commissioner, 132 T.C. No 15, 2009.
[7] IRC § 72(t)(2)(A)(ii).
[8] IRC § 72(t)(2)(A)(iii).
[9] IRC § 72(m)(7).
[10] IRC § 72(t)(2)(f); 72(t)(8)(A).
[11] IRC § 72(t)(2)(B).
[12] IRC § 72(t)(2)(D).
[13] IRS § 72(t)(2)(E); Notice 97-60.
[14] IRC § 72(t)(2)(A)(v).
[15] Pension Protection Act of 2005, Trade Preferences Extensions Act of 2015.

7

Required Minimum Distributions

Chapter Highlights

❖ Proper planning is essential to enjoying maximum tax deferral of IRAs and employer plans.

❖ Required minimum distributions from IRAs and employer plans must begin by April 1 of the year following your 70½ birthday.

❖ Your Roth IRAs are not subject to required minimum distributions during your lifetime; however, after your death, Roth IRA beneficiaries must take required minimum distributions based on their age.

❖ If you fail to withdraw your required minimum distribution, you will be subject to a 50 percent excise tax on the amount you should have withdrawn.

❖ During your lifetime, required minimum distributions are based on your age and your corresponding life expectancy factor in the Uniform Lifetime Table.

❖ If you die before April 1 of the year following your 70½ birthday, your beneficiary may take required minimum distributions based on his or her age.

❖ If you die on or after April 1 of the year following your 70½ birthday, required minimum distributions for your beneficiary may be based on your age or your beneficiary's age, whichever is lower.

❖ Your surviving spouse is the only person who may rollover your IRA or employer plan into his or her own IRA. A spousal rollover allows your spouse to treat your IRA as his or her own for distribution purposes; therefore, a spousal rollover generally provides your spouse with more flexibility and tax deferral.

❖ Multiple beneficiaries may each use their own age for required minimum distribution purposes if the Separate Account Rule applies. Your beneficiaries must take steps to ensure the Separate Account Rule applies because it is not automatic.

❖ A stretch IRA is an IRA with children and/or grandchildren beneficiaries, each using their own age for required minimum distribution purposes. Even if children or grandchildren are named beneficiaries, a stretch IRA is not guaranteed. Additional steps must be taken to preserve stretch IRA status.

❖ Naming a trust as an IRA beneficiary may provide additional control over IRA distributions and estate tax savings; however, required minimum distributions will be based on the oldest beneficiary's age only if special requirements are met.

❖ If no IRA beneficiary is named, your estate may be the default beneficiary. If your estate is the beneficiary, your will or the intestacy laws will determine the new owner, and the IRA must be distributed within five years.

TAX-DEFERRED RETIREMENT ACCOUNTS grow tax deferred until the account owner begins account withdrawals. Because these are retirement accounts, the account owner must begin distributions by April 1 of the year following his or her turning age 70½. Tax-deferred accounts include but are not limited to IRAs, 401(k)s, 403(b)s and 457 plans. This chapter reviews the rules for required minimum distributions from retirement plans for account owners and beneficiaries.

To help maximize wealth transfer to beneficiaries, proper beneficiary designations should be made. Some of these rules are very complex, especially when trusts are involved. Therefore, understanding these rules is vital when planning your retirement. Because your retirement plan assets may be your single largest asset, naming the correct beneficiary and coordinating your retirement assets with your estate plan are essential to making your retirement assets last. You should seek the advice of a competent professional when planning for retirement distributions.

Terminology

Qualified Retirement Plan: A retirement plan under IRC § 401. These plans include defined contribution plans, defined benefit plans, pension plans, profit sharing plans and ESOPs. This book sometimes refers to these plans as employer plans.

Defined Contribution Plan: An employer plan such as a 401(k) plan, a profit sharing plan, a money purchase plan, a target benefit plan or an ESOP.

Defined Benefit Plan: An employer plan, such as a pension plan, for which the employer promises to pay a certain amount to the retiree for life starting at retirement. The benefit amount is based on a formula usually factoring in years of service and highest compensation levels.

403(b) Plan: An employer plan available to tax-exempt employers. Although technically not a qualified retirement plan, it is similar to other qualified retirement plans in that the contributions are made on a pre-tax basis and are taxed when withdrawn. Accounts may only be invested in annuity contracts or mutual funds. These plans are frequently used by teachers and school employees to make salary deferral contributions.

Individual Retirement Account (IRA): An IRA is not a qualified retirement plan under IRC § 401(a) but is a self-directed account under IRC § 408. IRAs are funded by tax-free rollovers from other retirement plans, contributions by the IRA owner or contributions by a spouse.

Participant: The employee or account owner.

Required Minimum Distribution (RMD): Minimum withdrawals required from all qualified retirement plans, IRAs, 403(b) plans, 457 plans, etc. by the Required Beginning Date (RBD).[1]

Required Beginning Date (RBD): April 1 of the year following the calendar year the participant reaches 70½ years of age.[2] For qualified retirement plans, the RBD may be delayed until the participant retires if the plan document provides for this exception and the participant is not a 5 percent owner. This exception does not apply to IRAs.

Designated Beneficiary (DB): The person named on the beneficiary designation form of qualified retirement plans and IRAs.[3]

Beneficiary Designation Date (BDD): September 30 of the year following the participant's death.[4]

Inherited IRA: An IRA that remains in the deceased participant's name for the IRA beneficiary's benefit. Technically, an inherited IRA is an IRA with someone other than the surviving spouse as beneficiary. A spousal rollover is never referred to as an inherited IRA. For example, John Boudreaux owns an IRA and Pierre Thibodaux is his beneficiary. After John Boudreaux dies, the IRA will be titled "John Boudreaux IRA, deceased FBO Pierre Thibodaux." If a non-spouse attempts to re-title an IRA into his or her name, a full taxable distribution will occur.

Premature Distributions

Tax-deferred retirement plans impose a premature-distribution penalty if distributions are taken prior to age 59½.[5] Because these are retirement accounts, the IRS wants to discourage withdrawals prior to retirement. The 10 percent penalty discourages distributions prior to attaining 59½ (when you should be in or near retirement). Some of the benefits of tax-deferral are lost due to the penalty.

The 10 percent penalty applies to the distribution portion that is included in gross income.[6] Therefore, the 10 percent penalty generally applies to pre-tax contributions and gains in the account, and it is in addition to income taxes due on the distribution. Any distribution portion that represents a return of after-tax contributions is not subject to the premature-distribution penalty. The taxes on IRA distributions, including the 10 percent premature-distribution penalty, are the participant's responsibility and not the participant's spouse. This rule applies even if the IRA is community property.[7]

Exceptions to the 10 percent premature-distribution penalty exist. For example, qualified plan, 403(b) plan and government plan participants who separate from service after age 55 may withdraw from their accounts penalty free. In addition, government plan distributions to police officers, firefighters and emergency medical personnel are exempt from the premature-distribution penalty if they separate from service after age 50 rather than age 55.[8] This exception is not applicable to IRAs. In addition, Roth IRAs have special rules for premature distributions. See chapter 6 for more information regarding pre-59½ distributions that are exempt from the 10 percent penalty.

Required Minimum Distributions (RMDs)

Unfortunately, tax-deferred account owners are not allowed to enjoy tax-deferred growth forever. Because tax-deferred accounts are designed for retirement, once you attain age 70½, the IRS wants you to begin distributions. The goal of required minimum distributions (RMDs) is to prevent continued tax deferral and wealth transfer to the next generation. RMDs must commence by April 1 of the year following the participant attaining age 70½ (the required beginning date or RBD).[9] However, employees (other than 5 percent owners) still employed at age 70½ may wait to start RMDs from qualified plans until they terminate employment.[10] If your birthday is before July 1, you attain age 70½ in the same calendar year you attain age 70. Age 70 is used to calculate the first RMD. If your birthday is after June 30, you attain age 70½ in the same calendar year you attain age 71, and age 71 is used to calculate your first RMD.

EXAMPLE: Boudreaux was born on May 20, 1948, thus his 70th birthday is May 20, 2019. He turns 70½ on November 20, 2019, and must take his first RMD by April 1, 2020.

EXAMPLE: Thibodaux was born on August 20, 1948, thus his 70th birthday is August 2019. He turns 70½ on February 20, 2020, and must take his first RMD by April 1, 2021.

Calculating the Required Minimum Distribution

During your lifetime, the RMD is calculated using The Uniform Lifetime Distribution Table (See Appendix A). To calculate the RMD, divide the account balance as of the last valuation date of the prior year (usually December 31) by the applicable distribution period from the Uniform Lifetime Table.[11] If your spouse is named beneficiary and is more than 10 years younger, the joint life expectancy table may be used to calculate a lower required distribution.[12]

You may always distribute more than the RMD, but distributing less than the RMD results in a 50 percent excise tax on the amount that should have been distributed but was not.[13] Due to the significant penalties for not withdrawing the RMD, you should always withdraw the RMD. If you own two or more IRAs, the RMDs are calculated separately, but the total RMDs for all IRAs may be taken from one IRA or from multiple IRAs so long as the entire aggregate RMD from all

IRAs is withdrawn.[14] Owners of 403(b) plans may also take RMDs of multiple 403(b) plans from one 403(b) plan.[15]

Inherited IRAs (accounts paying to you as a beneficiary due to the participant's death) for RMD purposes cannot be aggregated with IRAs of which you are the participant.[16] Beneficiaries of 403(b) accounts are also restricted for RMD purposes from combining 403(b) accounts they own as a participant.[17] If you have two or more qualified retirement plan accounts (e.g. 401k plans), RMDs must be calculated and distributed separately. A 401k account may not satisfy the RMD for another 401k account owned by the same participant.[18]

In contrast to other retirement accounts, Roth IRAs are not subject to RMDs during your lifetime.[19] After your death, however, the beneficiaries must commence tax-free distributions based on the beneficiary's life expectancy.[20] The 50 percent excise tax applies to Roth IRA required minimum distributions that should have been distributed but were not. It does not get much worse than that—an otherwise tax-free distribution is subject to a 50 percent penalty for failure to withdraw the tax-free distribution. Roth IRA distributions after the participant's death are not considered income in respect of a decedent as no income tax is due upon distribution.

Distributions after Your Death

After your death, your selection of beneficiary will determine the post-death distribution schedule. A key point is that the Uniform Lifetime Table is only used by the participant for lifetime distributions. The Single Life Table is used by the beneficiary after the participant's death. The following distribution rules are the IRS rules for retirement plans that provide the maximum amount of tax deferral allowed by law. Keep in mind that your employer plan or IRA may have more restrictive rules that require more rapid distributions. Your employer plan or IRA may not allow more tax deferral than the following rules, but it may be more restrictive. For this reason, it is important to determine the distribution rules that apply to your employer plan or IRA. If your employer plan is too restrictive, consider a direct transfer to an IRA with more favorable distribution rules. The distribution rules discussed herein apply to both employer plans and IRAs, but the explanation will refer to IRAs unless stated otherwise. The following explanation assumes you are the IRA owner.

If You Die BEFORE Your Required Beginning Date

In general, if you die prior to April 1 following the year you reach 70½ years of age (the RBD), RMDs are based on your beneficiary's life expectancy if RMDs begin by December 31 the year after your death (Exception 1 below). If your beneficiary is your spouse, RMDs are based on the recalculated life expectancy of your spouse. Your surviving spouse must begin RMDs by December 31 of the year after your death or by December 31 of the year you would have been 70½ (Exception 2 below).

The specific rule is as follows: The entire account balance of your IRA must be distributed to the Designated Beneficiary by December 31 of the year than contains the fifth anniversary of your death (Five-Year Rule)[21] unless one of two exceptions apply.

EXCEPTION 1 (THE LIFE EXPECTANCY RULE): If the Designated Beneficiary is not your spouse and RMDs begin by December 31 of the year after your death, RMDs are based on the Designated Beneficiary's life expectancy.[22] The distribution period is the beneficiary's single life expectancy in the year following your death and is reduced by one for each year thereafter. This is the fixed-term method. The beneficiary never goes back to the table for the divisor. After the Designated Beneficiary dies, his or her beneficiary uses the same distribution schedule as the original Designated Beneficiary.

For example, if Boudreaux is the beneficiary and is 61 in the year following the participant's death, his life expectancy is 24.4. Boudreaux must withdraw 1/24.4 of the account the first year, 1/23.4 the second year, etc. If the Boudreaux dies 10 years later (at age 71), the new beneficiary continues distributions using Boudreaux's remaining life expectancy.

EXCEPTION 2: If the sole Designated Beneficiary by the Beneficiary Designation Date is your spouse, he or she must take RMDs over his or her life expectancy recalculated annually beginning on his or her required beginning date.[23] The Single Life Table is consulted each year to determine the recalculated life expectancy. (Do not subtract one as under the fixed method.) After your spouse dies, the beneficiary must take RMDs over your deceased spouse's remaining fixed-term life expectancy. This is based on your deceased spouse's attained age in the year of your spouse's death and reduced by one for each year thereafter.

For example, Clotile, Thibodaux's surviving spouse, is age 61 in the year following Thibodaux's death. She is the sole beneficiary of his IRA. Clotile's life expectancy is 24.4, so she must withdraw 1/24.4 of the account in her first distribution year. In the second distribution year, Clotile is 62, and she goes back to the Single Life Table for the divisor, 23.5. She must withdraw 1/23.5 in her second distribution year. In the third distribution year, Clotile is 63, and she goes back to the table for the divisor, 22.7. Notice that the divisor is reduced by less than 1 each year. This is due to recalculating her life expectancy and results in lower RMDs. Once Clotile dies, her beneficiary will continue distributions based on Clotile's life expectancy. If Clotile dies 15 years after the participant at age 75, the RMD must be taken for the year Clotile died based on her recalculated life expectancy. The following year, the new beneficiary begins distributions using the fixed-term method based on the age Clotile would have been (76) using the divisor from the Single Life Table, 12.7. The following year, the beneficiary simply subtracts 1 from 12.7 for a divisor of 11.7. The next year subtract 1 from 11.7 for a divisor of 10.7 and so on.

RMDs based on your surviving spouse's life expectancy must begin by the LATER of

- December 31 of the year following your spouse's death or

- December 31 of the year you would have been 70½.[24]

If your surviving spouse dies prior to commencing RMDs, the designated beneficiary must commence RMDs based on his or her life expectancy by December 31 of the year after your surviving spouse's death. Otherwise, the entire account must be distributed by December 31 of the year that contains the fifth anniversary of your surviving spouse's death.[25] The five-year rule does not require annual distributions so long as the entire account is distributed by the end of the five-year period.

The Five-Year Rule is not applicable if the participant began payments under an irrevocable annuity before the Required Beginning Date. Distributions must be taken using the rules for RMDs after age 70½ even if the participant never attained age 70½.[26]

If You Die ON or AFTER Your Required Beginning Date

In general, if you die on or after April 1 following the year you reach 70½ years of age, RMDs are based on your life expectancy or the life expectancy of your beneficiary, whichever is longer. If you die after RMDs begin, the RMD for the year of your death must occur by December 31.[27] Distributions after the year of your death will be determined by the beneficiary designation. <u>Keep in mind that the Five-Year Rule is never an option after RMDs have begun</u>. If there is no Designated Beneficiary (including charities and nonqualified trusts), post-death distributions are based on the participant's life expectancy, determined in the year of death and reduced by one for each year thereafter (the fixed term method using the Single Life Table).[28] In this case the Uniform Table is not used.

Non-spouse Designated Beneficiaries take distributions based on the beneficiary's life expectancy (Single Life Table). Life expectancy is determined in the year after your death and is reduced by one for each year thereafter (the fixed-term method). As the deceased participant, if your remaining life expectancy is longer than the applicable beneficiary's life expectancy, the beneficiary may use your life expectancy.[29] For non-spouse beneficiaries, the account always remains in your name (as the deceased participant) for the beneficiary's benefit. A deceased participant's IRA is never renamed in the non-spouse beneficiary's name. This would result in a full, immediate taxable distribution. Your spouse, however, may leave the account in your name or elect a spousal rollover.

After a non-spouse Designated Beneficiary dies, RMDs for the successor beneficiary will continue over the remaining life expectancy of the now deceased Designated Beneficiary or, if applicable, the deceased participant's remaining life expectancy.[30]

If your spouse is the Designated Beneficiary, the required distribution schedule will depend on whether your surviving spouse elects a spousal rollover. If the assets are left in your account (a spousal rollover is not elected) as a beneficiary account, RMDs will be based on the LONGER of[31]

1. The single life expectancy (Single Life Table) of your surviving spouse re-determined annually,[32] or

2. Your life expectancy (Single Life Table) using your attained age in the year of your death minus the elapsed years after the year of death (the fixed term method).[33]

Distributions to your surviving spouse must begin by December 31 of the year after your death. Your surviving spouse may name a new beneficiary, and after your surviving spouse dies, RMDs to the new beneficiary will continue as rapidly as your spouse's RMDs.[34]

The Spousal Rollover

A spousal rollover is a tax-free transfer of the deceased participant's IRA into the surviving spouse's IRA. All or part of the IRA may be selected for a spousal rollover; however, the deceased participant's required RMD for the year may not be rolled over. Your surviving spouse is the only person who is eligible for an IRA or employer plan spousal rollover after your death.[35] When electing a spousal rollover,

1. Your spouse must be the sole Designated Beneficiary.

2. RMDs are based on your surviving spouse's attained age using the more favorable Uniform Lifetime Table.

3. RMDs may be delayed until April 1 after your surviving spouse attains age 70 ½ (your spouse's RBD) rather than your RBD.

If your spouse elects a spousal rollover, he or she becomes the account owner rather than the beneficiary. A spousal rollover may be elected at anytime, even after your spouse's RBD.[36] Therefore, your spouse may leave the IRA in your name to receive penalty-free, pre 59½ distributions and elect a spousal rollover after reaching 59½ to prolong tax deferral.

To ensure that your spouse is eligible for a spousal rollover, he or she should be the sole primary beneficiary of your IRA. However, spousal rollovers have been allowed in situations where the surviving spouse was not the beneficiary. A spousal rollover has been allowed where the participant's estate was the beneficiary and the surviving spouse was the estate's sole beneficiary.[37] A spousal rollover was also allowed where a trust was the IRA beneficiary and the spouse had an unlimited right to withdraw principal. Distributions were first paid from the IRA into the trust. The surviving spouse then withdrew the distributions from the trust and rolled the distributions into an IRA.[38] These two examples from Private Letter Rulings indicate that, if the estate or a trust is the beneficiary and the spouse is the beneficiary of the estate or trust, the spouse may elect a spousal rollover even if he or she is not the IRA beneficiary so long as the surviving spouse is entitled to the benefits and controls the estate or trust to make the distribution. However, if you wish to ensure the choice of a spousal rollover to your surviving spouse, your spouse should be the sole Designated Beneficiary.

Spousal Rollover Benefits

- If you are older than your surviving spouse, RMDs can be delayed until your surviving spouse attains age 70½.

- The Uniform Lifetime Table can be used instead of the Single Life Table. RMDs calculated with the more favorable Uniform Lifetime Table result in lower RMDs and more tax deferral.

- Your spouse's beneficiaries (typically your children) can take RMDs based on their single life expectancies in the year of your surviving spouse's death, less the number of years since the year of death. Without the spousal rollover, RMDs are based on your surviving spouse's (not the new beneficiary's) single life expectancy established in the year of death. The RMDs for an inherited IRA (the spousal rollover was not elected) are based on your now deceased surviving spouse's life expectancy. The end result is that a spousal rollover often allows greater tax deferral.[39]

If your surviving spouse is under age 59½, however, he or she should consider leaving at least part of the IRA in your name after your death to avoid the 10 percent premature-distribution penalty. Upon your death, your spouse beneficiary may take penalty-free distributions from your IRA, even if neither you nor your surviving spouse ever attained age 59½. This is the exception to the premature-distribution penalty due to the participant's death. If your surviving spouse elects the spousal rollover, your spouse must wait until he or she attains 59½ to take distributions free of the premature-distribution penalty. After your surviving spouse attains the age of 59½, a spousal rollover may be elected for the remaining assets in your IRA to provide extended tax deferral. (RMDs begin when your surviving spouse attains 70½ years of age.)

EXAMPLE: Boudreaux dies and leaves 100 percent of his IRA to his wife, Clotile. Boudreaux was 57 at the time of his death, and Clotile was 54. Clotile may leave the IRA in Boudreaux's name and receive distributions from his IRA free of the premature-distribution penalty. If she elects the spousal rollover, she must wait until she reaches age 59½ to take penalty-free distributions. After Clotile reaches age 59½, she should then elect a spousal rollover. Once the IRA is in her name, RMDs do not commence until she is age 70½, and Clotile uses her life expectancy, rather than Boudreaux's life expectancy, to calculate RMDs. In addition, Clotile's beneficiaries may use their own life expectancies, rather than hers, to calculate RMDs after her death. As a result, the spousal rollover will allow more tax deferral.

For IRAs only, if your surviving spouse is the beneficiary, he or she may elect to treat the IRA as his or her own.[40] This is accomplished by your surviving spouse taking action inconsistent with that of an IRA beneficiary. For example, if your spouse makes a contribution to your IRA after your death, such action is inconsistent with the rights of an IRA beneficiary.[41] Another example is if your spouse does not take the RMD as required as an IRA Designated Beneficiary.[42] In both of these situations, an IRA may be deemed your spouse's IRA although a spousal rollover was not elected.

Choosing the Correct Beneficiary

The various choices of beneficiaries present powerful planning opportunities in addition to many traps for the uninformed. Selecting your retirement plan's beneficiary is one of the most important financial decisions you will make. Unfortunately, little thought or planning goes into the selection of beneficiaries. As a result, many individuals mimic what others have done regarding beneficiary selection and neglect their specific planning needs and objectives.

September 30 of the year following your death is the Beneficiary Designation Date (BDD), an important date for beneficiaries. To be entitled to all or part of an IRA or employer plan, a beneficiary must be a Designated Beneficiary. A Designated Beneficiary is a beneficiary still listed on the IRA or employer plan by the BDD (September 30 the year after the participant dies). As such, the designated beneficiaries are determined by the beneficiaries remaining as of the BDD.[43]

Typically, the surviving spouse is the primary beneficiary, and the children are the contingent or secondary beneficiaries. The financial needs of potential beneficiaries should be your primary determining factors when selecting your beneficiaries. Most married participants wish to provide maximum financial benefit and planning choices to their surviving spouse by naming their spouse as the primary beneficiary. In addition, the needs of your children or grandchildren may require that a trust be named as the beneficiary for their benefit.

Spouse as Beneficiary

For married participants, the most common beneficiary designation is 100 percent to the spouse. If your spouse does not have sufficient assets on which to live, your spouse should be named beneficiary, regardless of potential tax savings other beneficiary designations may provide. Your spouse may remain a beneficiary of your account or elect a spousal rollover. If your spouse will not need all of the IRA or if you wish to leave a portion of the IRA to another person, you should consider splitting the IRA into two IRAs. Your spouse is the beneficiary of one IRA, and a non-spouse beneficiary is named for the other IRA. You may also name another primary beneficiary with your spouse.

Children and Grandchildren as Primary Beneficiaries

If your spouse has sufficient assets to support his or her standard of living or if you are not married, consider naming your children or grandchildren as beneficiaries. If you have estate tax concerns, naming a non-spouse beneficiary will cause part of your estate tax exemption to be allocated to your IRA. Leaving your IRA to your spouse will qualify for the marital deduction and will increase your spouse's gross estate, potentially increasing the estate tax burden. However, the estate tax exemption portability rules will reduce the number of estates subject to tax. In addition, your children or grandchildren will likely be in a lower income tax bracket, and this may result in IRA distributions being taxed at a lower income tax rate after your death. If your IRA is composed of community property funds, in most cases, spousal consent will be required to name a non-spouse beneficiary.

If you have children from a prior marriage, a Qualified Terminal Interest Property (QTIP) trust may be used to provide income to your spouse while leaving the remaining assets to your children. Your spouse would receive the income from the IRA and the QTIP trust but would not have control over the distribution of principal.

Multiple Beneficiaries

When multiple beneficiaries are named, the distribution rules again provide many planning opportunities and numerous traps. If one of your beneficiaries dies after your death but prior to the BDD, the deceased beneficiary remains a beneficiary.[44] Your IRA plan document or beneficiary designation form will determine who receives the deceased beneficiary's portion.

By the BDD, unless all beneficiaries are individuals, your IRA or employer plan is treated as having no Designated Beneficiary, and the Five-Year Rule applies.[45] This means that your entire account must be distributed by the end of the year that contains the fifth anniversary of your death. Typically this outcome should be avoided whenever possible due to the loss of extended tax deferral. If you die after the required beginning date for RMDs, the Five-Year Rule does not apply. Rather, RMDs are based on your life expectancy. The time between your death and the BDD enables your beneficiaries to complete necessary planning to ensure stretch lifetime RMDs.

For example, if a charity and two grandchildren remain beneficiaries on September 30 the year following your death, the entire IRA must be distributed by the end of the calendar year in which the fifth anniversary of your death occurs. (The Five-Year Rule). All future tax deferral is lost because a nonindividual (the charity) was a beneficiary on the BDD. To avoid this outcome, the charity may be cashed out, or separate accounts may be created prior to the BDD. Separate accounts will also enable each Designated Beneficiary to use his or her own life expectancy for RMDs.

Unless the Separate Account Rule applies, if your IRA has more than one Designated Beneficiary, the oldest Designated Beneficiary's life expectancy is used to calculate the RMDs for all Designated Beneficiaries.[46] This may cause rapid distributions (less tax deferral) to the disadvantage of much younger beneficiaries. Beneficiaries cannot be added after your death, but beneficiaries may be removed by disclaimer under IRC § 2518 or by cashing out prior to the BDD.

The Separate Account Rule

If separate accounts are properly established, each beneficiary may use his or her own life expectancy for RMD purposes.[47] To establish separate accounts, the beneficiaries' shares must be in the form of a fraction or percentage, not dollar amounts. In addition, the separate account for each Designated Beneficiary must be established by December 31 of the year after your death. Creating separate inherited IRAs for each beneficiary is the best way to ensure the Separate Account Rule will apply. Alternately, an IRA custodian may create separate accounts by accounting for each beneficiary's gains, losses and distributions.[a] As long as the separate accounts are created by December 31 the year after your death, your beneficiaries may use the Separate Account Rule to calculate the RMD for the year following your death.[48] Any RMD in the year of your death that was not withdrawn prior to your death must be withdrawn by the end of the calendar year of your death.

The "Stretch IRA"

Although the RMD rules do not include the term "Stretch IRA," financial advisors refer to stretch IRAs as IRAs that have a child or grandchild named as the designated beneficiary. Stretch IRAs are sometimes referred to as Multigenerational IRAs, Super IRAs or Legacy IRAs, but they all rely on naming a relatively "young" beneficiary. The advantage of a stretch IRA is that it results in smaller RMDs which allow your IRA to continue compounded, tax-deferred growth for a longer period of time.

The stretch IRA is accomplished by naming children and/or grandchildren as primary beneficiaries of your IRA or, if your spouse elects a spousal rollover, as the beneficiaries of your spouse's IRA. The Separate Account Rule is very valuable when attempting a stretch IRA. Unfortunately, nearly all employer plans (e.g. 401(k) plans) disallow stretch IRAs. For this reason, most employer plans should be rolled into an IRA that allows the stretch IRA concept.

---

[a] The IRA custodian must allocate all post-death investment gains, losses, contributions and forfeitures for the period prior to the establishment of the separate accounts on a pro rata basis in a reasonable and consistent manner among the separate accounts. Reg § 1.401(a)(9)-8, A-2(a)(2).

An IRA for Each Beneficiary

Splitting your IRA into multiple IRAs, each with different beneficiaries, is ideal if your spouse will need some, but not all, of your IRA. A thorough retirement cash flow analysis can determine how much to fund each IRA. If your spouse's needs dictate that more retirement resources are required after the IRA is split, the assets can be transferred back to the IRA with the spousal beneficiary designation.

If you wish to guarantee that a beneficiary will receive a portion of your IRA, split your IRA, creating a separate IRA for that beneficiary. If you have children from a prior marriage, this technique can guarantee that the assets in the IRA that was "split off" will go to your children as the named beneficiaries. Compare this with naming your surviving spouse as the sole beneficiary and your children as contingent beneficiaries. After your death, your surviving spouse may change the beneficiaries. If your surviving spouse remarries, he or she may replace the beneficiaries (who may be your children) with the new spouse.

For example, Thibodaux names his wife Marie as the primary beneficiary of his IRA. Clotile (Thibodaux's daughter from a prior marriage) and Pierre (Thibodaux and Marie's child) are the contingent beneficiaries. While Thibodaux is alive, Marie assures Thibodaux that she will leave the remaining assets in the IRA to Clotile and Pierre equally. Once Thibodaux dies, Marie changes the beneficiary designation by removing Clotile's name. As a result, Clotile receives no portion of the IRA after Marie's death, even though the original IRA belonged to her father, Thibodaux.

To avoid this outcome, Thibodaux could have split off a portion of the IRA and named Clotile as the primary beneficiary. Upon Thibodaux's death, Clotile would have received 100 percent of this IRA and could not have been removed as beneficiary by Marie.

In addition, creating multiple IRAs, each with one primary beneficiary, will ensure that the beneficiary's life expectancy is used for RMD purposes. Such an arrangement eliminates the need to split your IRA into separate accounts after your death to ensure each beneficiary's life expectancy is used for RMDs. Furthermore, different investment policies may be developed for each IRA depending on the needs and risk tolerance of each beneficiary. All transfers between

IRAs should be via trustee-to-trustee transfer to avoid the 60-day rollover rule.

The Spouse as Beneficiary with the Option to Disclaim

A qualified disclaimer allows a beneficiary to elect not to receive all or part of the IRA benefits after your death. It allows significant post-death planning; however, it only works if the beneficiary follows through with the plan after your death. With a qualified disclaimer, you may name your surviving spouse as the primary beneficiary with the option to disclaim any portion of the IRA that will not be needed. Your surviving spouse has nine months after your death to determine how much of the IRA, if any, he or she will not need and elect a qualified disclaimer.[49] The disclaimed portion will go to your children, your grandchildren or to a trust for their benefit. Another option is to name your surviving spouse as the primary beneficiary with a credit shelter trust (CST) as the contingent beneficiary. The CST will allow the IRA to benefit your surviving spouse while funding the CST to attempt to optimize the use of your applicable federal estate tax exemption amount. This strategy allows for a "wait-and-see" approach and is not an all or nothing option for the surviving spouse. See the "Funding CSTs" section in this chapter for an explanation of using a qualified disclaimer to fund a CST.

Your surviving spouse does not have the obligation to disclaim any portion of the IRA; therefore, you must be comfortable with the possibility that your surviving spouse will not disclaim any portion of the IRA. As a result, your primary goal must be to provide for the surviving spouse in the event your spouse does not follow through with a qualified disclaimer. This strategy will generally not work when there is a second marriage and the contingent beneficiaries are not the children of the primary beneficiary surviving spouse.

Qualified Disclaimers

Qualified disclaimers are subject to the following criteria:[50]

1. The disclaimer must be irrevocable and unqualified (no strings attached);

2. The disclaimer must be in writing;

3. The disclaimer must be delivered to the appropriate party (the estate's legal representative, the trustee of the individual's trust, the transferor of the property or the individual or entity in possession of the property to be disclaimed) within nine months of the individual's death with respect to transfers occurring on death or within nine months of the date on which the interest in the beneficiary is created with respect to property interests which vest prior to the individuals death or, if later, the date on which the disclaiming party turns age 21;

4. The disclaiming party must not have accepted the disclaimed interest or any of its benefits; and

5. The interest disclaimed must pass to a person other than the disclaiming party, without any direction on the part of the person making the disclaimer. (The person disclaiming cannot direct who will receive the disclaimed asset.)

Failure to meet any of these requirements causes the disclaimer to fail, and the person who is attempting to disclaim will remain the asset's owner. In addition, a surviving spouse cannot roll the IRA into his or her own IRA and then disclaim.

The rules for qualified disclaimers are clear—the disclaiming party cannot receive any portion of the property being disclaimed. Thus, to disclaim, the beneficiary cannot receive any withdrawals from the IRA. However, a beneficiary may disclaim all or part of an IRA and still withdraw the deceased participant's year of death RMD.[51]

The disclaimed portion may be segregated into a separate account for the beneficiary. This option preserves tax deferral and allows the beneficiary to use his or her own life expectancy for RMDs. Earnings accrued from the participant's date of death to the date of the disclaimer are added to the disclaimed portion. Because RMDs are treated as pecuniary amounts, earnings must be included. A beneficiary may withdraw more than the RMD and disclaim the balance.[52]

If your children are named as the primary beneficiaries and your grandchildren as contingent beneficiaries, your children may disclaim all or part of the IRA for the benefit of their children (your grandchildren). If your children are not in need of the assets, this arrangement would allow the assets to pass to your grandchildren.

Your grandchildren would be subject to much smaller RMDs and greatly extended tax deferral.

If you name multiple beneficiaries and a large age difference exists between the beneficiaries, the beneficiary with the shortest life expectancy may disclaim his or her interest in the IRA by September 30 of the year following your death. The shortest life expectancy is now disregarded for RMD purposes, allowing for longer tax deferral for the remaining designated beneficiaries.

Keep in mind that for any strategy involving a disclaimer to work, the party with the power to disclaim must follow through with the disclaimer after your death. Obviously, no assurances exist that your surviving spouse or other beneficiary will disclaim. A beneficiary's promise to disclaim if it will save taxes often may be relied upon to the degree of the proverbial assurances that the check is in the mail.

Naming a Trust as Beneficiary

Naming a trust as the beneficiary of your IRA or other retirement account may provide additional control over distributions, asset protection, and investment management of retirement assets. In addition, a trust may provide significant tax-planning benefits. Due to the complex nature of naming a trust as a beneficiary, professional guidance is a must. Some techniques require detailed explanations due to the complex rules involved; however, this section will attempt to provide a straightforward explanation for each technique.

The general rule is that all beneficiaries must be individuals for RMDs to be based on the beneficiaries' life expectancies. An exception to this requirement is that a qualified trust may be a Designated Beneficiary if the following conditions are met:[53]

1. The trust is valid under state law.

2. The trust is irrevocable or becomes irrevocable upon the participant's death.

3. The trust beneficiaries are identifiable individuals as of September 30 of the year after the participant dies.

4. Documentation is provided to the plan administrator by October 31st of the year following the participant's death,

including a copy of the trust document for the trust named as beneficiary or a list of beneficiaries of the trust.

If all of these requirements are met, the oldest trust beneficiary's life expectancy is used to calculate RMDs paid to the trust.[54] If the trust fails to meet these requirements, the entire IRA or qualified retirement plan must be distributed by December 31 of the fifth year following the participant's death (The Five-Year Rule). Obviously, this outcome is to be avoided whenever possible.

If you die prior to 70½ and your surviving spouse is the trust's <u>sole designated beneficiary</u>, RMDs to the trust need not commence until you (the IRA owner) would have been 70½.[55] Your surviving spouse will be deemed the trust's sole designated beneficiary if all RMDs paid into the trust must be paid to your surviving spouse.

If some of the RMDs are retained in the trust for payment to your children (or other non-spouse beneficiaries), your surviving spouse will not be treated as the trust's sole designated beneficiary. In this case, RMDs must begin by December 31 of the year after your death and are based on the oldest beneficiary's non-recalculating life expectancy (typically your surviving spouse).[56]

Maintaining maximum tax deferral while naming a trust as beneficiary of your IRA or employer plan can be a very complex undertaking. Therefore, when possible, a trust should be funded with non-IRA/employer-plan assets as there are fewer traps for the unwary. If you must fund a trust with IRA or employer-plan assets (because there are no other assets to fund the trust or because there are minor beneficiaries involved), careful drafting of the trust document and beneficiary designations is essential.

Naming a Credit Shelter Trust (CST) as Beneficiary

A credit shelter trust (CST) (a.k.a. bypass trust, B trust, or family trust) allows the use of your federal estate tax exemption while providing support to your surviving spouse through income and/or principle distributions. A properly funded CST is generally used to help optimize the use of your available federal estate tax exemption. The CST must meet all requirements for naming a trust as beneficiary if the beneficiary's life expectancy is to be used for RMDs. Portability of the deceased spouse's unused applicable exemption amount will allow the use of both spouse's exemptions without the need for a CST. If estate tax savings is the primary objective for establishing a CST, exemption portability can more easily accomplish this goal. See Chapter 23 on Estate Taxation for more information.

As mentioned, the complexity of naming a trust as an IRA beneficiary warrants the funding of a CST with nonretirement assets when possible. In some situations there may be no alternative to using retirement assets to fund the trust. A non-tax driven benefit of funding a CST with an IRA is that a trust can provide professional management of a large pool of retirement assets if there is concern over your surviving spouse's ability to manage the assets. In addition, a CST may remain in existence after both you and your spouse are deceased to provide continued management and protection from creditors for your children and grandchildren.

Funding a Credit Shelter Trust

Although some employer plans allow the participant to name a CST as beneficiary, many employer plans prohibit naming a trust as beneficiary. Therefore, these explanations assume an IRA is funding the trust. The IRA will remain in your name as the deceased participant, and the distributions will be paid into the trust. The IRA is not renamed into the trust's name because such action would result in an immediate fully taxable distribution. Funding a CST with retirement assets may be accomplished in a few ways.

One way to fund a CST is to establish a separate IRA with the CST as the designated beneficiary. If the IRA grows in value, periodic monitoring of the IRA value is necessary to ensure that it does not exceed your unused applicable federal estate tax exemption.

A second method is to use a formula clause in the IRA beneficiary designation form that indicates how much of your IRA will be paid into the CST. For example, instructions are provided that require funding the CST with the maximum available amount of federal estate tax exemption. The balance, if the value of your IRA is over the available federal estate tax exemption, is paid to another beneficiary (e.g. your surviving spouse). If your surviving spouse is a beneficiary of an amount over the available estate tax exemption, upon your death, that amount will transfer free from federal estate taxes to your surviving spouse under the marital deduction.

If a formula clause is used to determine how much of your IRA is paid to the CST, it should be a fractional share formula and **not** a pecuniary formula (dollar amount) to avoid a technical rule that may require accelerated income taxation on IRA assets used to fund a pecuniary bequest in a will.

A third alternative is to use a qualified disclaimer to fund a CST. Your surviving spouse is named the retirement asset's sole beneficiary, and a CST is named the contingent beneficiary if your spouse survives you. Your children (or a trust for the benefit of your children) are named the second contingent beneficiaries to receive the IRA if your spouse dies prior to you. After your death, your surviving spouse determines how much of the retirement asset is needed to fully fund the CST, up to the federal estate tax exemption amount. This amount is disclaimed via a qualified disclaimer. The remaining assets in your IRA are paid to your spouse who may elect a spousal rollover or remain a beneficiary under your IRA.

This method allows a flexible, wait-and-see approach; however, your surviving spouse may have second thoughts about disclaiming part of the retirement assets. If your surviving spouse fails to disclaim, this method of funding the CST will be ineffective, and part of your federal estate tax exemption may go unused.

Advantages of Naming a Credit Shelter Trust as Beneficiary

Naming a CST as the IRA beneficiary allows your IRA to qualify for your federal estate tax exemption. It can guarantee the estate tax exemption does not go unused in the event portability of the deceased spouse's exemption is unavailable. Also, assets left to a credit shelter trust will not be subject to estate taxes regardless of future appreciation. If couples wish to fully utilize their generation skipping tax exemption, they must use a credit shelter trust at the first spouse's death to preserve both generation skipping tax exemptions. Exemption portability does not apply to generation skipping taxes. The CST can provide your surviving spouse with access to trust income and principal while providing these additional planning benefits. The new rules allowing portability of a deceased spouse's unused estate tax exemption provide the same tax benefits as a CST. Thus, in many cases a CST will no longer be necessary if estate tax savings is the primary goal. The estate tax exemption portability rules allow many couples to forego using a

CST to preserve both spouse's estate tax exemptions. Although exemption portability provides a straightforward way to maximize tax-deferral and estate tax savings, a CST has some advantages over portability. See Chapter 23 on Estate Taxation for more information about the pros and cons of portability and credit shelter trusts.

Disadvantages of Naming a Credit Shelter Trust as Beneficiary

A CST can provide significant benefits, but funding a CST with IRA funds has drawbacks. First, naming a CST as an IRA beneficiary may result in loss of some tax deferral because RMDs to the trust must begin by December 31 of the year after your death. If your surviving spouse is the IRA beneficiary, instead of the trust, RMDs may be delayed until April 1 following the year you or your surviving spouse attains age 70½, whichever occurs later. Therefore, naming a trust as beneficiary will cause a loss of some income tax deferral if neither you nor your spouse is 70½. In addition, RMDs will be made more rapidly as they will be based on the single life expectancy[b] of the oldest trust beneficiary (your surviving spouse). In short, individual beneficiaries generally provide for more favorable distribution options.

After your surviving spouse dies, your spouse's remaining life expectancy will be used for distributions to the trust beneficiaries. Once again, this outcome generally causes more rapid distributions.

Another disadvantage of using an IRA to fund a trust is that the spousal rollover is generally not available when a trust is named beneficiary. Compare this outcome with leaving the IRA to your spouse outright. Your children would take RMDs based on their own life expectancies after your spouse's death if your spouse elected to use a spousal rollover.

Finally, the trust income tax rates progress more rapidly than the individual income tax rates and may cause higher income taxes than if your spouse were named beneficiary. This may not be a problem if the trust pays out the retirement distributions annually to the trust beneficiaries because the distributions will be taxed to the beneficiaries rather than the trust.

---

[b] Not the more favorable Uniform Lifetime Table.

Qualified Terminal Interest Property (QTIP) Trust as Beneficiary

A QTIP trust allows your surviving spouse to receive all of the trust income for life with the trust principal paid to your children and/or grandchildren. Your surviving spouse may also be given distributions of trust principal based on the trustee's discretion or the needs of your surviving spouse. Thus, a QTIP trust may provide your surviving spouse with lifetime income and, if allowed by the trust, principal distributions. Your children are usually guaranteed to receive the QTIP trust principal. For this reason, a QTIP trust is a common tool in situations where a second marriage involves children from a previous marriage because it provides income to your spouse while the remaining trust assets go to your children after your spouse dies. For estate tax planning purposes, a QTIP trust allows the marital deduction to apply to the trust assets as long as all of the income is paid to your surviving spouse for life. If the marital deduction applies, the QTIP trust assets are included in your surviving spouse's estate for estate tax purposes.

To be eligible for the QTIP election, all of the QTIP guidelines must be followed.[57] These guidelines require that

1. All of the income be paid to your surviving spouse at least annually. In addition, your surviving spouse has the right to make nonproductive assets productive.

2. The assets in the QTIP trust and the trust itself must be designated as QTIP property by the executor on the estate tax return. Therefore, the QTIP election on Form 706 must be elected for both the IRA and the trust.

3. QTIP trust property may not be appointed to anyone other than your surviving spouse during his or her lifetime.

If these guidelines are not followed, the marital deduction for these assets is unavailable. A final point is that the QTIP requirements must be met by both the IRA and the QTIP trust.[58] See Chapter 24 for more information regarding QTIP trusts.

Satisfying the Income Requirement

When satisfying the QTIP requirements, you must remember that the income produced by the investments in your IRA is not the same as the RMD from your IRA. The income from your IRA investments is generally interest and dividends and not capital appreciation. Therefore, your IRA may produce income in an amount that is less or greater than the RMD. The QTIP rules require that all of the income be paid or made available to your surviving spouse which may amount to more or less than the RMD.

One method of satisfying the QTIP rules is to require the IRA to pay annually the greater of the RMD or the IRA income into the QTIP trust. The trustee must then pay the income of both the IRA and the QTIP trust to your surviving spouse at least annually.[59] For example, Boudreaux's IRA produces $35,000 of income, and the RMD is $45,000 for the year. The trustee must pay into the QTIP trust from the IRA $45,000 for the year which is the greater of the RMD and income from the IRA. Next, the trustee must determine the amount of QTIP trust income. The QTIP trust income is equal to the IRAs income of $35,000 plus the income generated by other assets in the QTIP trust. The QTIP trust income must be distributed to Boudreaux's spouse. When the IRA income is less than the RMD, the QTIP trust may retain the RMD in excess of the income to accumulate in the trust. The annual income from both the IRA and the accumulated QTIP trust assets must be distributed to your surviving spouse at least annually.

Another option is to require the IRA to pay to the QTIP trust the RMD for the year; however, the trustee is not required to distribute to your surviving spouse all of the realized income earned from the IRA each year. So long as your surviving spouse has the right to compel the trustee to pay out all of the realized income, at least annually, earned by the IRA, the QTIP guidelines are satisfied.[60] In addition, your surviving spouse must have the right to compel the trustee to pay the income from the assets in the QTIP trust (in addition to the IRA income) at least annually. Under this arrangement, the RMD must still be made from the IRA into the trust, and if your surviving spouse elects, no additional amounts are required to be paid from the IRA into the trust. Your surviving spouse may also elect not to compel the trustee to distribute the QTIP trust income. This arrangement may allow more tax deferral if the RMD is less than the IRA income for the year. This will allow the QTIP trust to accumulate assets for distribution to your children after your spouse dies. In addition, your surviving spouse should not be prohibited from withdrawing amounts in excess of the RMD. The distributions from the IRA and the QTIP trust may be reduced under this arrangement if your surviving spouse chooses not to withdraw all of the annual income from the IRA and the QTIP trust. However, if your children are from a prior marriage, your surviving spouse will likely withdraw the maximum rather than the minimum amount required by law. If maximum distributions are taken by your surviving spouse, assets will likely not accumulate in the QTIP trust, and IRA distributions of income may exceed the RMD.

Revenue Ruling 2006-26 provided additional guidance of necessary provisions of the QTIP trust document. The following arrangement will also satisfy the QTIP requirements:

- The IRA and the QTIP trust are considered separately for allocating income and principal and determining whether each satisfies the QTIP income requirements. The QTIP trust document or state law must be clear that the determination of income and principal for the QTIP trust and the IRA are made independently of each other. The definition of income should also be clear in the trust document.

- Your surviving spouse has the right to demand that the assets of both the IRA and the QTIP trust be made reasonably productive of income.

- Your surviving spouse also must have the right to require that the trustee of the QTIP trust withdraw all of the income from the IRA annually and that all of the withdrawn income immediately be distributed to your surviving spouse.

Careful planning is necessary to ensure that your surviving spouse is provided with adequate rights to income of the IRA assets and the QTIP trust. Failure to properly draft the trust will cause your IRA to be disqualified for the marital deduction. Furthermore, naming a QTIP trust as beneficiary will require significant coordination between the Trustee of the QTIP trust and the IRA custodian. It is advisable that you check with the IRA custodian to ensure they are both willing and capable of administering this type of plan. Some IRA custodians may not allow QTIP trusts to be named as the beneficiary due to the complexity this arrangement involves.

Defining the Meaning of "Income"

To qualify for the marital deduction, the QTIP trust should be drafted with provisions defining "income." For example, IRA income may be defined by Louisiana's power-to-adjust or Louisiana's unitrust provisions. See the chapter on trusts for an explanation of unitrust and power-to-adjust provisions. Although the RMD must be paid into the QTIP trust annually, income in an amount over the RMD is not required to be paid into the QTIP trust, but the surviving spouse must have the power to request the distribution of IRA income. In addition, the income of the other trust assets (e.g. RMDs and earnings that are not distributed to your spouse but remain in the trust) may be defined by Louisiana's power-to-adjust or Louisiana's unitrust provisions and must be distributed to your surviving spouse at least annually, or the spouse must have the power to compel the distribution. In addition, traditional notions of income under state law may be used to define income to qualify for the marital deduction.

The power to adjust between income and principal made separately as to the QTIP trust and the IRA is a reasonable apportionment of the income and principal under Reg. § 20.2056(b)-(5)(f)(1) and Reg. § 1-643(b)-1.[61] Therefore, a power-to-adjust provision may be used to define income to enable both the trust and the IRA to qualify for QTIP treatment. For example, if a $1 million IRA produces 2.5 percent ($25,000) of income from interest and dividends, the trustee may adjust this amount to $50,000 if he or she determines that $50,000 is a fair allocation to income.[62] If the RMD for the year is $70,000, the surviving spouse may (but does not have to) compel the trustee to distribute $50,000 to the surviving spouse (the income). Under the trust terms in Rev. Rul. 2006-26, the excess $20,000 remains in the trust where the trustee must determine the income portion of the $20,000 (with potential adjustment between income and principal) for distribution to the surviving spouse.

The Louisiana unitrust provisions[63] may be used to define income to enable both the trust and the IRA to qualify for QTIP treatment. The unitrust provisions should be not less than 3 percent and not more than 5 percent.[64] For example, a 4 percent unitrust provision may be used to determine the income of the QTIP trust and the IRA, respectively. Either the trustee must be required to distribute all of the income at least annually or your surviving spouse must have the power to demand the income from the IRA be distributed annually. Without the right to all of the income from the IRA at least annually, the marital deduction is not allowed. Continuing the example, a QTIP trust with a 4 percent unitrust provision is the beneficiary of an IRA worth $1,000,000. If the RMD for the IRA is $45,000, your surviving spouse may demand that $40,000 be distributed (4 percent of $1 million). If your surviving spouse does not demand the $40,000 distribution, the entire $45,000 remains in the trust. The trustee then uses a unitrust or power-to-adjust provision to determine the income on the $45,000 (and the other QTIP trust assets) which is paid to your surviving spouse. This arrangement qualifies for the marital deduction and QTIP treatment.[65]

If a state does not have unitrust or power-to-adjust provisions (Louisiana does), traditional definitions of trust income apply. If a $1,000,000 IRA produces 3.5 percent of interest and dividends totaling $35,000 and the RMD is $45,000, the RMD is paid into the QTIP trust, and the surviving spouse may demand $35,000 of IRA income be distributed. The remaining $10,000 is left in the trust, and the trustee must determine the income attributable to this amount that is paid to the surviving spouse. This arrangement also qualifies for QTIP treatment and the marital deduction.[66]

When drafting a QTIP trust, caution should be used not to rely on the Uniform Principal and Income Act (UPIA) §§ 409(c) and (d) to determine what is characterized as income. This is the UPIA 10 percent rule. Many states adopted the UPIA in its entirety (Louisiana has not), and the QTIP trust should be clear that UPIA §§ 409(c) and (d) will not apply when determining what portion of the IRA or of the QTIP trust assets is income.[67]

Finally, to satisfy the QTIP requirements, the income portion of investment returns should not be reduced by administrative expenses.[68]

Drawbacks of a QTIP Trust IRA Beneficiary

Drawbacks of funding a QTIP trust with retirement assets, other than complexity, are similar to the drawbacks of naming a CST as beneficiary. Specifically, the spousal rollover election is unavailable, and distributions usually must begin by December 31 of the year following your death. Furthermore, your surviving spouse's single life expectancy is used to calculate the RMDs. The ability to take RMDs over the life expectancies of a child or grandchild (the stretch IRA) is unavailable.

An additional disadvantage is that in a second marriage situation, where the retirement asset owner wishes to ultimately transfer the retirement assets to children of a prior marriage, it is possible that if the surviving spouse lives long enough and through the application of the RMD and QTIP rules, all of the IRA assets may be distributed out of the IRA and into the QTIP trust. In addition, if the QTIP trust is poorly drafted, all assets in the QTIP trust may be paid to the surviving spouse, leaving nothing for the deceased's children.

QTIP Trust Alternatives

A QTIP trust provides lifetime income to your spouse and the trust principal to your children after the death of your spouse. These objectives may also be achieved by splitting the IRA into two separate IRAs: One IRA for your surviving spouse and the other for your children or grandchildren. You determine how much to leave to each party, and you are assured that the beneficiary of each IRA will receive his or her intended share. Splitting the IRA may also alleviate friction between your surviving spouse and your children in second marriage situations. With a QTIP trust arrangement, your children's inheritance from the IRA is dependent upon your surviving spouse (and your surviving spouse's life expectancy). If your surviving spouse compels large distributions under the QTIP trust arrangement, animosity may develop between your surviving spouse and your children. Splitting the IRA removes the fate of your children's inheritance from the hands of your surviving spouse (your children's stepparent).

An IRA without a trust may be subject to QTIP treatment if the beneficiary designation pays out all of the income to your surviving spouse at least annually. A beneficiary designation that establishes a lifetime usufruct to your surviving spouse with your children as the naked owners also qualifies for QTIP treatment.

Utilizing a Trust to Guarantee Prolonged Tax Deferral

Unfortunately, a stretch IRA is not guaranteed even if you correctly establish the proper IRA beneficiaries. The beneficiaries may have plans other than a stretch IRA, and they may take a full taxable distribution, thereby foregoing additional tax-deferred growth. To ensure that maximum tax deferral (i.e. a stretch IRA) is achieved and to prevent the beneficiary from taking an immediate full taxable distribution, consider a conduit trust. The trustee of a conduit trust is required to withdraw the RMD from the IRA over the beneficiary's (or the oldest beneficiary's) life expectancy. No power is given to the trustee to hold or to accumulate retirement distributions in the trust. The trust also provides for professional management of the undistributed portion of the IRA. Because the trust beneficiaries cannot direct the trustee to take a full taxable IRA distribution, a conduit trust guarantees stretch IRA distributions under the trust terms.[69]

If a trust is the IRA beneficiary, the oldest trust beneficiary's age is used to determine RMDs for all trust beneficiaries. To use each trust beneficiary's age for RMDs, create and name sub-trusts as the IRA beneficiaries rather than naming the master trust as beneficiary.[70]

Distributions from a conduit trust will be dependent on the trust's wording. If your children are to receive the RMDs from the IRA, then use language that specifically directs the trustee to distribute the RMDs (rather than trust income).

If the trust is not required to pay out the RMDs to the trust beneficiaries at least annually, the primary and contingent beneficiaries' life expectancies may have to be used when calculating the RMD. This will generally not be a problem if the contingent beneficiaries are all younger than the primary beneficiaries. However, if the contingent beneficiaries are older than one or more of the primary beneficiaries, the RMDs will be larger due to the older contingent beneficiaries' shorter life expectancies.

Additional Planning Tips

The oldest beneficiary's life expectancy may be used for distributions from trusts as IRA beneficiaries, even if charities or elderly individuals are remote contingent beneficiaries.[71] For RMD purposes, you can limit the persons considered for RMD calculations once you reach an existing beneficiary who would inherit the IRA benefits upon the death of a prior beneficiary. Thus, if your surviving spouse is the primary beneficiary, your children are the contingent beneficiaries and a charity is the second (remote) contingent beneficiary, you can disregard the charity for RMD purposes. Therefore, the Five-Year Rule will not apply to conduit trusts if a nonindividual is a remote contingent beneficiary. Only the primary and first contingent beneficiaries are considered for the RMD calculation.

If charities or older beneficiaries are contingent beneficiaries with the children, either the Five-Year Rule (due to the charity) or the oldest beneficiary's age will be used to calculate the RMDs. Paying (cashing out) the charitable donation and removing the charity as a beneficiary prior to the beneficiary designation date will avoid the Five-Year Rule and enable RMDs to be based on the oldest beneficiary's age.

In several Private Letter Rulings[72] the IRS allowed trust beneficiaries to use the oldest child's life expectancy for RMDs, even though the trust allowed payment of estate debts and expenses (last illness, funeral, probate, administration expenses and estate taxes), when paid off by September 30 of the year following the IRA participant's death. By paying off estate debts and expenses, the estate (not considered an individual) may be removed as a beneficiary. This issue can be avoided by not allowing estate debts and expenses to be paid by a trust funded by an IRA.

When naming a trust as an employer plan or IRA beneficiary, professional tax advice is a must. This chapter attempts to provide the latest information concerning required minimum distributions; however, tax laws are subject to change without notice.

---

[1] IRC §§ 401(a)(9)(A), 403(b)(10), 408(a)(6), 457(d)(2), 4984.
[2] IRC § 401(a)(9)(C); Reg. § 1.401(a)(9)-5, A-1(c).
[3] IRC § 401(a)(9)(E).
[4] IRC § 1.401(a)(9)-4, A-4(a).
[5] IRC § 72(t)(2)(A)(i).
[6] IRC § 72(t)(1); Notice 87-16, 1987-1 C.B. 446, Question D9.
[7] Bunney, 114 T.C. 259, 262 (2000); Morris, T.C. Memo 2002-17.
[8] PPA 2006 § 838; § 72(t)(10).
[9] IRC § 401(a)(9)(C).
[10] IRC § 401(a)(9)(C); Reg. 1.401(a)(9)-2, A-2(a).
[11] Reg. § 1.401(a)(9)-5, A-4(a).
[12] Reg. § 1.401(a)(9)-5, A-4(b).

[13] IRC § 4974.
[14] Reg. § 1.408-8, A-9.
[15] Reg. § 1.403(b)-3, A-4.
[16] Reg. § 1.408-8, A-9.
[17] Reg. § 1.403(b)-3, A-4.
[18] Reg. § 1.401(a)(9)-8, A-1.
[19] IRC § 408(A)(c)(5)
[20] Reg. § 1.408A-6, A-14(b).
[21] IRC § 401(a)(9)(B)(ii)).
[22] Reg. § 1.401(a)(9)-3, A-3(a); IRC § 401(a)(9)(B)(iii).
[23] Reg. § 1.401(a)(9)-3, A-3(b).
[24] IRC § 401(a)(9)(B)(iv)(I); Reg. § 1.401(a)(9)-3, A-3(b).
[25] Reg. § 1.401(a)(9)-3, A-5, A-6 § 1.401(a)(9)-4, A-4(b).
[26] Reg. § 1.401(a)(9)-6, A-10, A-11.
[27] Reg. § 1.401(a)(9)-5, A-4(a).
[28] Reg. § 1.401(a)(9)-5, A-5(a)(2).
[29] Reg. § 1.401(a)(9)-5, A-5(a)(1).
[30] Reg. § 1.401(a)(9)-5, A-7(c)(2).
[31] Reg. § 1.401(a)(9)-5, A-5(a)(1).
[32] Reg. § 1.401(a)(9)-5, A-5(c)(2), A-6.
[33] Reg. § 1.401(a)(9)-5, A-5(a)(2), (c)(3).
[34] Reg. § 1.401(a)(9)-5, A-7(c)(2).
[35] Reg. § 1.408-8, A-5(a).
[36] Reg. §1.408-8(Q and A 5).
[37] PLRs 2003-04038, 2001-29036, 8911006, 9402023, 200950058, 201211034 and 201212021.
[38] PLRs 2003-04037, 2001-30056, 1999-25033, 9302022, 9426949 and 9427035.
[39] Reg. § 1.401(a)(9)-5, A-7(c)(2).
[40] Reg. § 1.408-8, A-5(a).
[41] Reg. § 1.408-8, A-5(b)(2).
[42] Reg. § 1.408-8, A-5(b)(1).
[43] Reg. § 1.401(a)(9)-4, A-4(a).

[44] Reg. § 1.401(a)(9)-4, A-4(c).
[45] Reg. § 1.401(a)(9)-4, A-3.
[46] Reg. § 1.401(a)(9)-5, A-7(a)(1).
[47] Reg. § 1.401(a)(9)-8, A-2(a)(2).
[48] Reg. § 1.401(a)(9)-8, A-2(a)(2).
[49] IRC § 2518.
[50] IRC § 2518; IRC Reg. §25.2518.2.
[51] Rev. Rul. 2005-36, PRL 201245004
[52] Rev. Rul. 2005-36.
[53] Reg. § 1.401(a)(9)-4, A-5(b).
[54] Reg. § 1.401(a)(9)-4, A-5(a).
[55] IRC § 401(a)(9)(B)(iii).
[56] Reg. § 1.401(a)(9)-5, Q and A-7(c), Examples 2 and 3.
[57] IRC § 2056(b)(7).
[58] Rev. Ruls. 2006-26, 2006-22 I.R.B. 939, 89-89.
[59] Rev. Rul. 89-89.
[60] Rev. Rul. 2000-2.
[61] Revenue Ruling 2006-26.
[62] La. Rev. Stat. Ann. 9:2158.
[63] La. Rev. Stat. Ann. 9:2068.
[64] Reg. § 1.643(b)-1.
[65] Rev. Rul. 2006-26.
[66] Rev. Rul. 2006-26.
[67] Rev. Rul. 2006-26.
[68] PLR 9043054.
[69] Reg. § 1.401(a)(9)-5, A-7(c)(3).
[70] PLRs 2004-49041; 2004-49042.
[71] PLR 200438044.
[72] PLRs 200432027, 200432028 and 200432029.

8

Employer-Plan Rollovers

Chapter Highlights

❖ Rolling your employer plan[a] into an IRA will provide more investment flexibility and can provide more planning flexibility.

❖ Non-spouse beneficiaries of employer plans may roll over the benefits to an inherited IRA upon the employee's death..

❖ If you are over age 55 when you separate from service but are under age 59½, you should consider leaving part of your 401(k) with the employer plan to avoid the premature-distribution penalty. When you attain age 59½, the balance of your 401(k) can then be rolled into an IRA to provide you with maximum flexibility.

❖ Firefighters, police officers and emergency medical personnel may avoid the premature-distribution penalty for withdrawals from government plans if they separate from service after age 50.

❖ If you, upon reaching retirement, have the option of receiving a lump-sum distribution of your employer plan, you must make an important decision: Whether to roll the distribution into a self-directed IRA or keep the plan assets in the employer plan. Most often a rollover is the best course of action; nonetheless, the pros and cons of both options should be considered before a rollover is selected.

SOME EMPLOYER-PLAN PARTICIPANTS are content with leaving their retirement assets with the company plan after retirement or changing employers. Some people are comfortable using the investment options available in their former employer plan and are familiar with the online account services. Others leave their retirement

---

[a] Employer plans include 401(k), profit sharing, pension, ESOP, 403(b), and 457 plans.

plan with a former employer due to procrastination or because they are unaware of their options. A common downside of leaving your retirement assets with the employer plan is the lack of suitable investment options and the lack of flexible distribution options, both of which result in reduced planning flexibility.

Planning Flexibility

An employee plan will often not have the flexibility if an IRA with regard to beneficiary designations. For example, you may wish to name a trust as a beneficiary of your employer plan. Some employer plans will not allow trusts as beneficiary. You must check your employer plan document to determine if a trust is a permissible beneficiary. Most IRA custodians allow trusts as beneficiary.

The investment flexibility allowed by IRAs must also be considered. Employer plans typically offer 18 to 25 investment options (some offer many more). The investment options of an IRA number in the thousands and provide complete flexibility to the IRA owner. Some employer plans allow participants to execute an in-service rollout of their plan assets to an IRA while still employed. This option allows the employee to invest their 401(k) assets in the investments of their choice outside of the 401(k) while continuing to make salary deferrals and receive a company match. Maximum flexibility and choice with regard to investment options is critical during difficult market environments.

You must check your employer plan's plan document to determine your available options. Rolling your employer-plan assets into a self-directed IRA can give you the maximum amount of control over planning options. It also can give you the maximum amount of control and number of choices over investment options.

But Which IRA?

Because all IRAs are not equal, consult the IRA custodial document and adoption agreement to determine if an IRA provides the flexibility to meet your planning needs. For example, consult these documents to determine if the beneficiary's distribution options are restricted. Unfortunately, many participants do not review the plan document or IRA adoption agreement. At a minimum, these documents should be reviewed to determine what will happen if a beneficiary predeceases the participant. Another key point is to determine if the default rule is per capita or per stirpes? This will determine whether the other designated beneficiaries split a predeceased beneficiary's portion or if this share goes to the predeceased beneficiary's descendants. Most clients prefer distributions to their beneficiaries under a per stirpes arrangement; but many IRA custodial agreements default to per capita distributions.

If a trust is or may end up as a beneficiary of your IRA, make sure the IRA custodian can accommodate such an arrangement. Custodians set their own rules, within the Internal Revenue Code guidelines, and some may not accept a trust as a beneficiary. Some custodians do not want to deal with the complexities of naming a trust as beneficiary. In addition, some IRA custodians cannot handle a usufruct/naked-ownership beneficiary designation or QTIP trust arrangement. You should specifically inquire whether these options are available.

As a practical matter, never assume the custodian handling the IRA is knowledgeable and that the advice received over the phone from a service representative regarding beneficiary designations or distribution options is correct to meet your planning goals. In fact, much of the misinformation received by do-it-yourselfers and professionals originates from the service representatives of IRA custodians.

Keep in mind that IRA documents vary, and many IRAs do not allow the fullest degree of planning options permitted by the Internal Revenue Code. Does your IRA allow the maximum number of planning choices allowed by law? If you are unsatisfied with your IRA's distribution options, you may directly transfer your IRA, tax-free, to an IRA custodian that allows the options to suit your planning needs.

Non-spousal Employer-plan Rollovers

The Worker, Retiree, and Employer Recovery Act (WRERA) of 2008 requires all employer plans to permit non-spouse beneficiaries to rollover the benefits to an inherited IRA beginning in 2010. A non-spouse beneficiary can elect to make a direct rollover of employer plan benefits to an inherited IRA. In addition they can directly convert the account into an inherited Roth IRA during the rollover.

The Advantages of a Direct IRA Rollover

When rolling your employer plan into an IRA, you should complete a direct rollover rather than a rollover. Although similar in terminology, the IRS treats each transaction differently. To complete a direct rollover, the employer plan sends the check directly to the IRA custodian, or the check is made payable to the order of the custodian for the employee's benefit. During a rollover, on the other hand, the check is made to the order of the employee. Regardless of whether the check was rolled into the IRA within 60 days, 20 percent of the rollover amount will be withheld. If you do not have sufficient cash on hand and are unable to "makeup" the 20 percent withholding, that amount is treated as a taxable distribution. To make matters worse, if you are under 59½ years of age, the 10 percent premature-distribution penalty will apply. If you are able to "makeup" the 20 percent withholding difference, you must now ask the IRS for a refund of the 20 percent withholding. If, for any reason, you do not complete the rollover within 60 days, a full taxable distribution occurs.

You may also transfer your IRA from one custodian to another by using a direct transfer. A direct transfer prevents the application of the 60-day rollover and 20 percent withholding rules.

An IRA owner may make an unlimited number of direct IRA-to-IRA transfers. On the other hand, an IRA owner is allowed only one IRA rollover per year where a distribution is taken from the first IRA and the proceeds are paid to the owner and are then placed in the second IRA within 60 days under the tax-free rollover rule. If the IRA owner has two IRAs, he or she may make a tax-free rollover from only one IRA within the one-year period. In addition, the distributions, not the rollovers, must be 12 months apart. It is best to avoid this issue by transferring assets between IRAs with a direct custodian-to-custodian transfer.

Employer Plan Options

If you retire between the ages of 55 and 59½, you have an additional planning decision. Depending on your situation, you should consider leaving assets within a 401(k) plan because individuals who separate from service after reaching age 55 may take withdrawals from their 401(k) plan without the 10 percent early withdrawal penalty.

Assets inside an IRA cannot be withdrawn prior to age 59½ without the 10 percent penalty unless an exception applies. Depending on your cash flow needs, it may be advantageous to leave part of the 401(k) intact (enough to support income needs until age 59½) and rollover the remaining balance to an IRA. At age 59½ you should consider rolling over the remaining 401(k) balance into an IRA because the 10 percent penalty is no longer applicable. Determining cash flow needs if retiring prior to age 59½ may reveal a need to keep this exception to the 10 percent early withdrawal penalty a viable option by leaving some assets in the 401(k) plan. An additional benefit of 401(k) plans is that you may take loans against your 401(k) if the plan document permits. Loans may not be taken from an IRA.

Pension Options

Pension benefits and pension rollouts present additional planning options. If your employer provides a pension plan, you generally have the option of receiving lifetime payments or electing a pension lump sum rollout. Retirees who elect to receive the pension over their lifetime typically select a benefit that will continue payments to their surviving spouse. Retirees may usually select a lesser amount (e.g. 50 or 75 percent) to be paid to their surviving spouse after the retiree's death. The higher the percentage paid to the surviving spouse, the lesser the retiree's lifetime pension payments. For example, a retiree may elect to take the maximum pension benefit payable for his or her lifetime. Upon the retiree's death, payments cease and there is no beneficiary. Another option is to receive a slightly reduced pension benefit during the retiree's lifetime with a lifetime pension benefit of one-half of this amount to the beneficiary (the 50% option). The retiree may wish to receive equal payments for the duration of both spouses' lives (the 100% option). In this case, the retiree's pension benefit is reduced more than the 50% option, but it provides a larger pension benefit to the surviving spouse. Remember, there are many variations to these examples, and each pension plan is unique.

The pension payments are fixed and cannot be increased, decreased, or turned off. In addition, the pension payments are fully taxable as ordinary income. Although pension payments are not subject to market risk, fixed pension payments may not provide an adequate inflation hedge or sufficient planning options. Some pensions, however, provide inflation adjustments to help keep pace with cost of living increases. In addition, if both spouses die prematurely, nothing will be paid to their children unless a period certain selection is made. A period certain selection will pay benefits to a beneficiary for a certain number of years if the retiree dies soon after retirement. A 15 year period certain will guarantee payments for a minimum of 15 years even if the retiree dies prior to 15 years elapsing. For example, if Boudreaux selects a joint and survivor annuity with a 15 year period certain, he and his wife are guaranteed payments for both lifetimes. If both Boudreaux and his wife die 10 years after payments begin, Boudreaux's beneficiaries (typically the children) will receive payments for 5 years. Longer guaranteed periods will reduce the retiree's lifetime pension payments.

Many retirees elect to receive their pension benefit as a lump sum payment which is rolled into an IRA. The retiree assumes the investment risk once the pension is received as a lump sum. Due to the relatively low rate of return of fixed pension payments, many retirees elect a lump sum pension distribution to invest in an attempt to achieve a higher rate of return. Receiving the pension as a lump sum also provides additional planning opportunities. For example, a lump sum pension payment may allow you to transfer these assets to a child or grandchild or to provide a pool of assets for any other purpose. In addition, distributions from the lump sum may be taken as needed which may result in delaying taxes until the assets are withdrawn from the IRA. Upon the death of both spouses, their beneficiaries will receive any amount remaining in the IRA.

When deciding how to receive their pension, each retiree must examine the relevant factors and their personal goals and needs. Factors to consider when deciding whether to rollover pension benefits include risk tolerance; required investment return; length of retirement; income needs; and other sources of income. To help determine the correct pension option, a comprehensive retirement cash-flow analysis is highly recommended.

9

Net Unrealized Appreciation

Chapter Highlights

❖ The net unrealized appreciation (NUA) strategy allows favorable tax treatment for employer stock that is not rolled into an IRA.

❖ To qualify for NUA treatment, the employer stock must be distributed as a lump sum.

❖ Ordinary income tax is paid on the cost basis of the employer stock selected for NUA treatment when it is transferred out of the employer plan.

❖ The difference between the cost basis of the employer stock and the fair market value is NUA and is taxed as a long-term capital gain when the stock is sold.

❖ All or part of the employer stock may be selected for NUA treatment.

❖ The lack of diversification by holding a large amount of employer stock must be weighed against the tax benefit of NUA treatment.

❖ The NUA strategy works best when the cost basis of the employer stock is low and the fair market value is high.

❖ If the employer stock is rolled into an IRA, the distributions are taxed as ordinary income. This may result in a higher amount of taxes paid on the employer stock.

❖ RMDs (required minimum distributions) do not apply to the NUA strategy.

❖ Heirs may also use the NUA strategy.

MANY PARTICIPANTS OF qualified plans have significant amounts of employer stock in their plan accounts. The tax code allows retirees to treat employer stock differently than other plan assets (mutual funds for example). This treatment is often referred to as net unrealized appreciation (NUA) treatment. NUA is the difference between the cost basis and the stock's price when distributed.[1] The retiree pays ordinary income taxes on the cost basis of the employer stock when distributed and long-term capital gain taxes on the NUA when sold.[2] This option involves distributing employer stock to the retiree and directly rolling over the remaining assets into a traditional IRA. This combination approach, although not for everyone, should be explored as it has significant advantages.

NUA treatment of employer stock provides an additional way to defer taxes on employer stock. It may result in a lower amount of taxes paid compared to rolling the employer stock into an IRA because NUA is taxed as a long-term capital gain. If employer stock is owned as stock units rather than the actual shares of stock, NUA treatment is available if the plan allows in-kind distribution of employer stock in exchange for stock units. Employer stock purchased with after-tax employee contributions is also eligible for NUA treatment. In addition, the employer stock must be received as part of an in-kind, lump-sum distribution.

Lump-Sum Distribution Requirements

If employer stock is distributed as a lump sum, all of the NUA is non-taxable at the time of distribution.[3] If the distribution does not qualify as a lump-sum distribution, only the NUA attributable to employee contributions, if any, is non-taxable at the time of distribution.[4] To be eligible for a lump-sum distribution, one of the following triggering events must occur:[5]

- You are at least 59½;

- You are an employee who separated from service (layoff, disability, retirement);

- You are self-employed and suffer from a total, permanent disability as defined in IRC § 72 (m)(7); or

- You are the beneficiary of a deceased retirement plan participant.

A lump-sum distribution means a complete distribution of all plan assets in one calendar year due to separation from service, death, disability or attaining 59½. It does not mean that the entire distribution must occur in one transaction but within a specific period of time.[6] A lump-sum distribution means that the account balance as of the first distribution after the most recent triggering event must be distributed within one calendar year.[7] Most employees who retire after 59½ have one opportunity to select NUA treatment. An employee who retires prior to 59½ has two opportunities: The first after separation from service and the second after attaining age 59½.

Caution should be used if the lump-sum distribution is attempted late in the calendar year. If additional assets are in the account in the following calendar year, the distribution is not a lump-sum distribution. This may occur if dividends or other amounts are applied to the account (even if due to plan administrator's error) in the following year. If employer stock attributable to employer contributions is received in-kind and is not part of a lump-sum distribution, NUA treatment is unavailable, and the entire amount is immediately taxable as ordinary income. For this reason, ensure that the lump-sum distribution rules are followed. To help ensure the entire account is distributed in one calendar year, do not attempt a lump-sum distribution near year's end. In addition, prior to the end of the year of your lump sum distribution, check your employer plan account to ensure that no assets remain.

Tax Treatment

By not including the employer stock in the traditional IRA rollover, you are exposed to income taxes immediately on the employer stock because you are receiving the shares of employer stock as a taxable distribution. However, you will be taxed only on the stock's cost basis. Use caution if you are under 55 or under 59½ (depending on when you separated from service), a 10 percent premature-distribution penalty will be assessed on the ordinary income realized (applied only to the stock's cost basis).

The stock may be sold immediately with the NUA taxed at long-term capital gain rates. The NUA portion will always be taxed at long-term capital gain rates, regardless of the holding period. The 3.8 percent surtax on net investment income will not apply to the capital gain on NUA.[a] If you retain the NUA stock, additional appreciation from the date of distribution value will be taxed at long-term capital gain rates if held at least one year. For shorter holding periods, short-term capital gain rates apply to the additional appreciation over the distribution value. The additional appreciation in excess of the NUA will be subject to the 3.8 percent surtax.

Until sold, the employer stock held outside the traditional IRA will continue to defer taxes on its appreciation. When you ultimately decide to sell the shares, you will pay long-term capital gain rates on the appreciation (the NUA portion). If the employer stock were rolled into an IRA, gain on the stock distribution would be taxed at ordinary income tax rates because IRA distributions do not qualify for NUA treatment.[8] In addition, there are no Required Minimum Distributions starting at age 70½ for the employer stock, allowing for more planning flexibility.

Your heirs may receive additional benefits by not rolling the employer stock into an IRA. First, if these same shares of employer stock were rolled into a traditional IRA, your heirs would ultimately owe ordinary income taxes on the employer stock, as they would on any asset held in a traditional IRA (as Income in Respect of a Decedent). By rolling the employer stock into a traditional IRA, your heirs are unable to utilize the benefits of long-term capital gain treatment when they decide to sell the stock. Compare this outcome with employer stock that received NUA treatment. At the retiree's death, the employer stock receives a step-up in basis on any appreciation in value which occurs from the time of the lump-sum distribution. Therefore, your heirs may sell the stock immediately after your death with no capital-gain tax liability on the increase in value from the date of distribution from the employer plan. The NUA portion of the employer stock remains NUA to your heirs, and they will pay taxes at long-term capital gain rates on the NUA portion.[9] Your heirs do not receive a § 1014 step-up in basis on the NUA.[10] In addition, there are no Required Minimum Distributions for your heirs as with traditional IRAs.

---

[a] The 2010 Affordable Care Act imposes a 3.8 percent surtax on investment income for taxpayers with adjusted gross income greater than $200,000 or $250,000 for couples filing a joint return.

For example, Boudreaux who works for ExxonMobil has $750,000 in his 401(k) plan of which $400,000 is ExxonMobil stock and $350,000 is held in other investments. For the purposes of this example, assume his cost basis of the employer stock is $10 per share and the fair market value is $80 per share (5000 shares). The total stock cost basis is $50,000 and the NUA is $350,000 ($400,000 market value - $50,000 cost basis). If the $350,000 in nonemployer-stock assets is rolled into an IRA, no taxes are due on the rollover. If the employer stock is taken in kind (not rolled into the IRA), Boudreaux will pay ordinary income taxes on the $50,000 cost basis. The $350,000 NUA is not taxed until the stock is sold. If the stock is sold immediately, Boudreaux will pay long-term capital gain taxes on $350,000. If Boudreaux does not sell the stock immediately, the additional gain (appreciation above the date of distribution value after the employer stock is distributed) on the employer stock will be taxed either as a long-term gain or as a short-term gain depending on the holding period. Continuing the example, the date of distribution value for Boudreaux's ExxonMobil stock is $80 per share. Boudreaux sells some of his shares of stock within one year of taking the lump-sum distribution when ExxonMobil stock is valued at $100 per share. For each share he sells, $10 is his basis which was taxed when distributed; $70 is NUA taxed as a long-term capital gain; and $20 is taxed as a short-term capital gain. What if Boudreaux sells some of his ExxonMobil shares for $120 per share after one year has elapsed since they were distributed to him? For each share he sells, $10 is his basis for which he was already taxed; $70 is NUA taxed as a long-term capital gain; and the remaining $40 is taxed as a long-term gain. All of the gain exceeding his cost basis is taxed as a long-term capital gain because the stock was sold more than one year after it was distributed.

To determine if the NUA option is feasible, it is important to know the actual cost basis of your employer stock. Your employer or plan administrator should have detailed records of the cost basis. You may have the option of cherry picking the lowest cost basis stock for NUA treatment of only that portion of the employer stock (specific identification method).

Exposing the employer stock to taxes now may be more advantageous in the long run if the employer stock's cost basis is much lower than the current market value. Of course this is always contingent upon the market value of the employer stock staying higher than the cost basis; therefore, this strategy is always subject to the risk of market value fluctuations.

Selective Net Unrealized Appreciation Treatment

Although the plan must be distributed in a lump sum, NUA treatment need not be selected for all employer stock. A portion of the employer stock, the higher-cost-basis stock for example, may be rolled into the IRA. The lower-cost-basis stock may be distributed in-kind for NUA treatment.

Tips for Implementing Net Unrealized Appreciation Treatment

If you decide to take NUA treatment for employer stock, you should first make sure that you qualify for a lump-sum distribution. In addition, to avoid the 20 percent withholding, you should transfer all of your nonemployer-stock assets and any employer stock not selected for NUA treatment to an IRA by direct rollover. By leaving only employer stock with the company plan, you will avoid the 20 percent withholding. Trustee-to-trustee transfers and transfers from an account holding only employer stock avoid the 20 percent tax withholding. Next, transfer the employer stock in kind to a retail (non-IRA) brokerage account.

If you made after-tax contributions (sometimes referred to as a tax-paid balance) that was invested in employer stock (or can be allocated to employer stock when you retire), you may offset the cost basis of the NUA stock to the extent of your after-tax contributions. This option allows you to receive employer stock without immediate income tax liability. For example, Boudreaux has after-tax contributions of $50,000, and he selects 3000 shares of employer stock for NUA treatment. His cost basis of these 3000 shares is $50,000. He may use his after-tax contributions to offset the cost basis of his NUA stock and owes no ordinary income tax on the distribution. As with any NUA strategy when the stock is sold, Boudreaux will owe long-term capital gain tax. This strategy is not suited for all employees, and a thorough analysis is recommended prior to selecting this or any other option regarding employer stock.

If the after-tax contributions are not used to reduce the income tax liability of an employer stock distribution, it may be distributed as cash without income tax consequences. In the alternative, after-tax contributions may be rolled into an IRA. You must keep track of the after-tax contributions that are rolled into an IRA to avoid paying income tax on the after-tax portion when distributed.

Factors to Consider

Diversification: If employer stock comprises a large portion of your assets, holding large blocks of employer stock may subject you to a large amount of company-specific investment risk. If the employer's stock value drops significantly, a large amount of wealth may be destroyed. Prudence dictates diversification in many cases.

Tax Savings: Calculate the potential tax savings if NUA treatment is selected. If tax savings are not significant, you will probably be better off rolling the employer stock into an IRA.

Sell Date: Employees who are likely to retain employer stock for many years and delay paying taxes on the NUA benefit the most.

Effect on Income Tax Bracket: By not rolling the employer stock into an IRA, you may end up in a higher tax bracket in the year of the distribution due to taxes paid on the cost basis of the stock.

Amount of retirement assets: NUA treatment is more suitable for retirees with larger amounts of retirement assets.

Cost basis in comparison to current market value: The larger the amount of NUA (the spread between the cost basis and current market value), the more beneficial NUA treatment is to the employee.

The bottom line: You must run the numbers to see if the long-term tax benefits outweigh paying some taxes now and the risks of holding the employer stock. Competent advice is a must when deciding to elect or not to elect NUA treatment for employer stock.

---

[1] Reg. § 1-402(a)-1(b)(2).
[2] Reg. § 1.402(a)-1(b)(1)(i); Notice 98-24, 1998-1 C.B. 929; PLR

2004-10023.

[3] §402(e)(4)(B).

[4] §402(e)(4)(A).

[5] §402(e)(4(D)(i).

[6] §402(e)(4)(D)(i).

[7] IRS Notice 89-25, 1989-1 C.B. 662; Prop. Reg. § 1.402(e)-2(d)(1)(ii); Rev. Rul. 69-495.

[8] Reg. § 1.402(c)-2, A-13(a).

[9] Rev. Rul. 69-297.

[10] Rev. Rul. 75-125.

Louisiana Public Retirement Systems

Chapter Highlights

❖ The Louisiana Public Retirement Systems may offer over eight retirement plan options, and many are irrevocable.

❖ The correct retirement option will depend on your retirement and estate planning "big picture." A retirement cash flow analysis can help determine which option is best for you and your beneficiary's needs.

❖ DROP allows you to accumulate a tax-deferred lump sum of assets that can help supplement your retirement income.

❖ Some DROP participants (especially participants of LaDROP) may benefit from an IRA rollover of their DROP account.

❖ The Windfall Elimination Provision may reduce a public retirement system member's Social Security benefits.

❖ The Government Pension Offset may reduce or eliminate spousal or survivor Social Security benefits of a public retirement system member.

EMPLOYEES UNDER THE Louisiana Consolidated Public Retirement System are faced with many unique issues when planning their retirement. Many different retirement systems cover employees and retirees of different areas of state and local government. This section will review the basic planning options available to most systems; however, not all options discussed in this section apply to all public retirement systems in Louisiana. Retirement systems under the Louisiana Consolidated Public Retirement System include

- Assessors' Retirement Fund
- Clerks of Court Relief and Retirement Fund
- District Attorneys' Retirement System

- Firefighters' Retirement System
- Harbor Police Retirement System
- Louisiana School Employees' Retirement System
- Louisiana State Employees' Retirement System
- Municipal Employees' Retirement System of Louisiana
- Municipal Police Employees' Retirement System
- Parochial Employees' Retirement System of Louisiana
- Registrars of Voters Employees' Retirement System
- Sheriffs' Pension and Relief Fund
- State Police Pension and Retirement System
- Teachers' Retirement System of Louisiana

Selecting the Correct Retirement Plan Option

The retirement systems each provide over eight retirement plan options, although not all plans have eight options and not all option benefits are identical. Selecting the correct plan option is extremely important because once the option is selected, the selection may be irrevocable. To illustrate some options, the following is a summary of some of the Teachers' Retirement System of Louisiana's retirement options.[a] Other retirement systems may have different options.

The Maximum Retirement Benefit

The maximum retirement benefit pays the highest eligible benefit amount for the member's lifetime. The Teachers' Retirement System of Louisiana (TRSL) will cease benefits at death and no additional payments are made to a beneficiary after the member's death. As such, the member does not name a beneficiary when selecting the maximum option. If the member dies prior to receiving all of his or her contributions through monthly benefits, the remaining contributions are paid to the member's estate. Some public retirement systems allow the member to name a beneficiary who receives the remaining amount the member contributed to the system, if any, in a lump sum.

---

[a] La. Rev. Stat. Ann. 11:783.

Option 1

Option 1 pays a benefit that is slightly less than the maximum benefit for the member's lifetime. Upon the member's death, Option 1 will pay a lump sum in the amount of the member's remaining contributions, if any, to the member's beneficiary. Generally, once the contributions are exhausted through benefits paid to the member, the beneficiary receives nothing. Option 1 is the only option that allows more than one beneficiary to be named, and the beneficiaries may be changed at any time. Option 1 may be beneficial to members who require flexibility with regard to changing beneficiaries or would like to name more than one beneficiary.

Lifetime Benefit Options

Additional options (e.g. Options 2 through 5) pay an amount less than the maximum for the member's lifetime and the member's beneficiary's lifetime. Generally, only one beneficiary may be named, and the beneficiary cannot be changed even if he or she dies.

The ability to change beneficiaries before and after retirement varies widely depending upon the option selected and the retirement system providing the benefit. The member should use caution when selecting a benefit option if there is a possibility he or she may require a beneficiary change at a later date. Under many benefit options, the plan member is unable to change the beneficiary once the selection is made. In addition, many benefit options allow only one beneficiary to be named which may cause a planning dilemma if the participant has two or more children or grandchildren he or she would like to name as beneficiaries.

Option 2

Option 2 provides the member with a reduced lifetime benefit. The benefit continues for the beneficiary's lifetime if the member predeceases. Option 2A (Pop-up) provides the member with a reduced monthly benefit which continues for the beneficiary's lifetime after the member's death. If the beneficiary predeceases the member, the benefit "pops up" to the Maximum Option benefit.

Option 3

Option 3 provides a reduced monthly benefit that is greater than Option 2 or Option 2A. After the member dies, the beneficiary will receive a benefit that is one-half of the member's benefit. Option 3A (Pop-up) provides a reduced monthly benefit that is greater than Option 2 or Option 2A but less than Option 3. After the member's death, the beneficiary will receive a benefit that is one-half of the member's benefit. If the beneficiary predeceases the member, the benefit "pops up" to the Maximum Option benefit.

Option 4

Option 4 provides a reduced monthly benefit that is determined by the cost of the benefit the member selects for the beneficiary. The amount selected for the beneficiary cannot exceed the Option 2 benefit amount. Option 4A (Pop-up) provides a reduced monthly benefit that is determined by the cost of the benefit the member selects for the beneficiary. The amount selected for the beneficiary cannot exceed the Option 2 benefit amount. If the beneficiary predeceases the member, the benefit "pops up" to the Maximum Option benefit.

When deciding which option to select, you must consider your entire retirement and estate "big picture." For example, IRAs, 403(b) accounts, other investments, your spouse's retirement plan, Social Security benefits and standard of living must be factored into a retirement cash flow analysis to determine the cash flow required from the retirement system. The amount of cash flow required during retirement and the needs of surviving beneficiaries are the dominant considerations. Your age and the age of your spouse, as well as the possibility of requiring a change of beneficiaries, are also factors.

The Initial Lump Sum Benefit Option

If you are eligible for but have not participated in DROP, you may select the Initial Lump Sum Benefit Option (ILSB). This provides a lump-sum payment equal to a maximum of 36 months of the Maximum Option monthly benefit. A lesser lump-sum amount may be chosen. You will receive a reduced monthly benefit for life if ILSB is selected; therefore, you must carefully analyze your required retirement cash flow to ensure the reduced monthly benefit will provide adequate income. If you select the ILSB, you may also choose the Maximum Option, 2, 2A, 3, 3A, 4 or 4A. Option 1 is not available if the ILSB Option is selected.

You may take a lump-sum taxable distribution, roll the lump sum into an IRA or qualified plan or allow the lump sum to remain invested at the retirement system similar to a DROP account.

The Deferred Retirement Option Plan

The Deferred Retirement Option Plan (DROP) is an optional program which allows members to accumulate an additional pool of retirement assets while continuing to work. If you participate in DROP, your retirement benefits are deposited into a special account at the retirement system while you continue to work and draw a salary. You may participate in DROP for a maximum of three years, and the decision to participate is irrevocable.

Why Participate In DROP?

If you are eligible for retirement but do not wish to retire, participating in DROP provides additional planning opportunities. DROP allows you to accumulate a pool of assets that may be taken as a lump sum in a full, taxable distribution or allowed to grow tax deferred to provide additional retirement resources. A drawback of DROP is that your retirement benefit is frozen at the beginning of DROP participation. Any pay raises you receive after beginning DROP will not be part of your monthly retirement benefit calculation. As a result, your monthly pension may be lower than if you do not participate in DROP. Members who experience long retirements and live past their life expectancy will be most affected if their pension payments are adversely affected by participating in DROP. On the other hand, members who die sooner, rather than later, after the onset of retirement benefit the most from DROP as they receive the lump sum DROP assets upfront. Members have the use of the DROP account assets to supplement their retirement. In addition, surviving beneficiaries will receive the DROP account assets and the survivor pension. Lastly, DROP participation favors those who prudently invest and spend the DROP account assets. It doesn't do much good to participate in DROP, potentially receive a lower monthly pension and waste the DROP account assets on frivolous spending. Because the decision to participate in DROP is irrevocable, you should weigh your options carefully.

You may participate in DROP for a maximum of three years, and once the duration of DROP is selected, it can only be shortened by retirement or death. If you want to participate in DROP for the maximum amount of time, you must begin participation when the DROP window begins. The DROP window begins when you are first eligible to retire. Consult your retirement system for your correct retirement eligibility date.

While participating in DROP, your account will not earn any interest or investment return. Once participation in DROP ends, if you were eligible to enter DROP prior to January 1, 2004, your DROP account earns interest at an annual rate of 0.5 percent less than the retirement system's realized rate of return. If the retirement system realizes a negative rate of return, the Louisiana Attorney General has determined that the value of DROP accounts may not be reduced by market losses. Thus, in negative return years, nothing is added to or subtracted from the DROP accounts.

If you are eligible to enter DROP on or after January 1, 2004, your DROP account is invested in LaDROP. This account is in essence a money market account, and DROP accounts will earn money market rates less 0.25 percent.

Rolling a DROP Account into an IRA

There are advantages and disadvantages of rolling a DROP account into an IRA. The advantages vary depending on the retirement system and when the member participated in DROP. If you are eligible for TRSL DROP prior to January 1, 2004, your DROP account will earn interest based on the system's actuarially realized rate of return less 0.5 percent. Your DROP account is invested in the market but cannot be reduced by market losses. However, if you are eligible for DROP on or after January 1, 2004, your DROP account is invested in LaDROP. LaDROP does not provide the upside market potential of the original DROP. If you wish to seek returns above the money market rate, you must rollout your DROP account into an IRA or take a full, taxable distribution. After the DROP funds are rolled over, the funds may be invested to suit your needs and risk tolerance. You and your beneficiaries will generally have more planning opportunities by rolling the DROP account into an IRA; however, consult with a competent financial advisor who is knowledgeable about DROP prior to making the rollover.

Unfortunately, some DROP account distribution rules are more restrictive than IRA distribution rules. For example, some retirement systems require distributions from DROP accounts to begin within one year of retirement. In addition, the distribution amount may only be changed once per year and cannot be reduced unless you retired prior to January 1, 2003, and are over 70½ years of age. By rolling the DROP account into an IRA you may experience extended tax deferral because distributions may be delayed until April 1 of the year after you attain 70½ years of age. You also have control of the investment choices with an IRA. Finally, IRA distributions may vary from year to year so long as the required minimum distribution rules are followed. The downside of the IRA rollover include distributions from IRAs are subject to Louisiana income taxation if over the annual exemption amount of $6,000 per taxpayer age 65 and over ($12,000 if both spouses are over age 65 receiving retirement income). DROP account distributions are not subject to Louisiana income taxation. Also, IRA assets may be subject to market losses.

11

Annuities

Chapter Highlights

❖ An annuity can provide benefits that no other investment can provide, such as guaranteed income for life and principal protection for assets invested in the stock market. These benefits may help an investor reach his or her planning goals.

❖ An immediate annuity begins payouts immediately rather than deferring payments.

❖ A deferred annuity grows tax deferred and pays a benefit to the investor or beneficiary at some later date.

❖ A fixed annuity appreciates at a minimum guaranteed fixed rate of return set by the contract terms.

❖ A variable annuity invests the annuity premiums in one or more annuity sub-accounts. The sub-accounts are analogous to mutual fund accounts with choices ranging from a fixed guaranteed account, fixed-income and stock-investment sub-accounts.

❖ Guaranteed Minimum Withdrawal Benefits (GMWBs) are designed to protect assets from market risk and to provide a guaranteed return of premiums.

❖ Guaranteed Minimum Income Benefits (GMIBs) may provide a lifetime income stream. The GMIB is calculated using a minimum account base which is typically the annuity premiums compounded at a growth rate of 4 or 5 percent.

❖ The guarantees provided by variable annuities come at an additional cost. The charges and expenses vary among annuities and among insurance companies, so cost comparisons are important.

❖ Fixed-indexed annuities calculate returns based on a stock market index. Fixed-indexed annuities may participate in a portion of the stock index gain but are generally not subject to market losses. The type of fixed-indexed annuity, the calculation method and the various caps, spreads and participation rates are all factors that determine fixed-indexed annuity performance.

❖ Withdrawals or payments from annuities are taxed as ordinary income regardless of the holding period. Investors must withdraw and pay taxes on all gains prior to withdrawing premium payments.

❖ Annuitized payments are received as part return of the premiums paid into the contract and part interest. The exclusion ratio is used to determine the taxable (interest) and non-taxable (premiums paid into the contract) amounts of each annuitized payment.

❖ If an annuity is gifted, the annuity owner may be liable for gift taxes in the amount of unrealized gains.

❖ Annuities do not receive a step-up in basis upon the owner's death; therefore, the annuity owner's gains in the annuity contract will be taxed to the beneficiary as ordinary income.

❖ An annuity may be exchanged for another annuity as a tax-free exchange. The 1035 exchange can be particularly helpful when attempting to "upgrade" to a more current annuity.

❖ When purchasing an annuity, care should be taken to ensure proper annuity structure to avoid an unintended payout and a loss of control over the annuity.

ANNUITIES CAN PROVIDE retirees and pre-retirees with tax-deferred accumulation, guaranteed growth, and unique guaranteed income benefits. Annuities can be very complex investment vehicles and are governed by unique income, gift and estate tax rules. Even with the dramatic growth in the use of annuities, many annuity investors are unaware of the unique opportunities and planning implications that arise when investing in annuities.

As with any investment, your needs and goals will help determine whether an annuity is right for you. An annuity can provide benefits that no other investment can provide, such as guaranteed income for life and principal protection for assets invested in the stock market. These benefits may help you reach your planning goals; however, there are no free lunches. Prior to investing in an annuity, you should understand the provisions of the annuity contract you are considering. Many types of annuities exist, and each is designed to fulfill certain objectives. An understanding of the differences between the various types of annuities may help to determine whether an annuity is right for your retirement planning. Annuities can vary widely, and the contracts are often very complex, so get the facts and a second opinion prior to deciding whether an annuity is right for your planning goals.

The growth of an annuity is tax deferred, so gains are taxed when funds are withdrawn.[1] Withdrawals may be subject to income taxes, and prior to age 59½, a 10 percent premature withdrawal penalty may apply. Withdrawals from annuities will affect both the account value and the death benefit. In addition, the annuity contract will pay periodic payments for life (if annuitized), payments when requested or a lump-sum payment. An annuity is the only type of investment vehicle that can guarantee that an investor will never run out of money, as the guarantees are based on the claims paying ability of the issuing insurance company. Upon the owner's death, the insurance company will distribute benefits to the beneficiary as defined in the contract. Another benefit of annuities is that they are protected under Louisiana law from seizure by creditors. See Chapter 25 for more information regarding the creditor protection features of annuities.

The increasing popularity of annuities has brought both scrutiny and praise by the financial press and financial advisors alike. This chapter explains the basic features of annuities in addition to the pros and cons of different types of annuities. While reading this chapter, keep in mind that claims about guarantees (e.g., death benefits, guaranteed fixed accounts, guaranteed income streams) are subject to the claims-paying ability of the insurer issuing the annuity.

Types of Annuities

Even though there are both private and commercial annuities, the primary focus of this chapter is on nonqualified, commercial, deferred annuities, whereby a lump sum or installments are paid to an insurance company.

Immediate Annuities

Immediate annuities, sometimes referred to as SPIAs (Single Premium Immediate Annuities), begin payouts immediately rather than deferring payments. For a given level of premium, the amount of each payment depends on, among other factors,

- Investor's age

- Whether the payout is based on one or two lives

- Whether payments are for a period certain, life with a period certain guarantee, or pure life

- The fixed return (depending on the current interest rate environment) or the variable return (depending on the sub-accounts' investment performance)

An immediate annuity is used to create a current income stream that is guaranteed for life or for a specific number of years (e.g. 20 years). This option is known as life plus 20 years period certain. For example, the life plus 20-years-period-certain option would continue payments to your beneficiary if you die prior to 20 years elapsing. For a given amount of premium, lifetime payments subject to a period-certain option are slightly less than straight life payments; however, the period-certain option provides protection against premature death and forfeiture of the remaining payments. A variety of period-certain terms are available (e.g. 5, 7, 10 and 20 years). Your spouse may also receive payments based on both lives, guaranteeing income payments until the last spouse dies.

Deferred Annuities

Deferred annuities grow tax deferred and pay a benefit to the owner or beneficiary at some later date. An investor may deposit a single premium payment (single premium deferred annuity) or multiple premium payments (flexible premium deferred annuity) into the annuity. The period of time prior to annuitization or full distribution is the accumulation phase, and gains in the annuity grow tax deferred. When the accumulation phase ends, the payout or distribution phase begins, and the annuity is annuitized or withdrawn.

The same lifetime payment options that are available to immediate annuities are available to deferred annuities once annuitization is selected. The vast majority of deferred annuities are never annuitized. Rather, the owner typically makes withdrawals from the annuity, or upon the owner's death, the beneficiary receives a lump-sum payment.

The beneficiary may also have the option of annuitizing the lump sum to receive periodic payments. In addition, some annuity contracts allow the annuity owner to specify how quickly the beneficiaries are to receive distributions from the annuity. This feature is designed to protect the beneficiary as it prevents the beneficiary from accessing all of the money at one time. For example, the owner may specify that upon his or her death the annuity will distribute the annuity to the beneficiary over 10 years. This option allows the contract owner to control the beneficiary's access to the funds without placing the funds in a trust.

Annuities can also be classified according to how the annuity premiums may be invested inside of the annuity. An annuity may be classified as a fixed, variable or fixed-indexed (equity-indexed) annuity.

Fixed Annuities

A fixed annuity is a long-term, tax-deferred insurance contract designed for retirement. Fixed annuities appreciate at a minimum, guaranteed fixed rate of return under the contract's terms. At inception, the owner is guaranteed a minimum return which is subject to the insurer's claims-paying ability. Only insolvency of the insurance company would cause the owner not to receive this minimum amount. The prevailing interest rate environment will heavily influence the guaranteed annuity rate. Caution should be used when comparing fixed annuities as many companies use a teaser rate which is higher during the first year and drops for the remainder of the contract.

Fixed annuities are typically offered for three, five, seven or ten years. At the end of the term, the fixed annuity will continue to grow tax deferred at the minimum, guaranteed rate. Because at the end of the term prevailing rates may be higher than the minimum, guaranteed rate of a current fixed annuity, it may be advantageous to exchange the fixed annuity for a new annuity offering a higher rate. A new surrender period will apply, so liquidity needs should be considered.

If the owner decides to annuitize the contract, payments will be fixed at the start of annuitization. An advantage of fixed annuities is that the contract owner assumes no market risk. The annuity guarantees a minimum, fixed rate of return.

The annuity grows tax deferred and, as opposed to certificates of deposit, can provide guaranteed tax-deferred accumulation. The income from certificates of deposit is taxed annually, and therefore, will accumulate more slowly than the fixed annuity. Keep in mind that withdrawals from an annuity may be subject to income taxes, and prior to age 59½, a 10 percent premature withdrawal penalty may apply.

A disadvantage of a fixed annuity is that over long periods inflation risk will deteriorate purchasing power. Therefore, it is advantageous to lock in longer-term fixed annuities near the peak of the interest rate cycle to obtain higher rates. It is also advantageous to annuitize a fixed annuity near the peak of the interest rate cycle as opposed to other periods.

Fixed annuities generally have surrender charges (called contingent deferred sales charges or CDSCs). Surrender charges can run 10 years or longer and decline over time. For example, a fixed annuity may have a seven-year surrender period with an initial CDSC of 7 percent. If the CDSC declines 1 percent annually, after seven years, withdrawals would not be subject to the CDSC. Fixed annuities also generally have a 10 percent-of-purchase-premium, penalty-free withdrawal feature. This feature provides some liquidity; however, fixed annuities are not short-term investments. If short-term liquidity is necessary, other investment choices should be considered. Investors can also shop around for fixed annuities with shorter surrender periods that are within their investment time horizon.

Impaired-Risk Immediate Annuities

Health-Adjusted or Impaired-Risk-Single-Premium Immediate Annuities are a type of immediate fixed annuity that offer an increased payout for a given amount of premium by using the annuitant's rated age rather than actual age. The annuity is medically underwritten to make an adjustment to the annuitant's life expectancy by considering medical conditions that reduce life expectancy. Typically, applicants must have a 25 percent reduction in life expectancy or would be rated using table two or higher for life insurance underwriting. Impaired-Risk SPIAs are beneficial because they can provide a greater amount of income for a given amount of premium. For example, $100,000 in premium would pay a 66-year-old male a monthly benefit of $676 for life. A 66-year-old male who has a rated life expectancy of a 72-year-old would receive a monthly benefit of $792 for life. If a female age 68 requires $1000 per month for life, a standard immediate annuity would require a premium payment of $151,378. If her health rated her age at

74 years, an impaired-risk immediate annuity would require a premium of $129,500. As a guaranteed source of income for a retiree, an impaired-risk SPIA requires fewer premium dollars than a standard SPIA for the same income stream.

Variable Annuities

Variable annuities invest the annuity premiums into one or more sub-accounts of the annuity. The sub-accounts are analogous to mutual fund accounts with choices such as a fixed guaranteed account, fixed income (bonds) and stock-investment sub-accounts. However, unlike mutual funds, variable annuities are subject to additional fees such as mortality fees and administrative fees. As opposed to owners of fixed annuities, the owner of a variable annuity assumes the investment risk. The investment return and principal value will fluctuate so that an investor's shares, when redeemed, may be worth more or less than their original cost. Although the variable annuity exposes one to market risk, a variable annuity can serve as a better hedge against inflation than fixed annuities. A trade-off exists, however, between guaranteed returns of a fixed annuity and potentially higher returns of a variable annuity. Another feature of variable annuities is the ability to reallocate money among the sub-accounts of the annuity. These reallocations are tax-free, internal transfers that allow the owner to invest more aggressively or more conservatively or to rebalance the portfolio.

Variable annuities can also differ from fixed annuities when annuitized. When a variable annuity is annuitized, the annuity payments can be linked to the sub-account performance. Higher returns on the sub-accounts will result in larger annuity payments and lower returns in smaller annuity payments. This feature may provide an inflation hedge to preserve purchasing power in later years. Investors may also choose to have all or part of the annuity payments paid as a fixed annuitization. In this case the payments remain the same for life or other period. In addition to tax deferral, variable annuities provide many types of guaranteed income, withdrawal and death benefits. As with any annuity, withdrawals may be subject to income taxes, and prior to age 59½, a 10 percent premature withdrawal penalty may apply. Withdrawals from the annuity will affect the account value, the withdrawal and income guarantees, and the death benefit. Before investing, investors should carefully consider the investment objectives, risks, charges and expenses of the variable annuity and its underlying investment options. The current contract prospectus and underlying fund prospectuses, which are contained in the same document, provide this and other important information. Please contact your representative or the Company to obtain the prospectuses. Please read the prospectuses carefully before investing or sending money. Variable annuities are generally considered long term investments.

➢ Death Benefits

Death benefits allow a minimum, guaranteed amount to be left to the beneficiary regardless of the market performance. If the owner dies without annuitizing the contract, the standard death benefit pays to the beneficiary the total amount of premiums paid minus any withdrawals. While there is no risk to the original principal (less any withdrawals), if the owner dies during the accumulation phase, both the investment return and the principal value will fluctuate in response to changing market conditions. Thus, the death benefit only protects the premiums if the owner dies without annuitizing the contract. The death benefit may also be based on the account high water mark, which is generally the highest anniversary value the annuity has ever achieved. There is usually an extra cost to provide death benefits tied to the high water mark.

An enhanced death benefit, often called a roll-up benefit, guarantees that the death benefit will grow at a minimum rate (e.g. 4 or 5 percent). The compounded growth of the roll-up benefit and the high water mark increases may cease when the contract owner reaches a certain age (usually age 80). Due to the additional cost for the high water mark and roll-up death benefits, as well as the age caps associated with these features, enhanced death benefits can be less advantageous for contract owners who are closer to age 80. The death benefits are designed to protect the beneficiary by paying an amount greater than the date of death account value if the owner dies when the market is down. Keep in mind that withdrawals from the annuity will reduce the death benefit amount and that the death benefit guarantees are subject to the insurer's claims-paying ability.

➢ Guaranteed Withdrawal Benefits

Guaranteed Minimum Withdrawal Benefits (GMWBs) are designed to protect assets from market risk and to provide a guaranteed return of premiums. Many variable annuity contracts allow the owner to withdraw annually a maximum percentage (e.g. 7 percent) of premium payments until the total premium payment amount is withdrawn, regardless of market performance. For example, if Thibodaux invests $100,000 in a variable annuity with a 7 percent GMWB, he may withdraw $7,000 per year until the total withdrawals equal $100,000. Until he receives all his premiums back, Thibodaux may continue to withdraw $7,000 per year even if the contract value falls to zero due to poor market performance.

The GMWB may also offer a step-up feature which locks in, on a periodic basis, any market gains. The GMWB would then be based on the step-up amount rather than the premiums paid. This feature may provide some protection from inflation in later years. For example, Thibodaux's GMWB has a step-up feature, and the account grows to $150,000. The GMWB allows Thibodaux to withdraw $10,500 per year (7 percent x $150,000).

In addition to a step-up feature, some GMWBs provide guaranteed withdrawals for life after the contract owner attains a certain age (usually age 60 or 65). The "for life" GMWB insures that payments continue for life even if the contract value falls to zero.

Multiple combinations of these benefits may also be selected. The GMWB is a safety net that guarantees a return of premium payments regardless of market performance. There is an additional cost for a GMWB, and an annual cap of 7 percent means it will take at least 14 years to withdraw of all premium payments. The GMWBs are also subject to the insurer's claims-paying ability.

➢ Guaranteed Minimum Income Benefits

Another exclusive benefit of variable annuities is the Guaranteed Minimum Income Benefit (GMIB). To receive this benefit, most annuities require annuitization. In addition, GMIB payments typically cannot begin immediately. One must wait a number of years (e.g. 10 years) to begin receiving GMIB payments. The GMIB features frequently evolve as annuity companies compete to provide better features. Changes to GMIBs may offer payments based on the contract's highest anniversary value to a certain age (e.g. 81). The minimum account base is usually equal to the premium payments compounded at a fixed rate of return (e.g. 4 or 5 percent). This minimum account base can be used to calculate annuity payments. If the contract value grows to more than the minimum account base, the contract value is used to calculate the annuity payments. Of course, one may elect not to annuitize but to take periodic payments or a lump sum payment. The GMIB is designed to provide a minimal amount of growth to the account base regardless of market performance. Like all other guarantees and enhanced benefits, GMIBs impose an additional cost on the contract and are subject to the insurer's claims-paying ability.

So how might a GMIB help an investor? Here is an example. Boudreaux invests $200,000 in a variable annuity with a GMIB feature. After 10 years, the contract value is worth $230,000 due to poor market performance. The minimum account base is equal to $325,778 (the premium payment compounded at 5 percent). Boudreaux may take withdrawals from the $230,000 contract value or use the GMIB to annuitize the minimum account base value of $325,778.

Many variable annuities are purchased for the guarantees provided by GMWBs and GMIBs rather than the tax deferral. A variable annuity is the only type of investment that provides these types of guarantees. If these guarantees are important to you, it may make sense to use a variable annuity with these guarantees for a retirement account. A variable annuity generally should not be used in a retirement account (e.g. an IRA) unless a GMWB, GMIB or an annuitization option is desired.

➢ Variable Annuity Charges

Several charges and expenses are associated with variable annuities. These charges and expenses vary among annuities and among insurance companies, so it is important to compare costs. Lower costs will result in less drag on the variable annuity's investment performance. A clear understanding of these charges is important prior to investing.

- **Surrender Charges:** If money is withdrawn from a variable annuity within the surrender period, a surrender charge usually applies. A surrender charge is also called a contingent deferred sales charge (CDSC). The surrender period is usually five to eight years but may be longer. The surrender charge is usually a percentage of the premium payments and declines gradually over the surrender period. For example, a seven-year surrender period may begin with a 7 percent surrender charge and decline 1 percent each year. Withdrawals after the surrender period are not subject to the surrender charge. In addition, the contract owner may annually withdraw 10 percent of the premium payments (or the contract value) free from the surrender charge. Some contracts allow earnings to be withdrawn at any time free from the surrender charge.

- **Mortality and Expense Risk Charge:** The mortality and expense risk charge (M&E) is an annual charge on the account value. The industry average M&E charge for variable annuities is around 1.25 percent. In addition, administrative fees may also be assessed as an account maintenance fee. This fee may be a flat fee (e.g. $30) or a percentage of the account value (e.g. 0.15 percent).

- **Fund Expenses:** In addition to the M&E charge, the portfolio sub-account manager charges a fee, typically ranging from .20 percent to over 1.5 percent annually, to manage the sub-account.

Annuities can provide guarantees to your principal and guaranteed lifetime income; however, these guarantees come at a price—the additional fees charged for each benefit and guarantee. The fees are the costs for protecting against market risk, inflation and running out of money. Some investors sleep better knowing they will at least get their money back or receive a minimum return regardless of how bad the market gets. The guarantees allow investors to keep their emotions in check in a volatile market by insuring that their principal and/or income stream is protected. The guarantees are designed to avoid a financial disaster, but they hopefully will never be used. Only after carefully weighing the pros and cons of each benefit and feature can you determine whether the guarantees' benefits outweigh the costs.

Fixed Indexed Annuities

Fixed-Indexed Annuities, also known as Equity-Indexed Annuities (EIAs), are the newest type of annuity (first introduced in the mid 1990s). These annuities calculate investment returns based on a stock market index (typically the S&P 500). A primary advantage of EIAs is that the account typically will not depreciate in value due to poor market performance. If the stock market index goes up, the account may appreciate in value (depending on the type of EIA and the calculation method). In addition, accumulated investment gains of certain types of EIAs are locked in and are not reduced if the index goes down. Most EIAs guarantee that the account owner cannot lose money (a benefit of fixed annuities) and can potentially hedge against inflation risk (a benefit of variable annuities). Equity-indexed annuities are not designed to keep pace with the market indexes over extended periods; rather, they are best suited for an investor who wants principal protection and an opportunity to outperform fixed-income investments (e.g. bonds and CDs).

An EIA generally does not have annual fees and expenses as do variable annuities. Some EIAs also guarantee a minimum fixed rate of return if the index performs poorly during the accumulation phase. For example, the EIA may guarantee a 3 percent return on 90 percent of the premium payments. As with other annuities, the guarantees are subject to the insurer's claims-paying ability. EIAs also grow on a tax-deferred basis, and withdrawals may be subject to income taxes. Prior to age 59½, a 10 percent premature withdrawal penalty may apply.

A drawback of EIAs is the account may not appreciate in value or may appreciate very little even if the equity index appreciates in value. The type of EIA, the calculation method and the various caps, spreads and participation rates are all factors influencing EIA performance. Another drawback of EIAs is their complexity. The formulas to calculate investment return vary by insurance company, and various restrictions exist. For these reasons, comparisons can be difficult, and thorough due diligence is a must. The following is a list (certainly not exhaustive) and description of some basic contract features:

- **Term:** The term is the period over which the index-linked interest is calculated. The term typically ranges from three to fifteen years; however, six to nine years is more common. At the end of the term, the contract owner may elect to continue the existing contract, to 1035 exchange into another contract, to annuitize or to cash out and pay taxes on any gains. Premature withdrawal penalties may apply if the owner is under age 59½.

- **Caps:** A cap is an upper limit on the amount of index-linked interest the EIA may earn. The cap may be an annual cap (e.g. 9 percent) or a monthly cap (e.g. 1.5 percent). For example, an annual cap of 9 percent will limit the returns to a maximum of 9 percent even if the stock market index returns more than 9 percent. The contract terms may allow the insurance company to adjust the cap from time to time.

- **Participation Rate:** The participation rate limits the index increase amount that will be used to calculate index-linked interest. For example, if the index is up 15 percent and the EIA has an 80 percent participation rate, only 12 percent is used in the calculation. Because the participation rate is generally set at the time the contract is issued, the participation rate for a given contract will depend on when it was issued. Insurance companies frequently change the participation rates for newly issued EIAs. Furthermore, an EIA may have both a participation rate and a cap restricting the investor's return.

- **Margins or Spreads:** An EIA may deduct a margin or spread from the stock market index rate of return to determine the amount of interest credited. These deductions will reduce the EIA return. For example, if an EIA has a spread of 2 percent and the market index return is 10 percent, the return credited to the EIA is 8 percent.

- **Vesting Schedules:** Some EIAs impose vesting schedules which reduce the amount of index-linked interest available for withdrawal if the owner makes withdrawals from the contract prior to the end of the term.

- **Point-to-Point Indexing Method:** Index-linked interest is calculated by subtracting the index's value at the start of the term from its value at the end of the term (normally five to twelve years). Only the index price is considered. Dividends are not included in EIA interest-crediting calculations. If the return is negative, nothing is added or subtracted from the EIA. If the return is positive, it is adjusted by one or more previously mentioned contract features (caps, spreads, participation rates, etc.). Point-to-point crediting methods typically work best in upward-trending markets.

- **Annual Reset Indexing Method:** Each year the index value at year's end is subtracted from the index's beginning value (excluding dividends). The prior years' index levels are irrelevant for future-index calculations. In addition, future market declines do not affect gains which have been credited to the account. Annual reset interest-crediting methods work best in a fluctuating market.

- **Averaging Indexing Method:** Some EIA indexing formulas average the stock market index over a period of time rather than using the index level at a given date. Averaging can work for or against the contract owner. It can protect the contract owner if the index was up most of the year and then drastically declined at the end of the index-calculation period for the year. It can also be to the owner's detriment if the index dramatically appreciates at the end of the index-calculation period for the year.

- **High-Water-Mark Indexing Method:** The high-water-mark method compares the index's highest point during the term to the index's value at the beginning of the term. If the number is positive (and after adjustments by the contract features), it is added to the EIA at the end of the term. The high-water-mark method locks in the highest equity-index level during the period regardless of the index's value at the end of the period.

Tax Treatment of Annuities

Annuities grow tax deferred during the accumulation phase if the owner is a "natural person." If an annuity is owned by a corporation, trust or other entity, the annuity loses its tax-deferred status.[2] However, exceptions to this general rule exist. Prior to February 26, 1986, annuities grew tax deferred regardless of whether the owner was a natural person or a non-natural person.

If an annuity is held by a trust as agent for a natural person, tax-deferred status is preserved. Tax-deferred status is allowed by the IRS where a grantor trust holds an annuity contract as the agent for natural persons and where the income on the contract is not includable in the participants' gross income.[3] In addition, the IRS takes the position that an annuity contract held by a trust (not a grantor trust), is holding the contract as an agent for a natural person. For such tax treatment, all beneficiaries (including remainder and reversionary interests) must be individuals.[4] A trust that has natural persons as beneficiaries is treated as an agent of a natural person and generally is eligible for tax-deferred treatment.[5]

Income Taxation of Withdrawals and Annuity Payments

When distributions are taken (through annuitization or withdrawals from the annuity), they are taxed as ordinary income regardless of the holding period. This is the trade-off for tax-deferred growth. Withdrawals from annuity contracts are taxed differently than annuitized payments from an annuity. Withdrawals provide flexibility with regard to the amount and timing of the cash flows. Annuitized payments are fixed as to the timing and cannot be stopped once payments begin. Annuitized payments can provide income for life but lack the flexibility of annuity withdrawals. Fixed annuitized payments will not vary as to the timing or the amount. Variable annuitized payments will not vary as to the timing but will fluctuate as to the amount with changes in the variable annuity sub-accounts' performance.

Annuity Withdrawals

For investments in annuity contracts <u>prior</u> to August 14, 1982, the IRS allows contract owners to withdraw their entire investment in the contract first (return of basis). Only when withdrawals exceed the amount invested in the contract will the owner have to pay taxes on the gains.[6]

For investments in contracts on or <u>after</u> August 13, 1982, the owner must withdraw amounts in excess of the investment in the contract first (interest first).[7] This means that taxation of gains in the annuity begins with the first dollar withdrawn. If a contract has accumulated income allocable to both pre-August 14, 1982, and post-August 13, 1982, investment in the contract, distributions are allocated in the following order:[8]

1. Pre-August 14, 1982, investment in the contract.

2. Income allocable to pre-August 14, 1982, investment in the contract.

3. Income allocable to post-August 13, 1982, investment in the contract.

4. Post-August 13, 1982, investment in the contract.

The Exclusion Ratio

Although annuitized payments lack the flexibility of annuity withdrawals, they receive more favorable tax treatment. Annuitized payments are received as part return of investment in the contract and part interest. The exclusion ratio is used to determine the taxable (the interest) and non-taxable (investment in the contract) amounts of each annuitized payment. The investment in the contract, the expected return and the expected number of payments (either fixed period or life expectancy) are all factors in calculating an exclusion ratio. The investment in the contract is typically the amount of premiums paid into the annuity. If the annuity has a refund or period-certain guarantee, an adjustment must be made to the investment in the contract.[9] See IRS Publication 939 for examples of how to calculate the investment in the contract.

For fixed annuities, the exclusion ratio is determined by dividing the investment in the contract by the total amount of payments. If payments continue for life, the total number of payments is determined by the annuitant's life expectancy. If payments are for a number of years, the total number of payments will be based on the period of years. For example, Thibodaux, age 60, annuitizes a fixed annuity which will pay him $600 per month for life. His life expectancy is 25 years[a]. He has invested a total of $100,000 into the annuity, and his total expected payments are $180,000 ($600 per payment x 12 payments per year x 25 years). The exclusion ratio is .556 ($100,000/$180,000). Therefore, Thibodaux may exclude $333.6 out of each $600 payment from his income. Only $266.4 is subject to income tax.

Annuitized payments from variable annuity contracts also use an exclusion ratio; however, because the annuity payments fluctuate with the investment sub-accounts' performance, the expected return is unknown. Thus, the exclusion ratio is calculated dividing the investment in the contract by the expected number of payments (fixed period or life expectancy).[10] For example, if Thibodaux, age 60, annuitizes a variable annuity, his payments will vary from month to month due to fluctuations in the annuity sub-accounts. Thibodaux's investment in the contract is $150,000, and the total number of monthly payments is 300 based on his life expectancy of 25 years (12 payments

---

[a] Determined by Table V of IRS Publication 939.

per year x 25 years). The exclusion ratio is determined by dividing the investment in the contract by the total number of payments. Therefore, Thibodaux may exclude $500 per month from each payment ($150,000/300 payments). If Thibodaux lives longer than his life expectancy, all future payments are fully taxable as he has recovered his entire investment in the contract. If annuitized payments began prior to January 1, 1987, the exclusion ratio applies to all payments even after the investment in the contract is recovered.[11]

The 10 percent premature distribution penalty applies to distributions prior to age 59½ on the amount includable as income.[12] Therefore, the 10 percent penalty does not apply to premium payments (the investment in the contract). A number of exceptions apply, including[13]

- owner's death

- disability (if satisfying the Social Security definition of disabled)

- investment prior to August 14, 1982, and interest on that investment

- series of substantially equal periodic payments and based on life expectancy (annuitizing the contract)

Gift Taxation of Annuities

If an annuity contract is gifted to another person (other than to a spouse or former spouse via divorce decree), the donor may realize some income tax consequences. For contracts dated after April 22, 1987, an annuity owner who donates an annuity to another person is treated as having received income in an amount that is equal to the contract's surrender value on the donation date minus the investment in the contract.[14] For example, if Thibodaux's investment in the contract is $50,000 and the surrender value on the date of donation to Marie is $75,000, Thibodaux's taxable income is $25,000. The donee's basis in the contract is the donor's investment in the contract plus income the donor realized upon donation. Therefore, Marie's basis is $75,000.

Contracts dated prior to April 23, 1987, follow a different rule. If the surrender value is greater than the investment in the contract and the donee later surrenders the contract, the donor must report the difference between the investment in the contract and the surrender value as of the donation date. Any additional gain (after the donation) is realized by the donee.[15]

Taxation upon the Owner's Death

Many annuity owners are unaware of the tax bill they may be leaving their beneficiaries. Annuities do not receive a step-up in basis upon the owner's death; therefore, the annuity owner's investment gain in the annuity contract will be taxed to the beneficiary as ordinary income. Many beneficiaries will have to pay significant taxes on annuity gains within a short time after the owner's death. Annuity owners should plan early to avoid or to minimize the tax burden on their beneficiaries.

An annuity issued after January 18, 1985, must distribute the remaining annuity (owner- or annuitant-driven) assets upon the owner's death.

If the contract was annuitized on or after the owner's death, the beneficiaries must take remaining distributions at least as quickly as under the owner's distribution schedule.[16] Therefore, if the owner annuitized the contract, the beneficiaries must take distributions based on the owner's remaining life expectancy. If the contract was not annuitized by the owner, the beneficiaries may annuitize the contract and take distributions based on the deceased owner's life expectancy.

If the owner dies prior to annuitization, the entire contract must be paid out within five years unless an annuitization option is selected by the beneficiary.[17] If the beneficiaries do not annuitize the contract, they must pay taxes on all annuity gains within five years of the owner's death.

Some annuity contracts allow beneficiaries to stretch distribution payments over their life expectancy so long as a required minimum distribution is taken annually.[18] This option provides flexibility, continued growth, and tax deferral of the annuity assets. Most importantly, it allows the tax burden to be stretched out over a number of years. Not all annuities provide this option.

If the surviving spouse is the sole designated beneficiary, the surviving spouse is treated as the owner for distribution purposes.[19]

The surviving spouse may continue the annuity's accumulation phase or take any other action consistent with an owner.

Income Taxation upon the Annuitant's Death

In most cases, the owner is the annuitant, so the rules in the above section apply. However, in cases where the owner and the annuitant are different people and where the annuitant's death prior to annuitization will cause a payout to the beneficiary, taxable income to the beneficiary is realized in the amount of the death benefits paid in excess of the investment in the contract. Although annuity companies consider a beneficiary claim to be a death benefit similar to life insurance, the entire amount over and above the cost basis is taxable as ordinary income.[20]

Estate Taxation

Annuities are included in the owner's gross estate. The value included in the gross estate will depend on several circumstances:

- If the annuity is still in the accumulation phase (not annuitized) upon the owner's death, the total death benefit is included in the gross estate.[21]

- If the annuitization phase has begun, the inclusion of the annuity's value in the owner's estate will depend on whether annuity payments continue after the owner's death. If the owner was receiving annuity payments under a straight-life arrangement, payments cease at the owner's death. In this case, no part of the annuity is included in the owner's estate. However, if payments will continue to a beneficiary after the owner's death, the value of the remaining payments due to the beneficiaries are included in the deceased owner's estate.[22]

- For an annuity owned by joint owners where both contributed to the investment in the contract, only the portion attributable to the decedent's contributions are included in the decedent's estate.

All tax discussion related to cost basis and exclusion ratio applies to nonqualified contracts only (accounts that are not IRAs or employer-sponsored retirement plans).

Annuity Exchanges

An annuity may be exchanged for another annuity as a tax-free exchange.[23] The 1035 exchange can be particularly helpful in "upgrading" to a more current annuity to have access to sub-accounts with better managers and/or to take advantage of new features and benefits that are available to the owner and/or beneficiary. If the current contract value is significantly more than the investment in the contract, a 1035 exchange can avoid income taxation on the transfer.

In addition, the cash value of life insurance policies can be transferred tax-free to an annuity policy under § 1035. If life insurance is no longer needed, a 1035 exchange to an annuity allows the owner to cash in the life insurance while avoiding taxation on the cash value until withdrawal or surrender of the annuity.

An annuity owner may also upgrade to a more current annuity by liquidating the contract and reinvesting the proceeds in a new annuity. Liquidating a contract is not a 1035 exchange; therefore, income taxes will be due to the extent that there are investment gains in the contract. The 10 percent premature-withdrawal penalty will apply if the owner is under age 59½.

One area still open to debate is whether losses incurred upon annuity surrender are allowed as a tax deduction. Revenue Ruling 61-201 permitted a loss on a refund annuity; however, some believe that this Revenue Ruling does not extend to surrendering a variable annuity in accumulation phase. In addition, the IRS has not given any official guidance on the subject. Assuming the loss is deductible, many annuity owners would benefit from a full surrender, rather than a 1035 exchange, when changing annuities.

An owner of a variable annuity that has a value of less than the premiums paid due to market losses may consider a variable annuity with better investment options or choose to switch to an equity-indexed or fixed annuity. For example, if Boudreaux's investment in the contract is $100,000 and the current contract value is $75,000, he has a deductible ordinary loss of $25,000. Any applicable contract CDSCs (surrender charges) are not deductible. The next issue is how to deduct the loss. If taken on Schedule A on Form 1040 as a miscellaneous itemized deduction, the loss is subject to the 2 percent floor, and deductions must be itemized. Another (arguably more aggressive) option is to take the loss on Form 4797 and as "other gains and losses" on the front of Form 1040. This option is not subject to the 2 percent floor.[24]

Proper Annuity Contract Structure

With the increasing popularity of nonqualified annuities and the various combinations of owner, annuitant and beneficiary, understanding proper contract structure is essential. Planning goals and the parties involved with the annuity contract will determine how to structure the contract.

Parties to an Annuity

A contract owner has full control over the contract. He or she may transfer the contract, change beneficiaries, make withdrawals or surrender the annuity contract. The annuitant is the person on whose life expectancy annuitized payments are based. Some annuities pay out to the beneficiaries upon the annuitant's death. In most cases, the owner is the annuitant which avoids the owner losing control over the annuity due to the annuitant's death while the owner is still alive. The beneficiary generally receives any death benefits.

Joint Ownership of an Annuity

Joint ownership of an annuity contract is not as advantageous for contracts issued after January 18, 1985. Prior to this date, joint owners could extend tax deferral over more than one lifetime by naming a younger joint owner. Current law requires distributions to be completed within five years of any owner's death with the exceptions of spousal continuation and annuitization options.[25]

The beneficiary spouse of a deceased holder may continue the annuity as the owner under the spousal continuation rule. The spouse must be the sole primary beneficiary. Therefore, if the spouse is named with another primary beneficiary, spousal continuation may be unavailable. Some contracts will allow spousal continuation on the surviving spouse's portion of the contract. This includes naming both spouses as beneficiaries.

A taxable gift occurs to the joint owner if one joint owner contributes all premiums. Upon the death of one joint owner, the entire contract value will be included in his or her estate unless the surviving joint owner can prove his or her premium contributions.

Owner-Driven and Annuitant-Driven Contracts

Another consideration is whether the contract is owner driven or annuitant driven. Most contracts are owner driven. An owner-driven contract pays out upon the owner's death. The owner has all contract rights and may change the annuitant and the beneficiary. To avoid unintended results, generally one spouse should be both the owner and annuitant, the other spouse the beneficiary and the children the contingent beneficiaries.

An annuitant-driven contract pays out upon the owner's or the annuitant's death. The owner's death will trigger a distribution of annuity assets (which may not include enhanced benefits). The annuitant's death will trigger a death benefit distribution that may include enhanced benefits. An annuitant-driven contract usually will pay the distribution to the beneficiary upon the annuitant's death. Keep in mind that contract functionality varies by the insurance carrier issuing the contract and that the contract will dictate whether the owner's or the annuitant's death triggers a payout.

Examples

The most common structure to avoid adverse consequences is for an owner-driven contract to name the husband or wife as owner, the annuitant is the owner, the beneficiary is the spouse, and the contingent beneficiaries are the children. This arrangement allows the surviving spouse to continue the contract and the children to become the surviving spouse's primary beneficiaries. The spouse may also exchange the contract, surrender the contract or annuitize the contract.

To allow spousal continuation at the greater of the contract value or the enhanced death benefit, the contract should be structured as follows: The contract owners are the husband and wife, the annuitants are the husband and wife, the primary beneficiary is the surviving spouse and the contingent beneficiaries are the children. Under this arrangement, either spouse would be able to continue the contract at the greater of the contract value or enhanced death benefit value. Not all annuities allow the spouse to continue at the greater of the contract value or the enhanced death benefit.

If a minor child will own the contract, the owner should be a Uniform Transfer to Minors Act account. The child should be the annuitant, and the beneficiary should be the child's estate.

If an irrevocable trust is used, the trust should be the owner. The trust beneficiary should be the annuitant, and the trust should be the beneficiary. This arrangement will allow tax deferral as the annuity is deemed to be held by a natural person.

If a trust is needed to protect the beneficiaries, a contract may be established, for example, with the husband as both the owner and the annuitant, the wife as the primary beneficiary and a trust as the contingent beneficiary. Upon the husband's death, the surviving spouse may continue the contract or take a full distribution.

Another option is to name the trust as the contract owner, the husband or wife as the annuitant and the trust as the primary beneficiary. Upon the annuitant's death, the death benefit is paid to the trust. The trust beneficiaries will receive the benefits as per the trust document. Spousal continuation may be allowable if the trust is a grantor trust and the spouse is the grantor.

Faulty Annuity Contract Structure

Example 1 of faulty contract structure: The contract is annuitant driven. The husband and wife are joint owners, the husband is the annuitant, and the children are the beneficiaries. If the husband predeceases the wife, the annuity may pay the proceeds to the children. Spousal continuation is unavailable, and the surviving spouse loses control of the annuity assets with some contracts.

Example 2 of faulty contract structure: A trust is the owner, the husband is the annuitant, the wife is the primary beneficiary and the children are the contingent beneficiaries. Upon the husband's death, the spouse will not be able to continue the contract, as she is not the owner's spouse.

Example 3 of faulty contract structure: A trust is the owner, the husband is the annuitant, and the children are the beneficiaries. Upon the husband's death, the children, rather than the trust, receive the proceeds.

Example 4 of faulty contract structure: The husband is the owner, the wife is the annuitant, and the children are the beneficiaries. An owner-driven contract, upon the husband's death, will pay the proceeds to the children, not the surviving spouse. If the contract is annuitant driven and the wife dies first, the proceeds are paid most often to the children. The husband receives nothing.

Example 5 of faulty contract structure: The husband and wife are joint owners, the husband is the annuitant, and the children are the primary beneficiaries. The Internal Revenue Code stipulates that upon the first owner's death, there must be a distribution. Some contracts will, upon the husband's death, pay the proceeds to the children (even with the wife as joint owner).

---

[1] Any withdrawals may be subject to income taxes and, prior to age 59 1/2, a 10% federal penalty tax may apply. Withdrawals from annuities will affect both the account value and the death benefit. The investment return and principal value will fluctuate so that an investor's shares, when redeemed, may be worth more or less than their original cost. An annual contingent deferred sales charge (CDSC) may apply.

[2] IRC §72(u)(1).

[3] PLRs 199905015, 9752035, 9639057, 9322011, 9316018.

[4] PLRs 9204010, 9204014.

[5] You should discuss any tax or legal matters with the appropriate professional.

[6] IRC § 72(e)(5)(B).

[7] IRC § 72(e)(2); 72(e)(3).

[8] Revenue Ruling 85-159.

[9] IRC § 72(c)(2); Treas. Reg. § 1.72-7.

[10] Treas. Reg. § 1.72-2(b)(3).

[11] IRC § 72(b)(2).

[12] IRC § 72(q).

[13] IRC § 72(q)(2).

[14] IRC § 72(e)(4)(C).

[15] Rev. Rul. 69-102, 1969-1 C.B. 32.

[16] IRC §72(s)(3).

[17] IRC § 72(s)(1).

[18] PLR 200151038.

[19] IRC § 72(s)(3).

[20] IRC § 72(e)(5)(E); Treas. Reg. §1.72-11(c); Rev. Rul. 55-313, 1955-1 C.B. 219.

[21] IRC §§ 2033; 2039.
[22] IRC § 2039(a).
[23] IRC § 1035.
[24] You should discuss any tax or legal matters with the appropriate professional.
[25] IRC § 72(s)(1).

Social Security

Chapter Highlights

❖ Social Security retirement benefits provide a financial security net that helps supplement your retirement income.

❖ Retirees born in 1929 and later must work 10 years to earn 40 work credits to become fully insured for retirement benefits.

❖ Social Security retirement benefits may begin at age 62; however, your benefits will be permanently reduced. Receiving Social Security retirement benefits at age 62 is called early retirement.

❖ Full retirement age is between 65 and 67 depending on when you were born.

❖ You may delay retirement until age 70 and receive an increased retirement benefit.

❖ Your Social Security benefits will be subject to income taxation if your income exceeds certain thresholds.

❖ If you work while receiving Social Security benefits prior to reaching full retirement age, your Social Security benefits will be reduced if your earned income exceeds certain thresholds.

❖ If you elect to receive early Social Security benefits, your total cumulative benefits may exceed the benefits you would have received if you waited until full retirement age.

❖ Choosing to begin Social Security payments early will result in reduced survivor benefits for your surviving spouse.

❖ Your surviving spouse and children are eligible for survivor benefits after your death based on your work credits.

FROM ITS ENACTMENT IN 1935, Social Security has provided retirement benefits to millions of Americans. Over the years, Social Security has expanded to provide additional programs such as survivor benefits for spouses and children and disability benefits for disabled workers meeting the qualifications for disability. Although there are several types of benefits provided by Social Security, this chapter will focus on Social Security retirement benefits or Old Age Survivors and Disability Insurance (OASDI).

Social Security consists of multiple programs or types of benefits, each with different rules and payment schedules. Social Security is not based on financial need; rather, it is based on your average wages, salary or self-employment income. Keep in mind that Social Security was not designed to provide a standard of living above the poverty line. Rather it was designed to lessen the Great Depression's effects by providing a financial safety net. However, combined with pension payments and other retirement savings, Social Security benefits remain a significant source of retirement income.

Will Social Security still exist 20 years from now? Obviously, no one has a crystal ball to predict the future. Considering the degree which Americans rely on Social Security, it is hard to imagine an existence without Social Security. However, demographic changes will prevent Social Security from existing in its current state. For example, in 2010 there were 2.9 workers paying Social Security taxes for each beneficiary. By 2040, there will be 2.1 workers paying Social Security taxes for each beneficiary.[1] With beneficiaries greatly outnumbering workers paying into the system, there is little doubt that additional changes will occur to the Social Security system due to extended life expectancies and aging baby boomers. To help minimize the financial jeopardy to the system, extending the age at which full benefits are available, reducing benefits or increasing Social Security taxes are all possibilities.

How Your Social Security Benefit Is Calculated

Your Social Security benefits are determined by a mathematical formula which calculates an inflation-adjusted benefit based on your earnings. To accomplish this goal, your actual earnings are adjusted for changes in average wages from the time the earnings were received. The purpose is to state past wages in terms of the level of today's wages. To compute Social Security benefits, the Average Indexed Monthly Earnings (AIME) of your 35 highest earning years must be determined. The AIME is an inflation-indexed average based on your lifetime earnings history. Only employment income on which Social Security taxes are paid is considered in calculating your Social Security Benefit. Several additional mathematical calculations are performed to determine your Primary Insurance Amount.

The amount of your Social Security benefit at full retirement age is equal to the Primary Insurance Amount (PIA). To obtain an estimate of your PIA, contact the Social Security Administration.

By creating an account at www.ssa.gov you can view your account and your earnings record. Your earnings record is the amount the Social Security Administration has recorded that you earned each year. You should check your earnings record periodically because mistakes which you do not correct may reduce your Social Security benefits.

Eligibility for Retirement Benefits

Eligibility for Social Security retirement benefits is based on earning the required amount of work credits (also known as quarters of coverage). A maximum of four credits per year are earned based on the amount of employment earnings. For example in 2019, one credit is earned for every $1,360 in employment earnings. To be eligible for Social Security retirement benefits, you must be fully insured. For retirees born in 1929 and later, you must work 10 years to earn 40 work credits to become fully insured.

Social Security retirement benefits may begin at age 62; however, your retirement benefits will be permanently reduced. Receiving Social Security retirement benefits at age 62 is called early retirement. If you begin Social Security retirement benefits early, and if you continue to work, your benefit may be further reduced if your earnings exceed certain limits. Once full retirement age is reached, your benefit is no longer reduced on account of your earned income. For individuals waiting until full retirement age is reached, Social Security will begin according to the following table:

Table 7 - Social Security Full Retirement Ages

Year of Birth	Full Retirement Age
1937 or earlier	65
1938	65 and 2 months
1939	65 and 4 months
1940	65 and 6 months
1941	65 and 8 months
1942	65 and 10 months
1943-1954	66
1955	66 and 2 months
1956	66 and 4 months
1957	66 and 6 months
1958	66 and 8 months
1959	66 and 10 months
1960 and later	67
People who were born on January 1 should refer to the previous year.	

An advantage of waiting until full retirement age is that Social Security benefits are not reduced. Yet another option is to delay Social Security retirement benefits beyond full retirement age. The advantage of delaying Social Security beyond full retirement age is that benefits increase by 8 percent each year from full retirement age to age 70. If you continue to work, Social Security benefits may increase as a result of higher earnings credited to your Social Security record in your final working years. If delayed Social Security is selected, remember to sign up for Medicare at age 65. This chapter will later review the pros and cons or beginning Social Security benefits early and electing delayed benefits.

Beginning Social Security Retirement Benefits

Social Security benefits do not start automatically when you reach normal retirement age. You must apply for Social Security. To allow time to process your application, you may want to apply for Social Security benefits three months prior to the date you would like benefits to begin. In addition, it may be possible to begin Social Security benefits in January although you do not retire until later in the year. This option should be discussed with the Social Security Administration. You may apply in person at your local Social Security office, or you may begin the application process online. Additional information may be obtained at www.ssa.gov or by calling 1-800-772-

1213. To apply, you will generally need your Social Security number, birth certificate or other evidence of your date of birth, W-2 or self-employment tax form and military discharge papers if you served in the military. You will also need to furnish an account number and a bank routing number to have your payments made by direct deposit.

How Your Social Security Benefits Are Taxed

The Omnibus Budget Reconciliation Act of 1993 subjects many retirees to taxation of their Social Security benefits.[a] To determine how much of your Social Security will be taxed, you must determine your provisional income. First determine your Preliminary Adjusted Gross Income (includes earnings, dividends, pensions and taxable interest). To this add interest on tax-free bonds and 50 percent of your Social Security benefits. Thus, your provisional (combined) income equals your adjusted gross income (not including Social Security), plus municipal bond income, plus one half of your Social Security benefits.

If you are married and your provisional income is under $32,000 ($25,000 for a single taxpayer), Social Security benefits are not taxable. If your provisional income is between $32,000 and $44,000 (or $25,000 and $34,000 for a single person), the taxable amount of Social Security equals the lesser of one half of Social Security benefits or one half of the difference between your provisional income and $32,000 ($25,000 if single). If your provisional income is over $44,000 ($34,000 if single), up to 85 percent of Social Security benefits are taxable. Louisiana residents are not subject to state income taxes on Social Security benefits after attaining age 65.

For example, Boudreaux and Clotile are married, have income of $31,000 and receive an additional $12,000 of Social Security benefits. Fifty percent of his Social Security benefit is $6,000. This amount is added to their income to determine their provisional income of $37,000. The amount of their Social Security that is taxed is the lesser of 50 percent of their Social Security ($12,000 x 50% = $6,000) or 50 percent of the amount of their provisional income that is in excess of the threshold amount (($37,000 - $32,000) x 50%= $2,500). Because

---

[a] Please note, changes in tax laws may occur at any time and could have a substantial impact upon each person's situation.

$2,500 is less than $6,000, only $2,500 of their Social Security benefit is taxed.

Assume Pierre is over 65, files single, utilizes the standard deduction, has a total adjusted gross income (exclusive of Social Security benefits) of $39,000 and receives $21,900 in Social Security benefits. His provisional income is $49,950 (39,000 + (21,900 x .5)). He exceeds the threshold, so taxable Social Security equals the lesser of $18,615 (85% of $21,900) or the sum of $13,558 (($49,950 - $34,000) x 85%) and $4,500. Since $18,058 is less than $18,615, the taxable amount of his Social Security benefits equals $18,058.

Retirees often attempt to maximize current income; however, maximizing current income may cause an increase in the amount of taxes and may cause taxation of Social Security benefits. Investments that produce large amounts of current income that is reinvested because it is not needed for current living expenses may be converted to tax-deferred or more tax efficient investments. Many retirees invest heavily in bonds and certificates of deposit for safety of principal. Unfortunately, the interest is included in current income each year. An alternative approach is to use a fixed annuity which may provide returns similar to certificates of deposit and protection of principal while deferring taxes on investment income. Another option is to invest for capital appreciation instead of income. Investing for capital appreciation involves more risk than fixed annuities. However, by reducing the amount of current income, taxation of Social Security benefits may be reduced or eliminated. Of course, all of these decisions are based on one's personal situation.

Effects of Earned Income on Your Social Security Benefit

Many Social Security recipients continue to work during their "retirement," either because they want to work to stay active or because they must work to make ends meet. Retirees who work and collect Social Security retirement benefits must plan their compensation carefully if they want to avoid losing some or all of their Social Security benefits.

In order to collect Social Security retirement benefits, you must be "retired." Congress has reasoned that if you earn more than a specified amount, you are not "retired" and, therefore, are subject to having some or all of your benefits eliminated. Congress does allow some earnings before benefits are reduced.

If you are under full retirement age, your Social Security will be reduced by $1 for every $2 earned over the exempt amount of $17,640 (2019). In the year you reach full retirement age, for every $3 over $46,920 (2019), $1 is withheld from your benefits until the month you reach full retirement age. Your Social Security is not reduced the month you reach full retirement age and thereafter.

A special rule applies in the year in which you retire. In the initial retirement year, no matter how much you earned for the year, no benefits will be lost for any month in which you earn $3,910 (1/12 of $46,920 (2019)) or less. One dollar in benefits will be withheld for every $3 in earnings above the limit.

For purposes of the retirement test, "earnings" are defined as "wages" earned as an employee or the "net earnings" of a self-employed person. The earnings must result from work performed after retirement. "In-kind" payments of goods or services in exchange for work are also considered earnings. However, retirement plan distributions, rents, capital gains, interest, dividends and other investment-related income do not count as "earnings" for this purpose. You are required to report estimated earnings in excess of the limits by April 15 of the following year. Benefits are then adjusted to reflect the amount owed, based on the estimate. Further adjustments may then be made based on actual results.

An example will illustrate how Social Security benefits are reduced when a retiree has "excess earnings." Boudreaux is a 63-year-old retired carpenter who receives $500 per month in social security benefits. During 2019, Boudreaux earns $21,000 for cabinets he makes and sells. Boudreaux's Social Security benefit will be reduced by $1,680 ((21,000 − 17,640)/2).

Spousal Benefits

If you have been married to your spouse for at least a year, you are eligible for spousal benefits. You need not be eligible for benefits based on your own work record to qualify for spousal benefits. If you wish to collect spousal benefits, your spouse needs to have filed for benefits, but need not be receiving benefits. At full retirement age, spousal benefits are equal to 50 percent of the worker's primary insurance amount. If a spouse collects benefits prior to full retirement age (must be at least age 62), spousal benefits will be reduced.

Taking Social Security Benefits Early

When planning and investing for retirement, you must address the decision of when to begin taking Social Security benefits. The decision of when to begin Social Security should not be taken lightly as your choice will affect your level of retirement income. Because the decision to take early benefits may also affect your surviving spouse's benefit, the circumstances of your spouse must also be considered. According to the Social Security Administration, approximately 74 percent of Americans elect to receive early Social Security benefits.[2] Factors to consider to decide when to begin Social Security include: life expectancy and health status, marital status and survivor needs, current and future income needs, other sources of income, and plans to continue working.

Three main questions are involved regarding when to take Social Security benefits

1. Is it beneficial to take early benefits at a reduced amount or wait until full retirement age to receive full benefits?

2. Should delayed retirement be selected to increase retirement benefits above full retirement benefits?

3. Would an alternative strategy such as file and suspend or claim now, claim more later result in increased lifetime benefits?

If you need the income now or expect a shortened life expectancy, the analysis can stop there. In those situations it is usually beneficial to begin Social Security at age 62.

A retired worker who is fully insured can elect to start receiving benefits at any time between age 62 and full retirement age (or later for delayed benefits). Your retirement benefit will be reduced by 5/9ths of 1 percent for every month between your retirement date and your full retirement age, up to 36 months, then by 5/12ths of 1 percent thereafter.

If your full retirement age is age 66, beginning at 62 will cause your benefits to be permanently reduced by approximately 25 percent. Furthermore, for those born after 1937 who choose to begin receiving benefits at age 62, the reduction-in-benefits penalty is increased from 25 percent to an eventual 30 percent. As a result if your full retirement age is 67, electing to receive benefits at age 62 will cause a 30 percent reduction in benefits.

The retiree who decides to receive early benefits may receive over three years of payments that someone who waits until full retirement age will never receive. Thus, it will take some time for the total benefits of the person who waits until full retirement age to catch up to those of the early retiree. Furthermore, for those born after 1937, full retirement age is being extended. Full retirement age is raised gradually until it reaches 67 in 2027. Thus, the recipient of early retirement benefits will receive even more payments than the retiree who waits for full benefits.

Most retirees elect to begin Social Security retirement benefits as early as possible. A number of studies have been performed which help provide insight on the effects of taking early, normal or late Social Security retirement benefits. There is no substitute for a case-by-case analysis of the optimal date to begin Social Security benefits. Unless early retirement benefits are favored due to health reasons (i.e. an anticipated less than average life expectancy) or because the income is needed at age 62, it may be financially beneficial to elect normal or delayed Social Security retirement benefits rather than early retirement.[3] This is due to a higher monthly benefit as a result of waiting to begin Social Security. If you elect to receive early Social Security benefits, it will take anywhere from 11 to 15 years (or more) after full retirement age to reach your break-even point. Several factors will influence the amount of time it takes to break-even. In addition to payments and cost of living adjustments, taxation of benefits; whether the early retirement benefits are invested or spent; benefit reduction due to earned income; and spousal benefits influence the break-even age. Considering only the accumulated value of payments reveals a break-even point of 77 years of age for early benefit takers. If we consider payments and cost of living adjustments, another study showed that the break-even age generally ranges from age 73 and 4 months, to age 74 and 7 months.[4] Breakeven age is further reduced if spousal benefits are included. After the breakeven age is attained, your total payments would be greater if you waited until full retirement age to begin Social Security payments. Thus, if you are in good health and foresee another 15 or more years of retirement after age 65, it may be beneficial to defer taking benefits until full retirement age.

The calculations get a bit more complicated if we consider factors beyond the accumulation values and cost of living adjustments. A more sophisticated analysis includes taxes, investment returns, and inflation. If your Social Security benefits are reduced due to earned income prior to full retirement age, the reduction in benefits should be included in the analysis. In addition, if the calculation assumes the early retirement benefits are invested, it pushes back the breakeven point. Another consideration is whether your Social Security benefits will be taxed. So taxes, inflation, investment return, and earned income add to the uncertainty of an unknown life expectancy when deciding whether to begin benefits at age 62. These additional factors can push the break-even age to as late as 81 to 86½ years of age.[5] If the early benefits are invested, one study found that the rate of return on the invested early benefits must generally exceed the rate of inflation by 5 percent or more to justify taking benefits at age 62 rather than at full retirement age. Higher inflation and marginal tax rates required higher rates of return (7 or 8 percent above inflation) to justify taking benefits at age 62. This study assumed the worker was the only person on the account, and the earnings test did not apply.[6]

There is also the possibility that working an extra three years may increase your Social Security benefits. This is so because additional earnings will be credited toward your Social Security account. Chances are that older low-earning years will be replaced in the benefit equation with a current higher earning year. The result is a higher Social Security benefit that will reduce the catch-up period to your breakeven point between early retirement and waiting until normal retirement age.

If you are in good health and have a family history of a long life expectancy, you should carefully weigh the decision to begin Social Security payments at age 62. Each year you live past the breakeven age, the more advantageous it is to have waited until full retirement age. In addition, because spousal benefits are based on your primary worker's benefit (based on a reduced Primary Insurance Amount (PIA)), beginning Social Security at age 62 will forever reduce your spouse's benefit. If you take early Social Security retirement benefits and die sooner, rather than later, your surviving spouse will be left with reduced spousal benefits.[7] Women have an additional consideration;

their average life expectancy is about three years longer than that for men. Therefore, women are more likely than men to live beyond the breakeven age and may benefit by not taking early retirement.[8] Longevity favors postponing Social Security benefits.

Of course, a universal rule for when to begin Social Security benefits is impractical. A combination of factors come into play, including your early retirement benefits breakeven point, your spouse's dependency on survivor benefits, the length of retirement, and the need to begin Social Security benefits at age 62. Depending upon your circumstances, it might make sense to begin taking benefits as soon as possible regardless of the net economic benefit in the future. For example, you may begin Social Security at age 62 because you cannot forego the current income. In that situation, breakeven analysis is a moot point. It may be necessary to begin Social Security at age 62 to help prevent prematurely drawing down your investment portfolio. However, if you continue working past age 62 or have sufficient assets or income to wait until full retirement age, it may make economic sense not to take early Social Security benefits. Obviously a detailed analysis of when you should begin Social Security benefits is required to factor in all of your circumstances.

Delayed Retirement Benefits

Another option available to you is delayed retirement. If you wait until age 70 to receive Social Security retirement benefits, you will receive higher benefits for waiting. Not including cost of living adjustments, the increase in benefits is 32 percent from full retirement age to age 70.[b] Studies have shown that gains from delaying benefits may be particularly large for primary earners in married couples due to the increase in survivor benefits that the secondary earner would receive in the event of widowhood.[9] People in the highest income tax bracket or with a family history of longevity may benefit by waiting for the larger payments. The decision and the benefit of delaying is dependent upon many of the same factors as the decision to take early retirement benefits. A straightforward calculation considering only the accumulation values show that a 66-year-old individual who waits until age 70 to begin taking maximum Social Security payments won't

---

[b] If full retirement age is age 66.

recoup the forgone money until they approach their early 80s. Other studies considering taxes, inflation and investment returns determined breakeven ranged from age 84 to age 87.[10]

Here's how the math works. Assume Thibodaux is age 66 and has attained full retirement age. Also assume that he would receive the maximum Social Security retirement benefit of $2,000, or $24,000 per year if he begins benefits at full retirement age. If Thibodaux opts to take late Social Security retirement benefits, he would earn a retirement benefit credit that amounts to an increase of 8.0 percent a year. By waiting until age 70 to start collecting, monthly retirement benefits increase to about $2,640, or slightly more than $31,680 a year—a 32 percent increase. But deferring payments means forgoing $96,000 he would have received during the wait until age 70. Although monthly income increases by $640 at age 70, it would take over 12 years to earn back the forgone payments. At the time of breaking even, Thibodaux would be over age 81. As with the analysis of taking early benefits or waiting until full retirement age, taxes, cost of living adjustments, whether the benefits are spent or invested, and spousal benefits impact the break-even point. Again, do not underestimate the impact of cost of living adjustments. These periodic increases continue to accrue while benefits are deferred. The larger monthly amounts to be received in the future will receive larger cost of living adjustments, in absolute numbers.

And as mentioned before, if longevity runs in your family, delaying benefits for a larger future check could make sense. As with all Social Security benefit decisions, each situation needs to be evaluated individually. Some retirees cannot forego the income until age 70 regardless of the long-term financial benefit. Delaying retirement benefits may significantly increase the survivor benefit and may be used in the file and suspend and claim now, claim more later strategies. The bottom line is the decision whether to delay benefits should be made only as part of a thorough retirement cash flow analysis.

File and Suspend Strategy

The Bipartisan Budget Act of 2015 eliminated the file and suspend strategy beginning April 30, 2016. The new rules suspend all benefits payable to other individuals based on the retiree's record; therefore, a spouse cannot receive a spousal benefit when their spouse has suspended their own benefits. As a result, the file and suspend strategy is no longer available after April 30, 2016. File and suspend strategies elected on or before April 29, 2016, will be grandfathered. Individuals attaining full retirement age on or before April 29, 2016, may elect the file and suspend strategy. Individuals born May 1, 1950 or later will not be eligible for the file and suspend strategy.

The file and suspend strategy for claiming Social Security benefits provides additional planning options if eligible and elected prior to April 30, 2016. A worker <u>who has reached full retirement age</u> but does not want to begin collecting benefits at that time may file for retirement benefits and immediately suspend their benefits. By filing for benefits, the worker's eligible spouse may file a restricted application for spousal benefits based on their spouse's earnings record. This strategy is often used when one spouse has a significantly lower earnings record (or no earnings record) and would receive a higher retirement benefit based on his or her spouse's earnings record. The spouse who filed for benefits and immediately suspended their benefits may accrue delayed retirement credits until age 70. This strategy allows the spouse with the higher earnings record to increase their retirement benefit by as much as 32 percent (excluding cost of living adjustments). The spouse with the lower earning's record immediately receives a higher spousal benefit. An additional benefit of this strategy is an increased survivor benefit for the spouse with the lower earnings record.

For example, Pierre is at full retirement age and he files for and immediately suspends his benefits. Pierre's retirement benefit at full retirement age is $2,200 per month. His wife, Clotile, has a retirement benefit at full retirement age of $500 per month based on her earnings record. Because Clotile is 62, her benefits are permanently reduced to $375 ($500 x .75) if she files for benefits.[c] By delaying his benefits until age 70, Pierre will increase his retirement benefits to $2,904 per month (a 32 percent increase excluding cost of living adjustments). Clotile will receive spousal retirement benefits of $1,100 per month versus $375 per month based on her earnings record. She will also be eligible for a higher survivor benefit if Pierre predeceases her. The

---

[c] If you are under full retirement age when you select a spousal benefit, you are deemed to be taking a benefit based on your own record - even if it is a spousal benefit. Thus, you will have a permanently reduced benefit due to beginning benefits prior to full retirement age.

strategy works best for one earner couples or those in which one spouse's earnings record is smaller in comparison to the other spouse.

Claim Now, Claim More Later

Pursuant to the Bipartisan Budget Act of 2015, when either spouse files for benefits, the spouse is deemed to file for their benefits and spousal benefits. Under Social Security rules, a spouse will receive the higher of their benefits or spousal benefits. As a result a spouse will no longer be able to file for spousal benefits and then switch to their own higher benefit later. Individuals born in 1953 or earlier are grandfathered and may file a restricted application.[d] Individuals born January 2, 1954, or later are not eligible to file a restricted application and the claim now, claim more later strategy is unavailable.

This strategy is typically used where both spouses have a significant earnings record. In addition, the more equal the lifetime earnings of the spouses, the more they have to gain from this strategy.[11] This strategy works by one spouse, after reaching full retirement age, filing a restricted application for spousal benefits and delaying the filing for his or her own retirement benefit until age 70. This strategy allows delayed retirement benefits to accrue while not postponing benefits altogether.

For example Pierre files for his own retirement benefits of $2,300 per month at full retirement age. His wife Clotile wishes to delay filing for her own benefit until she reaches age 70. When Clotile reaches full retirement age, she can file for spousal benefits based on Pierre's earnings record and will receive $1,150 per month (50 percent of Pierre's benefit). By delaying her filing for benefits based on her own earnings record ($2,200 per month at full retirement age) until age 70, Clotile's benefit will increase to $2,904 per month (excluding cost of living adjustments). At age 70, Clotile switches from a spousal benefit to her own larger retirement benefit. If Pierre survives Clotile, his survivor benefits will also be increased due to Clotile's higher benefit amount.

If both spouses have attained full retirement age, another option is available to allow both spouses to earn delayed retirement credits while one spouse receives a benefit. One spouse files and suspends their

---

[d] Individuals born on January 1, 1954 attains 62 as of December 31, 2015 for the purposes of Social Security.

benefit. The other spouse files a restricted application for spousal benefits. Now both spouses are earning delayed retirement credits. After the spouses attain age 70, the spouse who filed and suspended benefits receives their delayed retirement benefit. The spouse who filed the restricted application for spousal benefits switches to their own delayed retirement benefit. Both spouses receive a 32% increase in their full retirement age benefit (excluding cost of living adjustments).

Survivor Benefits

Your surviving spouse and children are eligible for survivor benefits after your death. Eligible family members receive survivor benefits based on your work credits. Younger workers must work fewer years to qualify; however, no one needs to work more than 10 years. A spouse's survivor benefits are 100 percent of their deceased spouse's benefits and are reduced if claimed prior to full retirement age. In addition, a one-time payment of $255 may be paid to your surviving spouse or minor children upon your death. This payment is to offset funeral expenses. Survivor benefits include the following:

- Your surviving spouse may receive reduced benefits at age 60 or age 50 if disabled. If born prior to 1940, full benefits are available at age 65. If your surviving spouse is born in or after 1940, the required age to receive full survivor benefits is gradually increased to age 67.

- If your surviving spouse is taking care of your child who is age 16 or younger or who is disabled, he or she may receive survivor benefits at any age. The surviving spouse must be unmarried and not already eligible for widow(er)'s benefits.

- Your unmarried children under age 18 are eligible for survivor benefits. Benefits extend to age 19 if your child is a full-time high school student.

- Your unmarried children who were disabled prior to age 22 and remain disabled are eligible for survivor benefits.

- Your surviving parents who are dependent on you for at least one-half of their support are eligible for Social Security survivor benefits.

If your surviving spouse is already receiving retirement benefits based on his or her work history, your surviving spouse will receive the greater of survivor benefits or retirement benefits. Retirement benefits based on your spouse's work history are converted to survivor benefits upon your death (if survivor benefits are greater than your spouse's retirement benefits). If your surviving spouse is at full retirement age, he or she will receive 100 percent of your basic benefit amount. Therefore, survivor benefits may be maximized by the working spouse not taking early retirement benefits as the working spouse's basic benefit amount is increased.[12] If your surviving spouse works and is age 60 or older but less than full retirement age, he or she receives a reduced amount. If your surviving spouse is caring for a child under age 16, he or she receives 75 percent of your basic benefit amount. Finally, your children receive 75 percent of your basic benefit amount. Benefits to your family are limited to between 150 percent and 180 percent of your basic benefit amount.

Benefits may be reduced for your surviving spouse if he or she is under full retirement age and he or she exceeds the earned income threshold. Benefits are reduced similar to the reduction in retirement benefits.

The Effects of Remarriage

A surviving spouse who remarries prior to age 60 loses the survivor's benefit; however, at age 62, a remarried spouse may be eligible for benefits on account of their new spouse.

If a surviving spouse remarries after age 60, he or she retains survivor benefits from their deceased spouse. If the new spouse's dependent benefits are greater than the survivor benefits, the surviving spouse should switch to the new spouse's dependent benefits.

If a person was divorced from a now deceased former spouse, survivor benefits are available even if the survivor remarried prior to age 60 if he or she is again divorced or widowed. The marriage, however, must have lasted for at least 10 years. After age 60, remarriage will not prevent the survivor's benefit.

Disability Benefits

Disabled workers may qualify for Social Security disability benefits. To qualify, workers must have earned at least 20 of the required work credits within the 10 years immediately prior to disability. Workers under the age of 31 are required to earn a reduced number of work credits to qualify for disability benefits.

Disability means a physical or mental disability that is expected to last or has lasted at least one year or is expected to result in death and prevents the worker from performing any substantial gainful work. Substantial gainful work is any work from which the worker earns $1,220 (2019) or more per month. Therefore, even though a worker may not be able to perform the duties to his or her usual job, he or she may be able to perform another job considered gainful work.

Disability benefits are converted to retirement benefits once the disabled worker attains full retirement age.

Eligibility for More Than One Benefit

Often, more than one benefit is available to an individual. For example, someone may be eligible for Social Security retirement benefits based on his or her own work history and for retirement benefits based on his or her spouse's work history. They should obviously choose the higher benefit. If an individual is receiving survivor benefits at age 60, he or she may switch to retirement benefits at age 62 based on his or her own work history if it provides a higher benefit.

The Windfall Elimination Provision

Retirees receiving a public retirement pension based on their earnings which were not covered by Social Security may have their Social Security retirement benefits reduced due to the Windfall Elimination Provision. The Windfall Elimination Provision adjusts the Social Security Primary Insurance Amount (PIA) formula for retirees who have both Social Security benefits and an uncovered pension. The Windfall Elimination Provision (WEP) reduces the Social Security benefit if the retiree has less than 30 years of "substantial earnings" on which Social Security taxes were paid. Substantial earnings increases annually and for 2019 is $24,675. The WEP does not apply to survivor benefits; however, it does apply to disabled worker beneficiaries and dependent beneficiaries of affected workers. Almost three-fourths of workers affected by the WEP were subject to the maximum PIA reduction[13, 14].

The Government Pension Offset

Pension recipients of an uncovered retirement system who are eligible for spousal or survival Social Security benefits may have their Social Security spousal or survivor benefits reduced by the Government Pension Offset. The Government Pension Offset (GPO) reduces Social Security spousal benefits by two-thirds of the pension amount and may result in a reduction of Social Security benefit to zero. For example, Clotile worked as a school teacher and receives a monthly pension of $1200. Her husband, Pierre, receives a Social Security benefit of $1400 per month based on his Primary Insurance Amount. Since two-thirds of Clotile's pension ($800) is more than her Social Security spousal benefit which is one-half of Pierre's Primary Insurance Amount ($700), Clotile's spousal Social Security benefit is reduced to zero. The GPO does not affect everyone, and it does not affect Medicare. Furthermore, the GPO only applies to a pension payable to a spouse based on his or her earnings; therefore, it does not apply to public retirement survivor benefits.

The impact of the WEP and the GPO can dramatically reduce the anticipated Social Security benefit. Relying solely on the Social Security statement will not indicate that the WEP and GPO will result in a reduction of benefits. Therefore if you are eligible for Social Security benefits and an uncovered pension, you should determine the impact of the WEP and GPO early during the retirement planning process. Learning about these reductions to Social Security benefits at retirement can be a devastating revelation.

---

[1] Social Security Administration.

[2] Social Security Administration Annual Statistical Supplement, 2012.

[3] Robert Muksuan, Ph.D., The Effect of Retirement Under Social Security at Age 62, Journal of Financial Planning, January 2004.

[4] Robert Muksuan, Ph.D., The Effect of Retirement Under Social Security at Age 62, Journal of Financial Planning, January 2004.

[5] Doug Lemmons, When to Start Collecting Social Security Benefits: A Break-Even Analysis. Journal of Financial Planning, Jan., 2012.

[6] Id.

[7] Robert Muksuan, Ph.D., The Effect of Retirement Under Social Security at Age 62, Journal of Financial Planning, January 2004.

[8] Alicia H. Munnell and Mauricio Soto, When Should Women Claim Social Security Benefits?, Journal of Financial Planning, June 2007.

[9] John B. Shoven, Ph.D. and Sita Nataraj Slavov, Ph.D., Recent Changes in the Gains from Delaying Social Security, Journal of Financial Planning, March 2014.

[10] Doug Lemmons, When to Start Collecting Social Security Benefits: A Break-Even Analysis. Journal of Financial Planning, January, 2012.

[11] Alicia H. Munnell, Ph.D, Alex Golub-Sass, and Nadia S. Karamcheva, Ph.D., Understanding Unusual Social Security Claiming Strategies, Journal of Financial Planning, August 2013.

[12] Alicia H. Munnell and Mauricio Soto, When Should Women Claim

Social Security Benefits?, Journal of Financial Planning, June 2007.
[13] Barbara Lingg, Social Security Beneficiaries Affected by the Windfall Elimination Provision in 2006, Social Security Bulletin, 68, 2008.
[14] Joseph P. McCormack, Ph.D., CFA, and Grady Perdue, Ph.D., CFP, Potentially Devastating Social Security Offsets, Journal of Financial Planning, November 2009.
Social Security: The Windfall Elimination Provision (WEP), Congressional Research Service, June 30, 2015.

13

Medicare

Chapter Highlights

❖ Medicare is a federal health insurance program for people over age 65, people with certain disabilities and people with end-stage renal disease. Medicare consists of Parts A, B, C, and D.

❖ You are eligible for Part A if you are age 65 or older and receiving Social Security benefits.

❖ Medicare Part A covers inpatient (overnight) hospital care which includes stays in a hospital, psychiatric hospital or skilled nursing facility. In addition, Part A covers home healthcare and hospice care. Medicare Part A is free to eligible individuals.

❖ Medicare Part B covers non-inpatient medical care including physician and surgeon fees, outpatient services, laboratory services, ambulance service and blood.

❖ Medicare Part C allows you to receive care through private, fee-for-service plans, managed health care plans (HMOs) and preferred provider organizations (PPOs). Part C is an alternative to Parts A and B.

❖ Medicare Part D provides prescription drug coverage if you are eligible for Medicare Plan A and enrolled in Part B.

❖ Medigap is insurance that fills the coverage gaps in Medicare coverage.

MEDICARE IS A federal health insurance program for people over age 65, people with certain disabilities and people with end-stage renal disease. The Medicare program is overseen by The Centers for Medicare and Medicaid Services (CMS), but the Social Security Administration processes Medicare applications and claims. Services covered by the Medicare program are provided by private companies under contract with the federal government. In fact, much of your contact is with the private company (e.g. Blue Cross/Blue Shield). Medicare consists of four parts: Parts A (hospitalization); Part B (outpatient services and physicians' services); Part C or Medicare Advantage (managed care); and Part D (prescription drug coverage).

Eligibility

If you are age 65 or older and receiving Social Security benefits, you are eligible for Part A. In addition, your surviving spouse or dependents are eligible for Part A once you attain age 65 and are entitled to Medicare Part A. Your dependents are eligible for Part A if you are under age 65 and are entitled to Social Security retirement benefits. Individuals of any age receiving Social Security disability benefits for 24 months or those with end-stage renal disease are also eligible for Part A.

You are automatically enrolled in Medicare at age 65 if you receive early Social Security retirement benefits or if you apply for Social Security retirement benefits at age 65. If you are over age 65 and are not eligible for free Part A coverage, you may enroll in Part A and pay a monthly premium. Eligibility for Part B requires only that you attain age 65 and be a United States citizen or have resided lawfully in the United States for the past five years. The Social Security Administration will send notification of enrollment to you if you are automatically enrolled. Notification is sent three months prior to age 65. You must remember to enroll in Medicare if you retire after age 65 because enrollment in Medicare is not automatic for individuals retiring after age 65. The Social Security Administration can provide additional information regarding enrollment and eligibility.

Your employer-sponsored health insurance may end when you attain age 65. Some employer-sponsored health plans pay for Medicare co-pays and deductibles as well as for services Medicare does not cover.

Medicare Part A: Hospital Insurance

Medicare Part A covers inpatient (overnight) hospital care which includes stays in a hospital, psychiatric hospital or skilled nursing facility. In addition, Part A covers home healthcare and hospice care. Medicare Part A is free to eligible individuals.

Inpatient Hospital Care

Medicare uses a benefit period or spell of illness to determine coverage. A benefit period begins on the day you enter the hospital as an inpatient and continues until you have been out for 60 consecutive days. The Part A deductible per benefit period is $1,364 (2019). After the deductible is paid for each benefit period, Medicare will pay the entire cost of the first 60 days of inpatient hospital care. After 60 days elapses, Medicare beneficiaries must pay coinsurance of $341 per day (2019) for an additional 30 days. In addition, a Medicare beneficiary has a lifetime reserve of 60 days. When the reserved days are used, Medicare beneficiaries pay $682 per day (2019) for days 91 to 150. After 150 days of inpatient care for a spell of illness, Medicare benefits are exhausted.

Medicare Part A covers the cost of a semiprivate room, meals, nursing services, laboratory tests, x-rays, medications, equipment and supplies, operating room charges and physical and speech therapy. Physicians' bills are covered by Part B not Part A. Services from a psychiatric hospital are generally covered in a similar fashion to inpatient hospital care.

Skilled Nursing Facility Care

A skilled nursing facility provides medically necessary nursing care but is distinguished from a nursing home which provides custodial care (assistance with activities of daily living)[a]. Coverage in a skilled nursing facility includes a semi-private room, meals, rehabilitation and medications. Prior to admission to a skilled nursing facility, you must have been an inpatient in the hospital for a minimum of three consecutive days. In addition, care in a skilled nursing facility requires

---

[a] Activities of Daily Living include bathing, continence, dressing, eating, toileting and transferring. Cognitive impairment includes memory loss, orientation difficulty and reasoning impairment.

certification that daily skilled care is necessary and that it can only be provided in a skilled nursing facility. Finally, admission to a skilled nursing facility must be within 30 days of discharge from the hospital. Skilled nursing care is limited to 100 days per benefit period. In addition, a coinsurance payment of $170.00 per day (2019) is required after 20 days in a skilled nursing facility.

Home HealthCare

Home healthcare coverage by Medicare requires that you be confined to your home, that your physician approves the care as medically necessary and that care is provided by a Medicare-approved agency. Coverage is provided for nursing services, speech therapy, physical therapy and occupational therapy. Home healthcare does not cover care that is primarily custodial.

Hospice Care

Hospice care is care for the terminally ill (having a life expectancy of six months or less). Coverage includes nursing care, medical equipment and supplies, medications, home health aide, homemaker services and medical social services. To receive coverage for hospice care, your doctor and the hospice care director must certify that you are terminally ill. In addition, you must elect hospice coverage instead of standard Medicare benefits.

Medicare Part B: Medical Coverage

If you are over age 65 and are a United States citizen or have resided lawfully in the United States for five consecutive years, you are eligible to enroll in Part B. The monthly premium for Part B is $135.50 (2019).[b] Single Medicare beneficiaries with modified adjusted gross income above $85,000 ($170,000 for married filing jointly beneficiaries) pay higher premiums for Part B.[c] In addition, you are required to pay an annual deductible of $185 (2019) and usually 20 percent of the medical costs. Part B covers non-inpatient medical care including physician and surgeon fees, outpatient services, laboratory services, ambulance service and blood (after the first three pints).

---

[b] Individuals subject to the Social Security hold harmless provision will pay 134.00.
[c] These thresholds apply through 2019.

Medicare Part B will also cover certain preventative services. Services that are not considered reasonable or medically necessary are not covered by Medicare Part B, such as cosmetic surgery, hearing aids, most eyeglasses and eye exams, most dentures and dental care, experimental procedures, self-administered prescription drugs and most chiropractic services.

Medicare Part C

Medicare Part C is also known as Medicare Advantage and is an alternative to Part A and Part B. Under Medicare Part A, you may choose any doctor who accepts Medicare (a private fee-for-service plan or PFFS). Under Part C, private health insurers offer Medicare benefits through their own policies. Part C allows you to receive care through private-fee-for-service plans, managed health care plans (HMOs) and preferred provider organizations (PPOs). Through Part C, insurance companies may offer benefits that were not available under Part A; however, an additional premium may be charged for these additional options. Overall, Part C offers more healthcare options with cost structure flexibility. In fact, overall cost may be lower than with Parts A and B. Factors to consider when evaluating a Medicare Advantage plan are premium cost, amount of deductibles, co-pays and coinsurance, and available healthcare providers participating in the plan.

To enroll in a Medicare Advantage plan, you must be eligible for Part A and enrolled in Part B. The plan must also be available in your area. If you join a new Medicare Advantage plan, you are automatically dis-enrolled from your current plan. You may join and leave a Medicare Advantage plan at any time.

Medicare Part D

Medicare Part D provides prescription drug coverage if you are eligible for Medicare Plan A and enrolled in Part B. In addition, Medicare Advantage provides prescription drug coverage through HMO, PPO or PFFS plans. Part D replaces drug coverage through medigap plans, Medicare discount cards and most Medicaid prescription drug coverage. Private companies offering Part D may design their own plan so long as certain guidelines are met. Although the cost for Part D will vary depending on the plan, the national average monthly premium was $32.50 (2019). In addition, there is an annual deductible that cannot exceed $415 (2019). Co-insurance varies by plan and by drug within each plan. After total drug costs reach $3,820 (2019), there is a coverage gap. During the coverage gap, you pay a portion of your prescription drug cost. When your out-of-pocket drug expenses during the donut hole (the coverage gap) reach $5,100[d], you switch to catastrophic coverage. During catastrophic coverage you pay 5% of each drug, or $3.30 for generics and $8.25 for brand-name drugs (whichever is greater).

These costs and limits are subject to change each year. When deciding which Part D plan to join, consider the prescription medications that are covered by each plan (the formulary). Obviously, a plan that does not cover your required medications is useless to you. Also consider the premium cost, deductibles and co-payments.

Medigap

Medigap coverage, as the name implies, fills the gaps in Medicare coverage. There are 12 Medigap policies (Plans A through L) which all provide basic benefits. Additional benefits are provided by different plans with various cost structures. For example, Medigap Plan A pays for Part A coinsurance and for 365 additional days of hospital care after Medicare coverage ends. Medigap Plan A also pays for Part B coinsurance and the first three pints of blood. Medigap Plans B through L cover various combinations of deductibles, co-payments, certain preventative care and care while out of the country. Additional benefits will add to the plan's cost.

---

[d] The $5,100 does not include monthly premiums, cost of drugs not listed in your plan, drugs purchased at pharmacies outside of your plan's network, or the 35% discount on generic drugs.

14

Long-Term Care Insurance

Chapter Highlights

❖ You should take steps to protect your assets, in particular your retirement assets, from the devastating effects of an extended long-term care stay for you or your spouse.

❖ A primary goal of long-term care planning is to protect the financial resources of your spouse and your family.

❖ Long-term care is non-acute, out-of-hospital care for individuals who cannot perform two or more activities of daily living and for physical illness, disability or cognitive impairment.

❖ Approximately 44 percent of people reaching age 65 are expected to enter a nursing home at least once in their lifetime. Of those entering a nursing home, approximately 53 percent will stay one year or more.[1]

❖ The average nursing home stay is 2.4 years. Of those entering a nursing home, 10% will stay five years or longer.

❖ In Louisiana, nursing home expenses for a semi-private room can easily cost in excess of $5,000-6000 per month.

❖ If you have significant assets to protect and meet the medical underwriting requirements, long-term care insurance can provide the most options and the best protection against long-term care expenses.

❖ Premiums for long-term care insurance may be tax deductible.

❖ Financial strength of the issuing company is an important criterion when choosing a long-term care policy.

❖ The company's history of rate increases is also important. If the initial premium seems too low in comparison to similar policies, the company may have a history of rate increases.

❖ Long-term care policy costs will vary according to your age, your health, the daily benefit amount, length of benefit period, elimination period, inflation riders and numerous additional features and benefits that may be added.

❖ Partnership Long-Term Care Policies are designed to help individuals pay for long-term care expenses and minimize the risk of Medicaid spend-down by allowing increased asset exemption levels for Medicaid applicants.

❖ Asset-based long-term care insurance, like traditional long-term care insurance, pays for long-term care expenses. However, if you never need long-term care, it pays a death benefit to the beneficiary of your choice. Asset-based long-term care insurance provides an alternative to paying premiums for insurance you may not use.

PROTECTING ASSETS FROM the devastating effects of long-term care expenses is one of the most important wealth preservation and wealth transfer issues facing retirees. Understanding the risks and the options available to you will allow you to make informed long-term care decisions. Most individuals have accumulated assets to fund their retirement; however, failing to protect these assets from long-term care expenses may result in not having sufficient resources to live through retirement.

To protect your family, you should plan for the possibility of a long-term care need. Long-term care insurance is primarily for your family's benefit, not yours. For example, married couples must protect assets from these expenses because the odds are significant that at least one spouse will require long-term care. If the assets earmarked for retirement are consumed to pay for your long-term care expenses, which assets will your spouse use to produce retirement income on which to live? In addition, you may have accumulated significant assets that you wish to eventually pass on to your children or grandchildren. Without proper planning, these assets may be depleted or significantly reduced by long-term care expenses.

In addition, long-term care insurance can provide resources to hire professional help and can prevent your family from having to provide around-the-clock care. Do not underestimate the emotional drain on your family and the sacrifices they will make by providing care. Most individuals wish to avoid a nursing home, but unfortunately, this is the end result without sufficient resources to hire caregivers or available family members to provide care in your home.

What is Long-Term Care?

Long-term care is non-acute, out-of-hospital care for individuals who cannot perform two or more activities of daily living and for physical illness, disability or cognitive impairment. Long-term care may be provided in your home, in a nursing home or in an assisted-living facility.

Regular health insurance and Medicare generally do not pay for long-term care services. As a result, if you do not have long-term care insurance, you will pay out of pocket and are at risk of depleting all or a significant portion of your retirement assets from an extended long-term care stay.

Three levels of long-term care exist. Skilled care is continuous, around-the-clock care which is ordered by a doctor and delivered by a skilled medical worker. Intermediate care is care that is needed daily or a few times a week, is provided by trained medical workers and is doctor supervised. Custodial or personal care is care provided to assist someone in performing activities of daily living (ADLs). ADLs include bathing, continence, dressing, eating, toileting and transferring. Cognitive impairment includes memory loss, orientation difficulty and reasoning impairment. Unlike skilled care, custodial care may be performed by unskilled persons.

Will You Need Long-Term Care?

Although you can never be certain that you will or will not need long-term care, recent studies can put the risks and probabilities of needing long-term care into perspective.

- Life expectancy after age 65 is 19.1 years.[2] With advances in medical technology, we are continuing to live longer. The longer a person lives, the greater the chances are they will need long-term care.

- Approximately 44 percent of people reaching age 65 are expected to enter a nursing home at least once in their lifetime. Of those entering a nursing home, approximately 53 percent will stay one year or more.[3]

- Other studies suggest that there is a 10 percent probability of a 65-year-old spending five or more years in a nursing home.[4]

- One study determined that over 20 percent of individuals aged 85-94 spend more than five years in a nursing home.[5]

- The average stay for a nursing home resident is 2.4 years.[6]

As you can see, the odds are significant that you will need long-term care at some time in your life. Due to the devastating financial effects of an extended long-term care need, it is prudent to know your options for protecting against this risk.

How Much Does Long-Term Care Cost?

The average cost for nursing home care in Louisiana can easily run in excess of $5,000 per month. Thus, the average long-term care stay may cost $144,000 ($5,000 x 12 x 2.4 years). A 60-year-old who is admitted to a nursing home today may, in 25 years, experience an average total cost of twice this amount (assuming a 3 percent inflation rate). Because these are the averages, some will experience lower costs while others will experience much higher costs for long-term care. Furthermore, if an individual moves to another state to retire and/or to live closer to their children, the cost may be two or three times this amount.

Louisiana has some of the lowest nursing home costs in the nation. The average semi-private daily room rate in Louisiana is $172 (2018) The average private daily room rate in Louisiana is $182 (2018). Obviously, some facilities had lower rates, and others had significantly higher rates. The national average for a semi-private room in 2018 was $245 ($89,297 annually). The national average for a private room in 2018 was $275 ($100,375 annually).

Many long-term care insurance policies also cover home care costs. In Louisiana, the average cost for a home health aide is $16 per hour. In 2018, the average cost for around the clock home health aide in Louisiana was $11,520 per month. Some people will require home health aide assistance for only part of the day which will reduce the cost. Most people prefer to stay in their home rather than in a long-term care facility; however, the cost for home health aide around the clock care can easily exceed the cost of a long-term care facility.

The cost for private long-term care insurance for a couple in their mid 60s in good health may cost $3000 a year or more. However, with the potential cost of an extended long-term care stay costing $250,000 or more, insuring against this risk requires serious consideration. Unfortunately, the underwriting guidelines preclude individuals with certain health issues from qualifying for long-term care insurance, and for many people, it is simply cost prohibitive.

If you have significant assets to protect and meet the medical underwriting requirements, long-term care insurance can provide the most options and protection against long-term care expenses. Long-term care insurance usually allows you to receive care in your home or in a long-term care facility. The main disadvantage of long-term care insurance is the premium cost. The cost goes up if the policy is issued for an older insured versus a younger insured assuming all else is equal. After the policy is in force, your premiums cannot be increased because of your age or changes in your health. However, the insurance company may increase the premiums for an entire class of insured. Procrastination can be dangerous when it comes to long-term care insurance. Waiting to purchase long-term care insurance may cause the premiums to become too expensive in later years, or you may later develop a medical condition and fail to meet the underwriting requirements.

Tax-Qualified and Non-tax-Qualified Plans

Many types of long-term care policies are offered, and many features and benefits may be added to each policy, so doing your homework is a must. The first question to ask is whether the policy is tax qualified or non-tax qualified. Most policies issued today are tax qualified. The Health Insurance Portability and Accountability Act (HIPPA) established the differences between the two types of policies, and a tax-qualified policy is clearly advantageous. Policies purchased prior to January 1, 1997, are generally grandfathered and considered tax-qualified, even if they do not meet all of the criteria required of a newly issued tax-qualified policy.

To be tax-qualified, the policy must be guaranteed renewable with a benefits trigger for policy holders who are chronically ill. "Chronically ill" is defined as an inability to perform at least two activities of daily living or the need for substantial supervision to protect health and safety due to cognitive impairment.

The benefits triggers are events that cause a long-term care policy to pay a benefit for eligible services. Activities of Daily Living (ADLs) are the most common benefits triggers. A policy that is "tax qualified" must use a benefits trigger that pays a benefit upon your inability to perform at least two ADLs. In addition, your condition must be chronic (expected to last at least 90 days).

Another benefits trigger required of tax-qualified policies is cognitive impairment. This benefits trigger is satisfied if you are unable to perform specific tests of cognitive function. Alzheimer's disease and other dementia are types of cognitive impairment. Cognitive impairment is generally defined as

- A loss of short or long-term memory,

- A loss of orientation of time, place or person or

- A loss of deductive or abstract reasoning

In 2019, premiums for tax-qualified policies can be included with other medical expenses (subject to the 10 percent AGI floor) and are deductible according to the following table:

Table 8 - Long-term care premium deductions

40 or under	$420
41-50	$790
51-60	$1,580
61-70	$4,220
Over age 70	$5,270

Age is based as of the end of the tax year. Sub-Chapter C corporations are allowed a 100 percent deduction for long-term care insurance premiums.

Benefits paid by an indemnity policy are tax free. Benefits paid by an expenses-incurred policy are tax free up to the amount of the expenses incurred. Policies that are non-tax qualified may use different benefits-triggering criteria, including the requirement that care be "medically necessary." Moreover, non-tax-qualified premiums are probably not deductible, and benefits received may or may not be counted as income. This area of the law is unclear.

Types of Traditional Policies

An indemnity policy will pay the daily dollar limit of the benefits purchased once the benefits trigger and elimination periods are satisfied. For example, an indemnity policy that pays $5,000 per month will pay this amount after the policy triggers are satisfied and the elimination period has expired regardless of the actual expenses incurred. After the policy triggers are satisfied, the indemnity payments may be used to pay for expenses that the policy does not cover, such as payments for care provided by family members. Indemnity policies provide flexibility to pay for the type of care desired.

An expense-incurred (also known as a reimbursement policy) policy will pay benefits only when the insurance company determines that you are eligible for benefits and the claim is for covered services. The insurance company will pay up to the lesser of the expenses incurred for covered services or the dollar limit of the policy. If the daily limit is $5,000 per month and the claim for care is $4,500, the policy will pay $4,500. The balance remains in the pool for future claims. An advantage of an expense-incurred policy is that premium costs may be lower than for an indemnity policy. Payment for services provided by family members may not be allowed if the family member is not a "licensed provider."

Other Factors to Consider

Individuals considering long-term care insurance should learn about the long-term care insurance choices available to make the best decision for their unique situation. Some issues related to the choice of insurance plans are discussed below.

Financial Strength of the Issuing Insurance Company

It is essential that you purchase a policy from a reputable company with strong financial ratings. Financial strength is critical because the company may have to pay benefits on the policy 30-plus years in the future. A number of ratings companies exist: A.M. Best, Fitch's, Duff & Phelps, Moodys, Standard & Poors and Weiss.

The choice of a long-term care insurance company is more "permanent" than with other types of insurance. In many cases, you cannot simply switch policies if rates increase or if the insurer's financial strength weakens. You may be uninsurable at a later time, and policy premiums will be higher as you age. Company selection, therefore, is critical, and the decision should not be based on price alone.

The company's history of rate increases is also important. Although you cannot be singled out for a rate increase, the insurer can increase rates for classes of policy holders. If the initial premiums seem too low in comparison to other similar policies, either the policies are not an apples-to-apples comparison or the company issuing the cheaper policy may have a history of rate increases.

Elimination Periods

Unfortunately, most policies do not start paying a benefit immediately after the benefits trigger has been satisfied. An elimination period will delay payment of benefits for a certain number of days. The elimination period is similar to a deductible for other types of insurance. During the elimination period, you will be responsible for paying 100 percent of your long-term care expenses. Typically, the elimination period is for 30, 60, 90 or 180 days but can be from zero days to one year. A shorter elimination period will cause the premium to increase for an otherwise identical policy; however, a longer elimination period will require you to pay more out of pocket for long-term care expenses.

In addition, the elimination period may be calculated a couple of different ways. If the elimination period is calculated using days of service, only the days you receive services will count towards the elimination period. If the calendar-days method is used, every day of the week counts, including days you do not receive long-term care services. Obviously, the calendar-days method is typically more beneficial.

Some long-term care policies require that you satisfy the elimination period once in your lifetime. Others require that the elimination period be satisfied each time you require long-term care. Prior to purchasing a policy, you should have a clear understanding of how the elimination period is calculated.

Optional Riders and Optional Benefits

Many features may be added to a long-term care policy as policy riders. The following is a nonexhaustive list of some of the features and benefits that may be added to a long-term care policy. Additional features and benefits will add to the cost of the policy.

Waiver of Premium riders allow you to discontinue premium payments when benefits are received. Some policies require a waiting period until the waiver of premium becomes effective. Dual waiver of premium waives the healthy spouse's premium when the other spouse is on claim.

Nonforfeiture Riders will refund some of your premium payments or result in reduced benefits in the event the policy is cancelled or discontinued.

Premium Refund at Death pays to your estate an amount equal to the premiums paid minus benefits paid. Typically, you must pay premiums for a minimum number of years, and death must occur prior to a certain age, usually 65, 70 or 75.

Shared care allows you to use your spouse's benefits when yours are exhausted. When one spouse dies, the surviving spouse's benefit increases by the deceased spouse's remaining benefits.

Transitional Benefits pays for claims incurred during the elimination period once the elimination period is satisfied.

Bed Reservation pays to reserve your bed in a facility if you temporarily leave the facility. For example, if you are admitted to the hospital and leave the nursing facility during your hospital stay, your bed at the nursing facility will be reserved for when you return.

Respite Care pays for facility care or home- and community-based care if the primary, unpaid caregiver such as your spouse needs to take a break from care giving.

Equipment and home modification benefits pay for modification to your home and for support equipment. For example, your home may have to be modified to make it handicapped accessible.

Types of Services Covered

Different types of long-term care policies cover various types of services. Common types of services include the following:

- Residential Care Facilities provide regular assistance but do not provide continuous nursing care. Emphasis is on social and lifestyle needs.

- Alternative Care Facilities provide significant supervision and assistance but do not provide medical care.

- Nursing Facilities provide medical care around the clock.

- Custodial care is assistance with ADLs provided by a trained aide.

- Intermediate care is occasional nursing services, preventive or rehabilitative, under the supervision of skilled medical personnel.

- Skilled care is nursing assistance by trained medical personnel under the supervision of a physician.

- Home Care is assistance with ADLs provided in the home by a trained aide.

- Home Health Care is medically necessary care provided in the home and performed through a home healthcare agency.

- Adult Day Care provides services on a less than 24-hour basis by centers outside of the home to those who cannot remain alone.

- Hospice Care is provided to the terminally ill to relieve physical and emotional discomforts at home or in a certified facility.

- Independent Caregivers are licensed caregivers who are not from a home healthcare agency. Independent caregivers provide additional choices and may reduce the cost of care.

You should make a special inquiry as to what types of services are covered and have it in writing. Ideally, look for a policy that will pay for personal care in your home. Taken a step further, some policies will pay for care in your home provided for by family members. Unfortunately, many policies are more restrictive with regard to care provided in the home. For example, some policies will only pay for care in the home if the care is provided by a licensed home health agency or a licensed home care provider.

Some policies place further restrictions on the type of facility covered. If you are admitted to a facility that is not covered by the policy, benefits will not be paid for eligible services. Definitions of the types of facilities may differ from policy to policy, so make sure the policy covers all of the options with regard to your potential future care needs.

Amount of Benefit

The amount of long-term care coverage may be stated in several ways. A key issue is how much coverage you will need and how long the benefit will be paid. The policy benefit limit is generally listed as a certain dollar amount per day over a period of years (one, three, five, seven or lifetime payments).

A good starting point to determine the amount of long-term care insurance to purchase is the cost per day. Because the average nursing home cost in Louisiana is around $5,232 (2018) per month for a semi-private room, individuals in Louisiana generally choose a daily benefit of around $175. If the benefit period is seven years, the maximum lifetime benefit amount will be $445,592. Inflation adjustments would provide higher daily benefits and a larger lifetime benefit over time. The lifetime benefit amount represents a "pool" of benefits from which eligible long-term care expenses are paid at a rate not exceeding the daily benefit limit. After the "pool" of benefits is exhausted, no additional benefits are paid. If the daily expenses are less than $5,232 per month, the benefits will last longer than seven years if the policy pays benefits under expense-incurred method (reimbursement method). Extra benefits may be accumulated by the insured for future long-term care needs beyond the seven-year benefit period.

An indemnity policy with a seven-year limit will pay the benefits over seven years regardless of whether daily expenses are less than the daily benefit limit.

When purchasing a long-term care policy, you must decide what daily benefit amount and length of coverage is right for you and your family. Several factors to consider when determining how long the policy benefit should be paid include price, amount of assets that require protection, amount of pension and Social Security benefits that can be used to pay for long-term care and amount of flexibility desired from the policy. Ideally, consider purchasing a comprehensive policy with a monthly benefit of at least $5,232 payable for five years and a compound inflation rider. This type of policy can provide adequate coverage in most situations, but it is also more expensive. Other, less expensive options include purchasing a policy with a lower daily limit and/or a shorter benefit period. For example, $3,000 per month benefit amount payable for three years. Although such a policy may not cover 100 percent of your long-term care expenses, it should cover most long-term care expenses and prevent a financial disaster.

The effects of inflation must also be addressed. The policy may have to pay out a benefit many years into the future when long-term care costs have significantly increased. Without protection against these increases, a policy benefit that is adequate today may be grossly inadequate many years from now. If an inflation rider is added, the benefit amount will be increased by the inflation adjustment amount. The inflation adjustment will either be calculated at a simple or compounded rate. A compound inflation rider provides a greater amount of protection from future increases in long-term care expenses; however, it is also a more expensive rider.

Additional Considerations

Costs vary among insurance companies for different age groups. It pays to shop around. Companies also vary with regard to medical underwriting requirements. A medical condition which may cause you to be uninsurable with one company may be acceptable with another. In addition, your family's unique situation must be considered.

Here are some considerations if you are married:

- A comprehensive home care benefit is very important to allow you to receive care in your home.

- Protecting the financial resources for your spouse is critical.

- Adequate respite care benefits are important to protect the healthy spouse's lifestyle.

- Equipment leasing and home modification benefits are not vital but are important if you don't want to pay out of pocket for these expenses.

- An indemnity plan will allow complete control and flexibility; however, a reimbursement plan will be more cost effective.

Here are some considerations if your children or grandchildren are able and willing to provide care:

- A comprehensive home care benefit is important to allow you to receive care in your home.

- Respite care benefits will provide relief for the family caregivers.

- Benefits for medical equipment leasing and home modification are not critical but are important if you don't want to pay out of pocket for these expenses.

- Consider an indemnity plan that will compensate family members who provide care as unlicensed caregivers.

Here are some considerations if you are single with no family members able or willing to provide care:

- Home care benefits may not be as important. Reducing these benefits may reduce your premium cost.

- An indemnity plan is not as important because care will most likely be administered in a facility by licensed caregivers. A reimbursement plan may be cheaper than an indemnity plan.

Partnership Policies

In an effort to promote the purchase of long-term care insurance, many states, including Louisiana, have adopted Long-Term Care Partnership Programs. The partnership program provides dollar for dollar asset protection from Medicaid spend down. To provide this protection, the Louisiana Medicaid program's eligibility rules are modified to provide a financial incentive to purchase long-term care insurance. If the insured requires long-term care, the policy pays its long-term care benefit. If the insured exhausts the policy benefits through an extended long-term care stay, the insured can apply for Medicaid. The normal asset threshold that Louisiana imposes on Medicaid applicants does not apply to the owner of a long-term care partnership policy. The applicant may keep assets in an amount equal to the benefits the long-term care policy provided. Assets that would otherwise be subject to spend-down are protected. Furthermore, these assets are exempt from Medicaid estate recovery after the insured's death.

Partnership Policy Requirements

The Deficit Reduction Act of 2005 (DRA) set forth the guidelines for Partnership policies and authorized all states to adopt long-term care partnership programs. Partnership policies are similar to traditional long-term care policies with regard to the features and benefits these policies provide. Pursuant to the DRA, Partnership policies must meet these criteria:

1. Partnership long-term care insurance policies must be tax-qualified. To meet the tax-qualified criteria, the policy must meet the guidelines specified by HIPPA as explained in the Tax-qualified and Non tax-qualified section of this chapter.
2. Provide Medicaid asset protection using the dollar-for-dollar model. The dollar-for-dollar asset protection model requires that the amount of assets protected from spend-down equals the dollar value of benefits paid by the policy in addition to the amount of assets exempted by the Louisiana Medicaid program.
3. Include automatic inflation protection if issued to an insured under age 76. If the insured is under age 61 when the policy is issued, the policy must include compound inflation protection. If the insured is between the ages of 61 and 76, the policy must provide some form of inflation protection, but it may be simple or compound inflation protection. If the insured is over age 76, no inflation protection is required.
4. Follow the consumer protection guidelines of the National Association of Insurance Commissioners (NAIC) Long-Term Care Insurance Model Act.

Asset-Based Long-Term Care Insurance

One of the objections you may have with traditional long-term care insurance is that premiums must be paid for coverage that may never be used. Although that is how homeowner's, automobile and health insurance provide coverage, many people don't see long-term care insurance in the same light. For example, you pay for fire insurance on your home every year, but I am sure that you do not think of fire insurance premiums as a waste of money if your home does not burn down. Even though the probability of needing long-term care is much greater than the probability of one's home being destroyed by fire, some people still opt to take their chances without long-term care insurance.

Asset-based coverage is an alternative to the "use it or lose it" proposition with traditional long-term care insurance. Asset-based coverage uses some of your assets that would be at risk to long-term care expenses and converts them into a long-term care policy funded with a life insurance policy or annuity that pays for long-term care expenses. The initial benefit period is usually three to four years. A rider may be added that provides additional lifetime coverage.

The policy will pay for long-term care when its benefits trigger has been met. The benefits trigger is typically the same as for traditional long-term care policies—two ADLs or cognitive impairment.

Asset-based coverage protects the rest of your assets if a long-term care need arises. The main advantage of asset based long-term care insurance is that if you never need long-term care, the policy pays the death benefit to your beneficiary. Depending on the contract, the death benefit may be equal to the premium payments, the premium payments plus a guaranteed amount of growth, some other guaranteed amount. If only part of the long-term care benefit is used, any remaining benefit is paid to your beneficiary.

The Pension Protection Act of 2006 allows tax-free distributions from qualifying annuities (e.g. asset-based long-term care annuities) for long-term care expenses. Existing annuities may be exchanged tax-free via a 1035 exchange to a qualifying long-term care annuity contract. The gains continue their tax-deferred status and all distributions for long-term care are tax-free.

Long-Term Care Riders

Riders to traditional life insurance policies may also provide long-term care benefits. A rider may be added to a life insurance policy which will use some of the death benefit to pay a long-term care daily benefit. A typical rider may pay out 2 or 4 percent of the death benefit per month. Each insurance policy and rider is subject to its own restrictions.

Many annuities provide for penalty-free withdrawals for long-term care expenses. Typically the annuity owner must be receiving care in a nursing home to receive these penalty-free withdrawals.

---

[1] Stillman and Lubitz, "Medical Care" 40 (10):965-967 (2002).

[2] Centers for Disease Control and Prevention, State Specific Healthy Life Expectancy at Age 65 Years - United States 2007-2009, July 19, 2013

[3] Stillman and Lubitz, "Medical Care" 40 (10):965-967 (2002).

[4] Kemper, Peter and Murtaugh, *Lifetime Use of Nursing Home Care*. The New England Journal of Medicine 1991, 324, 9 (February 28): 595-600.

[5] Spillman and Lubitz 2002, Table 3.

[6] MetLife 2011 Market Survey of Nursing Home, Assisted Living Costs, Adult Care Services and Home Care Cost, October, 2012.

15

Louisiana Medicaid Long-Term Care

Chapter Highlights

❖ To qualify for Louisiana Medicaid long-term care benefits, you must be a Louisiana resident, be at least 65 years of age or disabled and satisfy maximum income and asset thresholds.

❖ Certain assets are exempt for Medicaid qualification purposes. For example, the family home is an exempt asset; however, it may be subject to estate recovery after both spouses are deceased.

❖ The spouse who is not receiving Medicaid benefits is allowed to retain $126,420 in assets (2019) in addition to exempt assets.

❖ If the Medicaid applicant or their spouse transfers (donates) assets within five years prior to applying for Medicaid, the applicant will be ineligible for Medicaid during the disqualification period.

❖ The length of the disqualification period will depend on the value of the transferred assets.

❖ Transferring assets, converting assets into exempt assets and properly structured annuities are planning techniques that may help preserve assets when qualifying for Medicaid. Transfers to an irrevocable trust 5 years prior to applying for Medicaid can effectively protect all of the assets held in trust from Medicaid spend-down.

❖ Relatives of Medicaid recipients (or potential recipients) should use caution not to disqualify a Medicaid/SSI recipient by leaving assets to them in their will or by dying intestate that would place them over the asset limit.

❖ A special needs trust may be used to leave assets to individuals receiving governmental assistance without disqualifying them for benefits. For example, disabled heirs and disabled recipients of personal injury awards may benefit from special needs trusts.

MEDICAID IS A joint federal and state program which provides medical and long-term care services to qualified individuals. Medicaid is the nation's major public financing program for healthcare coverage for low income families and for long-term care provided to the impoverished elderly and the disabled. <u>Although Medicaid provides many types of benefits and services, this chapter will focus on Medicaid long-term care benefits.</u> Medicaid provides services in community-and home-based settings (outside of a nursing home) as well as in institutional settings (e.g. nursing home care). You are probably most familiar with Medicaid benefits that pay for long-term care services in a nursing home. In fact, Medicaid will only pay for long-term care benefits provided in a nursing home. Individuals receiving nursing home care paid for by Medicaid are "institutionalized."[a] The rules and qualification guidelines in this chapter are specific to Louisiana residents and are subject to frequent changes. Prior to making any decisions regarding Medicaid planning consult a qualified attorney.

Qualifying for Benefits

Although there are many ways to qualify for Medicaid, this chapter will primarily discuss qualifying for Medicaid long-term care benefits. Thus, we will be primarily discussing Medicaid benefits for individuals over age 65 who need long-term care. In addition to attaining age 65 and being in need of long-term care, one must also satisfy income and resource limitations which effectively restrict Medicaid benefits to the impoverished. Finally, recipients must be a Louisiana resident and United States citizen or a Qualified Alien.

---

[a] An institutionalized individual is an individual who is (1) an inpatient in a nursing facility; (2) an inpatient in a medical institution for whom payment is based on a level of care provided in a nursing facility; or (3) a home- and community-based services recipient.

Income Limitations

To qualify for Medicaid, the applicant's monthly income must not be greater than $2,313 (2019).[1] This amount is also known as the long-term care special income limit (SIL), and it includes the income of Medicaid recipient from all sources. If the Medicaid applicant's income is greater than $2,313 per month (2019) but less than the long-term care facility rate[b] and all of the other requirements are met, the applicant may still qualify after certain adjustments are made to their income. This alternate way of qualifying for Medicaid long-term care benefits is called the Spend-Down Medically Needy Program ("spend down"). For example, Boudreaux meets the resource test (discussed below), and his monthly income is $2,700 per month. Because his income is greater than the SIL ($2,313 per month in 2019), he does not qualify under the first test. However, if after certain deductions[c] are made to "spend-down" Boudreaux's income, his monthly income is less than his particular nursing home facility rate (e.g. $5,000), he passes the Spend-Down Medically Needy Program Test. After an individual is eligible for Medicaid, a portion of the institutionalized spouse's income is applied to the cost of care. This amount is the Patient Liability Amount.

The Minimum Monthly Maintenance Needs Allowance

The Minimum Monthly Maintenance Needs Allowance permits the institutionalized spouse to transfer income to the community spouse[d] to meet a minimum threshold of monthly income. If both spouses are institutionalized, there is no community spouse and the Minimum Monthly Maintenance Needs Allowance is not available. The purpose of the Minimum Monthly Maintenance Needs Allowance is to provide income to the community spouse to maintain a standard of living above the poverty level. If the community spouse's monthly income is less

---

[b] The monthly rate of the nursing home.

[c] Under the alternate test as of 2019, deductions from income include a standard deduction of $100 in urban parishes and $92 in rural parishes; the Supplemental Security Income Standard Deduction ($20); past due and current medical expenses incurred within three months of applying for Medicaid; and allowable health insurance premiums.

[d] The community spouse is the spouse at home defined as the legal husband or wife of an institutionalized individual living in a noninstitutionalized living arrangement (e.g. at home).

than $3,165.50 (2019),[2] the institutionalized spouse may transfer income to the community spouse to reach this minimum amount of monthly income. Income sheltered under the Minimum Monthly Maintenance Needs Allowance does not count towards the income limit and reduces the amount of countable income for Medicaid eligibility purposes. In addition the Minimum Monthly Maintenance Needs Allowance provides an exception to the Patient Liability Amount. If the community spouse has insufficient income to meet the Minimum Monthly Maintenance Needs Allowance threshold, income from the institutionalized spouse is diverted to the community spouse rather than used to pay a portion of the cost of care as the Patient Liability Amount.[e]

Resource Limits

In addition to the income test, Medicaid applicants must also pass a resource (asset) test to qualify for Medicaid. You cannot qualify for Medicaid if you have resources in an amount greater than $2,000.[3] If you and your spouse are institutionalized, your combined resources cannot be greater than $3,000. Resources include cash, bank accounts, real estate, investments, retirement accounts, and all assets or possessions which can be converted into cash.

The resources of both spouses are counted when you apply for Medicaid. For Medicaid purposes, there is no distinction between separate and community property. Therefore, all of the resources of both spouses are considered at the time of applying for Medicaid. If your resources exceed $2,000, you will be required to spend-down the excess resources by paying for your long-term care expenses out of pocket. After you spend-down your excess assets, you may qualify for Medicaid.

Income and/or principal distributions from trusts paid to either spouse are considered income in the month received. Furthermore, income from any source that is not spent is considered a countable

---

[e] DRA 2005 requires that "all income of the institutionalized spouse that could be made available to a community spouse, in accordance with the calculation of the community spouse monthly income allowance under this subsection, has been made available before the State allocates to the community spouse an amount of resources adequate to provide the difference between the minimum monthly maintenance needs allowance and all income available to the community spouse."

resource as are assets in trust that may be paid from the trust for the benefit of either spouse.

Basically, Medicaid will take a resource snapshot of both spouses at the time of application. If the asset and income tests are satisfied at that time, assets and income received solely by the community spouse subsequent to qualifying for Medicaid will not disqualify the institutionalized spouse for Medicaid.

Exempt Resources

Certain assets are exempt resources and are not included in the $2,000 resource limitation.[4] These exempt assets include

- Your home if you intend on returning home or if your spouse or a dependent resides in your home. Up to 160 acres of surrounding contiguous land may be included with your home. Proceeds from the sale of your home remain exempt if reinvested in another family home within three months. The institutionalized spouse may have no more than $585,000 (2019) of equity in their home (fair market value minus home equity loans, mortgages and reverse mortgages) to qualify for Medicaid. The limitation on home equity does not apply if the community spouse, a child under the age of 21 or a blind or disabled child is living in the home.

- Household furnishings regardless of value.

- Personal effects regardless of value.

- Wedding and engagement ring regardless of value.

- One vehicle per household if used for transportation by anyone in the institutionalized spouse's household.

- The cash value of permanent life insurance with a face value of up to $10,000. Term insurance is not a resource.

- Burial contracts that are irrevocable or cannot be sold without significant hardship.

- Burial funds (cash, securities, cash surrender value of life insurance policies or revocable burial contracts) which are clearly designated as burial funds. A maximum of $10,000 is allowed for each spouse. The face value of excluded life insurance and excluded burial contracts are applied first to this limit.

- A fully paid burial space or agreement which represents the purchase of a burial space held for the burial of the individual, his or her spouse, or immediate family. This exemption is unlimited and is in addition to the burial fund exemption. Burial spaces include: burial plots, gravesites, crypts, mausoleums, caskets, urns, vaults, headstones, plaques, burial containers and arrangements for opening and closing the gravesite.

- Property used in a trade or business and all property used by an employee in connection with employment as property essential to self-support. Property must be in current use or was in use, and there must be a reasonable expectation that the use will resume. Trade or business property includes real estate, buildings, inventory, equipment, tools, motor vehicles and livestock.

The Community Spouse Resource Allowance

The Community Spouse Resource Allowance enables your community spouse at home to retain assets to maintain his or her standard of living if you enter a nursing home. If you enter a nursing home and qualify for Medicaid, your spouse at home (the community spouse) is allowed to retain $126,420 (2019)[5] of nonexempt assets. Assets in value over this amount are deemed available when applying for Medicaid. After you qualify for Medicaid, your community spouse's resources may increase over the Community Spouse Resource Allowance without disqualifying your (the Medicaid recipient's) benefits. However, your (the Medicaid recipient's) resources may not exceed $2,000 at the time of applying for and while receiving Medicaid long-term care benefits.

Penalties for Transferring Assets: The Look-Back Period

Some applicants attempt to meet the resource limitations by removing assets from their estate through asset transfers (donations) to children or grandchildren. At one time, this was a straightforward strategy; however, the look-back rules currently impose penalty periods for certain transfers. The baseline date for transfers on or after February 8, 2008, is the date an individual applies for Medicaid and is determined eligible except for the occurrence of the transfer (the baseline date). To avoid the asset transfer penalty, transfers must be made at least 60 months prior to the baseline date (the look-back period).

The Deficit Reduction Act of 2005 (DRA 2005) which became effective on February 8, 2006, significantly changed the Medicaid rules for asset transfer penalties and look-back periods for long-term care benefits. For transfers occurring on or after February 8, 2006, the look-back period for all transfers is 60 months prior to the baseline date.

All gifts, even small gifts made in successive months, are added together to determine the penalty period. Under the old rule, small gifts were not problematic because the period of disqualification started when the gift was made and the penalty period likely expired by the time the donor entered a nursing home. Therefore, caution must also be used with transfers made to children and/or grandchildren, such as tuition payments or transfers under the annual exclusion. If such transfers are made within the five-year-look-back period, a period of ineligibility will commence when Medicaid eligibility would otherwise begin.

Transfers of noncountable assets for less than fair market value (even transfers into trusts) will not result in a penalty as they are not countable assets for transfer purposes. However, a home transferred into a trust or otherwise after one enters a nursing home will generally be deemed a countable resource (no longer exempt).[6]

Transfers Involving Revocable Trusts

Assets transferred *to* a <u>revocable</u> trust remain available resources and countable for Medicaid eligibility.

Assets transferred *from* a <u>revocable</u> trust to a person other than one's self are considered a transfer for less than fair market value subject to the 60-month-look-back period.

A transfer of assets placed into a revocable trust for the benefit of a third party is deemed to take place when the assets are transferred to the third party.

Transfers Involving Irrevocable Trusts

For irrevocable trusts, transfers made into the trust that could not under any circumstances be made to you (the Medicaid applicant) are subject to the 60-month-look-back period. The transfer is deemed to take place when the trust was established or when the ability to distribute assets to you terminated. Payments of principal or income for your benefit are considered income. Principal or income which could be paid to you is considered an available resource.

Calculating the Period of Ineligibility

If you make a transfer during the look-back period, you will be ineligible for Medicaid benefits for a period of time. The ineligibility period is calculated by dividing the transfer's fair market value by the private pay rate. The private pay rate is the average cost for a private pay nursing home resident in Louisiana ($5,000 in 2019). The length of the penalty period is without limitation. Therefore, if you make a very large transfer during the look-back period, it is possible to cause a period of ineligibility for the remainder of your lifetime. The penalty period runs from the date the applicant is eligible to receive Medicaid[f] (meets the asset and income tests), rather than from the date of transfer.

If Boudreaux makes a transfer of 150,000 to his children in January 2019, Boudreaux's penalty period of 30 months begins on the date he is eligible to receive Medicaid benefits (i.e. when he satisfies the income and resource limits). Boudreaux will be over the resource limit if he retains assets to pay for nursing home care during the penalty period. Boudreaux's period of ineligibility will begin when his resources are below $2,000, so his children or other relatives will have to pay for his nursing home care while he is ineligible due to the resource limit. To avoid the ineligibility period due to asset transfers, Boudreaux must wait 60 months until the look-back period expires to apply for Medicaid.

Estate Recovery

The State of Louisiana is required by the Federal Government pursuant to OBRA 1993 to seek reimbursement from your estate for certain services provided by Medicaid. Assets that were exempt when

---

[f] Applies to transfers made on or after February 8, 2006.

applying for Medicaid (e.g. your home) are available for estate recovery subject to certain restrictions.[7]

1. Recovery is limited to nursing home, community-based services and related hospital and prescription drug services for recipients age 55 or older when services were received.

2. The State cannot seek recovery from the Medicaid recipient's estate until after the surviving spouse is deceased or if the Medicaid recipient has a child under age 21 or has a child who is blind or disabled.

3. Recovery may be waived in cases where it is not cost effective. Estate recovery will be deemed cost effective when the amount reasonably expected to be recovered exceeds the cost of recovery and is greater than $1,000.

4. Estate recovery may be reduced by reasonable and necessary documented expenses incurred by the recipient's heirs to maintain the homestead while the recipient is in a long-term care facility or received home and community-based services if the homestead is part of the estate.

Estate recovery against the family home will not be instituted on the greater of the first $15,000 or one-half the median value of homesteads in each parish. The fair market value of the home is used to determine the home value rather than the assessed value.

Planning Options After DRA 2005

The changes to Medicaid's long-term care qualification rules make it more difficult to both preserve assets and rely on Medicaid to pay for long-term care services. The message from DRA 2005 is clear: If you have assets worth protecting, you should plan well in advance for the possibility of an extended long-term care need. One of the most effective strategies is to transfer assets to an irrevocable trust five years before applying for Medicaid. Other options include Medicaid compliant annuities, maximizing exempt assets, reverse half-a-loaf and personal care contracts. For some individuals, insuring against the risk of long-term care is the best option. Long-term care insurance planning is, therefore, an essential part of retirement planning. Hopefully, you will insure against this risk while you are in your low to mid-fifties rather than in your sixties or seventies. Purchasing long-term care insurance at a younger age will help increase the probability of meeting the underwriting requirements and may result in lower cumulative premium payments.

Self-Financing Long-Term Care

Self-financing long-term care will always be an option for some individuals; however, it is not always the best option. The retirement portfolios owned by you and your spouse may be consumed by long-term care expenses. If long-term care expenses exhaust your retirement portfolio, your spouse will be left with insufficient means to maintain his or her standard of living.

Self-financing is the most feasible for individuals with significant assets due to their ability to pay for long-term care expenses out of pocket for long periods of time. However, even the wealthy should consider insuring against this risk as they insure against other risks. For example, although a wealthy individual has the financial resources to rebuild their home many times over in the event it is destroyed by fire, they still insure against this risk through homeowner's insurance.

Transferring Assets

As discussed earlier, DRA 2005 places significant hurdles on transferring (donating) assets to qualify for Medicaid. The five-year-look-back period will require asset transfers prior to five years of applying for Medicaid to protect the assets.

Donating assets has its own inherent drawbacks. If you donate assets directly to one or more of your children (the donees), the donee will inherit your cost basis with no step-up available upon your death. Significant income taxes may be due upon the asset's subsequent sale by the donee. In addition, you lose control of the asset, and the asset will be subject to the donee's creditors. Prior to donating assets or attempting any Medicaid planning strategy, it is critical to consult a qualified elder law attorney.

In most situations it is beneficial to donate assets to an irrevocable trust to provide more protection and control over the assets. The trust can be drafted to provide a step-up in basis upon the donor's death and protection from creditors. The trust can also be drafted to have the income taxable to the parents, rather than the trust or the beneficiaries (typically the children). This typically results in lower income taxes on the trust assets. In addition, the settlor (creator) of the trust determines how the trust assets are to be managed and selects the trustee(s).

Converting Countable Resources into Exempt Resources

One planning option is to convert cash and investments that would otherwise be consumed by Medicaid spend down into an exempt resource, for example, the family home. The family home, as an exempt resource, is a valuable planning tool. Although DRA 2005 places a cap on home equity for Medicaid long-term care applicants, using countable assets to make home improvements or purchasing a more expensive home (using caution to stay under the home equity limit) is a viable option. The transfer of assets rule applies to transfers for less than full and adequate consideration. However, if a countable asset is used to purchase or acquire an exempt asset, the transfer penalties and look-back period do not apply. Converting cash and investments into exempt resources may be accomplished in the following ways:

1. Pay off the mortgage on your home.

2. Make improvements on your home such as a new roof, new paint, and/or updating the kitchen and bathrooms.

3. Make your home handicap accessible.

4. Purchase a more expensive home in the community spouse's name.

5. Purchase a new automobile and household goods.

6. Purchase a fully paid burial plan.

It is advantageous to pay off the mortgage on the family home versus other types of debt. Debt incurred to purchase an automobile, for example, will reduce the automobile's value by the debt amount. The debt on an automobile or other nonexempt resource will reduce the amount of total countable resources. Debt on the home will not reduce countable resources because the home is an exempt asset.

Due to the limitations on home equity value under DRA 2005, it may be necessary for some applicants, depending on their situation, to use a reverse mortgage to reduce the equity value of their homes. Other options include selling the home and purchasing a home with an equity value of less than $560,000 (2017).

Insuring the Look-Back Period

An additional alternative is to purchase long-term care insurance which pays a five-year benefit. Prior to entering a nursing home, you may transfer assets from your estate which causes a five-year-look-back period. The long-term care policy will pay for care during the look-back period. When the look-back period ends, you may apply for Medicaid.

Medicaid Annuities

Another planning option is to convert countable assets into an irrevocable income stream for the institutionalized spouse or the community spouse's benefit. The use of a properly structured annuity may allow you to qualify for Medicaid without going through spend-down or by significantly reducing the amount of assets you must spend-down. You may use countable assets to purchase an irrevocable immediate annuity payable for a term of years not longer than the annuitant's life expectancy.[g] Because the payments are based on the annuitant's life expectancy, the transaction is not considered a transfer for less than full and adequate consideration. Therefore, the look-back and asset-transfer penalty periods do not apply if certain requirements are met. The annuity income will count towards the community spouse's Minimum Monthly Maintenance Needs Allowance. This technique works best for married couples where one spouse is institutionalized and countable resources exceed eligibility thresholds. If the community spouse later becomes institutionalized, he or she will also have to satisfy the income and resource requirements.

For example, Boudreaux and Clotile have $300,000 of countable assets at the time Boudreaux applies for Medicaid (the snapshot date). Clotile may retain $126,420 (2019) as the Community Spouse Resource Allowance, and Boudreaux may retain $2,000. The

---

[g] Typically the community spouse will receive the payments.

remaining $171,580 may be used to purchase a properly structured immediate annuity that will make periodic payments of income to Clotile based on her life expectancy. The annuity payments are considered part of Clotile's Minimum Monthly Maintenance Needs Allowance. This strategy allows Boudreaux to immediately qualify for Medicaid without having to spend-down the remaining $171,580. It also provides Clotile with additional monthly income.

Funds used to purchase the annuity are no longer considered a countable resource because the annuity is irrevocable. Few annuities are irrevocable <u>and</u> contain the correct provisions for this technique, so do not attempt this technique without the guidance of a qualified elder law attorney. To avoid being considered a countable resource, an annuity purchased by an annuitant who applied for Medicaid must meet the following criteria:

1. The annuity must be irrevocable and nonassignable;

2. Annuity calculations must be actuarially sound based on the annuitant's life expectancy (Chart Z-1200);

3. The annuity must provide payments of principal and interest in equal installments (no deferred or balloon payments);

DRA 2005 also stipulates that any annuity purchased by the institutionalized spouse or the community spouse must name the State of Louisiana as the primary and permanent beneficiary for the total amount of Medicaid assistance paid unless there is a community spouse and/or a minor or disabled child. If there is a community spouse and/or a minor or disabled child, the State may be named the primary contingent beneficiary.

Protecting Your Home

Your home is an exempt asset so long as you intend to return to your home after a stay in a nursing home. After your death, your home may be subject to estate recovery, but estate recovery may not occur during your spouse's lifetime. Therefore, your home is an exempt resource for your lifetime and the lifetime of your spouse. Your home is also exempt if you have a surviving child under the age of 21 or a child who is blind or disabled as defined by the Social Security Administration.[8] Often, the home is the sole asset in the estate of a

Medicaid recipient. The State may attach a lien to the home to recover Medicaid payments as mandated by federal law.

Transferring the Full Ownership of the Family Home

The family home as an exempt asset is protected from Medicaid spend-down; however, it may be subject to estate recovery. There are several types of home ownership transfers that will not be deemed a gift for Medicaid transfer penalty purposes:[9]

- A transfer of a home to a child who is under age 21, is blind, or meets the definition of SSI disability.

- A transfer of a home to a sibling who has an equity interest in the home and who was residing in the home for a least one year immediately prior to the date of institutionalization.

- A transfer of a home to a child who is over age 21 and who was residing in the home for at least two years immediately prior to institutionalization.

Transferring the Naked Ownership of the Family Home

Although the State of Louisiana has begun to recover assets from the estates of Medicaid long-term care recipients as required by federal law, transferring the home's naked ownership may help protect some or all of the value in your home while allowing you and your spouse to continue to live in your home. The Louisiana Medicaid rules rely on state law to define the term "estate." Currently, Louisiana is not seeking recovery for a usufruct interest under an expanded definition of an "estate." Thus, if you only retain the usufruct which terminates at death, no portion of the home is included in the estate at death, and there are no remaining assets which may be subject to a lien.

As the usufructuary, Boudreaux will be responsible for property taxes on the home and for ordinary repairs. His children, as naked owners, will be responsible for extraordinary repairs.[h] Upon the death of Boudreaux's surviving spouse, no portion of the home is left in either estate to attach a lien for estate recovery. The usufruct terminates upon the surviving spouse's death.

---

[h] Extraordinary repairs are those for reconstruction of the whole or a substantial part of the property. All other repairs are ordinary repairs. La. Civ. Code Art. 578.

The transfer of the naked ownership is not an exempt transfer; however, the transfer's value is the value of the naked-ownership interest, not the home's full value.[10] This can reduce the penalty period if the transfer of the naked ownership occurs during the look-back period. Furthermore, gift taxes are due on the value of the transferred naked-ownership interest. In contrast to a transfer of the entire interest in the home, the naked owners will receive a step-up in basis upon the usufructuary's death.

An additional benefit of transferring the home's naked ownership is probate avoidance. Full ownership is transferred to the naked owners when the usufruct ends at death. Furthermore, if the definition of "estate" is expanded to include interests in usufructs for estate recovery, the usufruct value will be less than the home's full value. Thus, most of the home's value will avoid estate recovery.

If a high probability exists that the home will be sold, carefully weigh the tax implications. Your children, as naked owners, will have to pay the taxes on any capital gain on the portion of the home that represents their ownership interest. The capital gain exclusion for a home sale does not apply to the naked owners' interest if they do not reside in the home.

Do not make the mistake of transferring the home to a revocable trust to avoid probate (and attempting to avoid estate recovery). The home will no longer be an exempt asset if it is transferred to a revocable trust, and it will be immediately subject to spend-down as a countable resource.[11]

Leaving Assets to a Medicaid Recipient

Relatives of Medicaid recipients *or potential recipients* should review their wills or revocable trusts to prevent the Medicaid recipient from receiving assets and becoming disqualified for benefits. For example, if your spouse is or may receive Medicaid benefits, assets he or she inherits from you or from others will likely cause disqualification from Medicaid. In addition, the Medicaid recipient should not be the beneficiary of any asset (such as IRAs, life insurance, qualified retirement plans or annuities). Therefore, if your spouse is receiving Medicaid long-term care benefits, you should consider leaving your assets in a properly drafted trust for the benefit of your spouse.[12] The surviving spouse should not be the trustee, and the surviving spouse should not be given the power to compel distributions or access trust principal to benefit your surviving spouse. The trustee should be given power to make limited distributions to your spouse to avoid disqualifying your surviving spouse from Medicaid benefits. Otherwise, your assets must be left to a relative other than your institutionalized spouse to avoid disqualifying your institutionalized spouse from Medicaid. Unfortunately, the relative is under no legal obligation to use these assets for your spouse's care.

Related persons also should take caution not to die intestate, leaving the Medicaid recipient or potential recipient as an intestate heir. Relatives should draft a will leaving these assets to a trust or the Medicaid recipient's spouse, children or grandchildren.

Planning for Disabled Children

If a disabled child[i] who is receiving SSI and Medicaid benefits inherits assets, he or she may exceed the maximum asset threshold. Thus, a disabled child receiving an inheritance in excess of $2,000 will be disqualified from government benefits. For example, parents of disabled children are faced with the dilemma of disinheriting their children or potentially disqualifying their children from governmental benefits. Disinheriting a disabled child is generally not possible with Louisiana's forced heirship laws as the forced heir must receive at least the forced portion. For this reason Medicaid planning is more important in Louisiana than any other state. Even if forced heirship did not apply to disabled children, most parents do not wish to disinherit their children. The choice of some families is to leave assets to a sibling or other relative for the express purpose of caring for a disabled child. Several major problems exist with this arrangement: (1) there may be significant gift-tax issues; (2) the sibling or relative is under no legal obligation to use the assets for the disabled child's benefit; and (3) the assets are subject to the sibling's or relative's creditors. She Chapter 22 for more information about special needs trust.

Third-Party Trusts

One option is to leave assets in trust for a disabled child's benefit. Parents of a disabled child may leave assets to a special needs trust

---

[i] A "child" may be an adult or a minor.

created by their will. The trust should be drafted as a special needs trust to avoid the trust assets from being counted as a resource. Therefore, the trustee's discretion for distributing assets should be limited to providing for the beneficiary's needs which are not provided under the governmental assistance program (e.g. Medicaid or SSI). The trustee should be specifically prohibited from making any distribution which would jeopardize the benefits of the governmental assistance program. In addition, care should be taken not to make income distributions to the beneficiary that may place the beneficiary over the SSI/Medicaid income limit. The trust should be used to purchase items and provide supplemental support not otherwise provided by Medicaid. Spendthrift trust provisions are also included to protect the trust assets from creditors. Third party trusts are not required to reimburse the state for governmental assistance provided to the beneficiary. After beneficiary's death, the assets may be left to other children or grandchildren.

(d)(4)(A) Under-Age-65 Special Needs Trust

An Under-Age-65 Special Needs Trust[j] is a self-settled spendthrift trust created for an individual who is under age 65 and disabled when the trust is created. The trust is self-settled because it is funded with the beneficiary's assets rather than assets from a third party. This self-settled trust is typically established for a personal injury settlement or for other assets owned by a disabled individual who is under age 65 and requires medical benefits not covered by health insurance. The self-settled trust will help prevent the beneficiary from exhausting a personal injury settlement or other assets (countable resources) on his or her care prior to governmental assistance providing care. This type of trust will enable a disabled beneficiary to maintain a higher quality of life while maintaining eligibility for governmental entitled programs (e.g Medicaid and SSI). The disabled individual must be the sole beneficiary.

The disabled individual's assets are used to fund the self-settled trust. Assets from third parties generally should be used to fund a third-party trust[k] rather than a self-settled trust. The assets held in a self-

---

[j] May be referred to as a self-settled trust, Under age 65 trust, (d)(4)(A) trust.
[k] A third-party trust is not required to reimburse Medicaid for expenses incurred during the disabled beneficiary's lifetime.

settled trust will not be considered resources for SSI or Medicaid purposes; however, self-settled trusts are subject to payback provisions. The payback provisions provide that upon the disabled beneficiary's death, the trust must pay to the state all remaining assets in the trust, up to the amount of the state-provided care.

Even after the disabled individual surpasses age 65, the trust assets will not be considered resources. However, if additional assets are added after age 65, these assets will not be exempt resources.

The self-settled trust must be created by the disabled individual's parent, guardian, grandparent or a court. Although the disabled individual may have the legal capacity to create the trust, he or she cannot create the trust. In addition, the disabled individual's attorney-in-fact pursuant to a power of attorney cannot create the trust. The trust should have provisions to direct the trustee not to make distributions which would jeopardize the disabled individual's eligibility for governmental assistance.

---

[1] Louisiana Medicaid Eligibility Manual, Table Z-700.

[2] Louisiana Medicaid Eligibility Manual, Table Z-800.

[3] Louisiana Medicaid Eligibility Manual, Table Z-900.

[4] Louisiana Medicaid Eligibility Manual I-1630.

[5] Louisiana Medicaid Eligibility Manual, Table Z-800.

[6] HCFA Transmittal 64, § 3259.6(F).

[7] Louisiana Medicaid Eligibility Manual, U-300.

[8] Louisiana Medicaid Eligibility Manual U-310.

[9] Louisiana Medicaid Eligibility Manual I-1673.

[10] Louisiana Medicaid Eligibility Manual I-1673.

[11] Louisiana Medicaid Eligibility Manual I-1720.

[12] 42 U.S.C. § 1396p(c)(2)(B)(i); 42 U.S.C. § 1396p(d)(2)(A).

16

Types of Property Ownership

Chapter Highlights

❖ In Louisiana, property in a spouse's possession during marriage is presumed to be community property. Each spouse owns an undivided one-half interest in the community property.

❖ Property acquired through the effort, skill or industry of a spouse during marriage is community property. Community property also includes fruits of separate property such as dividends, rents and royalties.

❖ A declaration of separateness may be used to keep fruits of separate property separate.

❖ Upon the first spouse's death, the surviving spouse receives a step-up in basis on both halves of the community property.

❖ Separate property includes property acquired prior to marriage and property that is received by donation or inheritance.

❖ Two or more people may own the same property as co-owners or tenants-in-common.

❖ Louisiana does not recognize joint tenancy with rights of survivorship. In Louisiana, movable property owned by a Louisiana resident or immovable property in Louisiana that is titled as joint tenancy with rights of survivorship is treated as co-owned property or community property.

SEVERAL PROPERTY OWNERSHIP classifications are recognized in Louisiana. Understanding the differences between the types of property ownership is the first step to understanding your estate plan. The term property includes not only real estate but all assets[a] (movable and immovable). If your estate plan is based on the assumption that certain property will be classified as separate when, in actuality, it is community property or that certain property will automatically transfer by joint tenancy, disastrous, unintended results may occur. This chapter will briefly discuss the various types of property ownership recognized in Louisiana and the most common misconceptions regarding property ownership.

An example of how misconceptions of property ownership may cause problems is illustrated in the following hypothetical: Boudreaux and Clotile were married and had two children. Boudreaux inherited from his parents a large amount of rental properties that remained his separate property. Each month, the rental income was deposited into a separate savings account that Boudreaux left to his daughter in his will, along with the rental properties he inherited. In addition, Clotile had several large CDs in her name which were acquired during their marriage. Their son's name was listed on the CDs, but their son did not contribute any of the funds to purchase the CDs. Upon Boudreaux's death, the rental properties will belong to their daughter according to Boudreaux's will, but only one-half of the rental income savings account will belong to their daughter. The rental properties are Boudreaux's separate property, and he may leave all of it to his daughter. However, the rental payments from this separate property are community property. Half of the rental payment account belongs to Clotile. If Boudreaux intended to treat the rental income payments as separate property, he should have filed a Declaration of Separateness to classify the rental payments as separate property. Only then could all of the rental payments savings account be left to his daughter. Two years later, Clotile dies without a will. Upon Clotile's death, the CDs with her and her son's name on the registration will not automatically transfer to her son. Her son did not contribute any funds to the account, and merely placing his name on the account does not transfer ownership. The CDs will be transferred according to the intestacy laws of Louisiana and will be split between their son and daughter. As discussed herein, financial institutions may allow payable on death (POD) and survivorship arrangements with certain accounts (e.g.

---

[a] Different types of property include movable, immovable, corporeal (items with physical existence) or incorporeal (e.g. rents, credits, rights of action, copyright, or other right without physical existence).

certificates of deposit and savings accounts). However, these types of accounts do not change the nature of the assets from community to separate property.

The previous examples describe two very common property ownership misconceptions in Louisiana. Investors must know that income from separate property is community property, and adding a name to a CD or other account does not change or transfer ownership. You can easily avoid these problems with proper planning and with a correct understanding of property ownership law in Louisiana.

Community Property

In Louisiana, property in possession of a spouse during marriage is presumed to be community property.[1] Each spouse owns an undivided one-half interest in the community property.[2] The community regime is in effect during marriage unless altered by marriage contract (pre-nuptial agreement).[3] The community property regime ends upon the death of a spouse, upon declaration of the nullity of the marriage, upon judgment of divorce or separation of property[b] or by matrimonial agreement that terminates the community.[4]

Spouses who move to Louisiana may opt out of the default community property rules without the court's approval if done within one year of moving to Louisiana. After one year elapses, spouses who elect to opt out of the community property regime must petition the court for approval.[5]

Community Property includes the following:

1. Property acquired during the existence of the community regime through the effort, skill or industry of either spouse.

---

[b] A judgment decreeing separation of property terminates the community regime retroactively to the day of the filing of the petition. However, if a judgment is rendered that the spouses were living separate and apart after the filing of a petition for divorce without having reconciled, the judgment shall be retroactive to the date the original petition for divorce was filed. La. Civ. Code Art. 2375.

Thus wages, earnings and other compensation earned during marriage are community property.[6]

2. Property acquired with community assets.[7]

3. Property acquired with both community and separate property, unless the community property is inconsequential in comparison.[c]

4. Property donated to both spouses jointly is community property.[8]

5. Natural and civil fruits of community property. For example, dividends, interest, mineral royalties, rents and other "fruits" derived from community property are community property.[9]

6. Fruits and revenues of separate property. For example, rental income from separate rental property is community property.[10]

7. Damages awarded for loss or injury to community property.[11]

8. All other property not classified as separate property.[12]

Fruits and Products

The fruits and products[d] of separate property are community property; however, you may execute a declaration of separateness reserving fruits and products as separate property. To reserve fruits and products of immovable property, you must file the declaration in the parish of the immovable property's locale. For movable property, you

---

[c] The person claiming the property is separate property bears the burden of proving the property is separate. Determining if the community property used to purchase the asset was "inconsequential" in comparison to the separate property depends on the facts of a given situation. If the property is community, the spouse whose separate funds were used to acquire the community assets would be entitled to reimbursement for the value of the separate property upon the termination of the community. La. Civ. Code Arts. 2338, 2367.

[d] Fruits are produced from another thing without diminution of its substance. There are natural fruits and civil fruits. Natural fruits are products of the earth or animals. Civil fruits are revenues derived from a thing by operation of law or through juridical act such as rental income and dividend payments. La. Civ. Code Ann. Art. 551. Although minerals extracted from the ground results in the depletion of the property and are not considered fruits, minerals, bonuses, delay rentals, royalties and shut-in payments attributable to separate property are community property. La. Civ. Code Ann. Art. 2339.

must file the declaration in the parish of your residence.[13] If the fruits and products of separate property are not reserved as separate property, your heirs with a claim to a portion of your community property have a claim to a portion of these fruits and products. Inadequate planning may cause confusion and litigation between your heirs when determining property rights after your death.

Further confusion arises when spouses donate property to each other. If you donate <u>community</u> property to your spouse, the fruits and products are the separate property of the donee (receiving) spouse.[14] If you donate <u>separate</u> property to your spouse, the fruits and products are community property. A declaration of separateness is required to reserve the fruits and products as separate property.

Community or Separate: Which Law Applies?

Separate property brought into Louisiana by a married couple remains separate property; however, the property is presumed to be community property. The spouse claiming that the property is separate property bears the burden of proof.[15]

For married couples owning movable property, wherever situated, acquired by either spouse during the marriage, property rights are governed by the state laws of the acquiring spouse's domicile.[16] For married couples owning immovable property in Louisiana, property rights are governed by Louisiana law.[17]

With regard to successions, <u>movable</u>[e] property is governed by the laws of the state of the decedent's domiciled at the time of death. <u>Immovable</u>[f] property located in Louisiana is governed by Louisiana law. These are the general rules which may be overridden by several exceptions.

<u>EXCEPTION 1</u>: The law governing property rights for immovable property owned by a Louisiana resident which is located in another state can become rather complicated depending on the facts of each

---

[e] Movables are either corporeal or incorporeal movables that the law does not consider immovable property. Corporeal movables are things that normally can be moved from one place to another. La. Civ. Code Ann. Art. 471. Incorporeal movables are rights, obligations, and actions that apply to a movable thing. La. Civ. Code Ann. Art. 473. For example, stocks, bonds and annuities are incorporeal movables.
[f] Immovables are land and its component parts. La. Civ. Code Ann. Art. 462. Component parts are buildings and other constructions permanently attached to the ground. La. Civ. Code Ann. Art. 463.

situation. Generally, upon the termination of the community, if either spouse is domiciled in Louisiana, immovable property located in another state, but <u>which was acquired by either spouse while domiciled in Louisiana</u>, which would be community property if it were located in Louisiana, will be governed by Louisiana law.[18]

EXCEPTION 2: Upon the termination of the community or dissolution by death or divorce of spouses, either of whom is domiciled in Louisiana, property rights of immovable property in Louisiana and movable property wherever situated <u>that was acquired by either spouse during marriage while domiciled in another state</u> shall be determined as follows: (1) Property that is community property under Louisiana law shall be community property, and (2) property that is not community property under Louisiana law is the acquiring spouse's separate property. However, the other spouse shall be entitled, in value only, to the same rights with regard to this property as would be granted by the state laws of the acquiring spouse's domicile at the time of the acquisition.[19] This rule applies to movable and immovable property acquired during marriage by either spouse while domiciled in another state.

EXCEPTION 3: Upon the death of a spouse domiciled outside of Louisiana, that spouse's immovable property located in Louisiana and acquired by that spouse while domiciled outside of Louisiana, which is not community property under the laws of Louisiana, are subject to the same rights, in value only, in favor of the surviving spouse as provided by the law of the deceased's domicile at the time of death.[20] This rule only applies in death situations and when the acquiring spouse was domiciled outside of Louisiana both at the time the property was acquired and at death. The law of the domicile of the deceased at the time of death will determine property rights.

Community Property Basis Step-Up

Community property provides a tremendous income tax advantage to surviving spouses through the step-up in basis for the surviving spouse upon the first spouse's death.[21] For example, Boudreaux and Clotile own a tract of land as community property worth $100,000 with a cost basis of $10,000. Upon Boudreaux's death, half of the land's value is included in Boudreaux's estate; however, the entire tract of land receives a step-up in basis to the land's value on the date of

Boudreaux's death. Clotile may now sell the land without paying capital gain taxes on the land due to the step-up in basis to fair market value. If the property were the separate property of Clotile, there would be no step-up in basis upon Boudreaux's death, and the sale would cause a capital gain of $90,000.

Separate Property

In Louisiana, separate property includes all property that is not community property. If you wish to rebut the presumption that property acquired during your marriage is community property, you must do so by showing a "preponderance of the evidence." [22]

Separate property includes the following:[23]

1. Property acquired by a spouse prior to the start of a community regime. All property owned prior to marriage is separate property, unless the spouse converts the separate property to community property after marriage.

2. Property acquired with separate property by a spouse.

3. Property acquired with separate and community property when the community property's value is "inconsequential" in comparison to the separate property. The nonowner spouse is entitled to reimbursement for one-half of the value of the community property used to acquire the separate property.

4. Property acquired by a spouse by donation or inheritance to a spouse individually.

5. Property acquired by a spouse as a result of a voluntary partition of the community during marriage. For example, your estate plan may warrant converting community property to separate property owned by you or your spouse.

Although dividends and interest of separate property are community property, capital appreciation of separate property not achieved through the uncompensated common labor and industry of either spouse is generally not community property.[24] Thus the increase in value of a separate property stock investment is separate property, but dividends from this investment are community property unless a declaration of separateness is filed.

You may convert separate property to community property by donation between you and your spouse. Likewise, community property may be converted to separate property by donation of a spouse's community half to the other spouse. No gift taxes result from donations between spouses due to the unlimited marital deduction. This strategy may be used to help equalize the value of each spouse's estate to ensure that the lifetime federal estate tax exemption is not wasted if the first spouse to die has too few assets to utilize their entire exemption. Portability of the deceased spouse's unused estate tax exemption minimizes the need for this planning strategy for tax purposes. Donating a spouse's half of community property to the other spouse to create separate property may also help insulate the asset from lawsuits arising from the donating spouse's liability exposure.

Commingling Separate and Community Property

Many people are under the impression that if community property and separate property are commingled, all of the separate property is converted to community property. The mere commingling of separate property and community property does not automatically convert separate property into community property. For example, commingling separate funds with a checking account containing community funds does not automatically convert the separate funds into community property. However, the spouse claiming that the property is separate must rebut the presumption that the funds are community property with a "preponderance of the evidence." Clear documentation tracking the source of funds as separate property would provide such evidence. If, on the other hand, the separate funds cannot be differentiated from community funds, all of the funds are community property.[25]

For example, if Thibodaux deposits inherited separate property investments into a community property account owned by him and his wife, Marie, the *presumption* is that the entire account is community property. If Thibodaux can document with sufficient proof which assets are his separate property, he (or his separate property heirs) can prove these assets are Thibodaux's separate property. Account statements clearly showing the deposits of the separate property investment funds into the account should provide sufficient proof. In many cases, it is prudent to segregate separate property in separate property accounts to avoid this issue.

It is important to be aware of and to properly document the legal status of your property to prevent disputes among your loved ones. For example, if Boudreaux's will leaves half of his separate property to a child or all of his community property to his surviving spouse, unnecessary problems may arise if there is a dispute over whether certain assets owned by Boudreaux are classified as community or separate. Proper planning and documentation of the status of assets are essential to ensure a smooth transfer of assets to your loved ones.

Tenancy in Common (Co-Ownership)

A third type of property ownership is recognized in Louisiana, namely, tenancy in common (co-ownership). Louisiana law allows two or more individuals to own property "in indivision," with each having undivided fractional shares.[26] Co-ownership occurs when two or more people own the same asset. Unless proven otherwise, there is a presumption that the co-owners have equal shares of the co-owned property; however, co-ownership may be split among the owners in numerous ownership share combinations: 60/40, 75/25, 99/1, 20/30/50, etc.

As a co-owner, you may transfer, lease or burden with usufruct your share of the property held as tenants in common. However, the consent of all co-owners is required to transfer, encumber, or lease the entire co-owned property.[27]

Many people have the impression that merely placing a person's name on the account or property title is sufficient to make that person a co-owner. This is usually not the case, however. The consideration furnished test looks to the property that each "owner" contributed to determine ownership rights. For example, if Boudreaux and his son, Pierre, each contribute $5,000 to open a bank or investment account, each will have a 50 percent ownership interest in the account. If Boudreaux dies, 50 percent of the account value as of the date of death (assuming no withdrawals or additional contributions) will be included in his probate estate and gross estate. If Boudreaux contributes $7,000 and Pierre contributes $3,000 to open the account, then Boudreaux will have a 70 percent ownership interest, and Pierre a 30 percent ownership interest. If Boudreaux dies, 70 percent of the account value at the date of death will be included in his probate estate and gross estate. A common example of this issue is where a parent contributes 100 percent of the assets used to open a bank account, and the child contributes nothing. In this case, 100 percent of the account value at the date of death is included in the parent's probate estate and gross estate. None of the account would transfer to the child unless the child inherits by will or through intestacy. For ownership to transfer to the child, the child must either withdraw the funds from the account, or the parent must execute an act of donation.

Louisiana allows certain financial institutions (e.g. banks, savings and loan associations, credit unions) to provide accounts with payable on death (POD) or survivorship designations.[28] These statutes relieve the financial institution from liability for distributing the assets to the survivor named on the account or the POD designee. These statutes do not appear to prevent an individual from enforcing a property right against the person to whom the account was paid. For example, Boudreaux contributes $50,000 of community property assets to a certificate of deposit POD to Pierre, his child from a prior marriage. Upon Boudreaux's death, the financial institution will distribute the entire $50,000 to Pierre. Because the money used to open the account was community property, Boudreaux's wife, Clotile, may enforce her community property rights of half of the account value. Clotile would have to seek a remedy from Pierre rather than the financial institution.

If two or more people inherit the same tract of real estate and none is given a specific section of land, it is owned in indivision as co-owners. A co-owner is not required to continue ownership as a co-owner and may decide to end the co-ownership in several ways. All co-owners may agree to sell the entire tract to a third party and split the proceeds. In the alternative, one or more co-owners may agree to be bought out by other co-owners. In addition, one co-owner may decide to sell his or her undivided interest to a third party. Another option is a partition "in kind" whereby the property is divided into separate tracts of land where each co-owner will be the sole owner of their respective tract of land. If all of the co-owners agree as to how to partition the property, it may be divided without judicial intervention.[29] If they are unable to agree, a co-owner may petition the court to determine how to partition the property. If the property cannot be split into parcels of equal value, the property may be sold by partition by licitation (sheriff's sale).[30]

Upon the death of one or more co-owners, the deceased co-owner's undivided share will be transferred to the decedent's heirs by will or intestacy. The surviving co-owners do not automatically become the owners of the deceased co-owner's share, unless they inherit the deceased co-owner's share by will or through intestacy.

Property Owned as Joint Tenants

Another common pitfall is illustrated in the following example involving out-of-state immovable property, typically real estate. Immovable property is generally governed by the state laws of its locale. You must use caution when titling property located outside of Louisiana to ensure the property title does not frustrate your estate plan. For example, Thibodaux and his sister, Marie, own immovable property in Mississippi as joint tenants with rights of survivorship (JTWOS). Thibodaux's will bequeaths all of his property to his children. Thibodaux predeceases Marie. Marie is now the full owner of the immovable property he owned as JTWOS in Mississippi, and Thibodaux's children receive no portion of the property. Because the immovable property was located in Mississippi, which recognizes JTWOS, the surviving joint tenant, Marie, is the property's full owner after Thibodaux's death, regardless of the provisions in Thibodaux's will.

Many Louisiana residents have brokerage (investment) accounts registered as joint tenants with rights of survivorship or tenancy by the entirety. Neither one of these forms of property ownership have legal effect in Louisiana. If the property is actually community property, and the account registration is titled joint tenancy with rights of survivorship, the property remains community property. A similar outcome results when two Louisiana residents, who are not married to each other, contribute property to a brokerage account. In Louisiana, the brokerage account can only be recognized as a tenants-in-common account. Typically, however, the brokerage account is erroneously titled as joint tenants with rights of survivorship. Despite this, the assets in the account retain tenant-in-common status.

[1] La. Civ. Code Ann. Art. 2340.
[2] La. Civ. Code Ann. Art. 2336.
[3] La. Civ. Code Ann. Art. 2327.
[4] La. Civ. Code Ann. Art. 2356.
[5] La. Civ. Code Ann. Art. 2329.
[6] La. Civ. Code Ann. Art. 2338.
[7] Id.
[8] Id.
[9] Id.
[10] La. Civ. Code Ann. Art. 2339.
[11] La. Civ. Code Ann. Art. 2338.
[12] Id.
[13] La. Civ. Code Ann. Art. 2339.
[14] La. Civ. Code Ann. Art. 2343.
[15] La. Civ. Code Ann. Art. 2340.
[16] La. Civ. Code Ann. Art. 3523.
[17] La. Civ. Code Ann. Art. 3524.
[18] La Civ. Code Ann. Art. 3525.
[19] La. Civ. Code Ann. Art. 3526.
[20] La. Civ. Code Ann. Art. 3527.
[21] 26 U.S.C.A. § 1014(b)(6), (7).
[22] Talbot v. Talbot 864 So. 2d 590 (La. 2003).
[23] La. Civ. Code Ann. Art. 2341.
[24] La. Civ. Code Ann. Art. 2368.
[25] Curtis v. Curtis, 403 So. 2d 56 (La. 1981).
[26] La. Civ. Code Ann. Art. 797.
[27] La. Civ. Code Ann. Art. 805.
[28] La. Rev. Stat. Ann. §§ 6:312, 6:314, 6:653.1, 6:664, 6:765, 6:766.
[29] La. Civ. Code Ann. Art. 809.
[30] La. Civ. Code Ann. Art. 811.

17

Usufruct and Naked Ownership

Chapter Highlights

❖ Usufruct of an asset grants to a person the power to use the asset for the usufruct's duration. The usufruct may be for life or for a shorter period.

❖ A usufruct may be created by operation of law, by will or by act (e.g. donation or sale).

❖ The naked owners are the asset's owners subject to the usufruct.

❖ When the usufruct ends, the person with usufruct (the usufructuary) of a consumable asset must deliver to the naked owners either the value the asset had at the start of the usufruct or things of the same quality and quantity. At the end of a usufruct of a nonconsumable asset, the usufructuary must deliver the asset to the naked owner.

❖ The power to dispose of nonconsumable assets (e.g. real estate or investments) must be granted to the usufructuary, otherwise the naked owners must consent to the sale or donation.

❖ Many Louisiana residents leave their surviving spouse the usufruct for life over their estate. The children, as naked owners, will receive the full ownership of the property at the end of the usufruct.

❖ A usufruct for life qualifies for the QTIP election and offers unique planning opportunities.

A DISCUSSION OF estate planning in Louisiana would not be complete without a discussion of usufruct and naked ownership. The methods of creating usufruct as well as the laws governing usufruct of movable and immovable property have great importance to planning your estate. In addition, a general understanding of these concepts is vital to understanding estate planning concepts in Louisiana.

Full Ownership

A person with full ownership has the "direct, immediate and exclusive authority over a thing" and has the right to the use, enjoyment and disposal (sale, donation, etc.) of the thing owned.[1] A person with full ownership enjoys all of the benefits of ownership. For example, the owner of a home may live in the home, allow others to live in the home, rent the home to another person, sell, donate, or mortgage the home. The rights of full ownership may be split into usufruct and naked ownership. Likewise, the rights of usufruct and naked ownership may be combined to form full ownership.

Usufruct

A usufruct is a real right of limited duration of the property belonging to another individual.[2] Usufruct grants the right to use, possess and administer property and the right to the income, utility, profits and advantages produced from the property subject to usufruct. The usufructuary[a] may use the property for the usufruct's duration. Unless specifically allowed by law or by the person granting the usufruct, the usufructuary cannot sell, donate, encumber or transfer the property without the naked owner's consent. Usufruct may be over movable, immovable, consumable or nonconsumable property. In addition, a usufruct may last for a limited period of time (e.g. 7 years); until the occurrence of an event (e.g. remarriage); or for the usufructuary's lifetime. A usufruct may be granted in favor of successive usufructuaries.[3] For example, a usufruct on a tract of land in favor of a surviving spouse that will continue in favor of a child upon the death of the surviving spouse. In addition, usufruct may be established in favor of several usufructuaries.[4]

---

[a] The person who has the usufruct.

A usufruct may be created in the following ways:

By Operation of Law:

- A surviving spouse has a legal usufruct of community property inherited by the deceased spouse's descendants under intestate law.[5] Therefore, if you die without a will, your spouse will have a usufruct over your half of the community property. The usufruct terminates upon remarriage.

- Surviving parents have the usufruct of the separate property inherited by the decedent's siblings through intestacy if a decedent dies without descendants.[6] If you die without a will and without descendants, your brothers and sisters inherit your property, subject to your parents' usufruct. If your parents predecease you, your siblings inherit your property as full owners.

- Parents of minor children have the usufruct of property inherited by their children, but not property received by gift, nor to property acquired by their minor children's own labor and industry.[7]

By Testament (Will): A testator may bequeath the usufruct of any or all of his or her assets for the legatee's lifetime or for a shorter period of time. For wills executed on or after June 18, 1996, the usufruct is for life unless otherwise stipulated.[8]

By Act: A person may transfer the usufruct over his or her property by act of sale, donation or assignment. A person may also transfer the property's naked ownership and retain the usufruct.

Usufruct of Consumables

Consumables are assets that cannot be used without being consumed or without their substance being changed.[9] Examples of consumables include cash, harvested agricultural products, inventories, time deposits (CDs) and promissory notes. The usufructuary of consumables becomes the owner of such property and may spend the property as the owner but owes an obligation to the property's naked owners when the usufruct ends. The usufructuary must pay to the naked owner either the value that the thing had at the usufruct's start or deliver to the naked owner things of the same quantity and quality.[10]

For example, Boudreaux leaves a lifetime usufruct of $100,000 cash (a consumable) to Clotile, and his child Pierre is the naked owner. Clotile may consume the cash by spending it, or she may invest it and spend the interest and dividends. When the usufruct terminates at Clotile's death, Clotile's estate owes Pierre $100,000 for the cash value at the usufruct's start. What happens if Clotile spends the $100,000 and dies with little or no assets left in her estate? Pierre is likely out of luck and is left with no means of recovering the property he should now own as full owner. This is a major shortcoming of a usufruct over consumable property. Placing these assets in trust to benefit Clotile as the income beneficiary and Pierre as the principal beneficiary can avoid leaving Pierre in this unfortunate situation.

Usufruct of Nonconsumables

Nonconsumables are assets that may be enjoyed without alteration of their substance.[11] Examples of nonconsumables include land, the family home and other buildings, vehicles, shares of stock, bonds, mutual funds, and furniture. The usufructuary has the right of possession and the right to derive utility and profits but does not have ownership.[12] The usufructuary must act as a prudent administrator of the nonconsumable subject to the usufruct and must deliver the property to the naked owner at the usufruct's termination. For example, Boudreaux leaves to Clotile a usufruct for life of a tract of 100 acres of land (a nonconsumable asset). Pierre, their son, is the naked owner. Clotile may lease the land or plant crops on the land for her benefit. When the usufruct terminates at Clotile's death, the 100-acre tract of land must be delivered to Pierre as the full owner. A usufructuary over nonconsumables generally does not enjoy the right to unilaterally dispose[b] of the property; however, the usufructuary may be granted the right to dispose of nonconsumables without the naked owner's consent. For example, you may provide your spouse with the power to sell nonconsumable property (e.g. real estate or investments) without your children's consent. If you do not provide your spouse with the power to dispose of nonconsumable assets, your children may prevent your

---

[b] The right to sell, donate, encumber or destroy the property.

spouse from selling nonconsumable assets (e.g. the family home or investments). In some situations, this outcome is desirable; however, most people prefer to provide their surviving spouse with the power to dispose of nonconsumable assets to provide the usufructuary with maximum control and flexibility with regard to the usufruct.

When an asset subject to usufruct is sold, the usufruct attaches to the sale's proceeds, unless the parties agree otherwise.[13] The property received shall be classified as consumable or nonconsumable according to the Civil Code articles governing usufructs. Unless otherwise agreed, if the usufructuary with the power to dispose of nonconsumables sells a tract of land for cash, the usufruct attaches to the cash proceeds. The cash proceeds are a consumable and may be spent by the usufructuary, subject to the obligation to make the naked owner whole at the termination of the usufruct. Alternatively, the naked owner and the usufructuary may agree to divide the proceeds according to the value of their ownership interests.

The right to dispose of nonconsumable property includes the rights to sell, lease, alienate and encumber the property. It does not include the right to donate, unless that right is expressly granted.[14] If a thing subject to the usufruct is donated by the usufructuary, he is obligated to pay to the naked owner at the termination of the usufruct the value of the thing at the time of the donation.[15]

A usufructuary may dispose of corporeal movables that are gradually and substantially impaired by use, wear or decay. For example, vehicles, appliances and equipment may be sold without the express authorization to dispose of such items, provided the usufructuary acts as a prudent administrator.

Naked Ownership

Naked owners are the asset's owners subject to the usufructuary's rights. The naked owners will become full owners upon the end of the usufruct's term; upon the occurrence of a stipulated event; or upon the usufructuary's death. When the usufruct terminates, the naked owners of consumable assets are to receive the asset's value as of the time the usufruct commenced or property of the same kind and quantity. At the termination of a usufruct of nonconsumable assets, the naked owners are to receive the assets. The naked owner cannot interfere with the lawful exercise of a usufructuary's use and enjoyment of the asset.

Applying Usufruct in Planning

Most Louisiana residents who are married choose to provide a usufruct for life to their surviving spouse over the first-to-die spouse's half of the community property. If you are married, your surviving spouse is the owner of half of the community property and the usufruct provides your spouse the use of the other one-half. This arrangement serves several purposes.

First, your surviving spouse has the use of the property subject to usufruct for his or her lifetime. Thus, your surviving spouse may continue to live in the family home and may receive the income from and use other community property at his or her leisure. The naked owners, who are typically your children, cannot interfere with your surviving spouse's right to use and enjoy the property over which he or she has usufruct. You may also provide your surviving spouse with a usufruct for life over any separate property you own.

Second, with your children as naked owners, you, as the first-to-die spouse, have some assurance that your children will become full owners of your half of the community property when your surviving spouse dies. Upon your surviving spouse's death, the usufruct ends and your children become the property's full owners. So even if your surviving spouse leaves nothing by his or her will to your children, they shall become the full owners of the property you leave to them as naked owners. Compare this with leaving all of the community property to your surviving spouse in full ownership. In that scenario, your surviving spouse, as full owner of all of the community property, can leave all of the community property (which is now separate property) to whomever he or she chooses, gift the assets to another person or spend all of the community property. Unless forced heirship applies, your children may be completely disinherited of the entire estate, including your half of the community property and your separate property. This may be of particular concern to you if you have children of a previous marriage or if your surviving spouse is likely to remarry and may leave everything to his or her new spouse. Leaving the naked ownership of assets to your children and the usufruct to your spouse allows both to benefit from the assets. Alternatively, these same objectives may be accomplished with a trust which provides more control and certainty than usufruct and naked ownership.

It is important that spouses understand what happens with a usufruct arrangement upon the death of the first spouse to avoid unintended results. For example, Boudreaux is married to Clotile and they own a community property brokerage account that consists of stocks and bonds. Their wills leave the usufruct for life of their property to the surviving spouse with the naked ownership to their two children. Upon the first spouse's death, the brokerage account will be split into two accounts- half will be placed into an account for Clotile as her community property share. Her rights to her share of the community property are unrestricted. Boudreaux's half will be placed into a usufruct account with Clotile as usufructuary and their children as the naked owners. Clotile has the right to the income from the account. If Clotile does not have the power to dispose of nonconsumable property (the stocks and bonds) she must have the consent of the children as the naked owners to sell the stocks or bonds. The naked owners may decide not to consent to Clotile selling the stocks and bonds. If Clotile is not allowed to sell the stocks and bonds, she is entitled to spend the income from the stocks and bonds but may not spend the stocks and bonds. If, however, Clotile has the power to dispose of nonconsumables, she may sell the stocks and bonds without the consent of the naked owners. Selling the stocks and bonds converts these assets into cash which is a consumable that Clotile may spend. However, Clotile (or her estate) owes to the naked owners an amount equal to the value of the stocks and bonds sold minus taxes she paid as a result of the sale.

If the usufruct is over consumable property (e.g. cash or certificates of deposit) the usufructuary becomes the owner and may consume these assets as they wish. At the end of the usufruct, the usufructuary or their estate must pay to the naked owner the value that the consumable property had at the beginning of the usufruct.

Usufruct over Retirement Assets

Non-probate assets (such as employer plans, annuities and IRAs) are not included in the succession; rather, the account is simply distributed to the beneficiary outside of the succession. For example, if the nonparticipant spouse of a community-property IRA owner dies, the succession documents will typically not list the nonparticipant spouse's community interest in the IRA. If the nonparticipant spouse leaves the naked ownership of all of his or her assets to the children, the naked owners of the nonparticipant spouse's community share would find it difficult to later enforce their property rights (by way of an accounting). The amount due the naked owners through the accounting will depend on whether the usufruct is over a consumable or nonconsumable asset. The law is unclear whether an IRA, employer plan or annuity is a consumable or nonconsumable. The argument is stronger for classifying these assets as nonconsumables.

For example, assume Clotile and Pierre are married and Pierre has a community property IRA. When Clotile dies, she leaves the naked ownership of all of her assets to their children. If Pierre remarries and names his new wife, Marie, as the IRA beneficiary, upon Pierre's death, the IRA will be distributed to Marie as the beneficiary. But what about the naked-ownership portion of Clotile's half of the community property IRA? The naked owners have a claim against Pierre's estate for their share of the IRA. This situation can be avoided by properly coordinating your retirement assets with your will.

Additional Considerations

To avoid uncertainty with regard to classification as a consumable or nonconsumable asset, you may stipulate the usufruct's terms by testament or otherwise so long as the modification is consistent with the nature of usufruct.[16] For example, a nonparticipant spouse who wishes to leave the naked ownership of his or her community property interest to the children with usufruct to the surviving spouse may stipulate that the usufruct will be over a consumable (even if the assets are nonconsumables) or nonconsumable (even if the assets are consumables).

For federal estate tax purposes, the usufruct's classification as of a consumable or nonconsumable can have major tax implications. If classified as a consumable, the value included in the predeceasing spouse's estate is the value at the usufruct's start. This is also the amount that the surviving spouse deducts from his or her estate as a debt to the naked owners for the usufruct accounting. Compare this outcome to a usufruct of nonconsumables where the debt value owed to the naked owners is the value at the usufruct's termination. If there was significant appreciation in the nonconsumable from the time of the first spouse's death, the nonconsumable asset will provide a much larger deduction for the debt owed to the naked owners than would a usufruct of a consumable. To eliminate doubt as to whether the asset is classified as a consumable or nonconsumable, you should stipulate.

Granting usufruct for life also allows the use of the Qualified Terminal Interest Property (QTIP) election for federal estate tax purposes. See the discussion on the QTIP election in Chapter 23.

Another planning option provided by usufruct is to transfer the naked ownership of real estate (often your home) to your children while you and your spouse retain a joint and successive usufruct for life. Your children cannot force you out of the home, interfere with your use of the home or require that you pay rent. When the last spouse dies, the children become full owners of the property without going through probate.

[1] La. Civ. Code Ann. Art. 477.

[2] La. Civ. Code Ann. Art. 535.

[3] La. Civ. Code Ann. Art. 546.

[4] La. Civ. Code Ann. Art. 547.

[5] La. Civ. Code Ann. Art. 890.

[6] La. Civ. Code Ann. Art. 891.

[7] La. Civ. Code Ann. Arts. 223, 226.

[8] La. Civ. Code Ann. Art. 1499.

[9] La. Civ. Code Ann. Art. 536.

[10] La. Civ. Code Ann. Art 538.

[11] La. Civ. Code Ann. Art. 537.

[12] La. Civ. Code Ann. Art. 539.

[13] La. Civ. Code Ann. Art. 616.

[14] La. Civ. Code Ann. Art. 568.

[15] La. Civ. Code Ann. Art. 568.1.

[16] La. Civ. Code Ann. Art. 545.

18

Forced Heirship

Chapter Highlights

❖ Forced heirship is a unique Louisiana concept that requires certain categories of descendants to receive a minimum portion (the forced portion) of your estate.

❖ Forced heirs are entitled to the forced portion regardless of contrary provisions in your will.

❖ Generally, children under the age of 24 and children of any age who are disabled are forced heirs.

❖ Certain assets such as life insurance and retirement plans are exempt from forced heirship.

❖ The forced portion may be placed in trust, and your surviving spouse may be given the usufruct over the forced portion.

❖ A forced heir who does not receive the forced portion may enforce the claim to the forced portion unless otherwise prohibited by the will or other act.

❖ Parents with disabled children should consider establishing a special needs trust to receive the disabled child's forced portion.

THE STATE OF LOUISIANA IS unique in that its laws provide for forced heirship. When planning an estate in Louisiana, an understanding of forced heirship and its effects is crucial to avoid unintended results after the application of a forced heir's rights. Forced heirship provides certain rights to your forced heirs, including the right to claim a forced portion (the legitime) of your estate, the right to nullify certain lifetime gifts and the right to compel collation (equalization) of certain lifetime donations. The rules of forced heirship are as follows:[1]

1. All children[a] who have not attained age 24 are forced heirs.

2. All children (of any age) who, at the time of their parent's death, are permanently incapable of taking care of their person or administering their estate, due or mental or physical incapacity, are forced heirs.

3. Grandchildren are forced heirs of their grandparents if the grandparents' child (the grandchildren's parent) predeceased the grandparent and would not have reached the age of 24 at the time of the grandparents' death.

4. Grandchildren whose parent has predeceased the grandparents are forced heirs of their grandparents if the grandchildren are permanently incapable of taking care of their person or estate, due to mental or physical incapacity, at the time of the grandparents' death.

For the purposes of forced heirship, permanently incapable of taking care of their person or administering their estate at the time of the death of the decedent (e.g. the forced heir's parent) shall include descendants who, at the time of death of the decedent, have, according to medical documentation, an inherited, incurable disease or condition that may render them incapable of caring for their person or administering their estate in the future.[2]

The Forced Portion

The forced portion is one fourth of the legitime if there is one forced heir. If there is more than one forced heir, the forced portion is one half of the legitime.[3] However, if the fraction used to calculate the forced portion is greater than the fraction of the decedent's[b] estate that the forced heir would receive if the decedent died intestate, the forced

---

[a] A child means a natural or adopted child. It includes a child whose filiation is established.
[b] A decedent is a person who is deceased.

portion is calculated using the fraction of an intestate successor.[4] For example, Thibodaux dies leaving five children, one of which is a forced heir. The normal rule calculates the forced portion as one fourth of the legitime. However, because Thibodaux died leaving five children, the forced portion is one fifth of the legitime.[c]

What Does All of This Mean?

Although forced heirship does not prevent you from making a will, it may limit how your estate is distributed. At the time of your death, your children under the age of 24, incapacitated children and grandchildren in certain situations are forced heirs and have a claim against the forced portion of your estate. Keep in mind that all children are potentially forced heirs in the event of future disability. After the legitime is satisfied, the remainder of your estate (the disposable portion) may be distributed to anyone you choose.

What are a Forced Heir's Rights?

A forced heir must assert his or her right to the forced portion if he or she has not received assets sufficient to satisfy his or her inheritance rights under forced heirship. However, a forced heir may honor the testator's wishes by not asserting rights as a forced heir. If a forced heir's legitime is "impinged," the forced heir may assert his or her right of reduction.[5] A forced heir has five years from the decedent's death to assert his or her right to reduce excessive donations to the extent necessary to eliminate an impinged legitime.[6]

Property Exempt from Forced Heirship

Forced heirship does not apply to all of your property. Assets excluded from forced heirship include[7]

- Inter-vivos donations (gifts made during your lifetime) made at least three years prior to death.
- Retirement plans.

---

[c] If Thibodaux died intestate, each heir receives one fifth of his estate. Because one fifth is less than one fourth, one fifth is used to calculate the forced portion. If Thibodaux died leaving three children, one of which was a forced heir, the forced portion is one fourth of the legitime.

- IRAs.

- Insurance proceeds on your life, and premiums paid for such insurance.

In addition, forced heirship will not apply if your domicile is outside of Louisiana and you have no forced heirs domiciled in Louisiana at the time of your death.[8]

You may provide a usufruct to your surviving spouse[d] over the forced portion without impinging upon the forced portion. Thus, your surviving spouse may be given the usufruct for life over property which includes your child's forced portion.[9] If the surviving spouse with the usufruct of the forced portion is not the forced heir's parent, the forced heir may request security.[10] A forced heir may also request security if the usufruct of the forced portion affects separate property. Security may be required even if the usufructuary is the forced heir's parent.[11] In addition, the forced portion may be placed in trust, even for the forced heir's lifetime.[12]

The legitime is in terms of quantum or value. Thus, a forced heir is entitled to receive property of value at least equal to his or her legitime. In addition, the testator may select assets to satisfy the legitime, or he or she may delegate this authority to the executor.

One option to consider when working around the forced heirship requirements is that life insurance proceeds may be used to satisfy a forced heir's legitime. If the forced heir is unable to properly manage the insurance proceeds due to incapacity or immaturity, the proceeds should be placed in trust until the forced heir is capable of prudently managing such assets.

Collation

Louisiana law assumes parents wish to treat their children equally. If you made gifts to one or more children that transferred a disproportionate amount of your estate to that child, your other children may use collation to equalize how your estate is distributed. Collation is the actual or constructive return to the succession of certain donations by the decedent to be divided together with the other succession property.[13] This right is granted to children who qualify as

---

[d] Whether or not the surviving spouse is the parent of the forced heir.

the decedent's forced heirs. As the law currently stands, collation only applies to gifts made within three years of death and applies to the date of gift value.[14] To avoid the possibility of a child bringing an action for collation, you may dispense with collation in your will, act of donation or authentic act, making collation inapplicable.

Avoiding Disqualification from Governmental Entitlement Programs

If a disabled child is receiving or may receive governmental financial assistance, a Special Needs Trust should be considered to prevent the child from being disqualified from governmental entitlement programs. Because a disabled child of any age is a forced heir, simply disinheriting a disabled child may not be sufficient to avoid disqualification. In addition, you may prefer not to disinherit a disabled child but wish to provide assets for his or her benefit without disqualification from governmental benefits. A disabled child receiving a forced portion may exceed the income and resource limits to retain qualification for the governmental assistance. A Special Needs Trust for the forced portion of a disabled heir can prevent disqualification from governmental entitlement programs. In fact, a parent or grandparent may leave an amount in excess of the forced portion to a Special Needs Trust for the benefit of a disabled child or grandchild without jeopardizing governmental entitlement programs. A Special Needs Trust provides resources to the disabled heir to pay for needs other than food, shelter and other necessary expenses as provided for by the governmental entitlement program. The Special Needs Trust may pay for travel, entertainment, recreational equipment or other items or services not deemed as necessary expenses. So long as the Special Needs Trust does not pay for what is considered food and shelter, the disabled heir will not be disqualified from governmental entitlement programs regardless of the amount of assets in the Special Needs Trust. See Chapter 22 for more information about Special Needs Trusts.

---

[1] La. Civ. Code Ann. Art. 1493.
[2] La. Civ. Code Ann. Art. 1493(E).
[3] La. Civ. Code Ann. Art. 1495.
[4] Id.
[5] La. Civ. Code Ann. Art. 1504.
[6] La. Civ. Code Ann. Art. 3497.
[7] La. Civ. Code Ann. Art. 1505.
[8] La Civ. Code Ann. Art. 3533.
[9] La. Civ. Code Ann. Art. 1499.
[10] La. Civ. Code Ann. Art. 1514.
[11] Id.
[12] La. Civ. Code Ann. Art. 1502.
[13] La. Civ. Code Ann. Art. 1227.
[14] La. Civ. Code Ann. Art. 1235.

19

Community Property and Retirement Plans

Chapter Highlights

❖ Community property laws generally apply to employer plans and IRAs; therefore, amounts accumulated in these accounts are owned by each spouse as community property.

❖ The rules for community property rights of employer plans (e.g. 401k plans) are different for death and divorce. Upon divorce, each spouse is entitled to receive his or her share of the community property retirement asset. Upon death, community property rights are not as clear cut. If a nonparticipant spouse predeceases the participant spouse, the community property employer plan account is converted into the participant spouse's separate property.

❖ IRA accounts are generally not subject to different death and divorce rules. The nonparticipant spouse's community property share remains community property regardless of which spouse predeceases.

❖ Retirement accounts will pay to the named beneficiary regardless of community property rights. If there is a non-spouse beneficiary, the nonparticipant spouse or the nonparticipant spouse's heirs may have a right to be reimbursed for the community property portion due to them.

❖ If a nonparticipant spouse is the retirement account's beneficiary, most of the pitfalls discussed in this chapter can be avoided. Rolling an employer plan into an IRA may also help avoid some of the planning pitfalls.

❖ If a non-spouse is a named beneficiary due to the planning circumstances, proper planning is a must to avoid potential litigation to determine property rights. In addition, spousal consent may be required to name a non-spouse beneficiary.

LOUISIANA IS A community property state; therefore, each spouse has an undivided one-half interest in all community property assets. Community property assets include employer plans[a] and IRAs if the retirement assets are acquired during the community regime. The community regime generally applies during the marriage unless a prenuptial agreement is in effect or if the spouses otherwise elect out of the community property regime.

In the event of divorce, the nonparticipant spouse has a right to receive his or her community property interest in an IRA or employer plan. However, in the event of the employer plan participant's death or his or her spouse's death, the rules are not so clear cut. If the participant dies first, the IRA or employer plan account assets are distributed according to the beneficiary designation and not according to the participant's will, unless the estate is the beneficiary. A problem may arise when the *nonparticipant spouse dies first* and attempts to dispose of his or her community property interest in the *participant spouse's* retirement account by will or through intestacy. Proper planning and a thorough understanding of community property law and retirement plans can prevent unintended results.

For example, Pierre and Clotile have been married for 25 years and have lived in Louisiana the entire time. Pierre is employed by Valero and has a 401(k) account all of which is community property. If Clotile (the nonparticipant spouse) predeceases Pierre, she cannot leave her half of Pierre's 401(k) account to someone though her will. As explained further herein, Clotile's community property share disappears if she predeceases Pierre. In this example, the 401(k) account is converted to the separate property of Pierre as per the Supreme Court's ruling in *Boggs*.[1] If these assets were not employer-plan assets, Clotile could leave her half of the community property share to whomever she would choose.

In most situations, the nonparticipant spouse intends to leave his or her share of the participant's employer plan or IRA to the surviving

---

[a] Qualified retirement plans such as 401(k) plans, pension plans, profit sharing plans and 457 plans are referred to as "employer plans." Employer plans will also include 403(b) plans.

spouse, so the *Boggs* ruling will not apply. In addition, IRAs are generally treated as community property. The main problem area involves employer plan accounts (such as 401(k) plan accounts) when the nonparticipant spouse predeceases the participant.

Community Property and Retirement Plans

Louisiana has long recognized interests in employer plans and IRAs as community property if the earnings and contributions occur during the marriage.[2] The reasoning is that an employee's contractual pension right is not a gratuity but a property interest earned by the employee. To the extent the property right is derived from the spouse's employment during the marriage's existence, it is a community asset subject to division upon the marriage's dissolution.[3] When the marriage ends, the nonparticipant spouse is entitled to half of the value of the qualified plan assets earned during the marriage.[4] Funds in an employer plan attributable to employment during the marriage are community property.

Community property rules also apply to retirement benefits and survivor benefits under the Teachers' Retirement System of Louisiana and other Louisiana public retirement systems.[5] However, a nonparticipant ex-spouse or other individual attempting to assert their community property rights to a member's retirement benefits under a Louisiana public retirement system must wait until the member is entitled to receive payments as determined by the laws governing the retirement system.[6] The member is generally entitled to receive retirement funds upon retirement. Finally, DROP accounts of Louisiana public retirement systems are generally subject to community property law.[7]

In addition, the portion of an IRA purchased with community funds is community property.[8] An IRA funded with contributions made prior to marriage are the owner's separate property; however, the fruits of separate property are community property.[9] Thus the interest and dividends earned on separate property is community property as these are civil fruits. An owner of a separate property IRA owes an accounting to the nonparticipant spouse for the fruits and products of the separate property IRA. If the participant spouse is unable to determine what portion of the growth in the IRA is attributable to interest and dividends (community property) rather than capital appreciation (separate property), all of the growth of the separate property IRA which occurs during the marriage is presumed to be community property.[10] An accounting after the participant's death is due to the surviving spouse if the surviving spouse is not the IRA beneficiary. Upon divorce, each spouse is entitled to his or her IRA community property share.

Unfortunately, dividing a community property retirement asset upon the marriage's termination is not always as simple as dividing the asset in half. For example, only a portion of the asset was accumulated during marriage if the participant spouse made contributions to a retirement plan prior to marriage. In 1978 the Louisiana Supreme Court established the *Sims* formula for calculating the nonparticipant spouse's community interest in an employer plan account upon the termination of the community.[11] The nonparticipant spouse's share is calculated as the "amount of vested annuity payment or retirement benefit, multiplied by the pension's portion (or other benefit) attributable to credible service during the community's existence, divided by the pension (or other benefit) attributable to total credible service, divided by 2." EXAMPLE: Boudreaux has a 401(k) plan account with a balance of $700,000 at the time the community ended. Boudreaux contributed $100,000 to the account prior to his marriage to Clotile. During his marriage he contributed an additional $200,000. The community property portion of the 401(k) account is $233,000.[b]

Louisiana law also provides for a more loosely defined set of guidelines to determine each spouse's community property interest where the rigidity of the Sims formula would be inequitable.[12] One option is the present value method of calculating community property rights where the projected future pension benefits of the employee spouse are discounted to the present and "adjusted and discounted for contingencies such as mortality, interest, probability of vesting, probability of continued employment and retirement life expectancy."[13] The formula is to be used at the time of partition and not at the time of the community's termination.[14]

Retirement benefits in DROP accounts which were accumulated after the community's termination are subject to a nonparticipant

---

[b] Community property contributions $200,000 x account balance $700,000 / total contributions $300,000 x ½ = $233,333.

spouse's claim and division of the DROP account according to the *Sims* formula.[15]

Community Property and IRA Accounts

The Internal Revenue Code requires IRAs to ignore community property law.[16] The entire IRA is included in the decedent spouse's estate as the decedent's separate property. Upon the participant's death, the designated beneficiary will receive all distributions from the IRA, even if the entire IRA was accumulated during the community property regime. In spite of the Internal Revenue Code and La. R. S. 9:2449 which states that IRA benefits will be paid to the designated beneficiary as provided in the IRA agreement, IRAs are generally considered community property.[17] As such, each spouse includes his or her IRA community share in his or her estate.

If the surviving spouse is named the deceased spouse's IRA beneficiary, he or she receives both spouses' community shares. For federal estate tax purposes, if the surviving spouse is named the sole beneficiary, the value of the entire IRA is included in the surviving spouse's estate via the marital deduction. The portion of the deceased spouse's IRA that is not left to the surviving spouse is included in the deceased participant spouse's estate, subject to an accounting for the surviving spouse's community portion.

If the surviving spouse is not the beneficiary of a community property IRA, the IRA participant's estate may owe an accounting to the surviving spouse for his or her community property interest after the IRA owner dies.[18] The amount due to the surviving spouse is deductible against the decedent's estate. If the surviving spouse is the IRA beneficiary, no accounting would be required, and many of the issues discussed herein are avoided.

When a nonparticipant spouse dies, the estate may be due a receivable from the participant spouse for the nonparticipant spouse's community share. For example, Clotile predeceases Boudreaux and leaves the full ownership of all of her property to her children. Under Louisiana's community property law, her children own an interest in all of Clotile's property, including her community share of Boudreaux's IRA. If Boudreaux names his cousin Thibodaux as the IRA beneficiary, upon Boudreaux's death, Thibodaux will receive the IRA. None of the IRA will be paid to Clotile's children to satisfy

Clotile's community property interest in her husband's IRA. An accounting to Clotile's children from Boudreaux's estate is required.

Community Property, Qualified Plans and ERISA

The origin of much of the difficulty associated with community property rights and employer plans is the conflict between state law and federal law. The Supremacy Clause of the United States Constitution provides that federal law will prevail over state law when they are in conflict. Louisiana community property law provides that each spouse owns half of the community property and that each spouse owes an accounting to the other spouse at the community's termination.[19] The accounting is a heritable obligation.[c] Therefore, if an employer plan or IRA is community property, Louisiana law provides that each spouse, or his or her heirs, is entitled to his or her community share which is included in each spouse's estate. Taken a step further, each spouse should be able to bequeath his or her community share to whomever he or she chooses.

Federal law, in particular ERISA,[d] "...shall supersede any and all State laws insofar as they may now or hereafter relate to any employee benefit plan...." Therefore, the surviving participant spouse's property rights provided by ERISA override Louisiana community property law. The *Boggs* decision emphasized the importance of protecting a surviving spouse's retirement benefits and the income stream provided for by ERISA regulated plans (e.g. pensions and 401k plans). The Supreme Court placed more emphasis on protecting retirement benefits for surviving spouses than protecting a nonparticipant spouse's successors.

Specifically, a nonparticipant spouse who predeceases the participant spouse cannot bequeath his or her community share to another person. This is an obvious conflict between state law and federal law. As a result, Louisiana community property rights are pre-empted by ERISA when dealing with a nonparticipant spouse's rights

---

[c] A spouse or his or her heirs may demand an accounting from the other spouse or his or her heirs.

[d] The Employee Retirement Income Security Act of 1974 (ERISA) is a federal law that governs qualified retirement plans (i.e. employer plans). ERISA prohibits the assignment or alienation of employer-plan rights.

to benefits in his or her spouse's employer retirement plan as of the participant's date of death as determined by the U. S. Supreme Court in *Boggs*.[20]

Employer-plan assets that are earned and accumulated during marriage are generally considered community property. If the participant predeceases, the participant's surviving spouse is entitled to his or her half and the participant's half of the employer plan. In addition, plans that are governed by the Retirement Equity Act of 1984 (REA) require that benefits of a married participant be distributed in the form of a qualified joint and survivor annuity (QJSA), unless the participant's spouse receives 100 percent of the participant's account at the participant's death or waives the right to a QJSA.[e] Therefore, the nonparticipant spouse's consent is required to name someone other than the nonparticipant spouse as beneficiary. If the nonparticipant spouse consents to another beneficiary, the nonparticipant spouse waives his or her rights to the spouse's employer plan under REA.

This is where it gets a little tricky. If the nonparticipant spouse dies first, the employer-plan assets are transformed from a community property asset to a separate property asset. As a result, a predeceasing nonparticipant spouse cannot transfer his or her share to someone other than the participant spouse. The predeceasing nonparticipant spouse's estate does not have a claim for the nonparticipant spouse's community half. This is the effect of the *Boggs* decision.

Therefore, the rules for death and divorce are different. Upon divorce, each spouse is entitled to half of the employer-plan assets.[f] If a nonparticipant spouse predeceases the participant, the employer-plan asset is converted to the participant spouse's separate property. If the participant spouse dies first, the employer plan retains its community property status.

To avoid the elimination of the predeceasing, nonparticipant spouse's share, the Louisiana Legislature enacted La. R.S. 9:2801.1. This statute attempts to circumvent the effect of *Boggs*. La. R.S. 9:2801.1 provides:

---

[e] REA applies to pension plans and some profit sharing and stock bonus plans.
[f] Assuming all contributions and account appreciation in the account occurred during the community regime (during marriage).

When federal law or the provisions of a statutory pension or retirement plan, state or federal, preempt or preclude community classification of property that would have been classified as community property under the principles of the Civil Code, the spouse of the person entitled to such property shall be allocated or assigned the ownership of community property equal in value to such property prior to the division of the rest of the community property. Nevertheless, if such property consists of a spouse's right to receive social security benefits or the benefits themselves, then the court in its discretion may allocate or assign other community property equal in value to the other spouse.

This statute may not withstand a constitutional challenge under the Supremacy Clause. We will have to see how this will be settled in the courts. Hopefully, Congress will enact legislation to resolve this conflict between state and federal law.

IRAs and the Boggs Decision

A different outcome results when dealing with IRAs as IRAs are not subject to ERISA or REA.[g] The majority consensus is that *Boggs* does not apply to IRAs. However, until this issue is further resolved in the courts, there will be some uncertainty. If the surviving spouse is named as the IRA's sole beneficiary, he or she receives both halves of the community property interests in the IRA. If the surviving spouse does not at least receive his or her half of a community property IRA, the surviving spouse should have a claim for his or her one-half community property interest after the participant's death. This may occur if someone other than the surviving spouse is named the beneficiary of an IRA composed of community property assets.

If the predeceasing nonparticipant spouse leaves his or her community property interest in the participant spouse's IRA to the children outright or as naked owners, the children should have an enforceable property right. For example, Clotile, Boudreaux's predeceased nonparticipant spouse, leaves the naked ownership of her community share of Boudreaux's IRA to her children. Boudreaux, the

---

[g] Most 403(b) plans are not subject to ERISA or REA.

participant spouse, names Marie, his new spouse, as beneficiary. After Boudreaux's death, Marie receives the IRA benefits as the designated beneficiary. But what about Clotile's children who were the naked owners of Clotile's community share of the IRA. If Marie receives the entire IRA as beneficiary, Clotile's children receive no part of the IRA. Clotile's children should have a claim for their naked ownership interest from Boudreaux's estate.[h] This type of situation opens the door to litigation and is best avoided through proper planning.

It is important to distinguish when the IRA is funded to determine whether community property laws will apply. If benefits are rolled into an IRA from an employer plan after the nonparticipant spouse's death, then the IRA should be treated as separate property. The nonparticipant spouse's interest terminates at his or her death. However, if the benefits are rolled into an IRA from an employer plan prior to the nonparticipant spouse's death, then community property law should apply to the IRA.

Planning Options

One option is for each spouse to name the surviving spouse as the owner of any interest in each other's IRA or employer plan to reduce uncertainty when planning. If possible, one may want to leave nonretirement account assets to the children or to other non-spouse individuals.

Another option is to partition the IRA. If an IRA consists of community property owned by the spouses, the spouses may partition the IRA into separate IRAs equal to each spouse's community property interests. The original IRA participant is the owner of each IRA which prevents immediate taxation (due to a distribution) of the IRAs.[21] Each IRA may have separate beneficiaries. For example, the surviving spouse is the designated beneficiary for one IRA, and the children are the designated beneficiaries for the other IRA. The non-spousal beneficiaries (the children) receive the nonparticipant's community share IRA by virtue of being a designated beneficiary. This may be preferable to the nonparticipant spouse bequeathing his or her

---

[h] If the account were an employer plan (e.g. a 401k account), Clotile's community share of the 401k would disappear pursuant to the *Boggs* decision. In that case, there would be no accounting due Clotile's children.

community share of the IRA to the children as naked owners subject to the surviving spouse's usufruct.

To avoid the complexity and uncertainty in light of *Boggs*, participants may name their spouse as beneficiary of employer plans and IRAs. In addition, the nonparticipant spouse may want to bequeath to the participant spouse by testament his or her community property share. This would eliminate property rights children or other individuals have as naked owners against the surviving spouse's IRA, employer plan or annuity. Nonretirement assets can be used to satisfy bequests to non-spouses. The bottom line is that the best answer depends on your estate's asset composition and your planning goals.

---

[1] Boggs v. Boggs, 117 S.CT.1754 (1997).

[2] Frazier v. Harper, 600 So. 2d 59 (La. 1992); Robinson v. Robinson, 778 So. 2d 1105 (La. 2001); Bordes v. Bordes, 730 So. 2d 443 (La. 1999).

[3] La. Civ. Code; Hare v. Hodgins, 586 So. 2d 118 (La. 1991); Sims v. Sims, 358 So. 2d 919 (La. 1978); T.L. James v. Montgomery, 332 So. 2d 834 (La. 1975).

[4] La. Civ. Code Art. 2336; La. R.S. 2801.

[5] Johnson v. Wetherspoon, 694 So. 2d 203 (La. 1997).

[6] La. Rev. Stat. Ann. 11:291.

[7] Bailey v. Bailey, 708 So. 2d 354 (La. 1998); Stubbs v. Stubbs, 610 So. 2d 892 (La. Ct. App. 1st Cir. 1992).

[8] Frazier v. Harper, 600 So. 2d 59 (La. 1992).

[9] La. Civ. Code Ann. Art. 2339.

[10] McClanahan v. McClanahan, So. 2d 844 (La. Ct. App. 5th Cir. 2004.

[11] Sims v. Sims, 358 So. 2d 919 (La. 1978).

[12] Hare v. Hodgins, 586 So. 2d 118 (La. 1991).

[13] Id.

[14] Hare at 126.

[15] McKinstry v. McKinstry, 2002 LA 1216 (LACA, 2002); Bullock v.

Owens, 796 So. 2d 170 (La. App. 2 Cir. 9/26/01).

[16] Section 408(g).

[17] Succession of McVay v. McVay, 476 So. 2d 1070 (La. App. 3d Cir. 1985); Succession of Egan, 543 So. 2d 940 (La. App. 5th Cir. 1989).

[18] Succession of McVay v. McVay, 476 So. 2d 1070 (La. App. 3d Cir. 1985).

[19] La. Civ. Code Ann. Art. 2369.

[20] Boggs v. Boggs, 117 S.CT.1754 (1997).

[21] PLRs 9939021 and 9439030.

Wills

Chapter Highlights

❖ A will is a vital part of your estate plan because it allows you to maintain control over the distribution of your assets. Unfortunately, most individuals die without a will.

❖ If you die without a will, the State of Louisiana has one for you; however, your estate may not be distributed as you intended. As a result, your spouse or other loved ones may not be left with sufficient assets to maintain their standard of living.

❖ A will allows you to make specific bequests, provide usufruct to your spouse for life of all your assets, minimize potential estate taxes and create trusts to protect your children's assets from creditors and mismanagement.

❖ The two types of wills in Louisiana are the notarial will and the oligraphic (handwritten) will.

❖ You may revoke or amend your will at anytime.

❖ Wills should be reviewed by a competent estate planning attorney at least every five years or when there is a change in your family's circumstances or a revision in law. Your will should also be reviewed if it was executed in another state.

❖ You may name one or more executors in your will to represent your estate in the succession.

❖ When naming an executor, factors to consider include level of experience handling financial matters, geographic proximity, time available to devote to the succession, and overall maturity and willingness to accept the responsibilities of an executor.

❖ You may also authorize your succession to be administered as an independent administration to reduce probate expenses and delay.

A PROPERLY DRAFTED TESTAMENT (will) is the cornerstone of an effective estate plan. Unfortunately, it is estimated that 70 percent of Americans die without a will. A person who dies with a valid will dies testate, and a person who dies without a valid will dies intestate.[1] If you die intestate, the State of Louisiana's intestacy laws determine who will inherit your estate. The problem with the intestacy laws is that you lose all control with regard to who inherits your estate and how your assets will be inherited (e. g. outright or in trust). In addition, your estate may be subjected to unnecessary estate taxes that can be avoided with proper planning.

Contrary to popular belief, a will is not necessarily a lengthy, complex document. In fact, many wills are rather simple documents that define who will inherit which assets. In addition, the will typically names the executor and an attorney for the succession. Obviously, more complex estates normally require more complex wills and more in-depth estate planning.

If you have a properly funded revocable living trust, you can avoid the problems of dying without a will and avoid probate. You can also accomplish the same estate planning goals as with a will as explained in the section *Advantages of Having a Will* in this chapter. For an explanation of the pros and cons of revocable living trusts and avoiding probate see Chapter 22.

Dying Without a Valid Will

If you die without a valid will, the Louisiana intestacy laws provide the following rules for the distribution of your estate:

Intestate Heirs of <u>Community</u> Property

▪ Your descendants (children or their descendants) inherit your half of the community property, subject to the usufruct of your surviving spouse. The usufruct will terminate upon the remarriage of your surviving spouse.[2]

- If you do not have descendants, your surviving spouse inherits your half of the community property.[3]

Intestate Heirs of <u>Separate</u> Property

- Your descendants inherit your separate property in full ownership (no usufruct to your surviving spouse).[4]

- If you do not have descendants, your brothers and sisters (or their descendants) inherit your separate property, subject to a usufruct in favor of your surviving parents. [5] If your parents predecease you, your brothers and sisters (or their descendants) inherit your separate property in full ownership. If your siblings predecease you (leaving no descendants), your parents inherit your separate property in full ownership.[6]

- If none of the above survives you, your surviving spouse not judicially separated inherits your separate property in full ownership.[7]

- If you die without descendants, siblings or their descendants, or a spouse not judicially separated and your parents are deceased, your other ascendants (e.g. grandparents) inherit your separate property.[8]

- If none of the above survives, your closest collateral relation inherits your estate.[9]

Advantages of Having a Will

If you die with a properly drafted will, you maintain control over your estate distribution and can accomplish the following estate planning goals:

- Make special bequests of jewelry, cash or the family home to your spouse, child or other individual.

- Make bequests to your surviving spouse to delay or totally eliminate federal estate taxes.

- Provide your spouse with a usufruct of community <u>and</u> separate property for the remainder of his or her life.[a]

---

[a] If you die intestate, your spouse will not have usufruct over your separate property.

- Satisfy Louisiana's forced heirship requirement, even if you leave the full use (usufruct) of your estate to your surviving spouse for life or other period of time.

- Create a QTIP trust to provide for professional management of assets left to your surviving spouse, with all income paid at least annually to your surviving spouse for life. This trust will also ensure that after your surviving spouse dies, your children will ultimately receive these assets upon their reaching an age you deem appropriate.

- Grant to your spouse a usufruct for life of your property so it may qualify for the federal estate tax marital deduction. On the other hand, you may wish to terminate the usufruct upon your surviving spouse's remarriage, occurrence of other event or after a specific period of time depending on your goals.

- Grant to your spouse the "extra" usufruct rights of selling, exchanging or disposing of nonconsumable property (such as real estate) without the naked owners' (generally the children) consent. This is important to give your surviving spouse (the usufructuary) the freedom to sell real estate such as the family home without the children's consent. If your surviving spouse and a child (a naked owner) disagree about whether the family home should be sold, the child may withhold consent to sell the family home. To avoid this possibility, your will can provide that your surviving spouse may sell nonconsumable property without the naked owners' consent.

- Make specific bequests to grandchildren, charities or unrelated parties.

- Appoint two or more executors to "watch over" each other.

- Provide for alternative legatees if your spouse, children or other legatees predecease you.

- Direct your executor to make QTIP elections to defer or eliminate federal estate taxes.

- Establish trusts for children or grandchildren who are unable to manage their affairs or require professional management of assets. You select the ages the children or grandchildren will receive the property from the trust. Provisions requiring the trustee to pay for a child's educational and medical expenses or any other necessary expense may be incorporated into the trust.

- Establish a special needs trust for a disabled child.

- Provide for an independent administration of your estate.

Types of Wills in Louisiana

Two types of wills are currently utilized in Louisiana: the notarial will and the oligraphic will. Your will does not have to be recorded upon its execution, although it may be filed with the clerk of court for safekeeping. As Louisiana law does not allow joint wills, each person must execute his or her own will.[10]

Notarial Wills

A notarial will is executed in the presence of a notary and two witnesses. The testator[b] declares that he or she has read the will and acknowledges that this instrument is his or her Last Will and Testament.[11] This is the type of will your attorney will draft for you. It is signed and dated on each page and notarized.

Oligraphic Wills

The second type of will currently used in Louisiana is the oligraphic will. An oligraphic will is entirely handwritten in the testator's handwriting, signed and dated by the testator. It does not need to be notarized and requires no witnesses. Although the date may appear anywhere on an oligraphic will, the testator's signature must appear at the end. Anything written after the testator's signature will not invalidate the will, but the court has discretion to consider as part of the will anything written after the testator's signature.[12]

---

[b] A testator is the person executing the will; "testatrix" if of the feminine gender.

Due to the complex nature of estate planning, it is highly recommended that you seek competent legal advice before attempting to draft any type of will. Although oligraphic wills are easy to draft, the risk is very high that an oligraphic will drafted without the advice of an attorney will not address all of your planning issues. In fact, ambiguous language is an open invitation to litigation between your heirs and legatees.[c] While reviewing many wills, I have encountered wills with mistakes and/or omissions by attorneys and do-it-yourselfers alike—mistakes and/or omissions that produce an outcome totally unintended by the testator. Furthermore, personal situations change, and provisions that were proper five or ten years ago may not be proper under current circumstances. Testators who draft their will without the advice of an attorney are unlikely to be aware of changes in the law that would warrant updating their will.

How to Revoke Your Will

You may revoke or amend your will at any time.[13] The easiest way to revoke a will is to destroy the original will and any duplicate copies. A will may also be revoked by executing a subsequent will that expressly revokes a prior will.[14] Many wills begin with a statement that revokes all prior wills and codicils.[d] If the subsequent will does not expressly revoke the entire previous will, only dispositions of property that are incompatible or in conflict with the previous will are revoked.[15] In addition, property subject to a specific legacy in a will that is no longer in the estate (because, for example, it was sold, donated or destroyed) will cause the legacy to lapse. For example, if Boudreaux's will has a clause which leaves his 2019 Chevrolet to his nephew and Boudreaux sells the car prior to his death, the legacy lapses.

An additional way a testator may revoke a will is by stating clearly in writing that the will is revoked.[16] This statement must be entirely written and signed by the testator. Although there is no requirement that this statement be dated, it is a good idea to date such a statement. The testator may also revoke a will by a signed writing on the will itself.[17]

---

[c] Heirs are people who inherit through intestacy. Legatees are people who inherit through a will.

[d] A codicil is an amendment to a will.

After the will is executed, if the testator is divorced from the legatee at the time of his or her death, legacies to the former spouse are revoked.[18] In addition, if the spouse is named executor or trustee, these testamentary designations and appointments are likewise revoked upon divorce. The testator can provide that such provisions are not to be revoked in the event of divorce at the time of the testator's death.

If a will was executed in another state and the testator subsequently moves to Louisiana, the will is valid in Louisiana so long as it was properly executed according to the state laws of the testator's former domicile.[19] Likewise, if the testator moves from Louisiana to another state, the will is valid in that state, so long as the will was properly executed according to the laws of Louisiana. If you have a will that was executed in another state, have your will reviewed by a competent estate planning attorney to ensure that community property, usufruct and forced heirship issues are properly addressed.

If the original will cannot be found, there is a rebuttable presumption that the will was revoked. Courts have allowed a copy of the will to be probated when the original could not be found, when there was sufficient evidence to support that the testator did not wish to revoke the will. There is a presumption that the will was revoked by destruction.

Changes or Amendments to a Will

A will may be amended by a codicil, a written document executed with the same formalities as a will. Typically, a codicil is used if minor changes need to be made to a will. Given the efficiency of computers and word processors, few situations today justify a codicil. However, if the testator's mental capacity is in question, a codicil would allow the testator to amend an existing will without revoking the existing will and executing a new will. Minor changes to the will are generally not worth the risk of a challenge of the new will due to the testator's mental capacity. In this situation, a codicil would allow the minor changes to be made without risking a challenge to the will due to the testator's mental capacity.

Survivorship when Deaths are of a Common Disaster

When a common disaster involves the deaths of two people who are to inherit from one another and when it is impossible to prove which of the two survived the other, the estate of each decedent devolves as if each decedent survived the other.[20] In the will, a testator may provide that a legatee must survive the testator for a stipulated period (not exceeding 6 months). If the legatee dies within the stipulated period after the death of the testator, the legacy is left to a third person chosen by the testator.[21]

No Contest Clauses

In a will, a clause that revokes the legacy to a legatee who contests the will is a "no-contest" clause. No provisions exist in the Louisiana Civil Code or in the Revised Statutes that specifically address no-contest clauses, which are generally valid as long as they are not so broadly drafted so as to cause the estate to go to a third party if anyone contests the will.[22] This reasoning prevents an intestate heir who was not happy with the will from challenging the will and causing the estate to go to a third party, thereby depriving the legatees of their legacy. A properly drafted no-contest clause would revoke only the portion left to the legatee who contests the will.[23]

Selecting the Succession Representative

Typically, the surviving spouse is named the estate's succession representative[e] or executor.[f] If there is no surviving spouse or if the surviving spouse is unwilling or unable to serve as the succession representative, the testator typically relies on the children to act in this capacity. Often the eldest child is named succession representative; however, it is prudent to select someone who will best handle the duties of a succession representative.

Because each estate is different, the testator must consider their estate's complexity when naming a succession representative. In addition, how close in proximity the children live to the testator is a

---

[e] The succession representative also means executor or administrator.
[f] Executrix if of the feminine gender.

consideration. If the estate is complex and will require an administration, a prudent choice is to select a succession representative who is more comfortable with handling personal, business and financial affairs. Finally, the succession representative must have sufficient time to devote to the duties inherent of a succession representative. Keep in mind that the succession representative does not have to be familiar with financial or legal jargon. The succession attorney will advise and guide the succession representative throughout the succession process. As a practical matter, the succession representative takes few actions without the succession attorney's counsel.

Naming an Attorney for the Succession

In your will, you may name an attorney to represent your succession. However, because your selection of attorney is not legally binding on your legatees, they may select another attorney of their preference.[24]

---

[1] La. Civ. Code Ann. Art. 874, 875.
[2] La. Civ. Code Ann. Art. 880, 882, 888, 890.
[3] La. Civ. Code Ann. Art. 889.
[4] La. Civ. Code Ann. Art. 888.
[5] La. Civ. Code Ann. Art. 891.
[6] La. Civ. Code Ann. Art. 892.
[7] La. Civ. Code Ann. Art. 894.
[8] La. Civ. Code Ann. Art. 895.
[9] La. Civ. Code Ann. Art. 896.
[10] La. Civ. Code Ann. Art. 1571.
[11] La. Civ. Code Ann. Art. 1577.
[12] La. Civ. Code Ann. Art. 1575.
[13] La. Civ. Code Ann. Art. 1606.
[14] La. Civ. Code Ann. Art. 1607.

[15] La. Civ. Code Ann. Art. 1608.

[16] La. Civ. Code Ann. Art. 1607(3).

[17] La. Civ. Code Ann. Art. 1608(4).

[18] La. Civ. Code Ann. Art. 1608(5).

[19] La. Civ. Code Ann. Art. 3528.

[20] La. Civ. Code Ann. Art. 935, 1997 Revision Comment (g).

[21] La. Civ. Code Ann. Art. 1521.

[22] See Succession of Kern, 252 So. 2d 507. (La. App. 1971) where the court held that the no contest clause was invalid.

[23] See Succession of Wagner, 431 So. 2d 10 (La. App. 4th Cir. 1983) where the court upheld the no contest clause.

[24] Succession of Wallace, 574 So. 2d 348 (La. 1991).

21

Trusts

Chapter Highlights

❖ Trusts are flexible planning tools that allow you to plan for an infinite number of needs such as to protect assets, to help minimize taxes and to protect children, grandchildren or other beneficiaries from creditors and financial mismanagement.

❖ A trust is the relationship resulting from the transfer of property to the trustee to be managed for the trust beneficiaries' benefit.

❖ A trust is irrevocable unless the trust document states that it is revocable.

❖ The Settlor creates the trust; the grantor transfers property to the trust. The settlor and the grantor may or may not be the same person.

❖ The trustee must follow the instructions in the trust document regarding distributions of income and principal.

❖ Trustees are fiduciaries and are liable to the beneficiaries for breaches of their fiduciary duties and for imprudent acts.

❖ A class trust may be created for beneficiaries three generations removed from the settler, including generations not yet in existence.

❖ The trustee may be given discretion to adjust distributions between beneficiaries based on need.

❖ Crummey powers allow future-interest gifts to qualify for annual exclusion.

❖ A spendthrift trust can protect trust assets from the beneficiaries' creditors.

TRUSTS ARE SOME OF THE most useful planning tools available to help you achieve your retirement and estate planning goals. The planning possibilities with trusts include, but are not limited to,

- Managing assets in the event of incapacity
- Protecting beneficiaries from creditors
- Protecting beneficiaries from their own mismanagement of assets
- Reducing estate taxes
- Avoiding probate
- Preserving assets for a disabled beneficiary

Many Louisiana residents are unclear about how trusts work and are unaware of the many benefits trusts provide. The flexibility available to an estate planning attorney when drafting trusts provides an almost unlimited number of planning possibilities. Credit shelter trusts, marital trusts, generation-skipping trusts, life-insurance trusts, living trusts, minor's trusts, charitable remainder trusts and qualified terminal-interest property trusts (QTIP trusts) are just a few of the types of trusts used in estate planning.

Although trusts have many features and benefits, there are costs associated with establishing and maintaining a trust. For example, an attorney must be hired to draft the trust document, and a trustee may charge a trustee fee. In addition, the person transferring assets to a trust may or may not lose control of the assets.

This chapter reviews trusts in Louisiana and provides information on how trusts can benefit you and your family.

Trust Terminology and Trust Creation

A trust is the relationship resulting from the transfer of property[a] to a person (the trustee) to be administered for the trust beneficiary's benefit.[1] A trust is a set of instructions directing the trustee to manage and distribute the assets held in trust to the beneficiaries in a certain manner. When you create a trust, you get to choose the instructions

---

[a] Property as used herein is not limited to real estate but includes any asset (e.g. cash, stocks, bonds, real estate, etc.).

directing the trustee. Assets placed in the trust are re-titled in the trust's name. For example, if Boudreaux owns an investment account in his name and wishes to place the account into the Boudreaux Family Trust, he would have the account re-titled "The Boudreaux Family Trust." The investment account's assets would be managed by the trustee according to the trust document that created the trust.

A trust created while the settlor is alive is an inter-vivos trust. An inter-vivos trust must be created by an authentic act or by act under private signature; therefore, the trust document must be witnessed and notarized.[2] An inter-vivos trust is created when the trust document is executed.[3] The trustee's subsequent acceptance of an inter-vivos trust is retroactive to the trust's creation date.[4]

Frequently, a trust is not needed until the settlor's/testator's[b] death (e.g. one of the spouses dies). In this type of situation, a testamentary trust, which is created by a will, is ideal. A testamentary trust is embedded in the will and does not spring into action until after the settlor/testator dies. The only formalities to create a testamentary trust are those required to create a will.[5] This trust is created at the moment of the testator's death, without awaiting the trustee's acceptance of the trust.[6]

No special language is required to create a trust so long as it is clear that the creation of a trust is intended.[7] In addition, a trust may be revocable or irrevocable. If the trust document does not state that the trust is revocable, the trust is irrevocable.[8]

The Settlor

The settlor is the person who creates the trust.[9] More than one settlor can be named for an inter-vivos trust. Any person who has the capacity to execute a binding contract may be a settlor. A person who transfers property to an existing trust he or she did not create is a grantor, not a settlor. A settlor (as opposed to a grantor) may modify, revoke or terminate a trust if those rights were reserved (e.g. a revocable trust).

The Grantor

The grantor is the person who transfers property to the trust. Transferring assets to a trust is called funding a trust. Multiple grantors

---

[b] A Testator is the person who created the will.

may exist, and the settlor and grantor may be the same person. Any person may make additional contributions of assets to a trust by donation while alive or through a will. However, the trust document may limit or deny the ability to make additions.[10]

The Beneficiary

The beneficiary is a person or entity (e.g. a charity) for whose benefit the trust was created. Two types of beneficiaries exist: income beneficiaries and principal beneficiaries. A trust may have more than one beneficiary as to income or principal or both. In addition, separate beneficiaries of income and principal may exist, or the same person may be a beneficiary of both income and principal.

Unless otherwise provided in the Trust Code, a beneficiary must be in being and ascertainable on the trust's creation date. An unborn child is deemed a person and ascertainable if born alive.[11] A revocable trust instrument need not designate the beneficiaries upon the trust's creation but may instead provide a method whereby they are determined at a later time. However, the beneficiaries must be determined no later than the time when the trust becomes irrevocable.[12] This allows a beneficiary to be a person who is not in being when the trust is created, so long as he or she is in being when the beneficiaries are determined.[13] For example, Thibodaux creates a revocable trust which names his grandchildren as the beneficiaries. When Thibodaux creates the trust, he has two grandchildren. Upon Thibodaux's death, he has six grandchildren, and the trust becomes irrevocable. All six grandchildren are trust beneficiaries although only two were alive when Thibodaux created the trust. Lastly, a beneficiary does not have to accept the benefit conferred on him; his acceptance is presumed.[14]

Income beneficiaries receive income from the trust for life or for a shorter duration as defined in the trust document.[15] The principal beneficiaries receive the trust principal (the nonincome portion of the trust assets) in accordance with the trust document. This may occur before or after the income beneficiary's interest terminates. For example, Boudreaux's trust pays all of the trust's income to his surviving spouse, Marie, for life. Boudreaux names his children as the principal beneficiaries. During Marie's lifetime, no income is paid to the children as principal beneficiaries. Upon Marie's death, the children become beneficiaries of both income and principal, unless the trust states otherwise.

An interest in income terminates upon the income beneficiary's death or at the expiration of a term (e.g. 10 years) if the interest is for a period less than life. At the termination of an income interest, accumulated or undistributed income that has been or is required to be allocated to the income beneficiary will be paid to the income beneficiary or his or her heirs, legatees, assignees or legal representatives.[16]

The Louisiana Trust Code provides the following rules, which may be altered by the trust document, for the termination of an <u>income interest</u>. Unless the trust instrument provides otherwise,[17]

- Termination of the interest of the <u>sole income beneficiary</u> prior to the termination of the trust causes each principal beneficiary to become a beneficiary of income in an amount proportionate to his or her interest in the principal.

- Termination of an interest in income of <u>one of several income beneficiaries</u> causes the other income beneficiaries or their successors to become beneficiaries of that interest in income in proportion to their interests in the balance of trust income.

- If, however, termination of the income interest is by death and if descendants of the deceased income beneficiary are the beneficiaries of an interest in trust principal or succeed to such an interest upon the death of the income beneficiary, such descendants shall become beneficiaries of the deceased beneficiary's interest in trust income in proportion to the descendants' interests in their portion of trust principal.

Remember, these are the default rules if the trust document does not provide otherwise. Most trust documents will override the default rules to determine the remaining beneficiaries' rights after the termination of an income interest.

Likewise, upon a <u>principal beneficiary's</u> death, the interest generally vests in the principal beneficiary's heirs or legatees, subject to the trust. The trust may stipulate otherwise, however.[18]

In addition, the Trust Code allows the trust to shift a principal beneficiary's interest to a substitute principal beneficiary. Under certain conditions, the settlor may determine who receives a principal beneficiary's interest if he or she dies without descendants. The trust instrument may provide that the interest of a principal beneficiary who dies without a will and without descendants during the term of the trust or at its termination vests in some other person or persons, each of whom will be a substitute beneficiary.[19] If forced heirship does not apply to the assets held in trust, the trust instrument may provide that the interest of a principal beneficiary who dies without descendants during the term of the trust or at its termination vests in some other person or persons, each of whom will be a substitute beneficiary.[20] Therefore, if a principal beneficiary of a trust holding assets not subject to forced heirship dies with a will but without descendants, the trust instrument may redirect those assets to a substitute beneficiary. Without this Trust Code provision, the original principal beneficiary's interest will be controlled by the original principal beneficiary's will.

The trust may provide that the interest of a designated principal beneficiary of a revocable trust shifts to another person or persons, if the substitution occurs no later than the date when the trust becomes irrevocable.[21]

The Trustee

The trustee is the person to whom title to the trust property is transferred to be administered by him or her as a fiduciary. The trustee may accept the trust and the duties of a trustee in the trust document or in a separate document.[22] The trustee must follow the trust document's instructions with regard to the management and distribution of the trust assets for the trust beneficiaries' benefit. You may choose to name your spouse, children, friend, business associate, relative or yourself as the trustee. In the alternative, you may elect to name an institutional trustee or a combination of the two. There are pros and cons to both individual and institutional trustees. The selection of trustee will depend on the types of assets in the trust and the beneficiaries' identity and needs.

Multiple Trustees

The settlor may name two or more co-trustees to administer the trust. Co-trustees are sometimes used to "watch over" one another. If there are two trustees, both must agree to act with regard to trust property.[23] If there are three or more trustees, a majority of the trustees must agree to exercise trustee powers, unless the trust document provides otherwise.[24] In addition, the trust instrument may allow the trustees to act independently.

Co-trustees participate in the trust's administration and shall use reasonable care to prevent another co-trustee from committing a breach of trust.[25] A trustee who has not joined in exercising a power is not liable to the beneficiaries or to others for the consequences of that exercise, and a dissenting trustee is not liable for the consequences of an act in which he or she joins at the discretion of the majority of trustees, if he or she expresses his or her dissent in writing to the co-trustees at or before the time of the joinder.[26]

Only the following persons or entities may serve as a trustee of a trust:[27]

1. A natural person (individual trustee) enjoying full capacity to contract[c] who is a citizen or resident alien of the United States. The trustee may be the settlor, the beneficiary, or both;

2. A federally insured depository institution organized under the laws of Louisiana, another state, or of the United States (e.g. a bank), or a financial institution or trust company authorized to exercise trust or fiduciary powers under the laws of Louisiana or of the United States;

3. A nonprofit corporation or trust for educational, charitable, or religious purposes that is designated as income or principal beneficiary may serve as trustee of a trust for mixed private or charitable purposes.

Institutional vs. Individual Trustees

Advantages and disadvantages exist when using individual trustees (a natural person) and/or institutional trustees. The trust's complexity, the trust assets' composition and the beneficiaries' circumstances all matter in trustee choice. The availability of individual trustees is also a factor, as there may be no one available that the settlor deems suitable to serve as trustee. In this situation, an institutional (corporate) trustee may be ideal.

Institutional trustees provide the following advantages:

- A broad pool of resources and expertise in managing trusts.

- A knowledge of professional asset management.

---

[c] Mentally competent and at least 18 years of age.

- An inability to become incapacitated and/or to die.
- An inability to be influenced by coercive beneficiaries or other parties.
- A staff to prepare tax returns and investment performance reporting.
- A guarantee that they are audited and regulated.

Institutional trustees have several disadvantages:

- Institutional trustees charge a fee for their services.
- Institutional trustees are unfamiliar with family dynamics.
- Institutional trustees may be located in another state.

Individual trustees provide the following advantages:

- Knowledge of the beneficiaries and their family and their needs and the family. Such knowledge can be valuable if the trustee has discretion to invade corpus or sprinkle income for the benefit of one or more beneficiaries.
- A low or no-cost way to administer a trust.
- An ability to work out disputes among beneficiaries.

Individual trustees have the following disadvantages:

- May not have expertise in asset management.
- Individual trustees must be replaced due to death or incapacity.
- Individual trustees may be influenced by family members or the beneficiaries.

Removing a Trustee

For sufficient cause, a trustee can be removed in accordance with the provision in the trust document or by the proper court. A corporate trustee may be removed upon a settlor's or beneficiary's petition, if the court determines that removal is in the beneficiaries' best interest as a whole, if another corporate trustee that is qualified has agreed to serve as the trustee and if the trust document does not prohibit removal.[28]

A trustee-removal clause should be considered to prevent the beneficiaries from being "locked in" with an incompetent or difficult trustee. A trustee-removal clause can prevent the expense and delay of obtaining a court order to remove a trustee. Although it is not advisable to give the beneficiaries the unbounded power to remove a trustee, consider inserting an escape hatch into the trust document. The authority to remove a trustee may be granted to the income and principal beneficiaries if all agree, or an uninterested third party can be given the authority to remove a trustee for just cause upon a beneficiary's request. If a removal clause is not drafted in the trust, a court order will be required to remove a trustee. The trustee's removal may be warranted by

- A failure to place the beneficiaries' interest first.

- A failure to treat the beneficiaries equally unless otherwise directed by the trust document.

- Poor investment decisions regarding trust property.

- Excessive fees or multiple fees charged for asset management and trustee fees.

- Excessive fees paid to outside consultants such as attorneys and accountants.

- Poor decisions regarding discretionary distributions to the beneficiaries.

- Investment underperformance.

- Lack of adequate communication between the trustee and the beneficiaries.

- A lack of timely or proper distributions.

Succession of Trustees

In the trust document, the settlor should specify the method of selecting successor trustees. An original trustee, an alternate trustee and a successor trustee may be designated in the trust instrument or chosen by a method provided in the trust instrument.[29] The failure to name a successor trustee or a vacancy in the office of trustee does not cause the trust to be invalidated. If there is no trustee or successor trustee, the proper court appoints a trustee.[30]

Powers and Duties of the Trustee

Louisiana law provides a trustee with broad powers when dealing with trust property. The trust document will generally define the trustee's powers, which may be very broad or narrow in scope. As a result, a trustee does not have unbridled discretion but must act in a manner that is consistent with the trust document and the Trust Code. In many situations, the trust document will override the Trust Code. A settlor may expand or restrict the trustee's powers and duties to suit the settlor's desires regarding the administration and distribution of trust property so long as the Louisiana Trust Code does not prohibit such action. A trust may be drafted in very broad terms to accomplish a wide range of goals with few limitations on the trustee. In the alternative, the trust may severely limit the trustee's powers and permissible distributions. For example, the trustee may be given the following instructions:

1. Pay out all of the trust income to the income beneficiary at least quarterly.

2. Pay a certain dollar amount (e.g. $10,000) to each beneficiary annually.

3. For each beneficiary who is a full-time college student, pay all tuition, expenses, room, board, a reasonable allowance and reasonable transportation.

4. After considering all other sources of income, provide a reasonable standard of living of which the beneficiaries are accustomed.

5. Make no distributions to any beneficiary not advancing towards a college degree or gainfully employed.

6. Pay for all health, medical and educational expenses.

7. Pay all of the income to my surviving spouse and distribute principal for the payment of health, educational, maintenance and support expenses of my surviving spouse. If my spouse remarries, (his or her) interest in the trust terminates.

8. Provide a down payment for a beneficiary's first home.

9. Other than permissible distributions, retain the assets in trust until each beneficiary attains the age of 30 (or any age the settlor chooses).

10. Withhold certain distributions if a beneficiary does not maintain a certain grade point average.

11. Donate trust property with the settlor and the beneficiary's consent.[31]

12. Do not acquire, sell or lease trust property without the approval of a certain percentage of the beneficiaries.[32]

These are streamlined versions of typical trust clauses. They provide an idea of the types of provisions that may be included in a trust document. The actual clauses contain more detail and are more specific as to leave no room for interpretation of the settlor's intent.

The proper court may direct or permit a trustee to deviate from a trust document's provisions concerning the trust's administration if, because of circumstances not known to the settlor and not anticipated by him, compliance with the trust document would defeat or substantially impair the trust's purposes.[33] In addition, a court order may relieve a trustee from duties and restrictions that otherwise would be placed upon him by the administrative provisions of the Trust Code.[34] Careful and precise wording of the trust is vital to accurately reflect the settlor's intentions for trust distributions. The settlor and the attorney drafting the trust should go to great lengths to ensure that the trust is drafted to fulfill the settlor's intentions but to provide flexibility to the trustee to deal with unforeseen circumstances.

As an example of the dangers of not providing flexibility, consider where one Louisiana court would not permit the trustee to invade the trust corpus because the trust's purpose was to support the beneficiary for life and the withdrawal of $40,000 would defeat that purpose because there would be insufficient funds to care for the beneficiary later. The beneficiary's severe financial hardship was insufficient cause to override the settlor's intention to provide for the beneficiary for the remainder of her lifetime.[35]

If a trust is poorly drafted, relief may be sought to deviate from the trust provisions. For example, if convinced that adherence to the investments prescribed by the trust instrument would be likely to adversely affect the beneficiary's best interests, the proper court can, upon application by a trustee or a beneficiary, permit or direct the trustee to invest in securities not prescribed by the trust instrument.[36] In addition, the proper court can direct or permit a trustee to pay income or principal from the trust property for the necessary support, maintenance, educational, medical expenses or welfare of a beneficiary before the time he or she is entitled to the enjoyment of that income or principal, if the interest of no other trust beneficiary is impaired thereby.[37] Obviously, to minimize the possibility of having to petition the court for permission to deviate from a poorly drafted trust, it is best to use great care to properly draft the trust document.

The Trustee's Duties

A trustee is responsible for managing and distributing the trust property for the beneficiaries. When dealing with trust property, the trustee must strictly follow the trust document's instructions and guidelines. In addition, the trustee must make decisions regarding discretionary distributions and judgment calls if the trust document is unclear or silent. There is also the human side of the office of trustee. The trustee must balance the beneficiaries' needs and wants while acting within the trust document's guidelines.

A trustee's duties generally include safekeeping and investing trust property for the beneficiary's benefit. A trustee is under a duty to the beneficiaries to take reasonable steps to take, keep control of and preserve the trust property.[38] In most cases, a trust is a separate legal entity and must be treated as such. Therefore, a trustee will keep the trust property separate from his or her individual property. In addition, the trustee, so far as reasonable, should not commingle trust property with other property not subject to the trust. The property should be designated as trust property, unless the trust instrument provides otherwise.[39] In addition, the trustee should file timely income tax returns on the trust's behalf. If at any time the trust property of either an inter-vivos trust or a testamentary trust includes immovable property (e.g. real estate) or property whose title must be recorded in order to affect third parties, a trustee will file for record the trust instrument in each parish in which the property is located.[40]

Fiduciary Responsibility

Trustees are held to a fiduciary standard when dealing with trust property. As a fiduciary, trustees must not take their responsibilities lightly as they are held to the highest standard of care. The word fiduciary is derived from the Latin word for trust. The foremost obligation that a fiduciary owes to its beneficiaries is undivided loyalty to act solely in the beneficiaries' best interest.[41]

The golden rule for trustees is that a trustee will administer the trust solely in the beneficiaries' interests,[42] placing those interests first. Any violation of a duty owed to a beneficiary by the trustee is defined as a breach of trust.[43] When there is more than one beneficiary, a trustee will administer the trust impartially, based on what is fair and reasonable to all beneficiaries, except to the extent that the trust instrument directs or permits the trustee to favor one or more beneficiaries.[44]

The settlor may not attempt to limit a trustee's duty of loyalty to the beneficiaries. A provision of the trust instrument that purports to limit a trustee's duty of loyalty to a beneficiary is ineffective.[45] For example, a provision of a trust which contained a blanket release in favor of the trustees from any liability was found to be clearly inconsistent with the Trust Code.[46]

Prudent Administration

Not only must a trustee place the beneficiaries' interests first and exercise undivided loyalty to the beneficiaries, but trustees must also prudently administer the trust assets. The "prudent man rule" which required a trustee to exercise such skill and care as a man of ordinary prudence would exercise in dealing with his or her own property is no longer the standard. Trustees are currently held to the "prudent administration" standard.[47]

To satisfy the prudent administration standard, the trustee must exercise reasonable care and skill, considering the purposes, terms, distribution requirements and other circumstances of the trust. A trustee who has special skills or expertise or has held himself out as having special skills or expertise has a duty to use those special skills or expertise.[48] Therefore, a trustee who is also an investment advisor is held to a higher standard than a trustee who has little or no investment expertise.

A trustee is required to manage and invest trust property as a prudent investor <u>unless the trust document provides alternate instructions</u>. In meeting the prudent investor standard, a trustee must consider the purposes, terms, distribution requirements and other circumstances of the trust. The trustee's investment and management decisions are evaluated in the context of the trust property as a whole and as an overall investment strategy having risk-and-return objectives reasonably suited to the trust. Unless the trust document states to the contrary, the trustee may invest in any type of property.[49] The prudent investor statute evaluates trust assets as a whole rather than evaluating each asset. Prior to the adoption of the prudent investor statute, trustees were reluctant to invest in securities that subjected principal to risk (e.g. stocks). Small cap and international stocks were often avoided even though in the context of the overall portfolio including these securities provided the best risk/return tradeoff. The bottom line is that trustees may invest in any type of asset so long as in the context of the entire portfolio and considering the trust's purposes, the allocation is prudent.

The prudent investor rule differs from the prudent man rule in that the trustee's duty is determined by the trust's purposes and beneficiaries' circumstances, not in light of how a prudent man would manage his or her own property. In addition, prudence is determined with respect to the portfolio as a whole. The Uniform Prudent Investor Act provides that an investment that might be imprudent standing alone can become prudent if undertaken in sensible relation to other trust assets or other non-trust assets.[50] In addition, trustees should be able to demonstrate that a prudent <u>process</u> was used to invest trust assets, especially if a portfolio of stocks and bonds composes part of the trust assets.

Normally, prudence dictates that diversification is necessary to reduce risks. Circumstances can, however, overcome the duty to diversify. For example, if a tax-sensitive trust owns an under-diversified block of low-basis securities, the tax costs of recognizing the gain may outweigh the advantages of diversifying the securities. Retaining a family business as a trust asset is another situation where the trust's purposes outweigh the duty to diversify.[51]

Trustee Liability for a Breach of Trust

A breach of trust occurs if a trustee does not place the beneficiary's interest first, does not exercise undivided loyalty to the beneficiary, does not act as a prudent administrator or does not act as a prudent investor. A trustee who commits a breach of trust is liable to the beneficiary for losses. Due to the high standard of care and possible liability for a breach of this standard of care, a trustee should carefully consider accepting the responsibilities of the office of trustee. If a trustee commits a breach of trust, he or she will be chargeable with[52]

1. A loss or depreciation in value of the trust estate resulting from a breach of trust;

2. A profit made by the trustee through breach of trust; or

3. A profit that would have accrued to the trust estate if there had been no breach of trust.

Although trustees are held to a very high standard of care, a trustee is not liable for a loss or depreciation in value of the trust property or for a failure to make a profit if they are not a result of a breach of trust.[53] Furthermore, a trustee who is liable for a loss occasioned by one breach of trust cannot reduce the amount of his or her liability by deducting the amount of a gain that has accrued though another distinct breach of trust; but if the two breaches of trust are not distinct, a trustee is accountable only for the net gain or chargeable only for the net loss resulting from the breaches.[54]

Accounting by the Trustee

A trustee has a duty to the beneficiary to keep and render a clear and accurate account of the trust administration.[55] A trustee of a revocable trust has a duty to account to the settlor only.

A beneficiary of a trust has a right to know how the trust is administered. To this end, a trustee renders to a beneficiary or his or her legal representative, at least once a year, a clear and accurate account covering the administration for the preceding year. Each annual account shows, in detail, all receipts and disbursements of cash and all receipts and deliveries of trust property during the year. In addition, the annual account sets forth a list of all items of trust property at the end of the year.[56]

Upon the trust's termination, revocation or rescission or upon the trustee's resignation or removal, a final account is rendered to the beneficiary or his or her legal representative.[57]

A beneficiary may request complete and accurate information as to the nature and amount of the trust property, and he or she, or a person duly authorized by him or her, may inspect the subject matter of the trust and other documents relating to the trust.[58]

Revoking a Trust

A settlor may revoke a trust in whole or in part only if he or she has reserved the right to revoke the trust or has reserved an unrestricted right to modify the trust.[59] A settlor may also reserve the right to revoke the interest of any beneficiary, unless otherwise limited by the trust instrument.[60] Generally, if there are multiple settlors, all surviving settlers must agree to revoke a trust or the interest of a beneficiary in trust.[61]

The revocation of a trust results in the trust property returning to the settlor unless the trust instrument provides otherwise. The settlor may stipulate the effect of revocation or rescission of a disposition. Unless the trust instrument otherwise provides,[62]

1. Revocation or rescission shall cause the trust to fail, and the trust property held by the trustee at the time such revocation or rescission takes effect shall revert to the settlor or his or her heirs, legatees, or assignees;

2. Revocation or rescission of a disposition affecting an income beneficiary has the same effect as if the beneficiary had died on the effective date of the revocation or rescission;

3. Revocation or rescission of a disposition in favor of a principal beneficiary operates as a substitution of the settlor or his or her heirs, legatees, or assignees as the beneficiary of the interest involved, without affecting the income beneficiaries' interests; if there are two or more settlors, each disposition affecting principal shall be divided into as many separate dispositions as the number of settlors, and each settlor or his or her heirs,

legatees, or assignees shall receive a share in proportion to the amount of his or her contribution to the trust principal;

4. Acts of the trustee with regard to the trust property shall not be affected by the subsequent revocation or rescission of a disposition in trust. After a trust has been revoked or rescinded, the trustee shall have only those powers necessary to carry out the effects of the revocation or rescission.

5. A person receiving trust property as a result of the revocation or rescission of the trust shall be personally liable for the trust's obligations and liabilities existing on the date of revocation or rescission to the extent of the value of the trust property received by such beneficiary unless existing trust property is sufficient to satisfy the trust's obligations and liabilities.

Modification and Termination of the Trust

The settlors may agree to modify the trust's terms after its creation only to the extent they expressly reserve the right to do so.[63] If the settlor reserves the right to revoke the trust, the settlor has the right to modify the trust, and he or she may change, amend or terminate the trust.[64]

To aid the trustee in administering a trust, a trustee may, on written notice to all beneficiaries having a current interest in the trust or trusts, combine two or more trusts into one trust or divide a trust into two or more trusts. Such action is permissible if the combination or division does not impair the rights of any beneficiary or adversely affect the accomplishment of the purposes of the trust or trusts. The division of a trust will be based on the fair market value of the trust's assets on the division's effective date and need not result in a uniform interest in each asset. After the division, discretionary distributions need not be made uniformly from each of the separate trusts. A trust document may modify these rules, either to expand or to restrict the trustee's authority to combine or divide a trust.[65]

If the value of the trust's assets is less than $100,000 and, in relation to the costs of the trust's administration, the continuance of the trust unchanged would defeat or substantially impair the trust's purposes, the proper court may order the trustee to distribute the trust assets and dissolve the trust. The trust instrument may specifically prevent such a trust distribution regardless of the trust property's value.[66]

The settlors, trustees and beneficiaries cannot agree to terminate the trust or any disposition in trust, unless the trust instrument provides otherwise.[67] Therefore, an irrevocable trust generally cannot be modified or "undone." However, the proper court may order the termination or modification of a trust, in whole or in part, if the continuance of the trust unchanged would defeat or substantially impair the trust's purposes.[68] The proper court may order the termination or modification of the trust if the purpose for which it is created becomes illegal or impossible to accomplish.[69]

A modification, division, termination or revocation of a trust must be by authentic act or by act under private signature executed in the presence of two witnesses and duly acknowledged by the person who makes the modification, division or termination or by the affidavit of one of the attesting witnesses.[70] A modification, division, termination or revocation of a trust may also be by testament.[71]

Trust Protectors

The concept of "Trust Protectors" has long been associated with offshore or foreign asset protection trusts. A trust protector is typically someone not associated with the trust that is given the power to direct the trustee to take or not take certain actions, to modify the trust or to terminate the trust. In the context of offshore trusts, the trust protector was also generally given the power to transfer the trust to another offshore jurisdiction to frustrate a creditor's efforts to seize the trust assets.

More recently, trust protectors have been included in domestic trusts. In this context, the trust protector is used to provide flexibility to irrevocable trusts by empowering the trust protector to modify or terminate the trust. The concurrence of the existing trustee or the beneficiary is usually required to ratify the trust protector's actions. A trust protector can provide flexibility to handle circumstances occurring many years in the future—circumstances that were inconceivable at the time the irrevocable trust was drafted. Changes in tax law or changes related to beneficiaries may warrant modification of an irrevocable trust in future years.

The trust protector may provide the grantor or beneficiary the power to change the trustee (with the concurrence of the trust protector as an objective third party). If the grantor or beneficiary alone were allowed to change the trustee, the grantor or beneficiary would be deemed to have too much control over the trust assets. In such a situation, the trust assets may be included in the grantor's or the beneficiary's estate.

Due to the potentially enormous power given to the trust protector, the choice of trust protector must be given considerable thought. Foremost, the trust protector should be an independent party. Depending on the trust instrument, the trust protector may be given very narrow or very broad powers to modify the trust. Lastly, corporate trustees may not make good trust protectors as they may be reluctant to take action to modify a trust.

The trust instrument should clearly define the trust protector's role. In addition, the trust instrument can state that the trust protector is a fiduciary and has a duty of loyalty and impartiality to the beneficiaries. The grantor should consider placing restrictions on the trust protector's powers, restrictions such as

- Prohibiting the trust protector from naming himself or a related party as a beneficiary;

- Prohibiting the trust protector from naming the grantor as a beneficiary;

- Prohibiting any modification that would disallow the marital deduction or the charitable deduction; or

- Prohibiting modification that would cause unwanted tax consequences.

Distributions of Income

The trust document may provide instructions for how income is to be distributed among the beneficiaries. If it does not, all of the income must be paid to the income beneficiary at least semi-annually. If the beneficiary is a forced heir, the trustee must distribute income sufficient for the health, education, maintenance and support of the forced heir after considering other income and support received by the forced heir.[72] The trust document may stipulate that all or part of the income be accumulated for a certain period of time for distribution at a later date. For example, the trustee may be instructed to accumulate the income to pay for college tuition. If the trust document allows the trust to retain income received in a year and distribute it in a later year, the income retained at the end of the year is deemed to be accumulated, unless the trust document requires the undistributed income to be added to principal. Objective standards[d] are not required for the accumulation of income or for the distribution of accumulated income.[73]

In addition, the trustee may be given full discretion over the timing and amount of income distributions.[74] Additional flexibility may be given to trustees by allowing a trustee to "spray" or "sprinkle" income by allocating and disbursing income in different amounts to the income beneficiaries. Unallocated income may be accumulated and allocated to the income beneficiaries in a later year. In the alternative, the unallocated income may be added to principal each year or added to principal when the trust terminates.[75] This type of flexibility allows a trustee to use discretion to distribute more income to a beneficiary who is more in need than other beneficiaries. For example, if the surviving spouse and a child are the income beneficiaries, the trustee may allocate more income to the surviving spouse rather than divide the income equally between all income beneficiaries. This type of flexibility is helpful if the surviving spouse needs additional income from the trust.

Keep in mind that the default rule is not to add accumulated income to principal for purposes of entitlement to distribution.[76] Thus, accumulated income is to be distributed to the income beneficiaries rather than added to principal unless the trust document requires otherwise.

Distributions of Principal

Typically, the principal beneficiaries are the recipients of distributions of trust corpus or principal. The trustee must make distributions of principal in accordance with the trust document. For example the trustee may invade or use principal for the benefit of an

---

[d] Distributions based on objective standards are distributions typically based on health, education, maintenance or support needs of a beneficiary or any other objective standard.

income beneficiary under objective standards as provided in the trust document. The trustee may also be directed to pay accumulated income and principal to an income beneficiary for health, educational, maintenance, support needs or any purpose subject to an objective standard. In addition, the trust document may direct the trustee to pay all or part of the principal to an income beneficiary upon the beneficiary's request. Such a provision allows the trustee to distribute trust principal to the surviving spouse (although only an income beneficiary) at the surviving spouse's request. As a result, the trust can provide resources beyond the income to the surviving spouse income beneficiary. The principal remaining in the trust at the surviving spouse's death is distributed to the children (as principal beneficiaries). This is an example of the flexibility provided to the trustees and the beneficiaries if the trust is properly drafted.

An additional option is to direct the trustee to pay a stipulated amount or percentage to an income beneficiary even if the payments exceed trust income. For example, the trust may stipulate that 5 percent of the trust be distributed annually to the surviving spouse as income beneficiary. If the trust generates 3 percent income, an additional 2 percent from principal must be distributed to the surviving spouse.

If the same person is beneficiary of both income and principal, the trust instrument may direct or permit the trustee, in the trustee's complete discretion, to invade principal held for that beneficiary.[77]

The trust instrument may provide the manner in which and the share of the trust to which payments of principal to income beneficiaries will be charged; if it does not, all payments of principal made for the benefit of an income beneficiary will be charged against such income beneficiary's share in the trust as principal beneficiary or, if there is no such share, proportionately against the shares of all principal beneficiaries. If the trust document stipulates that principal may be distributed to the income beneficiary, principal that consists of the forced portion of a forced-heir principal beneficiary may not be distributed to an income beneficiary.

Typical Trust Clauses

- "I specifically request the Trustee to distribute income and to invade principal, if necessary, to pay all costs of education including all room, board, tuition, books, including a reasonable allowance to provide a standard of living to which the beneficiary is accustomed, and transportation, in the event a beneficiary is enrolled as a bona fide full-time student in an accredited college or university, including graduate work, or other career training."

- "I specifically request the Trustee to pay all costs of education including all room, board, tuition, books, including a reasonable allowance and transportation, in the event a beneficiary is enrolled as a bona fide full-time student maintaining a 2.00 grade point average (on a 4.00 scale) in an accredited college or university, including graduate work, after considering all other sources of funds available to the beneficiary to pay such expenses, such as grants or scholarships. If the trust income is insufficient or unavailable, due to the existence of the usufruct, to pay for the costs, fees and expenses listed in this section, the trustee is to invade (use) principal to pay for said costs, fees and expenses."

- "The Trustee may invade and distribute the principal of this Trust to the beneficiary, or his or her legal representative(s), when, in the Trustee's sole discretion, it is necessary to do so for the beneficiary's comfort, education, welfare, support or maintenance to support a lifestyle of which the beneficiary is accustomed."

- "The Trustee shall distribute to the beneficiary one-third (1/3) of the value of the trust principal when the beneficiary attains the age of thirty-two (32); one-third (1/3) of the value of the trust principal when the beneficiary attains the age of thirty-five (35); and the trust shall terminate when the beneficiary attains the age of forty (40)."

Class Trusts

Typically a trust must terminate at the last surviving income beneficiary's death or at the expiration of twenty years from the death of the settlor last to die, whichever last occurs.[78] Two exceptions in the Trust Code are provisions for trusts for mixed private and charitable purposes (e.g. a charitable remainder trust) and class trusts.[79] A class trust allows a settlor to create a trust for certain classes of descendants and has the potential to remain in existence for 100 years or more. The trust may include beneficiaries up to three generations younger than the settlor.

Class trusts provide multi-generational tax planning opportunities in certain situations. If the generation-skipping transfer-tax exemption is properly used, transfers to a class trust that benefit children, grandchildren and great-grandchildren may avoid estate and generation-skipping taxes.

A class trust is an inter-vivos or testamentary trust in favor of a class consisting of some or all of the settlor's children, grandchildren, great grandchildren, nieces, nephews, grandnieces, grandnephews, great grandnieces and great grandnephews, or any combination thereof. All members of the class need not be in being at the time of the trust's creation, provided at least one member of the class is then in being. Thus, if only one child of the settlor is born, a class trust may be established that includes grandchildren and great-grandchildren not yet in existence. Without the use of the class trust provisions, an irrevocable trust must limit the beneficiaries to those in being and ascertainable on the trust's creation date.[80]

For example, at Thibodaux's death his will creates a testamentary trust that will pay all of the trust income to his surviving spouse. His surviving spouse may also receive distributions of trust principal if necessary to support her standard of living. The trust beneficiaries may include Thibodaux's children, grandchildren and great-grand children born many years after Thibodaux's death. Without the use of a class trust, any grandchildren or great-grandchildren born after Thibodaux's death would be excluded as beneficiaries.

If the trust instrument so provides, the interest of each beneficiary in the class can be a separate trust after the class has closed.[81] If before the application of R.S. 9:1894,[e] the class consists only of members of one generation, the interests of the members of the class will be equal by roots from their common ancestor, unless the trust instrument provides otherwise. If before the application of R.S. 9:1894 the class consists of persons in more than one generation, their interests will be

---

[e] If a person, who would have been a member of the class if he had not died, dies before the creation of the trust, his descendants shall be considered members of the class by representation unless the instrument otherwise provides. La. R.S. 9:1894. This provision allows the descendants to step into the shoes of a predeceased class member.

equal by heads, unless the trust instrument provides otherwise.[82] In addition, a class can include those of the relationship whether by blood or adoption.[83]

A class trust may be created with respect to all or a portion of income or principal or both, but the members of the class must always be the sole beneficiaries of the portion of the trust of which they are beneficiaries. For example, a class trust may not create an income interest for the settlor's children and grandchildren. However, the trustee[f] may invade principal for the benefit of one or more individual income beneficiaries or one or more members of any class of income beneficiaries, even though such income beneficiary may not be a member of the class of principal beneficiaries.[84] Therefore, the class trust may distribute principal to the surviving spouse as income beneficiary, although the children or grandchildren are the principle beneficiaries.

The trust instrument may stipulate a date or a method for defining a date on which the class will close. Unless the trust instrument provides otherwise, the class will close when, because of the class definition, members may no longer be added to it.[85] For example, if Thibodaux creates a class trust with his children as income beneficiaries and his grandchildren are principal beneficiaries, the class of income beneficiaries closes when Thibodaux dies. The class of principal beneficiaries closes when Thibodaux's children die (no additional grandchildren may be born). In addition, a class trust will not terminate before the class's closing.[86] After the class closes, the trust will continue as to the class until the last surviving class member's death, unless an earlier termination date has been stipulated.[87]

Trustee Flexibility: Sprinkle Trusts and the Power to Adjust

Typical trusts with income and principal beneficiaries have traditionally invested for income and safety rather than for growth. The income beneficiary's needs are often considered a first priority over the principal beneficiary's needs. Often the surviving spouse is the income beneficiary, and the income requirements of a surviving spouse are considered a priority over the needs of the principal beneficiaries (e.g.

---

[f] Subject to La. R.S. 9:2068.

the children). In light of these needs, traditionally all or nearly all of the trust assets were invested in bonds for income and safety. A portfolio of bonds provides the greatest benefit to the income beneficiary but little or no capital appreciation for the principal beneficiaries. The trust instrument may specifically instruct the trustee to provide a maximum amount of income to the income beneficiary, even if it impairs the principal beneficiaries. However, if the trust instrument is silent, the trustee has a duty of impartiality between the beneficiaries. Investing primarily for income for the income beneficiary will be inherently unfair to the principal beneficiaries whose purchasing power will erode over time. Trying to hedge against inflation by investing in assets with more potential for capital appreciation will be inherently unfair to the income beneficiary. The power to adjust between income and principal provides a solution to this trustee dilemma as explained herein.

Sprinkle Trusts

A sprinkle[g] trust allows a trustee to allocate income among beneficiaries based on the trustee's sole discretion. For example, a trustee may sprinkle income to the beneficiaries according to their needs or where it will result in lower income taxation to beneficiaries in a lower tax bracket. A trustee may be given the power to "sprinkle" income in different amounts among the income beneficiaries without objective standards. Some or all of the income may also be allocated to principal.

A trust may allow a trustee, <u>who is not a trust beneficiary,</u> discretion to allocate income in different amounts among the income beneficiaries or to allocate some or all of the income to principal.[88] Income that is not allocated at year end may be accumulated and remain unallocated until a later year. If the trust terminates with unallocated income, the unallocated portion is allocated to principal. Sprinkle powers may not be imposed on a forced heir's legitime in trust.

The power to sprinkle income among beneficiaries gives the trustee broad powers to allocate income to compensate for changes in circumstances. A trust that is drafted many years prior to coming into existence or a trust that lasts for many years cannot address all possible

---

[g] Also known as spray trusts.

contingencies. Changes in circumstances occurring many years after the trust's creation warrant flexibility. The trustee may consider the beneficiaries' earning power, wealth, number of dependents, marital status, financial obligations, financial hardships or other factors.

Sprinkle powers allow the trustee to determine if one or more beneficiaries will receive more or less income. Alternately, the trustee may determine that the income is best allocated to principal to be saved for later. Empowering the trustee with discretion over income distributions provides flexibility; however, it opens the door to potential abuse. The settlor should carefully weigh the pros and cons of providing this amount of flexibility to the trustee. For this reason, trustee selection should not be taken lightly; choosing the right trustee is critical when discretionary powers are permitted. The exercise of the trustee's power to allocate income among the beneficiaries is subject to review by the court to prevent an abuse of discretion.[89]

Potential Income Tax Trap

Sprinkle powers present a potential income tax trap for trustees. The IRC grantor trust rules require the grantor of certain trusts to be considered the owner for income tax purposes and to report the trust's income on his or her tax return.[90] The grantor may be taxed on the trust income even if the income cannot be used personally by the grantor. If the grantor controls who will receive the income, the grantor-trust income tax rules apply. In addition, the grantor will be taxed on the trust income if he or she names the following people as trustee of a trust with spray powers:

1. The grantor;

2. The grantor's spouse; or

3. Related or subordinate parties who are not adverse parties. The Louisiana Trust Code does not allow a beneficiary to have sprinkle powers; therefore, there will not be an adverse party.

To avoid the income being taxed to the grantor, an independent trustee should be used. An independent trustee will not cause trust income to be taxed to the grantor.[91] An independent trustee may freely allocate income among beneficiaries without causing the grantor to be treated as the owner for income tax purposes. The grantor is not an independent trustee. If there are multiple trustees, the trustees are "independent" if not more than half of the trustees are related or subordinate parties who are subservient to the grantor. Related or subordinate parties include the grantor's parents, children or employees or a corporation or employee of a corporation in which the grantor and/or the trust have voting control and a subordinate employee of a corporation in which the grantor is an executive. The grantor's spouse living with the grantor is a related party.[92]

In addition, the grantor should not retain powers to remove, add or substitute himself or herself as trustee. Such powers may cause the grantor to be treated as owner for income tax purposes. A grantor may retain the power to replace the independent trustee with another independent trustee and not be considered the owner for income tax purposes.[93]

If the trust has a single beneficiary, the income will not be taxed to the grantor. A grantor/trustee who controls when a beneficiary will receive income will not be taxed on the trust income under the grantor trust rules. In this case, the trustee merely controls the timing of the enjoyment of the income, rather than shifting beneficial enjoyment of the income between multiple beneficiaries.

Estate and Gift Tax Implications of Sprinkle Powers

The grantor should not be the trustee of a trust with sprinkle powers if the trust assets are to be excluded from the grantor's estate. Section 2036 of the Internal Revenue Code includes sprinkle trust assets in the grantor's estate. A donor cannot retain the right to change the beneficiaries' interests as between themselves, unless the power is reserved as a fiduciary power limited by a fixed or ascertainable standard.[94]

For estate tax purposes, only look to the grantor to determine if the trust assets are to be included in the grantor's estate. Thus, if the grantor names his or her spouse as the trustee, the estate tax rules will generally not include the trust property in the grantor's estate. Likewise, a trustee need not be unrelated or nonsubordinate.

Remember that the power to sprinkle income is not limited by fixed or objective standards. The trustee may not be given the power to allocate principal between the beneficiaries subject to the trustee's discretion. The trustee may invade principal for the benefit of other beneficiaries; however, this power is limited to fixed or objective standards.

Planning Options with Sprinkle Powers

A trustee may use sprinkle powers to allocate income to beneficiaries in a lower tax bracket. This option may afford some tax planning by the trustee. If the trust will benefit multiple generations, presumably income beneficiaries with various degrees of financial need and/or in various tax brackets will exist.

Some additional planning options present themselves with sprinkle trusts. A credit shelter trust may be used with the surviving spouse and the children as income beneficiaries. The children would also be the principal beneficiaries. Because the credit shelter trust is not included in the surviving spouse's estate and is sheltered from estate taxes by the deceased spouse's applicable exemption amount, the marital deduction need not apply. Therefore, all of the trust income need not be paid to the surviving spouse. If the surviving spouse needs additional income, sprinkle powers may be used to allocate more income to the surviving spouse and less to the children. If the children require more income, the trustee may allocate more income to the children. This approach can give the trustee a huge amount of flexibility to administer the trust.

Compare this to the usufruct/naked-ownership arrangement where the income is owned by the usufructuary (the surviving spouse). None of the income can be "allocated" to the naked owners (the children). The usufruct/naked-ownership arrangement offers simplicity, but it is much less flexible.

A QTIP trust qualifying for the marital deduction must pay all of the income to the surviving spouse at least annually. A trustee of a QTIP trust cannot be given the power to allocate income to other beneficiaries.

The Power to Adjust

The power to adjust provides considerable flexibility to the trustee to make adjustments between income and principal when it is necessary for the trustee to satisfy his or her duty to be fair and reasonable to all beneficiaries.

The need to invest a significant portion of a portfolio in stocks to hedge against inflation is critical for portfolio survivability. If most of the portfolio is invested in stocks to provide longevity for young principal beneficiaries, the income beneficiary will not receive as much current income as a portfolio primarily invested in bonds would provide. Therein lies the conflict between the income beneficiary's needs and the needs of the principal beneficiary. The trustee is stuck between these two compelling needs because all beneficiaries must be treated impartially unless the trust states otherwise.

A trustee may make an adjustment between principal and income when the trustee determines, after taking into account the allocations for the year and the trust's purposes, that the adjustment is necessary to satisfy his or her duty to be fair and reasonable to all the beneficiaries. [95]

As an example, the trustee invests the trust principal of $1,000,000 in a diversified portfolio of stocks with a 1.5 percent dividend yield. The income beneficiary is the surviving spouse who relies on trust distributions to maintain her standard of living and will receive $15,000 of income annually (1.5% x $1,000,000). The principal beneficiaries are the grandchildren who are two and six years of age. The trustee is instructed to pay for the grandchildren's college education and down-payment on a home. In addition, the trust document gives the trustee the power to adjust between income and principal. If the current yield does not produce sufficient income for the surviving spouse, the trustee may allocate some of the principal to income to increase the yield to 5 percent for example. Now the surviving spouse will receive $50,000 instead of $15,000. The grandchildren's interests remain protected as the equity portfolio should provide an adequate hedge against inflation over the next 20 to 30 years. If the surviving spouse only requires $25,000 to maintain her standard of living, the trustee may only increase the yield to 2.5 percent. The trustee is afforded much flexibility with the power to adjust.

The Trust Code prohibits an adjustment between income and principal in the following situations:[96]

1. If the existence or exercise of the power to adjust would cause ineligibility for the estate-tax or gift-tax marital deduction or charitable deduction.

2. If the power to adjust diminishes the value for gift tax purposes of the income interest in a trust to which a person transfers property with intent to qualify for a gift tax exclusion.

3. If possessing or exercising the power to adjust causes an individual to be treated as the owner of all or part of the trust for income tax purposes and the individual would not be treated as the owner if the trustee did not possess the power to adjust.

4. If the terms of the trust instrument clearly deny the trustee the power to adjust.

A trustee may not make an adjustment that benefits him or her, directly or indirectly, unless all of the current beneficiaries consent or the proper court authorizes such adjustment after notice to all current beneficiaries.[97]

Limitations to the adjustment amount allowed to the trustee exist; however, the trustee may request a court order to exceed these limits. A court order is required for the trustee to make an adjustment from principal to income if the adjustment amount from principal, when added to the trust's net income for the year, exceeds 5 percent of the trust assets' net fair market value at the beginning of the year.[98] Likewise, a court order is required for the trustee to make an adjustment from income to principal if the amount of the adjustment from income reduces the net income for the year below 5 percent of the trust assets' net fair market value at the beginning of the year.[99]

If a trustee abuses his or her discretion when making or failing to make an adjustment, the beneficiaries may ask the court to restore the beneficiaries to the positions they would have occupied if the trustee had not abused his or her discretion, according to the following rules:[100]

1. When the abuse of discretion has resulted in no distribution to a beneficiary or a distribution that is too small, the court shall require the trustee to distribute from the trust to the beneficiary an amount that the court determines will restore the beneficiary to an appropriate economic position.

2. When the abuse of discretion has resulted in a distribution to a beneficiary that is too large, the court shall require the trustee to withhold an amount from one or more future distributions to

the beneficiary or require the beneficiary to return some or all of the distribution to the trust.

3. When the court is unable to restore the beneficiaries, the trust or both to the positions they would have occupied if the trustee had not abused his or her discretion, the court may require the trustee to pay an appropriate amount from his or her own funds to one or more of the beneficiaries or to the trust or both.

Crummey Powers

When a grantor funds an irrevocable trust, the transfer is subject to gift taxation. The annual exclusion will shelter the first $15,000 (2019) gifted annually to each donee. The annual exclusion is available for each trust beneficiary; therefore, if a trust has four beneficiaries, the grantor may transfer $60,000 (2019) into the trust each year free from gift taxes. However, to qualify for the annual gift-tax exclusion, the gift must be a present-interest gift. This means that the donee (the person receiving the gift) must have a current right to use and enjoy the donated asset. If the asset is donated to a trust for the beneficiary's future use and enjoyment, the donation is not a present-interest gift. An example of future-interest gifts are donations to an irrevocable trust which does not distribute income or principal until the beneficiary attains a certain age, for example age 21. In addition, transfers of assets into life insurance trusts are typically future-interest gifts because the beneficiaries receive no economic benefit from the trust until a future date (e.g. after the insured dies).

Any gift that is not a present-interest gift does not qualify for the annual exclusion. If the annual exclusion does not apply, the donor will be liable for gift taxes on the first dollar rather than the 15,001st dollar (2019). A trust drafted with "Crummey" powers enables gifts in trust of a future interest to qualify for the annual exclusion as a present-interest gift.

Frequently, "Crummey" powers are created by giving a beneficiary the power to withdraw assets transferred into the trust for a limited period of time. The duration of time varies among trusts; however, three days has been determined to be too short a duration. Thirty days minimum duration for a beneficiary to exercise his or her Crummey withdrawal right appears to be a sufficient duration.

For example, Thibodaux creates an irrevocable life insurance trust to pay for estate taxes upon his death. Each year, Thibodaux transfers $28,000 to the trust to fund the life insurance policy. The beneficiaries are Gaston and Jacques but they will not receive distributions or any other benefit from the trust until after Thibodaux's death. Therefore, their interest in the trust is a future interest, and transfers to the trust do not qualify for the annual exclusion. If the trust is drafted with Crummey powers, the annual exclusion will apply. Each year when Thibodaux transfers assets to the trust, Gaston and Jacques must be given the right to withdraw that year's transfer. The right to withdraw typically lasts 30 days. After 30 days elapses, Gaston and Jacques may no longer withdraw the assets. The trustee then uses these assets to pay the insurance premium.

Naked Crummey Powers

A large number of beneficiaries will provide a large number of annual exclusions. For example, a trust with 3 child beneficiaries and 7 grandchild beneficiaries qualifies for 10 annual exclusions. To qualify for the annual exclusion pursuant to Crummey powers, the beneficiary should have a beneficial interest in the trust. Thus, a contingent-remainder interest or a discretionary interest may not be sufficient to satisfy the beneficial-interest criteria needed to qualify for the annual exclusion. For example, Thibodaux creates an irrevocable life insurance trust with Crummey withdrawal rights. He names his children, Gaston and Jacques, as the trust beneficiaries. If either of his children dies while the trust is in existence, their children (Thibodaux's grandchildren) will receive the predeceasing child's share. Thibodaux's grandchildren are considered remote contingent beneficiaries. The IRS generally denies Crummey withdrawal powers to the grandchildren in this situation. Therefore, Thibodaux is allowed two annual exclusions and may donate $30,000[h] (2019) of assets to the trust each year free of gift taxes.

Naked Crummey powers exist when nominal beneficiaries (the grandchildren in the previous example) enjoy only a remote contingent right to the remainder and when there is no imaginable reason why one of them would not exercise his or her withdrawal rights, unless there exists an understanding with the donors that no one would do so or that

---

[h] The annual exclusion for Gaston and Jacques but not the grandchildren.

they know that doing so will result in undesirable consequences or both.[101] An example of this type of arrangement is if the beneficiary is told that they will be disinherited if they exercise their Crummey powers. The IRS has stated that with a naked withdrawal power it is presumed that some prearrangement existed to preclude its exercise (the beneficiary withdrawing the assets). The IRS has also stated that it will not contest the annual gift-tax exclusion for Crummey powers held by beneficiaries of current trust income and persons holding vested remainder interests but that it will deny the annual exclusion for withdrawal powers held by beneficiaries who have no other beneficial interest or whose beneficial interest is a contingent remainder interest (naked withdrawal rights). The IRS will examine all relevant facts and circumstances of each case and deny the annual exclusion whenever there is a prearranged understanding that the withdrawal rights will not be exercised or when the power holder will be faced with adverse consequences as a result of exercising the withdrawal powers.

Notice of Withdrawal Rights

The trustee must give notice to the beneficiary of his or her right to withdraw the donated asset. Notices of Crummey withdrawal rights are required in order for gifts to a trust to qualify for the §2503(b) annual exclusion.[102] A beneficiary must be given prompt notice of the right of withdrawal and a reasonable opportunity to exercise the right before it lapses. The IRS has indicated that both 30 days and 15 days are reasonable amounts of time.[103]

If the beneficiary does not receive notice of his or her right to withdraw, the right will be deemed illusory. Unfortunately, this results in the annual exclusion being disallowed for that transfer into the trust.[104] Proper notice includes the notice of the right to withdraw, the contribution amount to the trust and the amount of the withdrawal right.[105] Care must be taken to coordinate the transfers so that the trustee has sufficient time to distribute notices with adequate time remaining for the beneficiaries to exercise their withdrawal rights prior to the rights lapsing. Trustees should provide current notice when each transfer into the trust occurs. In addition, the Trustee should send notice via certified mail with return receipt.[106] If the beneficiary is a minor, notice should be given to the parent or guardian. Some trusts provide that the beneficiary may waive his or her right to notice of a withdrawal right as long as the beneficiary has the ability to regain the right to notice at some later time. Until this issue is settled by the courts, some uncertainty remains as to whether the waiver of notice will cause the interest to be a future interest, thus making the annual exclusion unavailable for that transfer.

Five-and-Five Powers

To further complicate matters, a beneficiary's failure to exercise his or her Crummey withdrawal right (causing the withdrawal right to lapse) may be treated as a taxable gift to the beneficiary to the extent that in any year the property value subject to the lapsed power exceeds the greater of $5,000 or 5 percent of the total asset value out of which the lapsed power could have been satisfied. The power to withdraw is a general power of appointment, and the release of such is treated as a transfer of the property subject to the withdrawal right by the releasing party.[107] If the gifts to the trusts are equal to or less than $5000 or 5 percent of the trust property per year, the "five-and-five" limitation will be sufficient for the transfers. For transfers to the trust greater than these limits, "hanging powers" may be used. A hanging power gives the beneficiary the power to withdraw the annual transfer to the trust up to the annual exclusion amount which lapses at the end of the withdrawal period but only up to $5,000 or 5 percent of the trust assets. Amounts greater than the "five-and-five" limitation do not lapse; rather they "hang" until a future year or years until the lapse of the hanging power will not be treated as a taxable gift under IRC § 2514(e). The hanging withdrawal rights are not completed gifts by the beneficiary and are not subject to gift taxation until completed gifts occur. If the beneficiary dies prior to all of the hanging powers lapsing, the unlapsed withdrawal rights will be included in the beneficiaries estate under IRC§ 2041(a)(2).

Creditor Protection

Often parents or grandparents wish to protect assets not only from their children's or grandchildren's mismanagement but also from their creditors. If the grantor wishes to protect his or her heirs' assets from creditors, a spendthrift trust can provide the necessary protection. A trust beneficiary may transfer or encumber his or her interest in the trust unless the trust document provides to the contrary. Therefore, consider drafting a trust that prevents a beneficiary from voluntarily or involuntarily alienating his or her interest in the trust. If there is a concern that a beneficiary may transfer or borrow against the interest in the trust, a spendthrift clause can prevent a creditor from seizing a beneficiary's interest in the trust. For example, Boudreaux creates a trust with a spendthrift clause and funds it with a portion of his assets. His children are the beneficiaries of trust income and principal. His children's creditors cannot seize the assets held in the trust. By adding a spendthrift clause in the trust, the trust assets are protected.

A creditor may seize only (1) an interest in income or principal that is subject to voluntary alienation by a beneficiary or (2) a beneficiary's interest in income and principal, to the extent that the beneficiary has donated property to the trust, directly or indirectly.[108] Therefore, property that the beneficiary transfers to the trust is not protected from the beneficiary's creditors. For this reason, Boudreaux cannot create a trust of which he is the beneficiary to protect his assets. However, property transferred to the trust by others is protected from Boudreaux's creditors. In addition, payments of alimony and child support are not provided protection regardless of the identity of the party transferring the assets into the trust.

A declaration in a trust instrument that the interest of a beneficiary will be held subject to a "spendthrift trust" is sufficient to restrain alienation by a beneficiary of the interest to the maximum extent permitted.[109]

---

[1] La. R.S. 9:1731.
[2] La. R.S. 9:1752.
[3] La. R. S. 9:1822.
[4] La. R.S. 9:1823.
[5] La. R.S. 9:1751.
[6] La. R.S. 9:1821.
[7] La. R.S. 9:1753.
[8] La. R.S. 9:2021.
[9] La. R.S. 9:1761.

[10] La. R.S. 9:1931.
[11] La. R. S. 1803.
[12] La. R.S. 2011.
[13] Id.
[14] La. R.S. 9:1808.
[15] La. R.S. 9: 1961.
[16] La. R.S. 9:1964.
[17] La. R. S. 9:1965.
[18] La. R.S. 9:1972.
[19] La. R.S. 9:1973(A).
[20] La. R.S. 9:1973(B).
[21] La. R.S. 9:1973(C).
[22] La. R.S. 9:1755.
[23] La. R.S. 9:2113.
[24] La. R.S. 9:2114.
[25] La. R.S. 9:2096.
[26] La. R.S. 9:2114.
[27] La. R.S. 9:1783.
[28] La. R. S. 9:1789.
[29] La. R.S. 9:1785.
[30] Id.
[31] Succession of Simpson, 311 So. 2d 67 (La.App. 2d Cir. 1975). Noted 11 La. Civ. Law Treatise, Trusts § 342.
[32] St. Charles Land Trust, Ashille Guibet v. St. Amant, 253 La. 243, 217 So. 2d 385 (1969). Noted 11 La. Civ. Law Treatise, Trusts § 342.
[33] La. R.S. 9:2064.
[34] La. R.S. 9:2065.
[35] Harriss v. Concordia Bank & Trust Co., 265 So. 2d 330 (La.App. 3d Cir. 1972).
[36] La. R.S. 9:2066.
[37] La. R.S. 9:2067.
[38] La. R.S. 9:2091.

[39] La. R.S. 9:2094.

[40] La. R.S. 9:2092.

[41] Pegram v. Herdrich, 530 U.S. 211, 224 (2000).

[42] La. R.S. 9:2082(A).

[43] La. R.S. 9:2081.

[44] La. R.S. 9:2082(B).

[45] La. R.S. 9:2062.

[46] Succession of Burgess, 359 So.2d 1006 (La.App. 4th Cir.1978)

[47] La. R.S. 9:2081, 2090.

[48] La. R.S. 9:2090.

[49] La. R. S. 9:2127.

[50] Uniform Prudent Investor Act Section 2 (b) and (c).

[51] Uniform Prudent Investor Act Section 3 Comments.

[52] La. R.S. 9:2201.

[53] La. R.S. 9:2203.

[54] La. R.S. 9:2202.

[55] La. R.S. 9:2088(A).

[56] La. R.S. 9:2088(B).

[57] La. R.S. 9:2088(C)

[58] La. R. S. 9:2089.

[59] La. R.S. 9:2041.

[60] La. R.S. 9:2042.

[61] La. R.S. 9:2044.

[62] La. R.S. 9:2046.

[63] La. R.S. 9:2021, 2024.

[64] La. R.S. 9:2022, 2023.

[65] La. R.S. 9:2030.

[66] La. R. S. 9:2026(2).

[67] La. R.S. 9:2028.

[68] La. R.S. 9:2026.

[69] La. R.S. 9:2027.

[70] La. R.S. 9:2051(A).

[71] La. R.S. 9:2051(B).

[72] La. R.S. 9:1841(1).

[73] La. R.S. 9:1963.

[74] La. R. S. 9:1963.

[75] La. R.S. 9:1961.

[76] La. R.S. 9:1963.

[77] La. R.S. 9:2068(B).

[78] La. R.S. § 1831.

[79] La. R.S. 9: 835.

[80] La. R.S. 9:1803.

[81] La. R.S. 9:1891(A).

[82] La. R.S. 9:1891(B).

[83] La. R.S. 9:1892.

[84] La. R.S. 9:1893.

[85] La. R.S. 9:1896.

[86] La. R. S. 9:1897.

[87] La. R.S. 9:1901.

[88] La. R.S. 9:1961.

[89] La. R.S. 9:2115.

[90] IRC § 671-678.

[91] IRC § 674(C).

[92] IRC 672(c).

[93] Treas. Regs. § 1.674(d)-2(a).

[94] Treas. Regs. §25.2511-2(c).

[95] La. R.S. 2158.

[96] La. R.S. 9:2159.

[97] La. R.S. 9:2160.

[98] La. R.S. 9:2161(A).

[99] La. R.S. 9:2161(B).

[100] La. R.S. 9:2163.

[101] PLR 9045002.

[102] Revenue Ruling 81-7.

[103] PLRs 9311021, 9232013, 9218040, 9030005, 8712014, 8134135, 8103074; Cristofani Estate v. Commissioner, 97 T.C. 74 (1991).

[104] Rev. Rul. 87-1, 1981-1 C.B. 474; PLRs 8229097, 8143045, 8143024, 8008040.
[105] Rev. Rul. 87-1, 1981-1 C.B. 474.
[106] TAM 9532001.
[107] IRC §§ 2041 and 2514.
[108] La. R.S. 9:2004.
[109] La. R.S. 9:2007.

Types of Trusts

Chapter Highlights

❖ Revocable trusts are trusts that may be amended or completely revoked by the settlor.

❖ A living trust is a revocable trust that allows assets in the trust to pass outside of the will or intestacy, thus avoiding probate.

❖ A revocable trust can also be used for asset management in the event of incapacity.

❖ Irrevocable trusts are trusts that generally cannot be amended or revoked by the settlor.

❖ An irrevocable life insurance trust removes the life insurance death benefit value and the cash value from the estate to help reduce estate taxes and pay for any taxes that are due.

❖ A credit shelter trust can help ensure the use of both spouses' estate tax exemptions to reduce estate taxes while providing the surviving spouse with the use of both spouses' assets.

❖ A Qualified Terminal Interest Property (QTIP) trust provides income for life to the surviving spouse while allowing the first-to-die spouse to control who will inherit the QTIP trust assets after the surviving spouse's death. A QTIP trust is useful to a spouse who wishes to guarantee certain assets will be left to children from a prior marriage.

❖ An IRA Beneficiary Trust is used to guarantee stretch IRA distributions, to provide creditor protection for inherited IRAs, and to retain control over investments and distributions for an IRA you leave to your beneficiary.

❖ Charitable Split Interest Trusts (e.g. charitable remainder trusts) provide income and gift and estate tax savings while paying an income stream to the donor. At the end of the trust term, the donated asset is delivered to the charity.

❖ Self-Settled (4)(d)(A) Special Needs Trusts are funded with assets of an individual under age 65, typically receiving Medicaid or SSI. This type of trust is ideal for inheritances or personal injury recoveries received by a disabled individual to avoid disqualification from Medicaid or SSI. The trust must reimburse the state for benefits paid on the beneficiary's behalf.

❖ A Third-Party Special Needs Trust is funded with assets of third parties for the benefit of an individual receiving Medicaid or SSI. The trust need not reimburse the state for benefits paid on the beneficiary's behalf.

TRUSTS ARE SOMETIMES referred to as the estate planning attorney's golf clubs because of the variety of trusts available to accomplish any number of planning goals. Similar to a golfer selecting a specific club for a specific golf shot, an estate planning attorney may select a specific type of trust to solve a specific planning issue. Trusts are extremely flexible and are limited only by the imagination as long as a trust provision is not prohibited by the trust code or is not in violation of law.

Some trust planning techniques are rather complex; therefore, a trust should not be used prior to consulting with a qualified estate planning attorney. In addition prior to establishing a trust, you should consider the cost of creating and maintaining a trust. Finally, the gift and estate tax implications of any type of trust used in estate planning must be evaluated.

Revocable Trusts

Revocable trusts are trusts that may be amended or completely revoked by the settlor. A trust becomes irrevocable upon the settlor relinquishing the right to revoke or amend the trust or upon the settlor's death.

Revocable trusts are typically tax neutral.[a] For income tax purposes, the grantor is taxed on the assets held in a revocable trust, and the trust assets are included in the grantor's estate. As a result, no gift-tax results when the grantor transfers assets to a revocable trust because the settlor/grantor[b] retains unrestricted use and control of the assets due to the ability to remove the assets or revoke the trust. If the trust becomes irrevocable during the settlor/grantor's lifetime, a gift occurs on the date the trust becomes irrevocable.

Revocable trusts are commonly used for asset management. For example, in the event the settlor/grantor becomes incapacitated and is unable to manage his or her affairs at a later date. When used as an asset management tool, revocable trusts are a viable alternative to powers of attorney. See Chapter 26 for more information on disability planning. Another common use of revocable trusts is to avoid probate. Assets held in a revocable trust (or an irrevocable trust) avoids probate.

Revocable Trusts as a Probate Avoidance Tool

A living trust is a revocable trust that allows assets in the trust to pass outside of the will or intestacy, thus avoiding probate. A living trust provides many benefits such as avoiding the expense and delay of probate, asset management in the event of incapacity, and increased privacy. This section will provide an overview of the benefits of a living trust as part of an estate plan.

Keep in mind that because living trusts are revocable, they do not have inherent tax saving advantages. Income from living trust assets is taxed to the grantor under the grantor trust rules as the grantor is considered the assets' owner. Estate tax saving provisions may also be incorporated into a living trust.

Typically, spouses will establish a living trust and transfer assets into the trust as a probate avoidance technique. The spouses are the grantors, settlors, trustees and beneficiaries. Their assets are transferred into the name of the trust to be administered, managed and distributed according to the terms of the trust. The settlor determines the beneficiaries and the terms of the trust. While revocable, the settlor may amend, change or dissolve the trust at any time. A living trust is

---

[a] Revocable Trusts are typically grantor trusts under the tax code.
[b] The grantor is usually the settlor, and the terms grantor and settlor are herein used interchangeably with regard to revocable trusts.

not a separate taxable entity and does not need its own tax identification number; rather, the settlor/grantor's Social Security number is used.

While the spouses are alive and capable, they are the trustees. When one spouse dies or becomes incapacitated, the other spouse assumes the role of sole trustee. After both spouses are deceased, the trust becomes a separate taxable entity requiring its own tax identification number. At that time the successor trustee chosen by the spouses and named in the trust document becomes the acting trustee. The trust will either continue for the benefit of the children, grandchildren or other beneficiaries, or the trust will dissolve and distribute the remaining trust assets to the beneficiaries (typically children and grandchildren). One option is to stipulate that the trust will remain in effect until the youngest beneficiary reaches a certain age. This option helps to ensure that the assets are properly managed and not squandered.

A living trust can be very useful for asset and financial management purposes if one or both spouses become incapacitated. The spouses may act as trustee and retain control of the assets. If one spouse becomes incapacitated, the competent spouse or successor trustee steps into the spouse's shoes as trustee. When the incapacitated spouse regains capacity, he or she resumes his or her role as trustee. Therefore the living trust can be an excellent alternative to a power of attorney.

Assets in a living trust will avoid probate but will be subject to applicable federal estate taxes. By avoiding probate, assets placed in a living trust are not governed by the will. In fact, the living trust serves as a substitute for a will to transfer assets to the heirs. Some of the benefits of avoiding probate include reducing probate expenses, avoiding the delay of probate proceedings, and avoiding publicity associated with probate. If you own real estate in another state, a living trust can avoid ancillary probate (multiple successions) in those states.

Avoiding Probate

Many individuals seek the use of a living trust to avoid probate expenses and the delays associated with probate. Probate (known as succession in Louisiana) is a court supervised process for the distribution of the decedent's assets and for payment of estate debts and expenses. Because successions are court supervised, there are procedures and formalities that must be followed. As a result, there are inherent delays associated with a succession. Sometimes the delays are a result of an heir refusing to sign a document required to complete the succession. The heir may be upset they did not receive a larger portion of the estate or refuses to sign to be "difficult" for no good reason. The result is more delays and often discord between family members.

Probate Expenses

One of the advantages of avoiding probate is avoiding the expenses associated with probate. The cost to complete a succession varies widely and is dependent primarily on the complexity and size of the estate. However, if an heir challenges the will or the classification of property as separate or community, the cost can escalate rapidly. Attorney's fees are the main cost associated with probate. Although most attorneys charge by the hour or a fixed amount, some charge a percentage of the estate assets. Due to the unique factors of each estate and the billing practices of different attorneys, there is no set rule of thumb for probate expenses. The potential for a legal dispute between family members, especially in second marriage situations, ads to the uncertainty. Your family situation may be harmonious now, but may not be when your succession is opened. Disagreements between heirs can quickly escalate into an expensive legal battle.

By eliminating the need for a succession with a living trust, a lot of the uncertainty surrounding the cost to settle your estate can be removed. In most cases, assets in a living trust can be quickly re-titled into the names of the beneficiaries after the grantor dies. The need for a court supervised succession with unknown cost is avoided. Of course, there are costs associated with drafting and funding a living trust. These expenses are known and paid for when the trust is created. So there is a tradeoff between unknown succession expenses paid after your death, and known expenses paid when the trust is created. Often the unknown succession expenses can greatly exceed the cost to draft a living trust.

Probate Delays

Another reason to avoid probate is to avoid the delay associated with probate proceedings. Because probate is a court-supervised process, certain document must be prepared and presented to the court for approval. If all goes well and the heirs sign off on the succession documents, a succession may be completed in three to six months.

However, many successions last much longer due to delays in gathering the information needed to complete the succession, a challenge to the will or the value of the assets, or uncooperative heirs. If any of these situations escalate into a legal battle, the delays can last years. That means that the heirs will not be placed into ownership of the assets for years after your death. Most living trusts can be settled in days or weeks.

Probate Publicity

Probate proceedings are public record, so anyone has access to all of the succession documents, including the will, a detailed descriptive list of assets and liabilities and the judgment of possession. The detailed descriptive list of assets and liabilities is an itemized list of everything the decedent owned and all of their debts. The judgment of possession designates the successors and the assets they inherit. Because a succession is public record, anyone can access the succession documents from the clerk of court's office. Living trusts by-pass probate and eliminate the need to file a detailed descriptive list of assets and liabilities and a judgment of possession. Living trusts, however, may not be entirely private. If the living trust holds immovable property, the trust document (or an extract thereof) must be filed in every parish where immovable property is located. Keep in mind that real estate holdings are typically a matter of public record whether held in trust or outright. For estates under independent administration, the independent administrator, heir or legatee may request the detailed descriptive list be sealed. Sealing the detailed descriptive list reduces some of the privacy concerns, but it is only available for independent administrations.

Ancillary Probate

An additional use for a living trust is to hold out-of-state property to avoid an ancillary probate proceeding. For example, if you own real estate in Mississippi, you may wish to place this property in the name of a living trust. The property in the trust's name will prevent your heirs from having to open a separate probate proceeding in Mississippi.

Final Thoughts

When creating a living trust is important to fund it properly. If it is not funded properly, a succession will be required to re-title assets not held in the living trust. Most assets, other than beneficiary designated assets,[c] not in the trust's name will have to go through probate. Bank accounts that have a payable on death (POD) registration[1] will be paid to the named beneficiary on the account. Thus a bank account with a POD registration will also avoid probate. In addition, automobiles may be transferred by an affidavit provided to the department of motor vehicles. So bank accounts with a POD registration, automobiles and investments with beneficiary designations may also bypass probate. By placing all of your nonbeneficiary-designated assets in the name of a revocable living trust you avoid probate. To accomplish this goal, the need to properly draft and fund a living trust cannot be over emphasized. If some probate assets are not held in the living trust, a succession will be needed to transfer these assets. For this reason, when a living trust is drafted, a pour-over will is also drafted. The pour-over will is used to pour all probate assets into the trust, and this is done through a succession.

An additional benefit of a living trust compared to a will is that a living trust may help deter a potential will contest as a trust is generally more difficult to challenge than a will. A living trust can also be challenged, however a will is easier to contest. In addition, a succession provides a forum for disgruntled heirs to raise objections and delay closing the estate.

If you plan on leaving assets to a testamentary trust[d] to benefit your children or grandchildren to protect the assets from creditors, predators or mismanagement, consider using a living trust instead. The cost to draft a testamentary trust will pay for all or at least a portion of the cost to draft a living trust. The assets left to your heirs avoid probate and receive both asset protection at your death.

If you wish to avoid the expense and delay of probate, protect your privacy, and avoid an ancillary probate for out of state assets, you

---

[c] Life insurance, IRAs, annuities, 401(k), 403(b), 457 plans and similar retirement accounts.

[d] A trust in your will.

should consider a living trust. If you want more information about the benefits of a living trust, seek the advice of an experienced estate planning attorney. Avoid out-of-state companies offering living trusts as these are often boilerplate documents and may not be drafted to work well with Louisiana law.

Irrevocable Trusts

Irrevocable trusts are trusts that generally cannot be amended or revoked by the settlor. A gift occurs upon funding an irrevocable trust, and the trust is treated as a separate taxable entity. Many uses for and many types of irrevocable trusts exist, but they are typically used to save taxes, to protect assets and to protect beneficiaries. Testamentary trusts are created by the testator's will and do not come into existence until the testator's death. Inter-vivos Trusts are created during the settlor's lifetime.

Irrevocable Life Insurance Trusts

Another very useful trust in the estate planner's tool box is the irrevocable life insurance trust (ILIT). Although this trust is primarily a trust to hold life insurance, the trust may hold other assets as well. If your estate will be subject to estate taxes, typically life insurance is the most economical source of funds to pay for estate taxes. If you or your spouse purchases the insurance policy, the death benefit proceeds are included in your estate, further increasing the size of your estate and increasing the federal estate taxes due. An alternative is to have a life insurance trust purchase and own the insurance policy. An ILIT can provide proper management and asset protection of the insurance proceeds. The ILIT may be drafted to provide lifetime resources to your children and/or grandchildren while protecting the assets from mismanagement, influence from third parties, and protection from creditor/lawsuits. Due to the enormous economic benefit that life insurance can provide, ILITs provide unique planning opportunities by leveraging your assets. An ILIT can also reduce or eliminate unnecessary estate taxes by removing existing life insurance from your estate.

The Importance of Life Insurance Planning

Life insurance has become an important component of many estate plans due to the financial resources and security it provides to the family upon the death of a primary breadwinner. The death benefit from a life insurance policy is generally not subject to income taxation; however, the death benefit is generally subject to federal estate taxation. Life insurance on your life or your spouse's life will be included in your gross estate if

- The death benefit is payable to or for the benefit of you or your spouse's estate[2] or if your executor is designated as the beneficiary of the life insurance.[3]

- If you have incidents of ownership at the time of death.[4] Incidents of ownership include the ability to change beneficiaries, borrow against the policy, assign the policy or terminate the policy.[5] Paying premiums, however, is not considered an incident of ownership. When removing life insurance from your estate, it is essential that you relinquish all "incidents of ownership." Otherwise, the death benefit will be included in your gross estate, thereby negating any benefits sought from removing the insurance from your estate. In addition, you are considered to have an "incident of ownership" in an insurance policy on your life in trust if, under the terms of the trust, you alone or in conjunction with another person or persons have the power as trustee or otherwise to change the beneficial ownership in the policy or its proceeds, or the time or manner of enjoyment thereof, even though you have no beneficial interest in the trust.[6]

- If a life insurance policy that you have an ownership interest or incidents of ownership in is transferred from your estate within three years of death, the death benefits are included in your estate.[7] If there is a concern that you, as the transferor of a life insurance policy, will not survive the three-year period, consider drafting the ILIT with a "back door" QTIP clause that would cause the insurance proceeds to be included in your surviving spouse's estate under the marital deduction with the proper QTIP election.

Because inclusion of life insurance death benefits in your gross estate can result in a significant increase in estate taxes, removing life insurance from your estate is one of the first steps to reducing estate taxes. In addition, if your estate will be subject to estate taxation, the proper use of life insurance can provide the most cost effective method to pay estate taxes. If you or your spouse already owns life insurance, removing the life insurance from your estate is one of the most powerful methods to reduce estate tax exposure. One of the easiest methods of removing the insurance policy is to transfer the policy to your children. A better alternative is to transfer the policy to a trust which will prevent your children from having control over the policy. This arrangement avoids the possibility of your children removing the cash value or terminating the policy. As with any transfer of life insurance, if the transfer is within three years of your death, the death benefit will be included in the your estate. However, if a new policy is purchased by the trustee and owned by the trust, the three-year waiting period does not apply. Transferring life insurance out of your estate is a taxable gift generally equal to the policy's cash value.

If properly arranged, none of the insurance proceeds will be subject to estate taxation. Some of the benefits of an ILIT are that

- The ILIT provides greater control and security to help ensure that the planning goals for the life insurance are attained.

- An ILIT can provide for ongoing management of the life insurance proceeds for less sophisticated beneficiaries.

- An ILIT can protect the life insurance death benefits from creditors through the use of spendthrift provisions.

- An ILIT can provide liquidity to offset financial hardship to a family-owned business upon the death of a key employee/owner. It can also provide funding for a buy/sell arrangement.

Some of the disadvantages of an ILIT are that

- The policy owner relinquishes control over the policy when it is transferred to the ILIT.

- There may be gift taxes due when transferring the policy to an ILIT.

- An ILIT will require attorney's fees and administration fees to create and manage the ILIT.

How Does an ILIT Work?

Once the ILIT is created, the parents transfer assets into the trust. The trustee will use these assets to pay the life insurance premiums. To enable the annual exclusion to apply,[e] the trust must be drafted with Crummey Powers. Crummey Powers allow the payments into the trust to be considered present-interest gifts. If the transfers are not present-interest gifts, the annual exclusion does not apply, and gift taxes would be due beginning with the first dollar transferred into the trust. A trust with properly drafted Crummey Powers preserves the use of the annual exclusion. Crummey Powers confer a right to the beneficiaries to withdraw the amount of the gift transferred into the trust. This right typically expires 30 days after notice of the right of withdrawal is given. After the 30-day window expires, the beneficiaries may no longer withdraw the transferred assets from the trust. See Chapter 21 for more information on Crummey Powers.

For example, Thibodaux creates an ILIT and names his three children as the beneficiaries. Each year Thibodaux transfers $45,000 into the ILIT for use by the trustee to pay premiums for life insurance on Thibodaux's life. Thibodaux may transfer up to $45,000 annually into the trust without gift tax implications if the annual exclusion is available for each child. If Thibodaux drafts Crummey Powers into the trust, the annual exclusion will apply. Each time Thibodaux transfers assets into the ILIT, the trustee must notify the beneficiaries of their right to withdraw the transferred assets within 30 days. If the beneficiaries do not exercise their right to withdraw within 30 days, the assets may not be withdrawn at a later date. After 30 days expire, the trustee uses the transferred assets to pay the life insurance premiums.

Upon the insured's death, the death benefit proceeds are paid to the trust for the benefit of the insured's spouse and children. The trustee is generally authorized, but not directed, to loan money to pay for estate taxes or to purchase property from the decedent's estate rather than paying the estate tax outright. Purchasing assets from the estate provides a ready source of cash for the estate, while keeping the

---

[e] Will allow each spouse to transfer $15,000 (2019) per beneficiary into the trust annually free of gift taxes.

purchased assets within the family. Once the estate has been settled, the trust may be allowed to dissolve and distribute its assets to the trust's beneficiaries. If the beneficiaries are in need of supervision over the assets due to being young in age or due to a lack of management skills, the trust may remain in effect until the beneficiaries are of a more mature age to manage the assets. In addition, a properly drafted trust can provide income to the surviving spouse for life and as much principal needed for health, education, maintenance and support.

If the surviving spouse will need some or all of the insurance proceeds to provide income for living expenses, a first-to-die policy can provide the needed cash. If estate taxes are the main concern, a second-to-die policy will pay the death benefit only upon the second spouse's death when taxes would generally be due on a properly planned estate. Of course a second-to-die policy has significantly lower premiums than a single-life policy.

Irrevocable Life Insurance Trusts: The Details

➤ The Trustee

The selection and powers of the trustee are critical to avoid estate taxation of the insurance proceeds. The insured should not act as trustee to avoid inclusion of the death benefits in the insured's estate. Generally, if the ILIT holds a second-to-die policy, neither spouse should act as trustee. In addition, any person who contributes assets to the ILIT should not be trustee. The safest option is to select a trustee that is neither the insured, the insured's spouse nor the ILIT beneficiaries.[f]

Care should be taken where a spouse is named co-trustee and the ILIT holds second-to-die insurance. Problems arise when the spouse is

---

[f] Revenue Ruling 84-179 stated that incidents of ownership would not be imputed to an insured who serves as trustee if the trustee cannot exercise incidents of ownership for his or her own benefit and if the fiduciary powers were transferred to the insured, rather than retained by the insured. For example, Boudreaux transfers a life insurance policy on Clotile's life to an ILIT with Clotile as the trustee, and Clotile is not a beneficiary of the ILIT. Clotile should not transfer assets to the ILIT. Pursuant to Revenue Ruling 84-179, the death benefits would not be included in Clotile's estate although she is the trustee. In addition, the policy proceeds were excluded from the estate of both the husband and wife under §2042(2) where the husband's ILIT purchased a second-to-die policy on their lives and the wife was the co-trustee of the ILIT. PLR 200404013.

also an income beneficiary or if principal may be expended on the spouse's behalf. Careful trust drafting is a must. If a spouse is named trustee, consider including language in the trust document that prohibits the spouse/trustee from exercising a power to sprinkle income or principal to the trust beneficiaries. In addition, the spouse/trustee's powers should be limited by objective standards.[8] The bottom line is that the trust should not give the spouse/trustee any discretionary power that would cause the death benefit to be included in the estate. Take the more conservative route when possible and avoid naming a spouse as trustee.

The IRS has traditionally held the position that if either the grantor or the beneficiaries have the power to remove a trustee, the trustee's powers were attributable to the grantor/beneficiaries. As a result, the insurance proceeds would be included in the grantor/beneficiaries' estate under § 2042(2).[9]

The IRS's position is that a grantor's retention of the right to remove a trustee and appoint an individual or corporate trustee would not be a retention of control over the trust, so long as the successor trustee was not related or subordinate to the grantor under §672(c).[g] In addition, a beneficiary may be afforded the same removal powers of a grantor.[10]

➤ The Beneficiaries

The children and/or grandchildren are typically named beneficiaries of the ILIT. The spouse may be given an income interest in the ILIT with the trustee empowered to invade principal for the spouse's benefit, restricted by objective standards. The children's needs and ages should be considered to determine how the ILIT must be drafted with regard to income and principal distributions and trust termination. For example, you may wish to delay the distribution of principal until the beneficiaries attain a certain age. Often a trust will not distribute principal until the second spouse's death. At that time,

---

[g] Under §672(c), a related or subordinate party includes a grantor's spouse, father, mother, issue, brother or sister or employee; a corporation or an employee of a corporation in which stock holdings of the grantor and the trust are significant in terms of voting control; or a subordinate employee of a corporation of which the grantor is an executive. Excluded from this group are "adverse parties" who are persons with a substantial beneficial interest in the trust which would be adversely affected by the exercise or nonexercise of the power. Rev. Rul. 95-58.

the insurance policy proceeds would be used to pay for estate taxes by loaning money to the estate or purchasing assets from the estate. If additional funds remain in the ILIT after the death of both spouses, principal distributions may be delayed until the beneficiary attains whichever age is deemed appropriate. Similar to other types of trusts, the trustee may be given discretion over when to terminate the trust as to a particular beneficiary. For example, a trustee may terminate the trust when the trustee determines that a beneficiary can manage his or her own affairs.

If the beneficiary lacks good judgment and may squander trust distributions, the trustee may be instructed to pay to the financial, educational, medical or other institution directly. Otherwise, the payments may be made to the beneficiary. In addition, to protect the beneficiaries from creditors, the settlor should consider drafting the ILIT as a spendthrift trust.[11]

➢ Gift Tax Implications

The transfer of an existing insurance policy and the direct or indirect payment of premiums on the policy are taxable gifts. The preservation of the annual exclusion ($15,000 in 2019) is an important objective when planning transfers to an ILIT. The value of the gift of a life insurance policy to an ILIT depends on the type of life insurance policy transferred. The gift tax value of life insurance is generally the value equal to the cost of replacing the policy on the date of the gift.[12] For permanent policies, this amount is the policy's interpolated internal reserve.[h] The outright transfer of a policy to the children (rather than the trust) is a gift of present interest and thus qualifies for the annual exclusion.

If the policy is too large to be covered by the annual exclusions available as determined by the number of donees, the policy may be split, allowing donations over multiple tax years. In addition, gifts may be split with the donor's spouse regardless of the spouse's ownership interest in the life insurance policy. Otherwise, the amount over the value covered by the annual exclusions will be subject to gift taxation. In the alternative, the donor's portion of the federal estate tax exemption may be used in lieu of paying gift taxes on the donation. To reduce the size of the gift, the policy owner may borrow against the

---

[h] Approximately the cash value.

policy. The loan may be paid back in subsequent tax years via the annual exclusion. When borrowing against a life insurance policy, use caution not to borrow more than the donor's cost basis as this will result in income recognition in the amount borrowed in excess of the cost basis.

Whether a transfer of an insurance policy to an ILIT qualifies for the annual exclusion will be determined by the ILIT document. If the trust creates no income interest until a time in the future (e.g. after the insured's death), the transfer is a gift of a future interest for which the annual exclusion is not available. In such a case, gift taxes will be due starting on the first dollar of value transferred, or a portion of the donor's federal estate tax exemption must be used. For obvious gift tax purposes, it is important to qualify insurance policy transfers and/or assets for premium payments for the annual exclusion.

An ILIT drafted with "Crummey" powers enables gifts of insurance and other assets to an ILIT to qualify for the annual exclusion as a present-interest gift. See Chapter 21 for more information on Crummey powers.

Credit Shelter Trusts

Credit shelter trusts (CST) are another common and very useful irrevocable trust. To preserve the federal estate tax credit shelter exemption[i] of the first-to-die spouse, assets must be left to someone other than the surviving spouse. Starting in 2011, the estate tax exemption portability rules allow the use of both spouses' exemptions without using a CST. See Chapter 23 for more information on exemption portability and the pros and cons of a CST to preserve both exemptions.

Without exemption portability, assets left to the surviving spouse are included in the marital deduction, and the credit shelter exemption will not apply to these assets. As a result, leaving the entire estate to the surviving spouse causes the predeceasing spouse's credit shelter exemption to be wasted. To avoid this outcome, assets may be left to the children or grandchildren, and the credit shelter exemption will apply to these assets. The problem with this arrangement is that the surviving spouse will not have the use of these assets because they now

---

[i] Also known as the federal estate tax exemption or applicable exemption amount.

belong to the children or grandchildren. For many individuals, the trade-off between using the exemption and providing the surviving spouse with sufficient assets to maintain his or her standard of living is not a decision they wish to make. A CST can help attain both tax savings and provide benefits to the surviving spouse. Beginning in 2011, exemption portability provides an alternative to CST to preserve both spouses' exemptions. With a CST, you can eat your cake and have it too. See Chapter 23 for more information on CSTs.

Marital Deduction Trusts

Marital Deduction Trusts (sometimes referred to as an "A" Trust) are typically used as part of an estate plan in coordination with a CST (sometimes referred to as a "B" Trust). The federal estate tax exemption available upon the first spouse's death is used to fund the CST. If any assets remain in the decedent's estate after funding the CST, those assets are used to fund a marital deduction trust. The surviving spouse has the full use of the assets in the marital deduction trust, and the assets are included in the surviving spouse's estate. Distributions subject to objective standards are not a requirement as the trust assets are included in the surviving spouse's estate. A marital deduction trust can be useful for asset management in the event the surviving spouse is unable to properly manage the assets. Furthermore, assets in the marital deduction trust avoid probate of the surviving spouse's estate.

Qualified Terminal Interest Property Trusts

Another very useful trust is a Qualified Terminal Interest Property Trust or QTIP trust (sometimes referred to as a "C" Trust). This type of trust allows the first-to-die spouse to name beneficiaries who will receive the property after the surviving spouse dies, and the property still qualifies for the marital deduction at the first spouse's death.[j] The QTIP rules require the income from the trust assets to be paid to the surviving spouse at least annually. Because the income must be paid to the surviving spouse, the assets in the trust will be included in the surviving spouse's estate under the marital deduction. The surviving spouse need not be given any other ownership interest in the trust, other

---

[j] The value of the assets is included in the second-to-die spouse's estate.

than the income paid at least annually. A QTIP trust is an excellent tool when children from a previous marriage are involved. You can guarantee children from a previous marriage will receive the assets in the trust after the surviving spouse's death while providing income to the surviving spouse. See Chapter 23 for more information on QTIP trusts.

IRA Beneficiary Trusts

If you wish to maintain control over the investment and distribution of your IRA after you are gone, consider naming an IRA trust as the beneficiary. The trust may be drafted to guarantee lifetime stretch distributions rather than allowing your beneficiary to take an immediate full taxable distribution from your IRA. In addition, the trust provides for asset management and creditor protection for inherited IRAs. See Chapter 7 for more information about naming a trust as a beneficiary of your IRA or other tax-deferred retirement account.

Charitable Split-Interest Trusts

Charitable split-interest trusts are trusts that have a charity and one or more individuals as beneficiaries. With a typical charitable split-interest trust, the grantor transfers assets to the trust, retains a current or future economic interest and provides a current or future economic benefit to the charity. In addition, the grantor is provided with estate, gift and income tax deductions. Charitable split-interest trusts are typically used when a donor has a highly appreciated asset that is producing little or no income. If the donor sells the appreciated asset to reinvest into income producing assets, a large capital gain will result. Charitable split-interest trusts allow the donor to create an income stream from the asset while reducing the adverse tax implications. The following is a brief overview of several types of charitable split-interest trusts.

Charitable Remainder Annuity Trusts

Charitable Remainder Annuity Trusts (CRATs) pay income to one or more beneficiaries for life or for a fixed period not to exceed 20 years. At the end of the term or upon the income beneficiary's death, the charity receives the assets remaining in the trust. CRATs are typically funded with low-basis, highly appreciated assets that are producing little or no income. If the owner sells such an asset to reinvest the proceeds into income producing assets, a taxable gain occurs. However, if the owner transfers this asset to a CRAT, the CRAT may sell the asset without paying capital gains taxes. Then 100 percent of the proceeds can be reinvested into income producing investments which will provide an income stream for the income beneficiaries.[k] The income stream (e.g. 6 percent of the trust assets or a fixed dollar amount) is fixed at the time the assets are transferred to the trust. A disadvantage of a CRAT is that no additional assets may be added to a CRAT.

The donor receives a charitable deduction for income taxes (subject to charitable deduction limitations) and for gift-tax purposes. In addition, the donated assets are removed from the donor's estate for estate tax purposes. In order to obtain the tax deductions, the present value of the remainder interest passing to charity must be no less than 10 percent of the initial value of the assets transferred to the CRAT. If the income stream is for the income beneficiary's life, the probability that the charity will not receive its interest cannot be greater than 5 percent.

Many would-be donors are reluctant to donate assets to a charitable split-interest trust because the asset donated to the charitable trust will be unavailable to the children when both spouses die. A wealth replacement trust may be used to replace the donated asset. To fund the wealth replacement trust,[l] a portion of the income stream received from the charitable split-interest trust is used to fund insurance premiums for an irrevocable life insurance trust for the benefit of the donor's children and/or grandchildren. If correctly done, the wealth-replacement trust's proceeds will be free of income taxes and estate taxes.

Charitable Remainder Unitrusts

Charitable Remainder Unitrusts (CRUTs) are similar to CRATs except that payments are a fixed percentage (e.g. 6 percent) of the trust assets valued annually. Due to fluctuations in the value of the trust assets, the income beneficiary's income stream will change with each valuation. Unlike CRATs, additional asset contributions may be made.

---

[k] Usually the beneficiaries are the transferors of the assets, and/or the children.
[l] A wealth replacement trust is a type of irrevocable life insurance trust.

Net Income with Make-up provision Charitable Remainder Unitrusts

Net Income with Make-up provision Charitable Remainder Unitrusts (NIMCRUTs) are similar to CRUTs except the income payments to the beneficiaries may be the lesser of the unitrust amount or trust income with make-up provisions in later years. A NIMCRUT allows the income stream to be turned off and then back on (via the make-up provisions) during later years. Significant income tax planning can be facilitated with NIMCRUTs.

Charitable Lead Annuity Trusts

Charitable Lead Annuity Trusts (CLATs) work the opposite of a charitable remainder trust by paying a guaranteed income stream to the charity for a number of years. At the term's expiration, the principal beneficiaries receive the assets remaining in the CLAT. The income stream to the charity is a fixed amount or a fixed percentage of trust assets—valued at the time the assets are transferred into the CLAT. No additional assets may be added to a CLAT.

The charity must receive the annuity payment each year. There is no prohibition against an amount that exceeds the annuity amount being paid to the charity; however, there are no additional tax benefits to the donor. The amount cannot be lower than the annuity amount. The donor receives a gift tax deduction for the present value of the annuity interest passing to the charity. To receive the charitable deduction for income tax purposes, the grantor must be taxed on the trust income under the grantor trust rules.

Charitable Lead Unitrusts

Charitable Lead Unitrusts (CLUTs) pay to the charity a fixed percentage of trust assets re-valued on an annual basis. The principal beneficiaries receive the remaining trust assets at the term expiration.

Trusts for Minors

Estate planners have several options to consider if establishing a trust for a child, grandchild or other minor.

Section 2503(c) Trusts

Also known as a "minor's" trust, this trust allows the grantor to make tax-free gifts to a minor in trust via the annual exclusion.[m] Trusts can provide more control and flexibility than UTMA accounts. However, they are more complex and more suitable for larger gifts.

Although the minor does not own the property held by a §2503(c) trust, the annual exclusion will apply if the trust meets the following criteria:

1. Trust income and principal may be paid to the beneficiary or spent on the beneficiary's behalf prior to age 21;

2. Assets not paid to the beneficiary or on behalf of the beneficiary are distributed to the beneficiary at age 21; and

3. If the beneficiary dies prior to age 21, assets remaining in the trust are either paid to the beneficiary's estate or pass under a general power of appointment granted to the donee.

➤ Features of §2503(c) trusts

The trust can restrict how assets are to be used for the beneficiary, such as for health, education, maintenance or support or for educational purposes only or for medical or financial emergencies only. The trustee can accumulate trust income to reduce the impact of the "Kiddie" tax. Once the child reaches age 19,[n] the income may be apportioned to the trust and the child in a manner that minimizes the tax burden. The trust must distribute the assets to the beneficiary at age 21, unlike age 18 for UTMA accounts.

➤ Establishing a §2503(c) trust

There can be only one beneficiary per trust, and the trustee should not be the donor or the donor's spouse. The trust may be allowed to continue beyond age 21 if the beneficiary is given the option to withdraw all of the trust assets at age 21 within an appropriate time frame and the beneficiary opts not to withdraw the assets during this window. The beneficiary is not forced to accept the assets at age 21.

---

[m] A donation by a grantor to a minor in trust for the minor's future enjoyment is typically a gift of a future interest which does not qualify for the annual exclusion.

[n] The Kiddie Tax applies to dependent children under the age of 19 and dependent full time students under the age of 24.

However, the beneficiary must be given notice of the right and the opportunity to withdraw the trust assets.[13] If the beneficiary does not withdraw the trust assets, the beneficiary is deemed to have withdrawn and re-contributed the assets, and the trust may be continued for any length of time. The beneficiary will now be deemed the grantor for income tax purposes.

Section 2503(b) Trusts

This type of minor's trust may continue after the beneficiary reaches the age of 21; however, the beneficiary must receive an income interest for a fixed number of years or for life. The actuarial value of the income interest qualifies for the annual exclusion, and the remainder is a future-interest gift for which gift taxes must be paid or a portion of the federal estate tax exemption must be used.

The income interest must begin immediately, and the trustee must distribute the income. Furthermore, the trustee must invest in income producing assets or risk rendering the income interest illusory. An illusory income interest will not qualify for the annual exclusion. Income may be paid to a UTMA account for the minor's benefit and allowed to accumulate until the minor attains age 18. The trustee may be given broad discretion to distribute principal for the beneficiary.

Only one beneficiary per §2503(b) trust is allowed. The trustee may be the grantor so long as principal distributions must be made pursuant to objective standards (health, education, maintenance and support). Finally, Kiddie tax rules apply for unearned income from the trust.

Crummey Minor's Trusts

A Crummey minor's trust qualifies for the annual exclusion through the Crummey withdrawal powers given to the beneficiaries. Upon each transfer into the trust, the beneficiaries are given notice of their power to withdraw the funds during a specified window of time.° A major advantage of Crummey minor's trusts is that the trust need not distribute assets to the beneficiaries at age 18 or 21, which is a disadvantage of UTMA accounts and § 2503 (c) Trusts. Unlike § 2503(b) Trusts, the income from the trust need not be distributed to the beneficiaries nor must the trust assets be invested to produce income.

° Similar to Crummey powers typically drafted into irrevocable life insurance trusts.

The trustee may be given broad discretion over income and principal distributions as well as broad discretion over trust asset investment.

Multiple beneficiaries may be named for each trust. Contingent beneficiaries may receive remainder interests of a predeceasing beneficiary to prevent the assets from reverting to the donor's estate.

Disadvantages of Crummey minor's trusts include the potential withdrawal of gifts to the trust by a beneficiary exercising Crummey powers and potential IRS challenges to an improperly established and improperly managed Crummey minor's trust.

Special Needs Trusts

Governmental assistance programs[p] provide benefits to disabled individuals with limited income and resources (assets). If a disabled individual receives an inheritance or personal injury recovery greater than the allowable resource limit, he or she will be disqualified from governmental assistance. Special Needs Trusts can enable a disabled individual to receive the benefit of an inheritance or personal injury award without disqualification from governmental benefits. In Louisiana, recipients of SSI are automatically eligible for Medicaid. In most cases the benefits provided by Medicaid far exceed the monthly SSI benefit. For this reason it is critical that eligibility for SSI be maintained even if the SSI benefit is minimal. Special Needs Trusts must be drafted carefully to instruct the trustee to spend income and principal for goods and services not otherwise provided by governmental assistance programs.

(d)(4)(A) Under-Age-65 Special Needs Trust

A self-settled trust can be created for an individual who is under age 65 and disabled when the trust is created. This type of trust can be ideal for a personal injury settlement or inheritance received by a disabled individual under age 65. The disabled individual must be the sole beneficiary. The disabled individual's assets and assets from third parties may be used to fund the trust.

The assets held in a (d)(4)(A) trust will not be considered resources for governmental assistance. Even after the disabled individual surpasses age 65, the trust assets will not be considered resources.

---

[p] Primarily Medicaid and SSI

However, if additional assets are added after age 65, these assets will not be exempt resources.

The trust's settlor may be the disabled individual, the disabled individual's parent, guardian or grandparent or the court. Upon the disabled individual's death, the trust must pay to the state all remaining assets in the trust, up to the amount of the state provided care. The trust should have provisions to direct the trustee not to make distributions which would jeopardize the disabled individual's eligibility for governmental assistance.

Third-Party Special Needs Trusts

Assets may be left in trust for the benefit of an individual receiving Medicaid or SSI benefits and his or her spouse. Trusts funded with the assets of others are not subject to the OBRA 1993 trust provisions. Therefore, a third party may fund a trust with his or her assets to provide for the special needs of a Medicaid or SSI recipient without disqualifying the individual from governmental assistance. For example, Boudreaux may leave assets to a third-party trust to benefit his brother who is a Medicaid recipient without disqualifying his brother from Medicaid. In addition, a spouse may leave assets in a testamentary trust after his or her death to benefit the spouse who is receiving Medicaid. Otherwise, the community spouse's assets must be left to someone other than the institutionalized spouse, or the community spouse risks disqualifying the institutionalized spouse from Medicaid.

The trust should be drafted as a special needs trust to avoid the trust assets from being counted as a resource. Therefore, the trustee's discretion for distributing assets should be limited to providing for the beneficiary's needs which are not provided for under the governmental assistance program. The trustee should be specifically prohibited from making any distribution which would jeopardize the benefits of the governmental assistance program.

Care should be taken not to make income distributions to the beneficiary that may place the beneficiary over the Medicaid income limit. Unlike a § (d)(4)(A) trust, a third-party trust is not required to reimburse the state for benefits paid by governmental assistance.

[1] LSA-R.S. 6:314, 6:653.1, 6:766.1
[2] IRC § 2042.
[3] IRC § 2042(1).
[4] IRC § 2042.
[5] IRC § 2042(2).
[6] Regs. Section 20.2042-1(c)(4).
[7] IRC § 2035(d)(2).
[8] IRC § 2041(b)(1)(A); Regs. §25.2511-1(g)(2).
[9] TAM 8922003.
[10] PLR 9735023.
[11] LSA-R.S. 9:2001-2007.
[12] Regs. §25.2512-6(a).
[13] Rev. Rul. 74-43; Heidrich v. Commissioner, 55 TC 746 (1971).

23

Estate Taxation

Chapter Highlights

- ❖ The Federal Gift and Estate Tax System is a unified system of taxation on gifts that you make during your lifetime and on the assets in your estate at your death.

- ❖ Your estate includes all of the assets you own at the time of your death, even if these assets are not subject to probate. Your estate also includes certain gifts made within three years of your death and gifts over which you retain too much control.

- ❖ The annual exclusion allows you to make gifts up to $15,000 (2019) to an unlimited number of people free from gift taxes.

- ❖ You may pay for tuition and medical treatment for any number of people directly to the provider without incurring gift taxes, regardless of the amount.

- ❖ Everyone has an exemption from federal estate taxes ($11,400,000 in 2019) which may be used during your lifetime or at death.

- ❖ The marital deduction allows you to transfer an unlimited amount of assets to your spouse during your lifetime or at death. However, leaving all of your assets to your spouse and "over-qualifying" the marital deduction may not be tax efficient.

- ❖ The surviving spouse of a person who dies in 2011 or later can use their deceased spouse's unused estate tax exemption in addition to their own (estate tax exemption portability).

- ❖ A credit shelter trust also allows you to maximize the use of your federal estate tax exemption and provide income and principal for your spouse.

- ❖ A QTIP trust allows you to provide lifetime income to your spouse while leaving the trust principal to another beneficiary.

The value of the trust assets is included in your surviving spouse's estate under the marital deduction. A QTIP trust can be helpful if there are children from a previous marriage.

❖ Louisiana has repealed its inheritance and gift taxes.

❖ A donee generally inherits the donor's cost basis for donated assets.

❖ Assets obtained by inheritance receive a step-up in basis to the date-of-death value.

❖ Both halves of the community property receive a step-up in basis to the date-of-death value upon the first spouse's death.

❖ Tax-deferred accounts such as IRAs, employer plans and annuities do not receive a step-up in basis upon the owner's death. These assets are known as income in respect of a decedent (IRD) assets.

AFTER SPENDING A LIFETIME paying income taxes, you may owe Uncle Sam one more time. The federal estate tax applies when you die. Most taxpayers spend a significant amount of time in the pursuit of reducing their income taxes. Reducing taxes is certainly a prudent activity as you are not obligated to pay more taxes than required by law. Unfortunately, the income tax is not the most devastating tax in the tax code. When you die or if you make donations (gifts) that exceed certain thresholds, you may be liable for estate and/or gift taxes. Estate tax rates are higher than income tax rates and are imposed on all of your assets at death. In 2019, the highest estate tax rate is 40 percent. In addition, the generation-skipping transfer tax imposes an <u>additional</u> 40 percent (2019) tax on transfers to grandchildren or younger generations.

The Federal Gift and Estate Tax System is a unified system of taxation on gifts made during life and at death. If your estate is large enough, you cannot give away all of your assets prior to your death in an attempt to avoid estate taxes. The reason is that the gift and estate tax system is designed to tax gifts during your lifetime and transfers at death. If your estate is taxable, the estate tax return (Form 706) is due nine months after your date of death.[1] Your beneficiaries may extend the filing deadline; however, estate taxes must be paid within nine months.[2]

The Estate Tax Calculation

The estate tax calculation is progressive; therefore, larger estates are taxed at higher rates than smaller estates. The estate tax calculation factors in not only assets included in your gross estate at death but also all of the taxable gifts that you made during your lifetime.[a] Your gross estate "shall include the value of all property to the extent of the interest therein of the decedent at the time of death."[3] The estate tax is calculated as follows:

Step 1: The estate tax calculation begins with determining the value of your gross estate by adding together the value of all the assets you own at the time of your death.

Step 2: From your gross estate, administration expenses, funeral expenses, and certain debts are subtracted to determine your adjusted gross estate.

Step 3: Your adjusted gross estate is reduced by the marital deduction and the allowable charitable deduction to determine your taxable estate. (If your entire estate is left to your surviving spouse, the marital deduction will result in a zero taxable estate. When this occurs, your federal exemption goes unused in Step 5.)

Step 4: To your taxable estate, add all lifetime taxable gifts (e.g. gifts in excess of the annual exclusion), compute the tentative tax base, and adjust for any prior gift taxes paid to determine the tentative tax. This step brings all taxable gifts you made during your lifetime into the estate tax calculation.

Step 5: From the tentative tax, the applicable exclusion amount (estate tax exemption), credit for any pre-1977 gifts, and credit for tax paid on any prior gifts are subtracted. The net result is the federal estate tax due.

---

[a] Taxable gifts are generally gifts that do not qualify for the annual exclusion.

Assets Included in the Gross Estate

One of the most common planning mistakes is underestimating the value of your gross estate. The federal gross estate is more expansive than the Louisiana probate estate as it includes all of your property interests in all assets at the time of death. Your probate estate includes only assets that are distributed through your will. Assets with beneficiary designations[b] are not controlled by your will. For example, assets such as life insurance and retirement plans must be included in your gross estate although they are excluded from the Louisiana probate estate. If your estate is the beneficiary, however, these assets are included in the Louisiana probate estate and are governed by your will. A common misconception is that life insurance is not taxable. Although life insurance is generally not subject to <u>income</u> taxation, the death benefit is generally subject to <u>estate</u> taxation. In addition to the assets owned at death, the following property interests are included in the gross estate and are subject to federal estate taxes:

- Property transferred with "strings attached," such as property over which the transferring party retains too much control or retains certain rights. For example, assets in the name of a revocable trust are included in the trustee's gross estate.

- Transfers of assets over which the donor retained the possession or right to income or enjoyment or the right to designate who will enjoy or possess the property either for life or a period that cannot be ascertained without reference to death or for a period that does end prior to death.[4] For example, if Thibodaux transfers the naked ownership of a tract of land to his children and retains the usufruct for life, when Thibodaux dies, his children automatically become the tract of land's full owners. The property over which Thibodaux retains the usufruct for life is not included in his <u>probate</u> estate; however, the land's value will be included in his gross estate for federal estate tax purposes.

- The value of an annuity receivable by a beneficiary which was payable for the decedent's life. For example, Boudreaux is receiving annuity payments for life, and upon Boudreaux's

---

[b] IRAs, 401(k)s, life insurance, other retirement plans, pensions and annuities.

death his daughter will continue to receive payments. The value of the payments to Boudreaux's daughter is included in Boudreaux's gross estate.

- The value of property over which the decedent had a general power of appointment. A general power of appointment is the power given to someone to select the person who will receive certain property at a later date. Powers of appointment are not recognized in Louisiana; therefore, for most Louisiana residents, powers of appointment will not be an issue.

- The value of property held as joint tenants with rights of survivorship, except to the extent the surviving joint tenant can be shown to have contributed to the property's acquisition.[5] For example, Thibodaux contributes 100 percent of the purchase amount to acquire a tract of real estate in Mississippi and names his son a joint tenant with rights of survivorship. Upon Thibodaux's death, the land's entire value is included in Thibodaux's gross estate. As Louisiana does not recognize joint tenancy with rights of survivorship, this will apply to immovable property outside of Louisiana.

- Life insurance proceeds paid to the estate.[6]

- Life insurance proceeds in which the decedent had incidents of ownership.[7] Incidents of ownership are the power to change the beneficiary, terminate the policy, or borrow against the policy.

- Property subject to the three-year rule.

The Three-Year Rule

If you transfer certain property within three years of death, it is included in your gross estate.[8] The following property, if donated within three years of death, is included in the decedent's gross estate:

- Life insurance on the donor's life. You must relinquish all "incidents of ownership" at least three years prior to death to exclude the death benefit from the gross estate.[9]

- Gift taxes paid by the donor or his estate on a gift made within three years of death are included in the donor's gross estate.[10]

- A gift of a retained interest within three years of death.[11] For example, Boudreaux gives his children the naked ownership of a tract of land and retains the usufruct for life. If Boudreaux then transfers the usufruct (the retained interest) within three years of death, the value of the tract of land is included in his gross estate. An outright transfer of the entire tract of land would have removed the land from his gross estate.

- Value of property where the decedent retained a reversionary right with a value over 5 percent of the property's value.[12] For example, Boudreaux transfers property to an irrevocable trust. Pierre is the lifetime income beneficiary. At Pierre's death the property is to revert back to Boudreaux. If Boudreaux does not survive Pierre, the property goes to Boudreaux's son, Clovis. Boudreaux dies before Pierre. The value of the remainder interest in the property is included in Boudreaux's gross estate if the reversion value, just prior to Boudreaux's death, is more than 5 percent of the value of Boudreaux's original transfer.

Gift Taxation

As part of the unified federal gift and estate tax system, a gift tax is imposed on direct or indirect transfers of assets by gift (donation).[13] Rather than paying gift taxes on a taxable gift, the donor may use part of their federal estate tax exemption during their lifetime. Exemption amounts used for gifts during the donor's lifetime will reduce the exemption amount available at death. The intent to donate is irrelevant for federal gift-tax purposes; therefore, if it "looks" like a gift, it will be taxed as a gift, even if the donor claims no gift is intended.[14] Any transfer for less than adequate consideration is a gift subject to taxation.[15] For example, if Boudreaux sells a tract of land with a fair market value of $100,000 to his son for $25,000, the transaction is treated as part sale and part gift. Boudreaux made a gift to his son in the amount of $75,000.

The gift is complete when the donor parts with dominion and control with no power over its disposition.[16] For example, when a revocable trust becomes irrevocable, the gift of the trust assets is complete.

Incomplete transfers result from a reservation of powers or "strings attached" to the gift. Reserving the power to vest the corpus (principal) in the donor or to change beneficiaries results in an incomplete gift.[17] Terminating the power or "strings attached" other than by the donor's death results in a completed gift.[18] For example, making an irrevocable beneficiary designation on a life insurance policy results in a completed gift.

Gifts Attributable to Trustee Powers

A donor or the donor's spouse may wish to act as a trustee of a trust they created. If the donor or the donor's spouse is the trustee, the trust should be drafted carefully to avoid unintended gift taxes. A donor may retain fiduciary powers as trustee if the powers are subject to fixed[c] or objective[d] standards. Fiduciary powers subject to fixed or objective standards do not prevent a completed gift.[19] A donor retaining a right (even in a fiduciary capacity) to use the assets to discharge a support obligation of the donor will be considered a retained right for the donor's benefit and result in an incomplete gift.

A person donating assets to a trust they serve as trustee should avoid discretionary powers and use objective standards to avoid the inclusion of the trust assets in their gross estate. For example, a trustee may "spray" income among the beneficiaries in the trustee's sole reasonable discretion.[20] If a completed gift was intended when the assets were transferred to the spray or sprinkle trust, the donor should not act as trustee or co-trustee.

Transfers Excluded From Gift Taxation

The annual exclusion allows a donor to make present-interest gifts of up to $15,000 (2019) annually to any number of donees. Only present-interest gifts qualify for the annual exclusion. To satisfy the present-interest requirement, the donee must have immediate and unrestrained use and enjoyment of the donated asset. Donations that are not present-interest gifts are future-interest gifts. If the gift is of a future interest, gift taxes will be due on the first dollar, rather than on amounts in excess of $15,000 (2019). Gift amounts greater than the annual exclusion or gifts that are not present-interest are taxable gifts.[21]

---

[c] For example, distribute 5 percent of the trust annually.
[d] Such as distributions for health, education or support.

The annual exclusion amount is indexed for inflation but only increases in $1,000 increments.[22]

Section 2503(c) Gifts

Transfers to individuals under the age of 21 are considered present-interest gifts[e] if the property and the income derived from it may be expended by or for the benefit of the person prior to age 21. In addition to the extent the gifted assets are not expended by age 21, the assets must be transferred to the person at age 21. See Chapter 22 for more information regarding gifts to Section 2503(c) trusts.

Tuition and Medical Expenses

You may pay the tuition or medical expenses (directly to the institution) for the benefit of any person free from gift taxes.[23] No limits are placed on the amount or number of annual tuition or medical payments. However, if the donation is made to the individual rather than the educational or medical institution, only $15,000 (2019) per donee is free from gift taxes.

Gift Tax Returns

The donor, not the recipient, of a taxable gift is responsible for payment of applicable gift taxes and for filing gift tax returns. A gift tax return must be filed for the prior year's donations by April 15, except under the following provisions:

1. An excluded transfer under the annual exclusion;[24]

2. A medical expense or tuition expense[25]; or

3. A deductible transfer under the marital deduction.[26]

For taxable gifts made after December 31, 1996, the donor must provide disclosure "adequate to apprise the Internal Revenue Service of the nature of the gift and the basis for the value reported."[27] Adequate disclosure starts the running of the three-year statute of limitations. Therefore, if you do not adequately disclose the gift's

---

[e] As a present-interest gift it qualifies for the annual exclusion.

nature, the IRS may attempt to revalue the gift at anytime after the three year statute of limitations. Adequate disclosure includes

1. The identities of and the relationship between transferor and transferee;

2. A description of the transferred property and consideration received;

3. The trust's Tax Identification Number and a description of the trust terms if property is transferred in trust;

4. A detailed description of the method used to determine the fair market value of the transferred property or an appraisal by a qualified appraiser; and

5. A statement explaining any position that is contrary to any proposed, temporary or final Treasury Regulation or Revenue Ruling.

The Federal Estate Tax Exemption

Each person has a $11,400,000 (2019) federal estate tax exemption. The exemption is technically referred to as the applicable exemption amount; however, this book will generally refer to the applicable exemption amount as the federal estate tax exemption. Property passing to anyone other than the surviving spouse may be applied to the federal estate tax exemption.

The Economic Growth and Taxpayer Relief Reconciliation Act of 2001 (EGTRRA) gradually phased out the federal estate tax (see Table 12). Unfortunately, the 2010 Tax Act retroactively reinstated the estate and generation skipping taxes for 2010, along with the step- up in basis rules. In 2010 the generation skipping tax was zero, but was reinstated after December 31, 2010. In 2011 the estate and gift taxes were reunified.

Table 9 - Estate Tax Exemptions

Year	Estate Exemption^	Gift Exemption	GST Exemption	Rates
2003	$1 million	$1 million	$1,060,000	49%
2004	$1.5 million	$1 million	$1.5 million	48%
2005	$1.5 million	$1 million	$1.5 million	47%
2006	$2 million	$1 million	$2 million	46%
2007	$2 million	$1 million	$2 million	45%
2008	$2 million	$1 million	$2 million	45%
2009	$3.5 million	$1 million	$3.5 million	45%
2010	$5 million	$5 million	Repealed	35%
2011	$5 million	$5 million	$5,000,000	35%
2012	$5,120,000*	$5,120,000	$5,120,000	35%
2013	$5,250,000*	$5,250,000	$5,250,000	40%
2014	$5,340,000*	$5,340,000	$5,340,000	40%
2015	$5,430,000*	$5,430,000	$5,430,000	40%
2016	$5,450,000*	$5,450,000	$5,450,000	40%
2017	$5,490,000*	$5,490,000	$5,490,000	40%
2018	$11,180,000	$11,180,000	$11,180,000	40%
2019	$11,400,000	$11,400,000	$11,400,000	40%

^ Under EGTRRA and the 2010 and 2012 Tax Acts
*Plus the deceased spouse's unused exemption amount (DSUEA)

The Marital Deduction

The unlimited marital deduction allows spouses to transfer an unlimited amount of assets between each other free of gift or estate taxes either during their lifetime or at death. The marital deduction applies automatically to assets transferred to the surviving spouse either outright or in trust.[28] For the marital deduction to apply, the recipient spouse must be given either full ownership of the property or a qualified terminal interest in the property. For example, property passing outright to the surviving spouse through the will or intestacy qualifies for the marital deduction. In addition, inter-vivos[f] gifts to a spouse and life insurance in the decedent's estate of which the surviving spouse is beneficiary qualifies for the marital deduction. Retirement plans, IRAs, and annuities naming the surviving spouse as the beneficiary qualify for the marital deduction. Finally, transfers of real property titled as joint tenants with rights of survivorship outside

---

[f] Gifts made during the donor's lifetime.

of Louisiana and a spouse's survivorship annuity also qualify for the marital deduction.[29]

The spouse must be a United States citizen to take advantage of the marital deduction. If the surviving spouse is not a United States citizen, a Qualified Domestic Trust (QDOT) may be used to preserve the full marital deduction.

Portability of the Exclusion Amount

Beginning in 2011, the applicable exclusion amount is portable between spouses. Portability allows a surviving spouse to use the deceased spouse's unused applicable exclusion amount (DSUEA) for gift and estate tax purposes. The applicable exclusion amount is now equal to the sum of the basic exclusion amount of the surviving spouse and the unused applicable exclusion amount of the last deceased spouse. For example, Marie dies in 2019 with a $7 million estate and her available exemption is $11,400,000. The excess $4,400,000 can be added to her surviving spouse's estate tax exemption. Prior to portability, the use both spouse's applicable exclusion amount, spouses had to set up a credit shelter trust or leave assets equal to the exclusion amount to someone other than the surviving spouse. Leaving assets to someone other than the surviving spouse deprived the surviving spouse from the use of those assets. Portability allows the surviving spouse to receive the deceased spouse's assets outright and utilize both exemption amounts without a credit shelter trust.

To take advantage of portability, the deceased spouse must have died after 2010, and an election must be made on an estate tax return (Form 706) to claim the deceased spouse's unused exclusion amount. An estate tax return must be filed to make the election even if estate taxes are not due at the first spouse's death. Form 706 must be filed within 9 months of the date of death unless an extension was granted. If Form 706 does not have to otherwise be filed, Form 706 may be filed up to two years after the decedent's death pursuant to Revenue Procedure 2017-34. If a surviving spouse remarries and the second spouse also predeceases, the surviving spouse must use the DSUEA of the second spouse. If a surviving spouse remarries and the second spouse also predeceases, the surviving spouse must use the DSUEA of the second spouse.

Portability allows the use of both spouses' applicable exclusion amounts without the need for a credit shelter trust. Portability will make it easier for couples to avoid estate taxes without the use of a credit shelter trust. Portability will be especially useful to individuals with large tax deferred retirement accounts who don't have sufficient non-retirement assets to optimally fund a credit shelter trust to preserve both exemptions. Spouses no longer have to choose between extended tax deferral (naming the surviving spouse as beneficiary) and utilizing both spouses' applicable exemption amount (naming a credit shelter trust or other non-spouse beneficiary).

However, a credit shelter trust can provide advantages to portability. First, portability is not guaranteed. An estate tax return must be filed after the first spouse's death. If the return is not filed, portability is lost. In addition, the surviving spouse could remarry and unintentionally lose the exemption as only the exemption of the last deceased spouse is available. The DSUEA is not indexed for inflation so appreciation of the assets may cause estate taxation in the surviving spouse's estate. In contrast, preserving the exemption with a credit shelter trust is not contingent upon filing an estate tax return, nor the availability of the exemption in the event of remarriage. Also, assets left to a credit shelter trust will not be subject to estate taxes regardless of future appreciation. Finally, the generation skipping transfer tax is not portable. If couples wish to fully utilize their generation skipping tax exemption, they must use a credit shelter trust at the first spouse's death to preserve both generation skipping tax exemptions. Although portability will be useful in many estates, credit shelter trusts will continue to play an important role in estate planning.

Credit Shelter Trusts (CSTs)

Many estate plans provide a bequest of all of the decedent's assets to the surviving spouse. This strategy works well if both spouses' combined estates are valued under or near the federal estate tax exemption amount. If the spouses' combined estates are less than $11,400,000 in 2019, leaving all of the assets to the surviving spouse will not expose the assets to estate taxes. If the DSUEA is used, a total of $22,800,000 (2019) can be transferred free of estate taxes.

When not relying on portability, here is how a credit shelter trust preserves both exemptions. When calculating estate taxes, the marital deduction is always applied prior to the federal estate tax exemption. If all of the deceased spouse's assets are transferred to the surviving spouse via the marital deduction, none of the first-to-die spouse's federal estate tax exemption will be used. To use some or all of the first-to-die spouse's federal estate tax exemption, assets must be left to someone other than the surviving spouse. For example, leaving a portion of the first-to-die spouse's estate to the children will use some of the first-to-die spouse's federal estate tax exemption. However, in many cases, it is not desirable to leave a large amount of assets to a non-spouse individual because the surviving spouse will need these assets to maintain his or her standard of living.

One option is to use a CST to preserve both estate tax exemptions and provide income and principal to the surviving spouse. A CST enables the first-to-die spouse to preserve the use of his or her federal estate tax exemption while providing income and principal to the surviving spouse. In addition, all future growth of the assets in the CST is free from estate taxation. A CST (aka "B" Trust or Bypass Trust) is typically drafted into a will or a revocable living trust and comes into existence at the testator's death, but the trust may be established and funded prior to death. The trust is typically funded with an amount equal to the federal estate tax exemption amount. A lesser amount may be used. The amount placed in the trust is not subject to federal estate taxes so long as the amount is not over the applicable exemption amount ($11,400,000 in 2019). Any future growth in the trust is not subject to estate taxes but will be subject to applicable income taxes. Typically, the children are the principal beneficiaries, and the surviving spouse is the income beneficiary. If the surviving spouse is the Trustee, the trust should be drafted to allow the trustee distribute assets to the surviving spouse by distributing income and/or principal subject to an objective ascertainable standard such as needs for health, education, maintenance and support. If the surviving spouse, for example, needs to replace the roof on the family home, assets from the trust may be used to pay for these repairs because this meets the requirements of an objective ascertainable standard for maintenance and support. Additional restrictions may be placed on the trustee's ability to make distributions, including no authority to make distributions to the surviving spouse or to distribute only the income to the surviving spouse. The key point is to avoid giving the surviving spouse trustee unlimited discretion to make distributions to him or herself without an objective ascertainable standard. If the spouse who is also the trustee is given unlimited discretion not subject to objective ascertainable standards, the trust's assets would be included in the surviving spouse's estate. If this occurs, the CST fails as an estate tax savings tool. A non-spouse trustee need not be limited by ascertainable standards.

Alternatively, the surviving spouse does not have to receive any income or principal from the CST. However, most CSTs provide income payments and access to principal to the surviving spouse. The trustee may also be given discretionary spray powers to allocate income between the surviving spouse and children beneficiaries. The correct trust provisions will depend on the spouses' planning goals and available resources.

Another option to provide the surviving spouse with property use for life with the children receiving the property at the surviving spouse's death is to provide a lifetime usufruct of certain assets to the surviving spouse. Leaving the naked ownership of assets to non-spouse legatees (e.g. the children) will use the deceased spouse's federal estate tax exemption. The amount of property left to non-spouse legatees as naked owners in excess of the federal estate tax exemption amount of the first spouse to die can be selected for QTIP treatment and included in the surviving spouse's estate. This will allow assets in amounts over the federal estate tax exemption to be included in the surviving spouse's estate. Estate taxation of these assets will depend on the federal estate tax exemption available and the value of the surviving spouse's estate at the time of the surviving spouse's death. The usufruct/naked-ownership arrangement allows both spouses' estate tax exemptions to be used without the use of a CST. A disadvantage of a usufruct/naked-ownership arrangement is that it provides less control over the assets compared to a CST.

Although credit shelter trusts and usufruct arrangements will continue to be important planning options, exemption portability will provide another way to preserve both spouses' exemptions.

Qualified Terminal Interest Property (QTIP)

Assets passing to anyone other than the surviving spouse will not fall under the marital deduction unless the asset is Qualified Terminal Interest Property (QTIP).[30] This is an exception to the rule that the marital deduction does not apply to property passing to anyone other than the surviving spouse. The QTIP election allows the first-to-die spouse to determine who will ultimately inherit Qualified Terminal Interest Property while giving the surviving spouse the income from the property for life. The QTIP election can be helpful in second-marriage situations. For example, Boudreaux has a child, Pierre, from a prior marriage to whom he wishes to leave certain assets after his death. Boudreaux also wants to provide financial resources to his surviving spouse, Clotile. If he leaves all of his assets in full ownership to his surviving spouse (who is not Pierre's mother), Boudreaux has no assurance that Pierre will receive any of Clotile's assets when she dies. Clotile may leave all of her assets and the assets she inherits from Boudreaux to her sister, child, friend, or anyone else she chooses. If Boudreaux leaves all or a portion of his estate to Pierre, Clotile may not have sufficient assets to maintain her standard of living. A properly established QTIP trust will help Boudreaux provide for his spouse and his child. A QTIP trust requires that all of the income from the trust be paid to the surviving spouse at least annually. When the surviving spouse dies, the remaining assets in the trust are distributed according to the wishes of the first-to-die spouse. The value of the remaining QTIP trust assets is included in the second-to-die spouse's estate via the marital deduction. In addition, the second-to-die spouse cannot redirect the assets to another individual. Continuing our example, once Clotile dies, the assets remaining in the QTIP trust are distributed to Pierre according to Boudreaux's wishes. The value of the remaining QTIP assets is included in Clotile's estate under the marital deduction, although she does not control who inherits the assets.

Some individuals rely on a verbal assurance that the surviving spouse will uphold an agreed upon arrangement such as Clotile's promise to leave Boudreaux's share of the estate to Pierre if Boudreaux pre-deceases Clotile. Frequently, the surviving spouse changes his or her mind after the first spouse dies. For example, Clotile may remarry and leave all of the assets to her new spouse. Influences such as the surviving spouse's own children or other relatives or diminished mental capacity may also cause the surviving spouse to deviate from a verbal agreement. For these reasons, promises like "of course I will leave your share to your children" should not be relied upon.

QTIP Requirements

The QTIP rules require that all income from QTIP assets be paid to the surviving spouse at least annually and no portion of the QTIP assets can be made available to anyone other than the surviving spouse. Income is generally dividends, interests and rents but not capital appreciation. In addition, the spouse must have the right to demand that assets not producing income be converted into income-producing assets. After the first spouse's death, the executor must list the property for the QTIP election on Schedule M and calculate the estate taxes with the deduction on a timely filed[g] estate tax return (Form 706). An affirmative election no longer has to be made on Form 706. For an inter-vivos QTIP election, the property subject to the QTIP election must be listed on Schedule A of a timely filed federal gift-tax return (Form 709).

A usufruct for life of property is eligible for the QTIP election.[31] Thus, a QTIP <u>trust</u> need not be used to obtain the tax advantages of the QTIP election so long as the usufruct is <u>for life</u>. A usufruct granted by Testament executed on or after June 18, 1996, is now presumed to be for life.[32] A usufruct created by Testaments drafted prior to this date that do not specifically indicate that the usufruct is for life will not be eligible for QTIP treatment. Transferring the naked ownership of assets to the children and the usufruct for life to the surviving spouse allows the assets to be eligible for QTIP treatment on an asset-by-asset basis.[33] Assets that are not selected for QTIP are included in the first-to-die spouse's estate and are offset by the federal estate tax exemption. Assets that are selected for QTIP will qualify for the marital deduction and will be included in the second-to-die spouse's estate.

Unless the usufructuary has the power to dispose of the property subject to usufruct, a usufruct of nonproductive, nonconsumable property is not eligible for QTIP treatment.[34] In addition, a usufructuary accounting debt deduction is disallowed on the surviving spouse's estate tax return for QTIP assets included in the surviving spouse's estate.[35]

For a QTIP trust, the election may be made over a fraction or percentage interest. The trust should authorize the executor to split the trust according to the fractional or percentage QTIP election to create a marital deduction (QTIP) share and a nonmarital share. The marital

---

[g] Including extensions

share is included in the surviving spouse's estate and the nonmarital share is included in the first-to-die spouse's estate. Due to the uncertainty of the estate tax exemption amounts, one option is to draft a testamentary trust with two or more subtrusts. The executor will fund subtrust A with the maximum amount of unused federal estate tax exemption available to the decedent. The remainder of the decedent's estate will fund subtrust B which will qualify for the QTIP election and will be included in the surviving spouse's estate for tax purposes. This is a typical arrangement which creates a CST (subtrust A) and a QTIP trust (subtrust B) and helps to maximize the use of both spouses' federal estate tax exemptions. Ideally, fund subtrust A with assets that are most likely to appreciate in value because any future growth is not subject to estate taxation in the surviving spouse's estate as are the assets in subtrust B.

Marital deduction and credit shelter planning are often accomplished with trusts such as the CST and QTIP trust. The key purposes are to structure the estate plan to optimize the use of the federal estate tax exemption of each spouse and to provide the surviving spouse with the use of these assets. Generally, a trust can provide better asset protection than portability or a usufruct/naked-ownership arrangement. It also provides the ability to control the asset from the grave through the trust's provisions.

Louisiana Inheritance Tax

The Louisiana Inheritance Tax was repealed for all inheritances effective January 1, 2008.

Louisiana Gift Taxes

Gifts made on or after July 1, 2008 are not subject to Louisiana gift taxes and gift tax returns need not be filed with the Department of Revenue.

Tax Basis of Assets

Inter-Vivos Donations

When assets are sold, the gain or loss on the sale is determined by the difference between the sale price and the cost basis. When assets are purchased, the cost basis is generally the purchase price. Improvements or additional construction on real estate, for example, will increase the cost basis.

A donee will generally use the donor's tax basis for tax purposes. For example, Thibodaux owns a tract of land that he acquired many years ago; its cost basis is $10,000. He donates the land to Boudreaux when the land's fair market value is $50,000. Boudreaux's cost basis is the same as Thibodaux's, $10,000. If Boudreaux later sells the land for $75,000 he will owe taxes on a capital gain of $65,000. The donor's cost basis will NOT be used under the following circumstances:

- When calculating a loss on a subsequent sale of donated property, if the property's value is less than the donor's basis, the donee's basis is the property's value on the date of gift.[36]

- When federal gift taxes are paid on the gift, the basis is increased by the portion of tax attributable to the increase in the property's value since it acquired that basis.[37]

- Under current law, property inherited from a decedent takes a tax basis equal to the property's fair market value on the date of death.[38] You may sell inherited property with no capital gain tax if there was no price appreciation from the date of death.

- The surviving spouse's half of the community receives a step-up in basis to the date-of-death fair market value.[39] Louisiana's community property regime provides a valuable tax advantage upon the first spouse's death. All community property receives a step-up in basis to the date-of-death value. Therefore, the surviving spouse may sell community property with no capital gain after the first spouse dies if there was no appreciation from the date of death to the time of the sale.

- Selection of the alternate valuation date causes the fair market value six months after the date of death to apply to carry over basis.

- Income in respect of a decedent (IRD) does not qualify for a step-up in basis.[40] An asset consisting of taxable income property that would have been taxable to the decedent had he or she lived to receive it and was not taxable while he or she was alive is IRD. It is taxable to the estate, beneficiary, legatee or heir when received.[41] Applies to IRAs, qualified retirement plans, annuities and outstanding payments on installment notes. IRD is not applicable to Roth IRAs.

- See Treas. Reg. § 1.1015-(a)(3) if the donee does not have basis information.

---

[1] IRC § 6075(a).

[2] IRC § 6081(a).

[3] IRC §§ 2001, 2033.

[4] IRC § 2036(a).

[5] IRC § 2040.

[6] IRC § 2042.

[7] IRC § 2042.

[8] IRC § 2035.

[9] IRC §§ 2035, 2042.

[10] IRC § 2035(b).

[11] IRC § 2035(a).

[12] IRC § 2037.

[13] IRC § 2501.

[14] Treas. Reg. § 25.2511-1(a)(1).

[15] Treas. Reg. § 25.2511-1(g)(1).

[16] Treas. Reg. § 25.2511-2.

[17] Treas. Reg. § 25.2511-2(c).

[18] Treas. Reg. § 25.25111-2(f).

[19] Treas. Reg. § 25.2511-2(g).

[20] La. Rev. Stat. Ann. § 9:1961(C).

[21] IRC § 2503(b)(1).

[22] IRC § 2503(b)(2).

[23] IRC § 2503(e).

[24] IRC § 2503(b).

[25] IRC §2503 (e).

[26] IRC § 2523.

[27] Treas. Reg. § 301.6501(c)-1(f)(2).

[28] IRC § 2056(a).

[29] IRC § 2039.

[30] IRC § 2056(b)(1).

[31] IRC §2056(b)(7).

[32] La. Civ. Code Art. 1499.

[33] PLR 8417087. 8304040.

[34] Regs. 20.2056(a)-7(d)(2); 20.2056(b)5(f); PLRs 8304040, 8312018, 8325056.

[35] IRC § 2053(c)(1)(C).

[36] IRC § 1015 (a).

[37] IRC § 1015 (d)(6).

[38] IRC § 1014.

[39] IRC § 1014(b)(6).

[40] IRC § 1014(c).

[41] IRC § 691.

24

Family Business Planning

Chapter Highlights

❖ Planning for the transition of a family-owned business to your children or grandchildren presents many tax and non-tax issues. Anyone with an interest in a family-owned business should have a business succession plan in place.

❖ Most family-owned businesses do not survive the second generation due to a lack of business succession planning.

❖ If you have more than one child, determining who will run the business must be addressed in a manner that preserves family harmony.

❖ If your estate will be subject to estate taxes, a business succession plan can provide a source of cash to pay for estate taxes.

❖ Buy-Sell agreements provide an orderly transfer of the business upon the owner's retirement, disability or death and can help ensure the business will continue as a viable ongoing concern.

❖ If you own a business with another individual and there is no buy-sell agreement that will provide for the transition of the business upon your business partner's death, your new business partners will be your deceased business partner's spouse and/or children.

❖ Limited liability partnerships and limited liability companies provide planning flexibility to family-owned businesses and are also widely used for estate planning and asset protection purposes for nonbusiness assets.

❖ Limited liability partnerships and limited liability companies can be established with unique asset protection features to help protect assets from lawsuits.

❖ Limited liability partnerships and limited liability companies allow you to transfer the majority of the value of the entity's assets to your children at a reduced gift and/or estate tax value while maintaining full control over the assets.

PLANNING FOR A FAMILY BUSINESS is as much about maintaining family harmony as it is about reducing taxes and providing for a smooth transition of the business. A business owner must have an exit plan that balances business, family and tax-savings needs. Furthermore, because a closely held business often comprises a large percentage of the owner's estate, it may give rise to potentially significant estate tax liability. Often there is insufficient cash available to pay the estate taxes, and as a result, the business must be sold to provide cash to pay the estate taxes due. To make matters worse, estate taxes are due nine months after death. If sufficient cash is not available, the business may have to be sold at a fire-sale price to quickly produce the required cash. Avoiding this outcome is critical if the business is to survive into future generations.

Non-tax Issues

In addition to estate tax issues, many non-tax issues must also be resolved. For example, there is the question of who will own and run the business after the owner's retirement, disability or death. If the owner has more than one child, some of the children may not wish to take over the family business. In addition, one child may be willing to take over the business, but the child may not have the financial means to buyout the siblings' ownership interests. A mechanism to facilitate a smooth transition upon the owner's retirement, disability or death must be in place. Lastly, if a child has no desire to be a part owner of the business, other assets may be earmarked for this child to equalize inheritances.

Nearly 70 percent of all businesses fail during the transition from the first generation to the next, and 85 percent of businesses will not make it to the third generation.[1] Failure of these businesses can be attributed to many factors, but the primary cause is a failure to develop a business succession plan. When developing a business succession plan, some of the most common issues are

- Conflicts among the children and other nonfamily members.

- Power struggles over who will control the business.

- Insufficient liquid assets to pay estate taxes.

- Insufficient capital to withstand financial hardship due to the loss of a founder/key employee.

- Ways to keep ownership of the business "in the family."

When developing a business succession plan, some of the most common questions are

- Should all of the children participate in running the business? If not, will nonparticipating children receive ownership interests in the business? If they will not, how will the estate plan be structured to treat all of the children fairly?

- Should the business be sold to a third party or to nonfamily business partners?

- If the owner retires, will he or she continue to rely on the business resources for retirement income?

Valuation of the Business

A frequently overlooked step to the planning process is obtaining a proper valuation of the business which will help determine whether estate taxes will be assessed against the estate. An accurate valuation is critical when a closely held business is involved, and a qualified appraisal is a must to obtain an accurate valuation. Estimating the valuation is critical due to possible estate tax exposure on undervalued business entities. For example, if life insurance will be used to pay for estate taxes attributable to the business, an accurate valuation is needed to determine the amount of life insurance required. An accurate valuation is also important when structuring the terms of the buy-sell agreement.

Buy-Sell Agreements

A Buy-Sell agreement is a planning technique used to arrange the disposition of the owner's business interest. Buy-Sell agreements provide an orderly transfer of the business upon the retirement, disability or death of the owner and help ensure the business will continue as a viable ongoing concern. A buy-sell agreement creates a market for the retired/disabled/deceased owner's share at a pre-determined price. It also helps to ensure that surviving family members of a deceased owner are treated fairly. Two basic types of Buy-Sell agreements exist: Stock Redemption Agreements and Cross-Purchase Agreements.

A closely held business owned by two or more people should consider a buy-sell agreement to prevent the surviving owners from having new business partners (the heirs of the current business partner). A buy-sell agreement provides the following advantages:

1. It helps to ensure the smooth transfer of a closely held business by providing for the orderly transfer upon the retirement, disability or death of an owner.

2. It allows the owners to fix the price for sale and purchase of the business.

3. It provides a funding mechanism to buy out the heirs who do not wish to own or run the business.

4. It provides funds to pay estate taxes.

Buy-sell agreements have the following trade offs:

1. The terms of the agreement may restrict an owner's access to outside credit.

2. The owners are bound by the agreement unless all parties agree to change the terms. This may restrict an owner's estate planning options.

3. Periodic business valuations may be required.

Cross-Purchase Buy-Sell Agreements

In a cross-purchase buy-sell agreement, one of the simplest forms of buy-sell agreements, the owners agree to buy each other's ownership interest in the business for a pre-determined price. Because a cross-purchase buy-sell agreement is a private agreement between the owners, the business is not a party to the agreement. The agreement states the price and terms at which the remaining owners will buy the retired/disabled/deceased owner's interest. The exiting owner (or the family of a deceased owner) receives cash for the exiting owner's interest in the business. The remaining owners own all of the business when the cross purchase is complete.

To provide cash to purchase a deceased owner's interest, life insurance is often used to fund the cross-purchase. Life insurance is often used as it is the cheapest, most liquid source of cash upon the owner's death. If life insurance is not used, the purchasing party must have sufficient available cash to purchase the retired/disabled/deceased owner's interest upon a triggering event (e.g. retirement, disability or death). Cross-purchase agreements funded with life insurance require every owner to purchase a separate life insurance policy on each of the other owners. The business does not own the policies. The insurance premiums are nondeductible (considered personal expenses), but the death benefits are income tax free. Because the insurance policies are self-funded, money to pay the premiums must come out of each owner's pocket. Additional compensation may be taken by the owners to offset the premium expenses. However, the additional compensation will obviously increase the owner's taxable income.

A drawback of cross-purchase buy-sell agreements funded with life insurance is that each owner must purchase an insurance policy for all of the other owners. If there are numerous owners, many life insurance policies are required. Four owners require 12 policies. Also, a life insurance policy will provide funding only upon the death of an owner.

The remaining owners receive an increase in their income tax basis in their total holdings in an amount equal to the price for the shares they purchase. An increase in the tax basis will result in a lower amount of taxes paid if the owners wish to sell their ownership interest at a later date. If the cross purchase occurs at death, the stock will be purchased from the deceased owner's estate at its step-up market value. If the cross purchase occurs during the lifetime of the owner (for example, due to retirement or disability), the basis is what the buyer paid for the stock.

Redemption Agreements

A redemption buy-sell agreement provides that the business buys from the selling party upon the occurrence of a triggering event (retirement, disability or death). The purchasing parties must have an available source of cash to purchase the retired/disabled/deceased owner's interest upon a triggering event. Again, life insurance is typically used to fund redemption agreements as it is often the cheapest source of available cash upon the death of an owner. The policies are owned by and the premiums are paid by the business. The business may not deduct the insurance premiums under IRC § 264 (a)(1).

Upon the retirement/disability/death of an owner, the deceased owner's interest in the entity is purchased. The surviving owners remain, and their ownership interests are adjusted according to their ownership interest and the percentage of the deceased/disabled/retired owner's interest which is purchased.

Long term, for any type of buy-sell agreement, the owners should consider funding at least a portion of the purchase with something other than life insurance. If the buyout occurs because of a nondeath event (retirement or disability), nonlife insurance sources of cash must be available. Furthermore, rather than paying the purchase price in a lump sum, the buy-sell agreement may allow installment payments over a period of time. Such an arrangement may make it easier on the cash-flow of the business and the purchasing owners.

Many complex rules and tax implications exist that are beyond the purposes of this chapter. Different types of buy-sell agreements in addition to the cross-purchase and redemption agreements also exist. As with all areas of estate planning, competent professional help is a must when structuring a business succession plan.

Limited Liability Partnerships and Limited Liability Companies

Limited liability partnerships (LLPs) and limited liability companies (LLCs) generally provide the most estate planning benefits to families owning closely held businesses. These two business entities provide much flexibility and are widely used for estate planning and asset protection purposes.

Limited liability partnerships (LLPs) and limited liability companies (LLCs) are often used to fractionalize ownership of business interests, real estate or other assets, to take advantage of valuation discounts and to provide for centralized management. The use of valuation discounts can significantly reduce gift and estate taxes. In addition, LLPs and LLCs can be used to transfer assets out of the parents' estates while the parents maintain full control and managerial authority over the assets. Parents may remove nearly all of the value and future appreciation of the LLP or LLC from their estates while retaining control of the assets in the LLP or LLC. The additional benefits of valuation discounts, income shifting to the children, and asset protection further add to the appeal of these planning vehicles.

Family Liability Partnerships

A family limited partnership (FLP) is a limited liability partnership with at least one general partner exposed to unlimited liability. For this reason, FLPs are often established with a corporation or an LLC controlled by the parents as the general partner. This technique limits the liability of the general partner to the assets of the corporation or LLC and prevents unlimited liability exposure to the partners. In addition, a FLP must have at least one limited partner. The partners who are not general partners are limited partners whose liability is limited to their capital contribution to the partnership. The limited partner has the role of passive contributor whose powers are generally restricted to nonmanagerial duties. Management power lies in the hands of the general partners.

Partner contributions are mandatory, and the partnership agreement must describe the contributions and state its agreed value or method of determining the value. If the partnership agreement fails to require or describe a contribution, the limited partner is liable as a general partner. The contributions may consist of money, movable property, immovable property or the performance of nonmanagerial services. Finally, a limited partner is liable for the obligations of the partnership only up to the amount of the agreed contribution.

Limited Liability Companies

A limited liability company (LLC) is an entity that is an unincorporated association having one or more members. It is a hybrid entity with characteristics of both partnerships and corporations.

Unlike an LLP, an LLC need only have one member.[2] For income tax purposes, an LLC will be taxed as a corporation unless the proper election is made to tax the LLC as a partnership. Most family-owned business entities formed as an LLC are taxed as a partnership or as an sub chapter S corporation. This prevents income taxation at both the LLC level and the individual level for distributions similar to double taxation of corporations which are not classified as sub chapter S corporations. Additionally, LLCs are not subject to Louisiana Franchise Taxes.

In exchange for membership units, a member may contribute cash, property, services, a promissory note or other binding obligation to contribute cash or property or to perform services.

The LLCs' operating agreement sets the guidelines by which the LLC is managed. The operating agreement is analogous to the by-laws of a corporation. The members of the LLC may amend the operating agreement according to its rules for amendment. In the absence of an operating agreement, Louisiana law provides for default rules of operation.

The main advantage of an LLC over an FLP is that an LLC does not require a general partner who would have unlimited liability for the debts of and claims against the LLC. A limited liability partnership requires at least one general partner who is exposed to unlimited liability for the FLPs' liabilities.

Benefits of LLCs and FLPs

- LLCs/FLPs facilitate gifting of large assets by transferring fractional interests of the LLC/FLP rather than a fractional interest in the underlying asset (e.g. real estate or a business). As a practical matter, it is more feasible to transfer 5 percent of an LLC/FLP than 5 percent of a tract of land. If 5 percent of the land is transferred, the new owner can force a partition or sheriff's sale of the land. Transferring an interest of a LLC/FLP over which the parents retain control avoids this problem.

- Parents may retain control of the LLC/FLP and the underlying assets although most of the value of the LLC/LLP is transferred to children. Control of the LLC/FLP may be retained by the parents although they own as little as 1 percent of the LLC/FLP.

The parents direct how the assets are invested and managed. The parents also determine when and if distributions are to be made.

- Investment costs may be reduced by keeping the LLC/FLP assets pooled together for investment purposes while transferring the LLC/FLP interests.

- Parents may place restrictions on the right to transfer entity interests to nonfamily members. Restrictions may include to whom children may sell or donate their LLC/FLP interest. The parents or the LLC/FLP may be given a right of first refusal to purchase the LLC/FLP interests if a child wishes to sell.

- Out-of-state immovable property owned by an LLC/FLP avoids ancillary probate.

- A properly established LLC/FLP helps to protect assets from creditors.

- Valuation discounts generally reduce asset values for estate- and gift-tax purposes.

- Income from the LLC/FLP may be transferred to the children who will likely be in a lower tax bracket than the parents.

- An LLC/FLP can provide more flexibility than an irrevocable trust when transferring assets to children or grandchildren. The managing members determine how the assets are to be managed and distributed which prevents mismanagement by the child or grandchild (similar to donations to a trust). An irrevocable trust lack flexibility because the terms of the trust generally cannot be changed.

Trade Offs of LLCs and FLPs

- Creating an LLC/FLP generally requires the assistance of an attorney. Although not all operating agreements are complex, drafting a complex operating agreement can be expensive.

- An LLC/FLP requires the preparation of additional income tax returns which add to administration fees.

- Direct control of the assets transferred to an LLC/FLP may be lost depending on the terms of the LLC/FLP.

Membership Interests

A membership interest in an LLC is an incorporeal movable, making LLCs an ideal vehicle for owning out-of-state real estate. Typically, real estate owned outside of Louisiana must go through ancillary probate or be held in a living trust to avoid probate all together. An alternative is to place real estate located outside of Louisiana into an LLC. The LLC interests, as incorporeal movables, do not require ancillary probate proceedings. The LLC interests are inherited rather than the underlying assets held in the LLC.

The remainder of this chapter will focus on LLCs rather than FLPs. Most of the principles and techniques described herein for LLCs may also be applied to FLPs.

Management of Limited Liability Companies

The management duties of an LLC are generally determined by the operating agreement. In addition, the management structure of an LLC may be established with Class A and Class B membership units. Generally, the parents retain the Class A membership units (voting units) and use the Class B membership units (nonvoting units) for transfers to the children. Management of the LLC is typically restricted to the parents, enabling them to retain control of the assets owned by the LLC. This arrangement allows the parents to transfer the majority of the value of the LLC to the children while retaining full control over the LLC and the underlying assets. Nonmanager members (the children) have no authority with regard to the LLC, although they may own 99 percent of the LLC. In addition, nonvoting members may be restricted from accessing financial information if so provided in the operating agreement or articles of organization.

Asset Protection Benefits of Limited Liability Companies

One of the most appealing benefits of LLCs[a] is their asset protection benefits. A properly structured LLC can help to deter lawsuits and protect an LLC member from liabilities arising from the

---

[a] Family limited partnerships also benefit from these asset protection features. In fact, the charging order as it applies to LLCs originated in partnership law.

assets or business owned by the LLC. For example, if the LLC consists of a business that may be the source of a lawsuit, the LLC helps to protect the LLC owner from personal liability arising from the LLC. The assets within the LLC may be subject to seizure if the cause of action arises from the business within the LLC, but the owner of the LLC is generally not subject to personal liability.

In addition, an LLC helps to protect the assets owned by the LLC from causes of action arising from outside of the LLC. For example, Boudreaux has LLC X which owns an investment portfolio and LLC Y which owns rental properties. If Boudreaux is sued by a tenant who was injured on property owned by LLC Y, the assets in LLC X should be protected from the lawsuit. The reason multiple LLCs are often used is to separate nonrisky assets (e.g. an investment portfolio) from risky assets (e.g. rental property). If the LLCs are properly drafted, LLC X will be protected from lawsuits arising from LLC Y or elsewhere. Individuals who are in a high risk profession such as a medical doctor or engineer and who are vulnerable to lawsuits benefit from isolating risky assets from nonrisky assets.

Unless otherwise provided in the articles of organization or the operating agreement, a membership interest is assignable. However, an assignee is only entitled to receive the distributions and to receive the allocation of income, gains and losses to which the assignor was entitled. An assignee does not become a member nor does an assignee have any of the rights or powers of a member until he or she is admitted as a member. Therefore, unless the operating agreement otherwise provides, the person to whom the LLC units are transferred only has the rights of an assignee.

A key point is that all LLCs are not equal, and many will not provide adequate asset protection. The operating agreement must be properly drafted to provide the maximum amount of protection from creditors. With a properly drafted LLC, an assignee does not become a member or participate in management unless the members unanimously consent in writing. The assignor continues to be a member until the assignee is admitted as a member. A judgment creditor would be entitled to a charging order and would only have the rights of an assignee. An assignee is only entitled to receive the distributions and the allocation of income, gains and losses to which the assignor was entitled.

Because a judgment creditor's only rights to property held in an LLC is that of an assignee by way of a charging order offers some unique asset protection benefits. If an LLC member is sued and a judgment creditor wins a monetary judgment against the LLC member, the judgment creditor is only entitled to a charging order. The charging order requires that any distributions from the LLC that would have been paid to the LLC member must now be paid to the judgment creditor as an assignee.[3] Of course with a properly drafted LLC, the managers of the LLC would not be required to make distributions and would simply reinvest income into the LLC. The end result is that the judgment creditor receives no distributions from the LLC but is responsible for income taxes on the reinvested income attributable to their assigned interest. The judgment creditor cannot force a distribution or liquidation of the LLC, is not entitled to review the books of the LLC and is not entitled to management rights. If income is needed from the LLC, the managing members may pay a salary to themselves to extract income from the LLC without making a distribution to all LLC members. Obviously, a charging order can be a very unpalatable asset to own, and a creditor may be more willing to settle or not pursue a legal remedy in light of this outcome.

Estate Planning Techniques Using Limited Liability Companies

Techniques to Help Reduce the Gross Estate Value

An LLC[b] facilitates the gifting of large assets by donating a fractional interest in the LLC to the children while the parent(s) retains full control of the LLC. Gifting of the fractional interests is often accomplished through the use of the annual exclusion and the applicable exemption amount.

For example, Boudreaux and Clotile own a closely held business or a portfolio of marketable securities worth $1,000,000 which is transferred to an LLC. In exchange for the business, they receive 990 nonvoting membership units and ten voting manager membership units. Because they owned 100 percent of both the business and the LLC, the exchange is tax-free. They wish to maintain control over the

---

[b] The same valuation discounts are also available for family limited partnerships.

business by retaining the voting manager membership units. They intend to donate nonvoting membership units to their children while taking advantage of valuation discounts to reduce their gift and estate tax exposure. Boudreaux and Clotile set up the ownership of the LLC as follows:

	Father	Mother	Total
Voting Managing Membership Units	5	5	10
Nonvoting Membership Units	45	45	90
Total	50%	50%	100%

Boudreaux and Clotile each give to their two children 5 percent of their nonvoting membership units for the following gift valuation:

Value of LLC	$1,000,000
5% of LLC Gift per spouse	* .05
Value of 5% Membership of the units Prior to Discounts	$50,000
Less 20% Minority discount	-$10,000 (.20x$50,000)
Value prior to Marketability Discount	$40,000
Less 30% Marketability discount	-$12,000 (.30x$40,000)
Taxable value of gift for **EACH** spouse	$28,000

Each spouse may use his or her annual gift exclusion ($15,000 in 2019) to further reduce the taxable gift to $13,000. Of course, Boudreaux and Clotile may transfer a lesser amount each year to avoid creating a taxable gift. In the alternative, they may wish to gift larger amounts to rapidly remove the asset from their estates. To avoid paying gift taxes on gifts in an amount greater than the annual exclusion, they may use their applicable estate tax exclusion amount. If both spouses transfer a 5 percent interest to each child, $100,000 can be removed from their estates for a taxable gift of $26,000.[c] Over a period of nine years, the value of 90 percent of the LLC, plus all future appreciation, can be removed from their estates. Because the parents continue to own the voting managing membership units in the LLC, they retain full control even though they own 10 percent of the LLC.

---

[c] Each spouse transfers 5 percent of the LLC for a taxable gift of $26,000 per spouse or $52,000 for both spouses. Subtracting each spouse's $15,000 annual exclusion results in a taxable gift of $26,000.

Valuation Discounts

As described earlier, another advantage of LLCs is the availability of valuation discounts for gift and estate tax purposes. Valuation discounts through the use of the minority discount and the lack of marketability discount are some of the most important benefits of an LLC. A key observation is that the assets being valued are the LLC interests and not the underlying assets in the entity. The LLC interests are included in the gross estate rather than the assets owned by the LLC. Valuation discounts vary on the particular facts, but it is common to achieve cumulative discounts of 25 to 45 percent.

The Minority Discount

The minority discount is a discount due to a member's lack of control over the LLC assets and management decisions. The minority discount is recognized because the holder of a minority interest lacks control over management policy and cannot control the LLC, determine when distributions occur or terminate the LLC. For these reasons, a third party seeking to purchase a 40 percent interest in an LLC would not be willing to pay an amount equal to 40 percent of the value of the LLCs' assets. The purchaser may be willing to pay some lesser amount due to the discount for only purchasing a noncontrolling minority interest.[4] Minority interests in partnerships are treated similarly to minority interests in LLCs and corporations.[5]

The Lack of Marketability Discount

The lack of marketability discount, which is separate from the minority discount, is based on the premise that the fair market value of an asset, in this case an LLC interest, is the price at which the interest would change hands between a willing buyer and a willing seller, neither being under the compulsion to buy or sell and both having reasonable knowledge of relevant facts.[6] An interest in an LLC is not easily transferable, as there is no readily available market to sell, and a transferee is often given the rights of an assignee with no assurance that he or she will be admitted as a member. For these reasons, a buyer of an LLC interest would not be willing to pay an amount equal to the fair market value for the LLCs' underlying assets.

The valuation discounts carry a wide range of variation. The amounts of the discounts are fact specific; therefore, working with a competent appraiser who is familiar with valuation discounts is necessary to help minimize the risk of an IRS challenge for using overly optimistic valuation discounts.

Common Mistakes to Avoid

To avoid valuation-discount and completed-gift challenges by the IRS, the LLC should have both economic substance and a sufficient non-tax business purpose and should not be created merely to utilize valuation discounts.[d] In addition, to avoid a challenge to the valuation discount and inclusion of the full value of the LLCs' assets in the estate, there cannot be an implied agreement that the donor of assets to an LLC would retain the economic benefit of the transferred assets.[7] A parent who transfers assets to an LLC must treat the assets as owned by the LLC. Any benefit the parent receives from the transferred asset must be by virtue of ownership of the LLC interests not the underlying assets.

Another pitfall to avoid is retaining too much control as a direct owner of the assets in an LLC, rather than as a manager of an LLC which owns the asset. Although the distinction seems small, it is important in the context of estate planning. The value of LLC membership interests which are transferred to the children may be included in the parents' estates if too much control is retained by the parents. In addition, if the parents retain all of the income from LLC assets, the IRS may include the entire value of the LLC in the parents' estates. For example, assume Boudreaux creates an LLC to which he transfers several rental properties. After transferring 90 percent of the nonvoting units of the LLC to his children, Boudreaux distributes all of the income from the LLC assets to himself. Because his children own 90 percent of the LLC membership units, they should receive 90 percent of the distributable income. If Boudreaux retains all of the income, the IRS will include the value of the entire LLC in his estate. Boudreaux cannot retain beneficial use and enjoyment of assets he no longer owns (90 percent of the LLC membership units were transferred to his children). If Boudreaux wishes to receive more income than his

---

[d] These same mistakes to avoid apply to family limited partnerships.

10 percent share of his LLC membership units provides, he could compensate himself for his duties as a manager and for maintaining the rental properties owned by the LLC.

To help ensure the full benefits of valuation discounts and avoid the inclusion of transferred FLP/LLC interests in your estate, the following guidelines should be considered:

- Retain adequate assets outside of the LLC to provide adequate cash flow to support your standard of living. To avoid an IRS challenge that you retained beneficial ownership of the LLC assets, you should avoid the need to distribute to yourself a percentage of the LLC income that is greater than your ownership interest in the LLC.

- Establish the LLC while in good health. The IRS has challenged "death bed" LLC formation where the sole objective appeared to be tax avoidance.

- Establish a clear business purpose for the LLC. A business objective other than tax avoidance must be evident. For example, management consolidation of rental properties or investments is a valid business objective.

- Document negotiations regarding the terms of the LLC. Because these entities involve family dealings, adequate documentation can help prove arm's length dealings.

- Refrain from making non-pro rata distributions to the owners, especially to yourself or your spouse as the donors. This avoids the issue of beneficial ownership of donated assets.

- Do not commingle the LLC funds with personal funds. The entity must be established as a bona-fide business with a valid business purpose. Businesses involving multiple owners do not commingle funds with the owners' personal accounts.

- Refrain from using LLC assets to pay for personal expenses to avoid the issue of beneficial use of donated assets. Once assets are transferred to an LLC, you no longer directly own the assets. Additional income to pay for personal expenses may be provided by pro-rata distributions to you from the LLC. You may then pay for personal expenses with your share of the LLC distribution.

- Have the limited partners donate assets to the LLC in exchange for partnership interests. This helps to establish that a bona-fide business was created among family members.

- Maintain accurate books and records.

- Do not waive your fiduciary duties as the manager/general partner.

- Comply with all aspects of the operating/partnership agreement. The IRS may "set aside" the LLC for tax purposes if business formalities are not followed.

- Ensure that the assets transferred to the LLC are re-titled to reflect the LLCs ownership. Assets donated to the LLC must reflect their new ownership.

- No implied agreement that you will retain sole economic benefit of the underlying assets should exist.

[1] www.sba.gov, Succession Planning-Passing on the Mantle.
[2] La. Rev. Stat. Ann. 12:1301(A)(10).
[3] Rev. Rul. 77-137, 1977-1 CB 178.
[4] Ward v. Commissioner of Internal Revenue, 87 T.C. 78 (1986).
[5] Harwood v. Commissioner of Internal Revenue, 82 T.C. 239 (1984).
[6] Treas. Reg. § 20.2031-1(b).
[7] Estate of Harper v. Commissioner, T.C. Memo 2002-121.

25

Asset Protection

Chapter Highlights

❖ Asset protection planning is a legal and legitimate way to help insulate assets from future creditors. Asset protection planning is not an attempt to defraud creditors, hide assets or evade taxes.

❖ Business owners, physicians, attorneys, architects, accountants, corporate officers, corporate directors and other licensed professionals are particularly susceptible to lawsuits. However, proper planning can help anyone with assets worth protecting insulate their assets from seizure by a judgment creditor.

❖ Successful asset protection planning must begin prior to the creation of a liability. A transfer of assets after a liability arises may be treated as a fraudulent transfer and may be nullified.

❖ The first line of defense of asset protection planning is adequate liability insurance.

❖ Exempt assets provide additional protection, although some assets have low dollar limits on the exemptions.

❖ Life Insurance, annuities and IRAs are provided generous exemptions from seizure by Louisiana law.

❖ Federal law provides exemptions from seizure for employer plans.

❖ Transferring assets to the spouse with a lower exposure to liability can help to protect assets.

❖ Other techniques such as trusts, corporations, limited liability partnerships and limited liability companies provide additional insulation from lawsuits and creditors.

ASSET PROTECTION TECHNIQUES have been used for many years to help protect assets from seizure by creditors. However, in recent years asset protection has come to the financial planning forefront as the number of lawsuits, both frivolous and meritorious, has increased. Due to the increasing need to protect assets from creditors, asset protection planning has become an integral part of retirement planning and estate planning. Most people wish to protect their home from loss due to fire, so they purchase homeowner's insurance. In addition, many people protect their assets from catastrophic medical expenses through adequate health insurance. Just as assets must be protected from risk of catastrophic medical expenses or loss by fire or other risk, assets must be protected from seizure by creditors. Liability insurance provides some protection from personal injury claims and other liability exposure; however, certain liabilities are usually excluded (e.g. intentional acts). In addition, liability exposure may exceed policy limits. A $1 million policy does not do much good if a jury awards a plaintiff a $10 million judgment.

Asset protection planning is a legal and legitimate way to help insulate assets from future creditors. To reach this end, asset protection planning does not attempt to defraud creditors, hide assets or evade taxes. Rather, assets may be protected through adequate liability insurance, by making assets less appealing to creditors, and by placing assets out of the reach of creditors. The last two objectives help to deter potential lawsuits and encourage settlements for more reasonable amounts.

A key point to remember is that successful asset protection planning must begin prior to the creation of a liability. A transfer of assets after a liability arises may be treated as a fraudulent transfer and may be nullified. Generally, if a creditor is not an existing creditor at the time of the transfer, the creditor must show that the transfer was made with the actual intent to hinder, delay or defraud the creditor.

Asset protection planning is not only for the wealthy. In fact, anyone who owns non-IRA/401(k) assets[a] should take steps to adequately protect these nonexempt assets. Consider this example. Boudreaux is in an automobile accident, and it is determined that he is at fault. Boudreaux acknowledges that he is at fault, but he believes the plaintiff's injuries are highly exaggerated. The plaintiff is suing for chronic neck and back pain; however, the medical experts disagree to the severity of the injury caused by the accident. Boudreaux's

---

[a] Retirement accounts are generally exempt from seizure.

automobile insurance will pay up to its policy limits; however, what if the injured plaintiff has won a judgment for an amount far greater than his policy limit? The plaintiff can seize Boudreaux's personal assets to satisfy the remainder of the judgment. An investment portfolio or rental property that Boudreaux relied upon for retirement income may have to be sold to pay the judgment creditor[b]. Without proper planning, no one with assets worth seizing is immune from a similar fate.

A similar outcome may result from a business owner, engineer, architect, lawyer, doctor or other professional who is liable to a judgment creditor in an amount exceeding liability/malpractice insurance limits. A judgment creditor may collect the monetary award through liens, seizure and other means of collection. It is no secret that individuals and businesses with deep pockets are highly susceptible to lawsuits. Proper planning can help anyone with assets worth protecting insulate their assets from seizure.

Sources of Liability

Of the many sources of liability, it is often the liability that arises "out of the blue" that creates the problem. Unplanned liabilities are often underinsured or not insured at all.

Some common sources of liability include

- Tort liability from your actions or lack of actions. Tort liability includes intentional torts and unintentional torts (negligence). A personal injury claim arising out of an automobile accident is a common example. In addition, malpractice liability for failure to follow the professional standard of care is another type of tort liability.

- Premises liability though the ownership of real estate or business interests. Homeowners and business owners may be liable for the injuries sustained by persons on their property.

- Parents are liable for the acts of their minor or unemancipated children. The liability is absolute and is not based on a presumption of fault or on a failure to properly supervise or train.[1]

---

[b] A judgment creditor (sometimes referred to as creditor) is a winning plaintiff in a lawsuit to whom the defendant owes a monetary award.

- Business owners have vicarious liability for the acts of their employees.

- Landowners have environmental liability for above or below ground hazards regardless of the landowner's knowledge of the hazard.

- General partners are personally liable for the acts of other partners. In addition, a defective limited liability partnership or corporation may be treated as a general partnership exposing the "partners" to unlimited personal liability.

- Corporate shareholders may face unlimited personal liability when a judgment creditor succeeds in "piercing the corporate veil" if corporate formalities are not followed.

Asset Protection Techniques

Liability Insurance

The first line of defense of asset protection planning is liability insurance. The most common forms of liability insurance include automobile insurance, malpractice insurance, errors and omissions insurance, the liability insurance component of homeowner's insurance and umbrella liability insurance. Although you may have one or more of these liability policies, you should verify that you have adequate coverage and that there are no "holes" in your coverage that leave you exposed to liability.

An umbrella policy is liability insurance that picks up where automobile, homeowner's or other insurance policies end. It provides coverage in excess of your automobile and homeowner's coverage, and it covers sources of liability your automobile and homeowner's policies do not cover. For example, it may also cover liabilities for liable, slander and defamation of character. Umbrella policies are relatively inexpensive and can raise your liability protection into the millions.

Exempt Assets

Certain assets are exempt from seizure under Louisiana law and Federal bankruptcy law. Although these exemptions provide some protection, their utility, in some cases, is limited due to the dollar limitations of some exemptions. Converting nonexempt assets into exempt assets is one of the easiest asset protection techniques. Louisiana residents fortunately enjoy generous exemptions for life insurance and annuities. These exemptions allow you to easily convert a large sum of assets into exempt assets.

➤ The Family Home

In Louisiana your home is exempt from seizure up to a value of $35,000. The homestead includes up to five contiguous acres of urban property or up to 200 acres of contiguous property if your home is not located in a municipality. The homestead includes the land and any permanent structures. If the liability exceeds the exemption amount, your home may be seized and sold, and you retain sale proceeds up to $35,000. The entire value of the homestead is exempt for uninsured claims of healthcare providers arising of illness or injury if the medical expenses exceed $10,000 and are greater than 50 percent of the debtor's annual adjusted gross income for the preceding three years.[2]

➤ Personal Property Exemptions

The following items are exempt from seizure

- Tools, instruments, books, one utility trailer and one firearm up to $500 in value that are used in one's trade or profession.

- Personal servitudes of habitation and usufruct under Article 223 of the Civil Code.

- Clothing, bedding, linen, chinaware, nonsterling silverware, glassware, a cooking stove, heating and cooling equipment, one noncommercial sewing machine, equipment for required therapy, kitchen utensils, pressing irons, washers, dryers, refrigerators, deep freezers (electric or otherwise) and living room, bedroom, and dining room furniture used by the debtor or a member of his or her family.

- Family portraits.

- Arms and military accoutrements (military equipment other than weapons and uniforms).

- Musical instruments played by the debtor or a member of his or her family.

- Poultry, fowl and one cow kept by the debtor for the use by his or her family.

- All dogs, cats and other household pets.

- Any wedding or engagement rings worn by either spouse, provided the value of the ring does not exceed five thousand dollars.

- Federal earned income tax credit, except for seizure by the Department of Revenue or if the debtor is in arrears in child support payments.

- Seven thousand five hundred dollars in equity value for one motor vehicle per household used by the debtor and his or her family household for any purpose. The equity value of the motor vehicle shall be based on the NADA retail value for the particular year, make and model.

- Seven thousand five hundred dollars in equity value for one motor vehicle per household if the vehicle is substantially modified, equipped or fitted for use by a physically disabled debtor or family member for transportation.

➢ Life Insurance

Louisiana provides generous exemptions for life insurance that allow the protection of a significant amount of wealth. A life insurance policy's cash value and death benefit are exempt from the claims of the insured's and the beneficiary's creditors under Louisiana law. The exemption applies to all liability for any debt of any beneficiary existing at the time the death benefit or the cash value is made available for the beneficiary's use. Group life insurance benefits and policies owned by trusts are also protected. The exemption is limited to $35,000 of cash value for any policy issued within nine months from the date of seizure or bankruptcy proceedings.[3] Because the cash value and death benefits have an unlimited exemption if purchased more than nine months prior to seizure or filing for bankruptcy, a significant amount of wealth may be protected from the policy owner's and the beneficiary's creditors by purchasing a single premium life insurance policy.

➤ Annuities

Annuities are also protected from seizure with generous exemptions under Louisiana law. The exemption applies to all annuities: deferred, immediate, fixed, variable and equity-indexed, whether in accumulation or pay-out phase. Annuity contracts and payments from annuity contracts are exempt from creditor claims of the owner, annuitant, beneficiary or payee. However, alimony and child support obligations are not exempt.[4] Contributions to an annuity contract are exempt if made more than one year prior to seizure or filing for bankruptcy. In addition, a transfer from one annuity contract to another is not considered a contribution.[5]

The protection provided to annuities allows an easy and inexpensive way to protect assets from creditors by converting nonexempt assets into an exempt asset (an annuity). An added benefit is that the assets in an annuity are protected without the use of trusts, LLCs or other limited liability entities. The law provides protection only for annuities issued by insurance companies; therefore, private annuities are not protected from seizure. An unlimited amount of assets held in annuities and payments from annuities are exempt from creditors so long as the contribution was made more than one year from the date of seizure or filing for bankruptcy.

➤ Retirement Accounts

Qualified retirement plan accounts[c] receive protection from seizure under the federal exemption provided by ERISA. Individual retirement accounts (IRAs) are not governed by ERISA; therefore, they are not protected by the ERISA exemption. We must look to State law to provide creditor protection for IRAs. Louisiana law protects IRAs[d] and other tax-deferred retirement plans[e] and proceeds and payments from such plans from seizure. Alimony and child support obligations are not

---

[c] 401(k) plans, pension, profit sharing or other ERISA covered plans.
[d] Includes Roth IRAs, Education IRAs, SEP IRAs and SIMPLE IRAs.
[e] Includes 401(k), 457, 403(b), profit sharing, pension plans, etc.

protected. In addition, contributions made within one year from the date of seizure or filing for bankruptcy are not protected. The one-year limitation does not apply to rollovers and transfers.[6]

The Bankruptcy Abuse Prevention and Consumer Protection Act of 2005 is a Federal law that provides retirement assets with additional protection from bankruptcy. Retirement accounts[f] are exempt from bankruptcy under Federal law. This broad exemption covers 401(k) plans, IRAs, Pensions, 403(b) plans and retirement plans of tax-exempt organizations and governmental plans. No limits to the value in employer-sponsored plans or IRA rollovers from employer-sponsored plans are imposed. Contributions and earnings on contributions to IRAs and Roth IRAs are protected up to $1 million. Amounts rolled into IRAs from employer-sponsored plans are not subject to the $1 million cap. There is a division among federal Circuit Courts regarding the application of bankruptcy protection for inherited IRAs. The Fifth and Eighth Circuits have ruled in favor of the debtor (the inherited IRA beneficiary). The Seventh Circuit has ruled that an inherited IRA is not protected from a creditor's claim in bankruptcy.[7] In 2014, the U.S. Supreme Court appeared to have settled the issue when it ruled in *Clark v. Rameker* that an Inherited IRA is not protected in bankruptcy.[8] However, the United State Bankruptcy Court for the District of New Jersey ruled that an inherited IRA was not available to bankruptcy creditors under New Jersey law.[9]

Creditor protection pursuant to The Bankruptcy Abuse Prevention and Consumer Protection Act of 2005 applies to bankruptcy only, not to other judgments or creditors. Thus, we must continue to rely on state law to protect IRAs and other non-ERISA covered plans from nonbankruptcy creditors. The Bankruptcy Abuse Prevention and Consumer Protection Act of 2005 will provide the most benefit to residents of states that do not provide IRAs with adequate bankruptcy protection. Fortunately, Louisiana law provides protection from seizure from all creditors, including bankruptcy creditors, to IRAs.

Correctly Titling Assets

Changing the title to assets, such as converting a community property asset to a separate property asset, is another asset protection

---

[f] Included retirement accounts under I.R.C. §§ 401, 403, 408, 408A, 414, 457 and 501(a).

technique. A separate or community liability of a spouse may be satisfied from community property and from the separate property of the spouse who incurred the liability.[10] Therefore, a spouse is not required to use his or her separate property to satisfy a separate or community liability of his or her spouse. This technique works best if one spouse has a higher liability exposure than the other spouse. For example, if Boudreaux's profession exposes him to excessive liability, he may transfer most of the assets to his wife as her separate property. Boudreaux's creditors will not be able to seize his wife's separate property. His creditors will only be able to seize his separate property and the community property. This technique is simple, but it is not perfect. His wife's separate property assets are reachable by her creditors, and there is the possibility of divorce. In spite of its weaknesses, this technique is a way to hedge your bets by placing assets out of reach of the creditors of the spouse most likely to be sued.

Trusts

A properly drafted trust can protect the trust assets from seizure arising from a beneficiary's liabilities. This type of trust is a spendthrift trust. A spendthrift trust cannot be used to protect assets you donate to a trust created for your benefit. However, you may create, for the benefit of your children and grandchildren, a spendthrift trust funded with your assets that will be protected from their creditors.

If your children or spouse has creditor issues or if you want to protect their inheritance from their potential creditors, consider establishing a spendthrift trust in your will. Many people use trusts to manage property for a minor, disabled or irresponsible beneficiary. However, beneficiaries who are capable of managing their own affairs also benefit by obtaining creditor protection for the assets they inherit from you. Rather than leaving assets to your children or grandchildren directly, leave the assets to a spendthrift trust for their benefit. A properly drafted spendthrift trust can protect your children's inheritance from mismanagement, bankruptcy, judgment creditors and future ex-spouses. The benefits of spendthrift trusts are more fully described in Chapter 21.

Domestic Asset Protection Trusts

Several states, including Alaska, Delaware, Missouri, Nevada and Rhode Island, have passed legislation extending spendthrift protection to persons who transfer property to a trust. Such trusts are known as domestic asset protection trusts. A domestic asset protection trust allows you to protect your assets from your creditors by transferring assets to a trust for your benefit. Typical trusts do not allow you to protect your assets from your creditors. Generally, you should not retain the authority to compel a distribution of trust assets for your benefit. However, the trust is drafted to permit (rather than require) the trustee to distribute assets to you when you request. In addition, the trust must be administered in the state whose laws allow such trusts, and at least one trustee must be located in the state. Domestic asset protection trusts allow the assets to remain in the United States, an arrangement with which many settlors are more comfortable. They may not provide, however, as much protection as offshore asset protection trusts. Because domestic asset protection trusts are relatively new, future litigation will continue to test the strength, or lack thereof, of the asset protection features of domestic asset protection trusts.

Offshore Asset Protection Trusts

Offshore asset protection trusts are trusts established in a foreign jurisdiction such as the Bahamas, The Isle of Man, The Cayman Islands, The Cook Islands, Nevis or other favorable jurisdictions outside of the reach of United States courts. Favorable offshore jurisdictions will not recognize a judgment of a United States court and often have laws that make it more difficult for a creditor to seize the trust assets. For example, the offshore jurisdiction may have a very short statute of limitations for fraudulent transfers which may preclude a creditor from seizing assets due to a fraudulent transfer. An additional obstacle for creditors is the unwillingness of an offshore jurisdiction to recognize a judgment of a United States court. Because the offshore jurisdiction will not recognize a United States court judgment, the creditor must begin a new lawsuit in the offshore jurisdiction. The additional expense incurred to hire local counsel and begin a new lawsuit in a foreign jurisdiction is, in itself, a significant obstacle. Even if a creditor files a lawsuit in a foreign jurisdiction, the laws are usually less than friendly to creditors, and seizing the assets will be difficult at best. In light of these significant obstacles, a creditor may be more willing to accept a lesser settlement amount to settle the claim.

Funding an Offshore Trust

One method of funding an offshore trust is to transfer assets directly to the offshore trust. Another method is to transfer assets to an LLC (or FLP) located in the United States. The nonmanaging members' interests in the LLC are transferred to and owned by the offshore trust. The managing members' interests (usually one or 2 percent of the LLC) is retained by the owner of the asset. This arrangement allows the underlying assets to remain in the United States as they are owned by the LLC. In addition, the owner continues to freely manage and control the assets of the LLC. If a creditor threat appears imminent, the LLC assets are liquidated and placed into the offshore trust. In the alternative, assets may also be transferred directly to the offshore trust without the use of an LLC.

Weaknesses of Offshore Trusts

Although offshore trusts appear to be a formidable asset protection tool, court decisions have been rendered where the courts ordered the settlors to bring the assets in the offshore trust back to the United States.[g] When the defendants refused or claimed that the trust did not allow them to bring the assets back into the United States, the settlors were jailed until they complied.[11] The increasing willingness of judges to jail a settlor until assets are returned to the United States will reduce the usefulness of offshore trusts.

Furthermore, the Bankruptcy Abuse Prevention and Consumer Protection Act of 2005 allows the bankruptcy estate to reclaim assets transferred to asset protection trusts within 10 years of filing for bankruptcy if the transfer was made with the intent to hinder, delay or defraud creditors. This legislation will certainly have a negative effect on asset protection trusts.

Also, beware of offshore asset protection "kits" as they are often useless and provide little or no asset protection. In spite of their weaknesses, offshore asset protection trusts may be warranted when asset amounts are sufficient to justify the cost of establishing and

---

[g] Known as a repatriation order.

maintaining an offshore trust and planning is done sufficiently in advance of a creditor's claim.

Entity Protection: Corporations

Most people think of corporations when they think of limited liability business entities. A corporation will generally limit the liability of shareholders to their investment in corporate stock from liabilities arising from the corporation. Unfortunately, corporate liability protection is not absolute if the "corporate veil" is pierced. To avoid a creditor from "piercing the corporate veil," corporate formalities should be followed, and the corporation should be adequately funded by maintaining sufficient capital to operate.

Although corporations provide liability protection from claims arising from the corporation, they will not protect you from liability arising from your own acts. For example, licensed professionals, including doctors, attorneys, accountants and architects, do not enjoy unlimited liability protection from their acts. Professional practices established as a limited liability entity will help protect a licensed professional from the acts of his or her partners but not from his or her own acts. To achieve additional liability protection from liability arising from their own actions, additional planning techniques are required. One technique is to use multiple entities to insulate assets from creditors.

In addition to corporations, limited liability companies and limited liability partnerships are used to limit an owner's liability to his or her investment in the entity. These entities can be used to protect non-risky assets such as an investment portfolio from liability arising from risky assets (i.e. assets that may produce liability). A basic technique of asset protection planning is to separate business assets from personal assets through the use of limited liability entities.

For example, a physician may own an LLC which owns the land and office building which is leased to his medical practice established as a professional corporation or other limited liability entity. A second LLC may own equipment that is leased to his medical corporation. In addition, his personal investment assets may be owned by a third LLC which owns only non-risky assets. The use of multiple entities will help protect assets from liability arising from malpractice claims or arising from another cause of action (e.g. an automobile accident).

See Chapter 24 for additional information on the asset protection benefits of limited liability companies and limited liability partnerships.

Fraudulent Conveyances

As discussed at the beginning of the chapter, asset protection techniques will generally fail when transfers are made or actions are taken that are considered fraudulent conveyances. A creditor may rely on a revocatory action to annul a debtor's act or failure to act which causes or increases the debtor's insolvency. The debtor's intent to deprive a creditor is not relevant. A revocatory action is only available to parties who are creditors of the debtor when the transfer occurred. In addition, the revocatory action must be brought within one year from the date the creditor learned or should have learned of the act or transfer. Otherwise, the revocatory action should be brought within three years of the debtor's act or transfer.[12]

[1] La. Civ. Code Art. 2318.

[2] La. Rev. Stat. Ann. 20:1.

[3] La. Rev. Stat. Ann. 22:647.

[4] La. Rev. Stat. Ann. 13:3881(D)(1).

[5] La. Rev. Stat. Ann. 13:3881(D)(2).

[6] La. Rev. Stat. Ann. 13:3881.

[7] Clark v. Rameker, 714 F.3d 559 (7th Cir. 2013).

[8] Clark et ux. v. Rameker, Trustee, et al., Supreme Court of the United States, No. 13-299, June 12, 2014.

[9] In Christopher P. Andolino, Chapter 3, Case No. 13-17238 (RG), 2/25/15.

[10] La. Civ. Code Ann. Art. 2345.

[11] FTC v. Affordable Media, LLC, 179 F.3d 1228 (9th Cir. 1999); In re Stephen J. Lawrence, 279 F.3d 1294 (11th Cir. 2002).

[12] La. Civ. Code Ann. Arts. 2036, 2037, 2041, 2043, 2044.

Additional References:

Rosen, Howard and Rothschild, Gideon, *Asset Protection Planning*, BNA Tax Management 810-2nd (2005).

Rothschild, Gideon, *More Clients Should Choose Trusts*, Estate Planning and Taxation.

Rothschild, Gideon and Rubin, Daniel, *Estate Tax Savings With Self Settled Trusts*, Personal Financial Monthly, Vol. 2 No. 8, August 2002.

Hickey, McDaniel, Sigler, Kalmbach, Raglin and Moragas, Estate Planning in Louisiana, West (2017).

Osborne, Asset Protection: Domestic and International Law and Tactics, West (2006).

26

Disability Planning

Chapter Highlights

❖ Planning for incapacity is an often overlooked but highly important part of your retirement and estate plans.

❖ A power of attorney allows you to name one or more attorneys-in-fact to manage your affairs or otherwise act on your behalf if you are unable or otherwise unavailable.

❖ Power of attorney can give very broad or limited authority to the attorney-in-fact.

❖ You may name a single attorney-in-fact or multiple attorneys-in-fact who are required to act in unison or independently of each other.

❖ As the principal, you may amend or revoke your power of attorney at any time. In addition, the power of attorney terminates upon the death of the principal or the attorney-in-fact.

❖ A power of attorney may be drafted as a "springing" power of attorney that does not give the attorney-in-fact the authority to act on your behalf until you become incapacitated.

❖ Express powers such as the power to donate assets or to contract a loan must be specifically listed in the power of attorney.

❖ Special powers such as the ability to change beneficiaries of retirement plans or life insurance policies may also be granted; however, these powers should be carefully drafted.

❖ A medical power of attorney authorizes the attorney-in-fact to make health care decisions on behalf of an incapacitated individual.

❖ A revocable trust is a trust that may be amended or terminated at anytime. Revocable trusts are often used to avoid probate (a.k.a.

living trusts) or as an asset management tool in the event of incapacity.

❖ A living will enables an individual to declare his or her intentions with regard to the withholding or withdrawal of life-sustaining procedures in the event of a terminal and irreversible condition.

❖ A living will may be revoked at any time by the declarant without regard to his or her mental state or competency by canceling or destroying the declaration.

❖ An interdiction is a legal proceeding that declares an individual incapable of managing his or her person or estate and names a curator to act on behalf of the interdict. An interdiction may be avoided with a properly drafted power of attorney or revocable trust.

DISABILITY PLANNING FOCUSES on planning for the possibility that you become incapacitated and are unable to manage your financial affairs or you become unable to make healthcare decisions or both. Due to the continuing advances of medical science, the average life expectancy has been steadily increasing. Along with an aging population comes an increasing occurrence of incapacity— the inability to manage one's affairs or care for their person. A frequently overlooked area of retirement and estate planning is what will happen to you and your assets in the event of disability or incapacity.

Without proper planning, if you become incapacitated and are unable to manage your affairs, a judge will have to name a curator[a] in an interdiction proceeding. An interdiction proceeding is not private and is more expensive than other alternatives. Furthermore, the incapacitated individual does not control who will become the curator during the interdiction. Of significant importance to many individuals is to maintain control of their affairs. Unfortunately, an interdiction proceeding removes all control and choices out of the incapacitated person's hands.

This chapter will examine several alternatives for disability planning. Because there is no best answer to disability planning, a combination of techniques often works best. One option that allows

---

[a] The curator is the person who manages the affairs of someone who is interdicted.

you to maintain control over your affairs is to establish a general power of attorney and a power of attorney for healthcare decisions. Revocable trusts provide an additional, although more complex, option for managing your affairs if you become incapacitated. This chapter will also examine living wills and their place in the retirement and estate planning puzzle. Lastly, the least desirable alternative, interdiction, is explored.

Powers of Attorney

A power of attorney[b] enables a competent individual (the principal) to name a representative or attorney-in-fact to manage his or her affairs. The attorney-in-fact does not have to be an attorney. The Civil Code allows a competent person to select another individual who will act on his or her behalf through power of attorney in the event of incapacity. A power of attorney is a less expensive and nonpublic method for someone to manage the affairs of another. A key question is who will be selected as attorney-in-fact. Consideration should be given to the degree of maturity and financial sophistication when selecting an attorney-in-fact to manage financial decisions. However, financial sophistication is not generally an issue when selecting an attorney-in-fact for healthcare decisions.

The attorney-in-fact may be given authority to handle specific matters or to manage all of the principal's affairs. The document granting power of attorney stipulates the scope of the attorney-in-fact's powers. Although there is no legal requirement that the power of attorney be reduced to writing, when the law prescribes a certain form for an act, a power of attorney authorizing the act must also be in that form.[1] For example, if the principal wishes to grant the power to donate, sell or mortgage immovable property, the power of attorney must be in writing. As a practical matter, powers of attorney should always be in writing. The preferred method of granting power of attorney is by notarial act.

Unless the power of attorney provides otherwise, the power of attorney is a "durable" power of attorney. A "durable" power of attorney remains in effect even after the principal is incapacitated. Louisiana has long recognized powers of attorney as "durable." Prior

---

[b] Also known as mandate or procuration in Louisiana.

to other states enacting durable power of attorney statutes, powers of attorney executed in many other states terminated upon the principal becoming incapacitated. Obviously, when an individual becomes incapacitated, the power of attorney is most needed.

Express Powers

Certain powers must be expressly granted in the power of attorney. For example, express authority must be given to donate, sell, mortgage, acquire or lease a thing; however, neither the property description nor its location need be expressly given.[2] In addition, express authority in the document conferring power of attorney must be given for the following actions:

- To make donations either outright or to a new or existing trust or custodial arrangement;

- To accept or renounce a succession;

- To contract a loan, acknowledge or make remission of a debt or become a surety;

- To draw or endorse promissory notes and negotiable instruments;

- To enter into a compromise or refer a matter to arbitration;

- To make healthcare decisions, such as surgeries, medications and nursing home residency.

- Prevent or limit reasonable communications, visitation, or interaction between the principal and relative by blood, adoption, or affinity within the third degree, or another individual who has a relationship based on or productive of strong affection.[3]

- Entering into a self-dealing transaction by the attorney-in-fact.

A power of attorney does not give the attorney-in-fact unbridled freedom when acting on behalf of the principal. The attorney-in-fact is bound to fulfill their duties with prudence and diligence. In fact, the attorney-in-fact is responsible to the principal for the loss that the principal sustained as a result of the attorney-in-fact's failure to perform as well as for exceeding his or her authority.[4] The principal may terminate or amend the power of attorney at any time.[5] In addition, the power of attorney terminates due to the following:

1. Death of the principal or attorney-in-fact;

2. Interdiction of the attorney-in-fact; or

3. Qualification of the curator after interdiction of the principal.

Selecting an Attorney-in-Fact

Typically, the spouses are selected as the attorney-in-fact for each other. If the spouse is unavailable or unable to fulfill the duties of attorney-in-fact, often one or more of the children are selected as successor attorneys-in-fact. There is also the option of selecting two or more attorneys-in-fact. If more than one person is selected as attorney-in-fact, the principal may stipulate that a majority must agree to take certain types of action or that all must agree. On the other hand, the principal may stipulate that multiple attorneys-in-fact may act independently of each other. This may be important if one or more attorneys-in-fact live out of town and may not be readily accessible. Contingent attorneys-in-fact should be selected in the event the primary attorney-in-fact is unwilling or unable to fulfill the duties of attorney-in-fact.

Springing Powers of Attorney

You may not wish to appoint an attorney-in-fact who is immediately empowered to act on your behalf. One option is to draft a conditional or springing power of attorney. A springing power of attorney becomes effective only upon the principal's incapacity. Some people are more comfortable with a springing power of attorney because the attorney-in-fact has no authority to act on the principal's behalf until the principal becomes incapacitated. The power of attorney becomes effective upon the incapacity of the principal, established by authentic act stating that "due to an infirmity, the principal is unable consistently to make or to communicate reasoned decisions regarding the care of the principal's person or property." Two physicians licensed to practice medicine in Louisiana who have personally examined the principal must sign the authentic act.[6]

Only after such an act is signed may the attorney-in-fact act on the principal's behalf. In contrast, a standard power of attorney gives the attorney-in-fact the ability to act immediately on the principal's behalf regardless of the principal's ability to manage his or her affairs.

Determining when an individual is incapacitated, especially if the principal is in and out of incapacity, may be problematic. To avoid this issue of determining when the principal becomes incapacitated, use an immediate (nonspringing) power of attorney. The attorney-in-fact is immediately empowered to act on the principal's behalf. A principal who places trust in an attorney-in-fact to act on his or her behalf when the principal is incapacitated should be comfortable with giving the attorney-in-fact the immediate power to manage his or her affairs when the principal is capable. It boils down to the principal selecting an attorney-in-fact with whom the principal has complete trust.

Special Powers to Consider

When drafting a power of attorney, you must consider the extent of the powers to confer upon the attorney-in-fact. For example, will the attorney-in-fact have the power to change beneficiaries of insurance policies or retirement plans, to take distributions from retirement plans or to make investment decisions for retirement plans or other investments? If the children of a prior marriage are the beneficiaries of a retirement plan or annuity, will the current spouse as attorney-in-fact (who is not the parent of the beneficiaries) have the power to change these beneficiary designations? If the attorney-in-fact is granted the power to change beneficiaries, one option is to limit the choices of individuals who may be named beneficiary. Another option is to specifically prohibit changing beneficiary designations. In addition, if the attorney-in-fact has the power to donate assets, the principal may consider limiting the donees to which property may be donated.

If your estate plan calls for gifting assets out of your estate, consider including specific language in the power of attorney document that grants to the attorney-in-fact the specific power to donate assets from your estate. Without the specific power to donate assets from your estate, any donation will be treated as a revocable donation, and the asset will be included in your gross estate for estate tax purposes.

For example, Boudreaux makes annual gifts to an irrevocable life insurance trust. Boudreaux's power of attorney does not specifically give his wife, Clotile, the power to donate assets. If Boudreaux becomes incapacitated, and Clotile continues the annual gifts to the life insurance trust, all of the gifts Clotile makes as Boudreaux's attorney-in-fact are incomplete gifts. The value of these gifts will be included in Boudreaux's estate. To avoid this problem, Boudreaux's power of attorney must specifically authorize the attorney-in-fact to donate assets. Likewise, powers of attorney with gifting powers can also be helpful if Medicaid planning must be done after an individual becomes incapacitated. Although the power to gift has many benefits, granting the power to gift to the attorney-in-fact should not be taken lightly. The principal must have complete trust that the attorney-in-fact will act in the principal's best interest.

Self-Dealing by the Agent

If future planning may involve donating assets to the agent or a change of beneficiary in favor of the agent, the power of attorney should provide for self-dealing (i.e. the agent contracting with himself). For example, the principal may wish to qualify for Medicaid long-term care and donating assets to the children may avoid spending-down all of their assets. If the agent is a child of the principal, the agent may not donate assets to themselves without the express authority of the power of attorney to self-deal.[7]

Power of Attorney for Healthcare

A special type of power of attorney known as a medical power of attorney authorizes the attorney-in-fact to give consent for medical procedures or obtain medical records when the principal is unable to make such decisions. This is a type of limited power of attorney that restricts the attorney-in-fact's authority to make medical decisions on the principal's behalf.

Limitations of Powers of Attorney

Powers of attorney are essential planning tools; however, they are only effective if the third party is willing to recognize the attorney-in-fact's authority. For example, a "stale" power of attorney may not be recognized by a third party. A bank or brokerage firm may not accept the power of attorney if they are unsure of its current validity. The institution may require the power of attorney to be re-executed or an in-house power of attorney form to be executed. This is obviously a problem if the principal is incapacitated. Therefore, it is recommended that the power of attorney be re-executed from time to time. In addition, third parties in another state may not recognize powers of attorney not drafted according to their state's formal requirements.

Revocable Trusts (Living Trusts)

A living trust is a revocable trust that allows assets in the trust to pass outside of the will or intestacy thus avoiding probate. In addition to avoiding probate, living trusts are used as an asset management tool in the event of incapacity. For example, Pierre and his wife Marie transfer assets to a revocable trust of which Pierre and Marie are co-trustees. Assets may be added or removed from the trust at any time, and Pierre and Marie retain full use and control of the assets. In the event that Pierre or Marie becomes incapacitated, the co-trustee manages the trust assets. If both Pierre and Marie are incapacitated, the successor trustee selected by Pierre and Marie and named in the trust document assumes management of the trust assets. When Pierre and/or Marie regain their ability to manage their affairs, they resume their role as trustees. In addition, the assets in the trust are managed according to the trust instrument as per Pierre and Marie's instructions. Although revocable trusts are more complicated and more expensive than powers of attorney, they are generally more readily accepted by financial institutions and other third parties when dealing with trust assets. The "stale" power of attorney issue discussed herein is not an issue with revocable trusts. See chapter 22 for additional information regarding revocable trusts.

Living Wills

All persons have a fundamental right to control the decisions relating to their medical care, including the decision to have life-sustaining procedures withheld or withdrawn under certain circumstances, through a properly drafted living will. A living will enables an individual to declare his or her intentions with regard to the withholding or withdrawal of life-sustaining procedures in the event of a terminal and irreversible condition. A living will should be distinguished from a medical power of attorney, as a living will only directs medical decisions when a person is terminally ill. Medical powers of attorney are generally applicable for all other medically related issues.

The State of Louisiana allows a competent individual to execute a written declaration (a living will) directing the withdrawal or withholding of life-sustaining procedures in the event of a terminal and irreversible condition.[8] A terminal and irreversible condition is defined as a continual profound comatose state with no reasonable chance of recovery or a condition caused by injury, disease or illness which, within reasonable medical judgment, would produce death and for which the application of life-sustaining procedures would serve only to postpone the moment of death.[9]

Life-sustaining procedures include the invasive admission of nutrition and hydration[c] but do not include steps taken to provide comfort care and pain relief. Beware of boilerplate living wills issued by medical institutions as they may not contain language adequate to express your true intentions with regard to withholding medical treatment.

The living will must be signed in the presence of two competent witnesses who cannot be related by blood or marriage and who cannot inherit from the declarant's[d] estate. The declarant may make an oral or nonverbal declaration in the presence of two witnesses at any time subsequent to the diagnosis of a terminal and irreversible condition. It is the responsibility of the declarant to notify the attending physician of the declaration. If the declarant is comatose, incompetent or otherwise incapable of communication, any other person may notify the physician.[10]

A living will may be revoked at any time by the declarant without regard to his or her mental state or competency by canceling or destroying the declaration. Another person may cancel or destroy the living will in the presence of and at the direction of the declarant. In addition, a living will may be revoked by written revocation that is signed and dated by the declarant. Finally, a living will may be revoked

---

[c] Feeding tubes.

[d] The person who is making the declaration in their living will regarding their intent to withhold medical treatment.

by an oral or nonverbal expression of the intention to revoke the living will.[11]

If a person does not have a living will and cannot express his or her wishes orally or through other nonverbal communication in the presence of two witnesses after the diagnosis of a terminal and irreversible condition, the following order of individuals are authorized to make a declaration:[12]

1. A previously appointed tutor or curator of the patient;

2. Any person previously designated by the patient to make such a declaration on the patient's behalf. The declaration must be made by the patient while an adult by written instrument signed by the patient in the presence of two witnesses. If more than one person is authorized, the patient may indicate the order in which the persons designated shall have authority to make the declaration;

3. The patient's spouse, not judicially separated;

4. An adult child of the patient;

5. The parents of the patient;

6. The patient's sibling;

7. The patient's other ascendants or descendants.

Louisiana Physician's Order for Scope of Treatment (LaPOST)

A patient or their representative may communicate end of life decisions regarding medical care through a physician's order. The Louisiana Department of Health and Hospitals issues a bright gold form that is completed and signed by a physician based on the patient's preferences. One of the goals of LaPOST is to encourage discussions between a patient and their physician regarding treatment options and preferences for end of life decisions. LaPOST is for patients with life-limiting and irreversible conditions with death expected within six months.[13]

Interdiction

Interdiction requires a judicial proceeding and should only be considered when no other options are available to protect an individual's person or property. An interdiction proceeding is more expensive and the least private of all other options; therefore, it is the least desirable.

For a person to be interdicted, he or she must be unable to make reasoned decisions due to an infirmity, including chronic substance abuse. However, a decision is not unreasoned merely because it appears risky, unwise or imprudent, and advanced age alone is not an infirmity. A person suffering from an infirmity who may experience lucid intervals may still be eligible for interdiction.

If you wish to have someone interdicted, a lawsuit must be filed against that person. You must provide evidence to prove that the person is unable to consistently make reasoned decisions as described above. The person you are trying to have interdicted has an opportunity to show why they should not be interdicted. This process occurs in open court and can be expensive. If contested, an interdiction proceeding can also cause a dispute between family members and the person being interdicted

Full interdiction is a last resort and warranted only when a person's interests cannot be protected by less restrictive means. Less restrictive means include power of attorney, the use of a trust or limited interdiction. A failure to properly plan through powers of attorney and revocable trusts may result in an interdiction proceeding if incapacity causes an individual's inability to manage their affairs or his or her person. Once a person loses the legal capacity to form a binding contract, he or she no longer has the ability to execute a power of attorney or a trust for asset management. For this reason, the importance of proper planning with powers of attorney and revocable trusts cannot be over emphasized.

Full Interdiction

A court may order the full interdiction of a person of the age of majority or an emancipated minor who, due to an infirmity, is unable consistently to make reasoned decisions regarding the care of his or her person <u>and</u> property or to communicate those decisions and whose interests cannot be protected by less restrictive means.[14] Less restrictive means include powers of attorney and trusts that provide management of an individual's assets. A person who merely acts imprudently when caring for his or her person or property but does not suffer from an infirmity is not a candidate for full interdiction.

Limited Interdiction

A court may order the limited interdiction of a natural person of the age of majority or an emancipated minor who, due to an infirmity, is unable to consistently make reasoned decisions regarding the care of his or her person or property or to communicate those decisions and whose interests cannot be protected by less restrictive means.[15]

Curators

When someone is interdicted, the court will appoint a curator to represent the interdict and to care for the person or the affairs of the interdict or any aspect of either. Because the court determines who will act as curator, the interdict loses control over who will manage their person or their assets. The curator is required to exercise reasonable care, diligence and prudence and to act in the interdict's best interest. The court may confer upon a curator of a limited interdict only those powers required to protect the interdict's interests.[16] An undercurator is also appointed to act in place of the curator if the curator is unable.[17]

A full interdict lacks capacity to make a juridical act; however, the validity of juridical acts made prior to interdiction is not affected by the interdiction.[18] A limited interdict lacks capacity to make a juridical act pertaining to the property or aspects of personal care that the judgment of limited interdiction places under the authority of his or her curator.

Due to the public nature, expense and invasiveness of an interdiction proceeding, you should eliminate the potential of interdiction through a properly drafted power of attorney or trust for asset management. These options allow you to retain control over who will manage your person and your affairs if you become incapacitated.

[1] La. Civ. Code art. 2993.
[2] La. Civ. Code art. 2996.
[3] La. Civ. Code art. 2997.
[4] La. Civ. Code arts. 3001, 3008.
[5] La. Civ. Code art. 3025.
[6] La. R.S. Ann. 9 § 3890.
[7] La. Civ. Code art 2997.
[8] La. Rev. Stat. Ann. 40:1299.58.
[9] La. Rev. Stat. Ann. 40:1299.58.2(15).
[10] La. Rev. Stat. Ann. 40:1299.58.3.
[11] La. Rev. Stat. Ann. 40:1299.58.4.
[12] La. Rev. Stat. Ann. 40:1299.58.5.
[13] La. Rev. Stat. Ann. 40:1299.64.1.
[14] La. Civ. Code art. 389.
[15] La. Civ. Code art 390.
[16] La. Civ. Code art 392.
[17] La. Civ. Code art 393.
[18] La. Civ. Code art 394.

27

Successions

Chapter Highlights

❖ A succession (aka probate) is the court supervised process for the orderly distribution of a deceased person's assets and for the payment of estate debts and expenses.

❖ A primary function of a succession is to determine the identity of the deceased person's successors, and to place the successors into possession and ownership of the decedent's assets.

❖ A succession must be completed whether the decedent died testate (with a will) or intestate (without a will).

❖ A succession may require an administration if the estate is complex or large in size, consists of business assets, there is a legal dispute among the successors, or creditors require an administration.

❖ An administrator is the person appointed by the court to manage the assets and liabilities of the decedent and to distribute the decedent's assets to the successors according to law. If appointed by the decedent in their will, this person is an executor.

❖ Louisiana allows the independent administration of successions which streamlines the succession process. An independent executor can be appointed in the decedent's will. The successors may also agree to an independent administration unless prohibited by the decedent's will.

❖ Non-probate assets such as IRAs, 401(k)s, life insurance, annuities, payable on death accounts and assets held in trust are distributed outside of the succession.

WHEN SOMEONE DIES, there is a process for the orderly distribution of the deceased person's assets and payment of estate debts and expenses. In Louisiana, this process is called a succession. A succession is the transmission of the estate of a deceased person to his successors, the people inheriting the assets. Immediately upon the death of the decedent[a], successors acquire ownership of the estate assets.[1] Nevertheless, the successors must obtain proof that they are the legal owners of the decedent's assets. The proof is necessary to identify the new owner(s) to third parties in order to sell, lease, mortgage or otherwise use the property of the decedent as the new owner(s). A primary function of a succession is to determine the identity of the deceased person's successors and to re-title and place them into possession and ownership of the estate assets. For example, financial institutions will not release funds and investments to the successor until proper documentation of a succession is provided. Likewise, a buyer of real estate will require proof of good title to property a successor inherits. A Judgment of Possession rendered at the conclusion of a succession provides the buyer with proof of the transfer to the successor. In addition, a succession provides an orderly process to pay the outstanding debts owed by the decedent.

Other states refer to this process as probate. Sometimes successions are referred to as probate in Louisiana as well. The term "probate" means to prove the validity of a will. Probate and succession are often used interchangeably to mean the process of placing the successors into possession and ownership of the decedent's estate.

The Decedent's Estate

A person's estate consists of property (all assets not solely real estate), rights and obligations (debts) a decedent leaves at death. An estate with debt and charges but no assets is still an estate.[2] Estate debts include debts of the decedent and administration expenses. Debts of the decedent are debts existing at the time of death such as credit card debts, medical bills, utilities and mortgages. Administration expenses arise after the death of the decedent such as attorney and accountant fees for the succession and funeral expenses.[3] Successors are responsible for estate debts in an amount that does not exceed the value of their inheritance.[4] For example, if the sole heir's inheritance is valued at $50,000, the heir is liable up to this amount even if the decedent's debts exceed $50,000.

---

[a] A decedent is an individual who has died.

Testate and Intestate Successions

A succession is required to re-title and transfer property whether the decedent died testate or intestate. If the decedent died with a valid will, the succession is a testate succession. If the decedent did not have a valid will at the time of his or her death, the succession is an intestate succession. A successor who inherits property through a testate succession is known as a legatee. A successor who inherits property through an intestate succession is known as an heir. See Chapter 20 for an explanation of the succession rights of heirs of an intestate succession.

Succession Procedures

Louisiana recognizes three types of succession procedures: small successions, simple possession and administered successions. If the succession does not qualify for a small succession or for a simple possession proceeding, the succession must be administered. The composition and complexity of the estate and the identity of the successors determine which procedure may be used.

Small Successions

A small succession is the succession or ancillary succession of a person leaving property in Louisiana having a gross value of $125,000 or less valued as of the date of death.[5] The successors of a person who dies intestate or testate and with an estate value under $125,000 may be able to take advantage of a small succession. Small successions usually are less expensive and often are resolved quicker than normal succession proceedings.

The affidavit procedure may be used for small successions where judicial opening of the succession is unnecessary.[6] When the estate qualifies, the successors may be placed into possession by affidavit. The affidavit is presented to financial institutions as proof of the successor's ownership. A multiple original of the succession affidavit is filed in the parish where the decedent's immovable property is located not prior to 90 days after the decedent's death.[7] Filing the succession affidavit serves as proof of chain of title for real estate. The affidavit procedure for small successions may be used for a succession

1. Of a person <u>domiciled in Louisiana</u> who died intestate if the heirs of the decedent are his descendants, ascendants, brothers of sisters or their descendants, or the surviving spouse; or

2. Of a person <u>domiciled outside of Louisiana</u> whose testament has been probated by court order of another state if the sole heirs are the decedent's legatees under a testament probated by a court of another state.

The affidavit small succession is <u>not</u> available for a succession of a decedent domiciled in Louisiana who dies testate or for a decedent domiciled in another state who dies intestate leaving property in Louisiana.

For example, a Louisiana resident dies intestate with a bank account valued at $45,000 as the sole asset. The heirs are his two children. The children can have the bank account placed into their name with a small succession rather than going through the normal succession procedure. In fact, this succession would qualify for the affidavit procedure. If a succession does not qualify for the affidavit procedure, the succession will have to be judicially opened as a simple possession succession or an administered succession.

Does the Estate Require Administration?

Many successions are not formally administered because they are uncomplicated and easily resolved. If the estate is relatively free from debt, and the successors accept the succession, the succession may be completed without an administration. The succession is relatively free from debt when its only debts are administration expenses, mortgages not in arrears, and the debts of the decedent are small in comparison to the assets of the succession.[8] However if these criteria are not satisfied, the estate is large in size requiring payment of estate taxes, consists of business assets, there is a dispute among the successors, or other circumstances exist that prevent the use of an un-administered succession proceeding, the succession must be administered.

Simple Possession Successions

Simple possession is a procedure where the succession documents are typically filed all at once, and the succession is opened and closed in the same day. If no estate taxes are due, no creditors demand an administration, and all heirs/legatees accept the succession, the simple possession procedure may be used. First, an Affidavit of Death and Heirship is filed to open the succession. If the decedent died testate (with a valid will), a petition is filed asking the judge to probate the will. The executor named in the will typically is not confirmed and officially appointed because there is no role for an executor in an un-administered succession. A list of all of the assets and liabilities is filed. Next, a petition is filed asking the judge to place the successors into possession of their respective portions of the estate. Finally, the judge signs the Judgment of Possession which places the successors into possession of the decedent's estate.

Administered Successions

Estates that do not qualify for a small succession or simple possession succession must be administered. Typically successions require administration due to their large size that results in payment of estate taxes, their complex nature of assets, business ownership, the existence of outstanding debts, or other circumstances that prevent the use of an un-administered succession proceeding. An administered succession requires the appointment of a succession representative. A succession representative is also known as a executor (executrix if female) for testate successions and an administrator (administratrix if female) for intestate successions.

Is a Succession Necessary?

Sometimes the heirs or legatees decide not to open a succession. Often a title examination prior to a real estate sale many years after the decedent's death triggers the need to open a succession. For example, if a person dies intestate with a surviving child. All of the decedent's assets will be inherited by the child; however, the child cannot exercise certain rights of ownership over the assets (e.g. sell or mortgage the real estate) until a succession is completed. The child cannot sell real estate owned by the decedent, because the real estate is still in the name of the decedent. For example if the child tries to sell the property 15 years after the decedent's death, the title examination will show that the child does not have clear title to the property and cannot sell the property. The only acceptable proof that the child is the rightful successor to the real estate is a recorded Judgment of Possession[b]. The Judgment of Possession re-titles the decedent's property into the child's name. After the Judgment of Possession is recorded in the conveyance records, the child may sell the property as the new owner. Sometimes real estate is passed down through multiple generations without a succession after each death. When a successor tries to sell or borrow against the property, successions must be done for each decedent to show proper chain of title to the last successor.

Duties of the Succession Representative

The succession representative manages the assets and liabilities of the decedent with the attorney's guidance and instructions from the court. If appointed by the court, this person is called an administrator. If named in the decedent's will, this person is called an executor. The succession representative is responsible for carrying out the testator's directions in the will as ordered by the court. The succession representative is typically the person who contacts the attorney to start the succession process. In addition, the succession representative is responsible for gathering information about the estate's assets that is used by the attorney to prepare the descriptive list.[c] When the succession representative is appointed, he or she is regarded as a fiduciary with the duty of collecting, preserving and managing the succession property. The succession representative must act as a prudent administrator and is personally responsible for damages resulting from failing to act as such. If necessary, the succession representative may sell succession property after petitioning the court for proper authority. If real estate is being sold, notice of the sale must be published in the parish where the succession proceeding is pending. If real estate is located outside of the parish of the succession proceeding, notice must also be published in the parish where the property is located.

The succession representative will have to obtain a tax identification number to open bank or brokerage accounts in the name of the estate. In addition, the estate will need a tax identification number to file a fiduciary income tax return.

---

[b] Or Succession Affidavit if the estate qualifies.

[c] The descriptive list is a list of the assets and liabilities of the decedent.

Independent Administrations

In an effort to streamline the succession process, Louisiana allows the independent administration of successions.[9] As a testator, you may choose to have the succession representative serve as an independent administrator by stating in your will that the succession representative will serve as an independent administrator.[d] An independent administrator has all of the rights and powers of a standard succession representative but without the requirement of petitioning the court or the requirement of publishing notices for the sale of succession property. Providing for an independent administration can greatly streamline the succession process by allowing the independent administrator to act without court authority. Moreover, an independent administration can reduce the cost of a succession by eliminating the need to file petitions with the court to take certain actions.

If the will does not provide for an independent administrator or if the independent administrator named in the will is unwilling or unable to serve, all of the general or universal legatees may collectively agree to designate an independent administrator.[10] Furthermore, if a decedent dies intestate, all of the intestate heirs may agree to select someone to serve as an independent administrator.[11]

Although independent administration streamlines probate, the reduction of court supervision may cause concern to testators or other interested parties. For that reason, a testator may specifically prohibit an independent administration in their will.[12] In addition, any interested party may request that the independent administrator furnish security.[13] The court may order that adequate security be furnished if it is deemed necessary. Furthermore, the annual accountings are not required for an independent administration; however, any interested party may demand an annual accounting.[14] A final accounting by the independent administrator is required unless it is waived by the heirs or legatees.[15]

What to do When a Loved One Dies

The death of a loved one is a difficult time even for well-planned estates. It is an emotional time for the decedent's family members who often have many questions concerning the steps to take after a death in

---

[d] Independent executor means the same as independent administrator.

the family. Although every situation is different, this list provides some of the steps necessary to finalize the affairs of a deceased loved one. Typically the surviving spouse is the executor named in the decedent's will or the co-trustee of a living trust. Another family member may also serve in this capacity. For un-administered successions, the executor need not be formally appointed but may act in the capacity of a point person for wrapping up the decedent's affairs. Thus, many of the executor's "duties" are carried out by the surviving spouse or other family member when an executor is not appointed.

Things to do Immediately

1. Determine if the decedent had specific wishes regarding their funeral or memorial service. Instructions may have been left in the decedent's will or in a separate list of final instructions.

2. Determine if all or part of the decedent's funeral costs have been pre-paid.

3. Contact the funeral home to make funeral arrangements.

4. Call the newspaper to arrange for an obituary.

5. It the executor's job to collect and preserve the estate assets. As soon as practicable, the executor should take an inventory of all of the assets and the date-of-death value. If there is a concern that personal effects may "walk off", personal effects (jewelry, guns, cash, etc.) should be placed into safekeeping.

6. Notify the agent/attorney-in-fact pursuant to powers of attorney that their responsibility ended with the principal's death.

Things to do After the Funeral

1. If not yet found, locate the decedent's will and/or other final instructions. Check with the clerk of court's office to determine if the will was filed for safekeeping. If a will is not found, the decedent died intestate. In some cases copies of a will may be

probated. Bring original wills or copies to your meeting with the succession attorney.

2. Contact an attorney to open the succession. Set up an appointment to discuss matters that require immediate attention. It should also be determined whether the succession must be administered. Go to my website www.LouisianaEstatePlanner.com and print a copy of my Succession Checklist. Or you may email me at john@jsiroislaw.com for a copy. Bring as much information listed on the Succession Checklist as you have available.

3. If the decedent died with a properly funded revocable trust, a succession will not be necessary. The trustee of the trust will distribute or retain the trust assets as defined in the trust document. Contact a competent estate attorney for assistance or if you have questions about the trust distributions.

4. Order death certificates if not already ordered. The number of certificates will depend on the composition of the estate assets. Check with your attorney for an estimate of the appropriate number; however, a minimum of five to ten is recommended. Ideally, have the funeral home order the death certificates.

5. If the estate will be administered and the decedent has an executor named in their will, the executor must be confirmed by the court. If the decedent died intestate, someone (usually the surviving spouse, a close family member, or other suitable person) must be appointed administrator.

6. If not yet completed, the executor/administrator should take an inventory of all of the assets and the date-of-death value.

7. Check that the home, automobile and other assets have adequate insurance coverage.

8. If the decedent was receiving Social Security benefits, notify the Social Security Administration and provide them with a death certificate. Benefits paid after death must be returned.

Determine if a surviving spouse is eligible for an increased benefit. Minor children may be eligible for a survivor benefit.

9. If the decedent was receiving a pension, notify the pension administrator and provide them with a death certificate. Determine if payments continue to another beneficiary.

10. If the decedent was employed, notify the employer's human resources department of the employee's death. Check for group life insurance benefits, pension benefits and retirement accounts. Also check with former employers for similar benefits.

11. Notify health insurance carriers of the insured's death.

12. Notify credit card companies of the decedent's death and cancel where appropriate.

13. Notify credit reporting agencies of the decedent's death. Contact Experian, 1-888-397-3742; Equifax, 1-800-525-6285; and TransUnion, 1-800-680-7289. Have all accounts coded as "Closed, Account holder is deceased".

14. Contact life insurance and annuity companies to obtain death benefit claim forms.

15. If the decedent lived alone cancel/alter their phone, cable television, etc. Have the decedent's mail rerouted mail to an alternate address.

16. Contact the Veterans' Administration if the decedent was a veteran. Check for benefits payable.

17. Check with the decedent's tax preparer or CPA to determine if a tax return for the year of death has been filed.

Information Needed to Open a Succession

Here is a basic succession checklist of information needed to open a succession. Visit www.LouisianaEstatePlanner.com, call my office at 985-580-2520 or email me at john@jsiroislaw.com to obtain a copy of my comprehensive Succession Checklist.

1. A copy of the act of sale or other document containing the property description of the home and other real estate owned by the decedent.

2. Funeral and cemetery bills.

3. Physician and hospital bills for the last illness and insurance claims made.

4. Certified copy of the death certificate.

5. Original Last Will and Testament if the decedent died testate. If the original Last Will and Testament cannot be found bring any available photocopies.

6. Names, addresses, dates of birth and social security numbers of all children and other heirs or legatees.

7. A complete list of all of the assets owned by decedent such as cash, bank accounts, savings accounts, savings certificates or bonds of any kind, stocks, mutual funds, annuities, etc. Include accounts on which the decedent's name appears alone or with other names and any account containing money belonging to the decedent or the decedent's spouse. The date of death value of all of the assets will also be needed.

8. Copies of titles to automobiles, boats, trailers, etc.

9. Safety deposit box information and key (do not enter the box).

10. Copies of life insurance policies.

11. Copies of any insurance policies under which hospital, medical or accident benefits may be claimed for the estate.

12. Copies of retirement plan benefits, pensions, IRAs, 401(k), 403(b), etc.

13. A list of all the personal effects of the decedent such as jewelry, furniture, collectables, clothing, any and all movable property.

14. A list of all mortgages and other debts existing on the date of death. Check with your attorney prior to paying any debts.

Nonprobate Assets

Some assets owned by a decedent are not part of the probate estate; therefore, it is important to distinguish between probate assets and non-probate assets. The *federal* gross estate includes all assets in which the decedent had an ownership interest. Federal estate taxes are based on the value of the federal gross estate. The *probate* estate consists of all assets that are distributed by the decedent's will or through intestacy. Non-probate assets like retirement accounts, annuities, and life insurance proceeds paid to a named beneficiary and federal savings bonds titled "A or B" are not part of the probate estate. Likewise assets held in a revocable or irrevocable trust are not part of the probate estate. These non-probate assets are included in the federal gross estate for estate tax purposes. Non-probate assets are not controlled by will or the intestacy laws but are paid to the named beneficiary of the asset.

Payable on Death Accounts

A bank savings account, certificate of deposit, or credit union account may be established as a "payable on death to" account. When the account owner dies, the financial institution will pay to the named beneficiary upon receiving a death certificate of the account owner. Payable on death accounts avoid probate and facilitate a quick distribution of the account to the named payee.[16]

Access to Safe Deposit Boxes

When a safe deposit box is leased under the names of two or more persons with each having the right of access, any survivor has the right to remove the contents of the safe deposit box. Thus, after the death of one of the lessors of the safe deposit box, any surviving lessor may remove all of the contents. Unless you intend to leave all of the contents of the safe deposit box to the surviving named lessor, use caution when providing access to a safe deposit box to another individual.[17]

If the decedent is the sole individual leasing a safe deposit box, the bank should be notified of the death of the person as soon as practicable. Access to the box will be restricted until sufficient proof of the right to access the box is presented to the bank. The succession representative will have access to the safe deposit box after presenting letters of administration[e] (letters testamentary if the decedent died testate) to the bank. A Judgment of Possession recognizing and putting the successors into possession of the contents of the safe deposit box would also be conclusive proof to the bank to allow the transfer of the contents of the box to the named individuals.[18]

---

[1] La. Civ. Code Ann. Art. 935.
[2] La Civ. Code Ann. Art. 872.
[3] La. Civ. Code Ann. Art. 1415.
[4] La. Civ. Code Ann. Art. 1416.
[5] La. Code. Civ. Proc. Art. 3421.
[6] La. Code Civ. Proc. Art. 3431.
[7] La. Code Civ. Proc. Art. 3434(C)(1).
[8] La. Code Civ. Proc. Art. 3001.
[9] La. Code Civ. Proc. Art. 3396.
[10] La. Code Civ. Proc. Art. 3396.3.
[11] La. Code Civ. Proc. Art. 3396.5.
[12] La. Code Civ. Proc. Art. 3396.13.

---

[e] Letters of Administration are issued by the court when the executor/administrator is appointed.

[13] La. Code Civ. Proc. Art. 3396.14.
[14] La. Code Civ. Proc. Art. 3396.17.
[15] La. Code Civ. Proc. Art. 3396.19.
[16] La. Rev. Stat. Ann. 6:314, 6:653.1, 6:766.1.
[17] La. Rev. Stat. Ann. 6:321.
[18] La. Rev. Stat. Ann. 6:325.

Final Thoughts

By reading this book, I hope you have become more knowledgeable about the issues you will encounter as you navigate through retirement and plan your estate. I also hope this book serves as a useful guide to you throughout your planning endeavors. Remember that professional guidance is highly recommended prior to attempting any retirement, estate, or long-term care planning. You should be enjoying your retirement not trying to keep up-to-date with changing tax laws and a turbulent stock market. Leave those issues to the professionals. Your goal should be that with thorough planning and professional guidance you will enjoy worry-free golden years.

APPENDIX A

Uniform Lifetime Table

This Table is used by all IRA owners unless their spousal designated beneficiary is more than 10 years younger than the participant. In that case the actual joint life expectancy of the participant and spouse is used with the joint life expectancy table. The Uniform Lifetime Table is never used to calculate distributions to a beneficiary.

Age of IRA Owner or QRP Participant	Life Expectancy (Years)	Age of IRA Owner of QRP Participant	Life Expectancy (Years)
70	27.4	93	9.6
71	26.5	94	9.1
72	25.6	95	8.6
73	24.7	96	8.1
74	23.8	97	7.6
75	22.9	98	7.1
76	22.0	99	6.7
77	21.2	100	6.3
78	20.3	101	5.9
79	19.5	102	5.5
80	18.7	103	5.2
81	17.9	104	4.9
82	17.1	105	4.5
83	16.3	106	4.2
84	15.5	107	3.9
85	14.8	108	3.7
86	14.1	109	3.4
87	13.4	110	3.1
88	12.7	111	2.9
89	12.0	112	2.6
90	11.4	113	2.4
91	10.8	114	2.1
92	10.2	115	1.9

APPENDIX B

Single-Life Table
Use this table to calculate a beneficiary's life expectancy

Age	Life Expectancy	Age	Life Expectancy	Age	Life Expectancy
0	82.4	38	45.6	76	12.7
1	81.6	39	44.6	77	12.1
2	80.6	40	43.6	78	11.4
3	79.9	41	42.7	79	10.8
4	78.7	42	41.7	80	10.2
5	77.7	43	40.7	81	9.7
6	76.7	44	39.8	82	9.1
7	75.7	45	38.8	83	8.6
8	74.8	46	37.9	84	8.1
9	73.8	47	37.0	85	7.6
10	72.8	48	36.0	86	7.1
11	71.8	49	35.1	87	6.7
12	70.8	50	34.2	88	6.3
13	69.9	51	33.3	89	5.9
14	68.9	52	32.3	90	5.5
15	67.9	53	31.4	91	5.2
16	66.9	54	30.5	92	4.9
17	66.0	55	29.6	93	4.6
18	65.0	56	28.7	94	4.3
19	64.0	57	27.9	95	4.1
20	63.0	58	27.0	96	3.8
21	62.1	59	26.1	97	3.6
22	61.1	60	25.2	98	3.4
23	60.1	61	24.4	99	3.1
24	59.1	62	23.5	100	2.9
25	58.2	63	22.7	101	2.7
26	57.2	64	21.8	102	2.5
27	56.2	65	21.0	103	2.3
28	55.3	66	20.2	104	2.1
29	54.3	67	19.4	105	1.9
30	53.3	68	18.6	106	1.7
31	52.4	69	17.8	107	1.5
32	51.4	70	17.0	108	1.4
33	50.4	71	16.3	109	1.2
34	49.9	72	15.5	110	1.1
35	48.5	73	14.8	111+	1.0
36	47.5	74	14.1		
37	46.5	75	13.4		

About the Author

John E. Sirois, JD, MBA, CFP®, CIMA, CIMC is a CERTIFIED FINANCIAL PLANNER™ and Certified Investment Management Analyst specializing in retirement planning and investment management. He has offices in Metairie and Houma and works with clients throughout Louisiana. John is also an estate and elder law attorney primarily practicing in the areas of estate planning, successions, long-term care planning, Medicaid qualification and special needs planning. John uses his diverse knowledge of retirement planning, estate planning, elder law and investment management to guide Louisiana residents through both the transition into retirement and throughout their retirement years. He helps his clients accumulate, protect and distribute their assets according to their wishes.

John is an avid speaker and has spoken to various groups and organizations. He has taught courses at Nicholls State University covering retirement planning, investments and estate planning. In addition, he has appeared as a guest speaker at Money Watch Live and teaches continuing education courses for attorneys, CPAs, financial planners, insurance agents and social workers through NBI, Lorman, Tulane School of Law and Loyola School of Law. John received a Bachelors of Science in Business and a Masters of Business Administration from Nicholls State University. He received a Juris Doctor from Tulane University.

John was born and raised in South Louisiana where he resides with his wife, Katherine and daughter, Sophia. His step-daughter, Lauren, lives in New Orleans. He enjoys spending time with his family, hunting, fishing, cooking, and reading, writing and educating others about retirement, investment, estate and elder-care planning.

To book John as a speaker for your organization; for in-house CPE or CLE programs; for employer sponsored pre-retirement planning workshops or for retirement or estate planning questions, contact John at 1-888-574-7647 or E-mail at john@jsiroislaw.com.

To order additional copies of this book or for questions regarding retirement, estate or investment planning, call 1-888-574-7647 or E-mail John at john@jsiroislaw.com.

Additional copies may also be purchased by visiting John's website at www.LouisianaEstatePlanner.com or at Amazon.com.